Critical Studies of the Asia Pacific Series

Series Editor: **Mark Beeson**, Professor in the Department of Political Science and International Studies at the University of Birmingham, UK

Critical Studies of the Asia Pacific showcases new research and scholarship on what is arguably the most important region in the world in the twenty-first century. The rise of China and the continuing strategic importance of this dynamic economic area to the United States mean that the Asia-Pacific will remain crucially important to policymakers and scholars alike. The unifying theme of the series is a desire to publish the best theoretically-informed, original research on the region. Titles in the series cover the politics, economics and security of the region, as well as focussing on its institutional processes, individual countries, issues and leaders.

Titles include:

Hiro Katsumata
ASEAN'S COOPERATIVE SECURITY ENTERPRISE

Barry Wain
MALAYSIAN MAVERICK
Mahathir Mohamad in Turbulent Times

Critical Studies of the Asia Pacific Series
Series Standing Order ISBN 978–0–230–22896–2 (hardback) 978–0–230–22897–9 (paperback)
(*outside North America only*)

You can receive future titles in this series as they are published by placing a standing order. Please contact your bookseller or, in case of difficulty, write to us at the address below with your name and address, the title of the series and the ISBN quoted above.

Customer Services Department, Macmillan Distribution Ltd, Houndmills, Basingstoke, Hampshire RG21 6XS, England

Also by Barry Wain

THE REFUSED
The Agony of the Indochina Refugees

Malaysian Maverick

Mahathir Mohamad in Turbulent Times

Barry Wain
Institute of Southeast Asian Studies, Singapore

First published 2009
PALGRAVE MACMILLAN

Palgrave Macmillan in the UK is an imprint of Macmillan Publishers Limited, registered in England, company number 785998, of Houndmills, Basingstoke, Hampshire RG21 6XS.

Palgrave Macmillan in the US is a division of St Martin's Press LLC, 175 Fifth Avenue, New York, NY 10010.

Palgrave Macmillan is the global academic imprint of the above companies and has companies and representatives throughout the world.

Palgrave® and Macmillan® are registered trademarks in the United States, the United Kingdom, Europe and other countries

ISBN-13: 978–0–230–23873–2   hardback

This book is printed on paper suitable for recycling and made from fully managed and sustained forest sources. Logging, pulping and manufacturing processes are expected to conform to the environmental regulations of the country of origin.

A catalogue record for this book is available from the British Library.

A catalogue record for this book is available from the Library of Congress.

10   9   8
18 17 16 15 14 13 12 11 10

Printed in China

Contents

Foreword

Mahathir Mohamad can be elusive. While he has been a public figure in Malaysia for half a century and well known abroad for almost as long, he has presented himself as a bundle of contradictions: a Malay champion, who was the Malays' fiercest critic and an ally of Chinese-Malaysian businessmen; a tireless campaigner against Western economic domination who assiduously courted American and European capitalists; a blunt, combative individual who extolled the virtues of consensual Asian values.

Much, of course, can be explained by political expediency: Like all successful politicians, Dr. Mahathir compromised where necessary to meet the competing and shifting demands of politics. But he remains a complex character, "a series of personae", as Khoo Book Teik put it in his 1995 study of the man and his ideology.[1] Critics and admirers, who loathe and love him with equal passion, are both correct sometimes. In the words of one sage who has known and observed Dr. Mahathir since his student days, he is "so likeable and worthy of respect at times and so utterly ruthless at others".[2]

Unlike Khoo, I do not analyse Dr. Mahathir's performance within a theoretical framework. As a journalist, I tell his story from ground level, examining the interesting and significant events in his life and the impact they had on him and the country. I follow him from birth in 1925 in modest circumstances to his practice as a provincial doctor, from outcast first-term parliamentarian to Malaysia's longest serving prime minister and Third World spokesman, and from the heights of authoritarian power to the depths of political recrimination in retirement after 2003. I take a fresh look at the controversies that characterized his political career and examine what 22 years of strongman rule have meant for this former British territory.

I first encountered Dr. Mahathir when I was posted to Kuala Lumpur from 1977 to 1979 as a staff correspondent for the *Asian Wall Street Journal* and he was deputy prime minister. He was outspoken and testy about negative publicity, especially after he switched from the education portfolio to trade and industry, responsible for attracting foreign investment. He remained ever ready to denounce critical foreign press reporting during his premiership. In the interests of disclosure, I should mention that I held managerial posts and responsibilities for the *Journal's* coverage of Malaysia from 1984 to 1992.

Dr. Mahathir speaks for himself. As the author of dozens of books, studies and reports, the willing voice in hundreds of interviews, several thousand speeches and an almost endless stream of commentary, he has had his say on nearly every conceivable subject. His memoirs will follow when he is finally satisfied with the drafts and resists the temptation to rewrite them one more time.[3] I weigh his words against his record, relying heavily on reporting, by myself and others, supplemented by personal interviews.

In an effort to fill the gaps, reconcile differences and illuminate the shadows, I interviewed Dr. Mahathir three times for the book. Two meetings took place in his city office on the 86th floor of the Petronas Twin Towers in the heart of Kuala Lumpur, and the other in his regular office at the Perdana Leadership Foundation at Putrajaya. Between the second and third interviews he had open-heart surgery and a follow-up operation for a serious infection in the wound. He also answered additional questions submitted by email. Similarly, his wife, Siti Hasmah Mohamad Ali, readily agreed to an interview and responded promptly to email queries. The two of their seven children I approached, Marina and Mukhriz Mahathir, also submitted to questioning.

The fourth prime minister of Malaysia and the first commoner to hold the title, Dr. Mahathir in many ways was an outsider. A nationalist and modernizer, essentially pragmatic, he had little time for rules, customs and traditions that might obstruct his ambitious plans. Ever the maverick, he delighted in bucking the system and opting for the unconventional course, especially if told he could not, or should not. Even while exercising tight political control, Dr. Mahathir never embraced the Malaysian establishment, preferring to try and create a new social and political order more to his liking.

Some aspects of Dr. Mahathir's early life hitherto have remained obscure, which might be considered surprising given how long he towered over Malaysia and projected himself internationally. Part of the explanation for the mystery is his presumed sensitivity to being the grandson of an Indian immigrant, which raised cultural barriers that fellow Malaysians have been reluctant to breach by questioning him directly. With me, Dr. Mahathir discussed his family freely and noted the influences that shaped his outlook and steered him into politics. Part I covers events on his way to becoming prime minister at the age of 56.

Part II, the body of the book, is a thematic treatment of Dr. Mahathir's leadership of Malaysia. It opens with an account of how he defeated successive political challenges, and explores his vision, an all-consuming desire to turn Malaysia into a modern, industrialized nation commanding worldwide respect. Dr. Mahathir's decision to direct the ruling party into business in a major way, while the government practised affirmative action, changed the nature of the party and accelerated the spread of corruption. One manifestation was the eruption of successive financial scandals, massive by any standards, which nevertheless left Dr. Mahathir unfazed and unapologetic. To help ensure the numerically superior but economically lagging Malays shared national success, Dr. Mahathir re-interpreted Islam to cater for their material as well as spiritual needs. Because of its repercussions, his dismissal in 1998 of his deputy and heir apparent, Anwar Ibrahim, is accorded close and

separate scrutiny. Other chapters examine Dr. Mahathir's "think big" philosophy, which prompted a public craze for setting all sorts of world records,
his showdown with the nine royal households that constitute the Malaysian monarchy, and his emergence on the global stage as an advocate of
developing countries and Islamic issues.

Retiring at 78 after having ruled for almost as long as his three predecessors
combined, Dr. Mahathir might have been expected to join the international
lecture circuit and enjoy his mix of celebrity and notoriety. But, in a twist that
was unexpected but entirely consistent with his unorthodox streak, he
plunged back into the politics he had forsworn, as a savage and unrelenting
critic of his handpicked successor, Abdullah Badawi. He contributed to efforts
that forced Abdullah into retirement early in his second term. Within sight of
his 84th birthday, Dr. Mahathir was still making his political presence felt.
Part III assesses Dr. Mahathir's legacy and looks at his place in history.

Researching this book gave me the opportunity to make contact with
many Malaysians, quite a number of them old friends. Most were only too
willing to help. It was an affirmation of the cheerful cooperation and courtesy I have found throughout a long association with the country.

Param Cumaraswamy was generous with his time in discussing the inter-
section of legal and political issues. Abdul Wahab Mohamed Osman rounded
up an assortment of locals in Alor Star to relive the early Mahathir years.
Abdullah Ahmad was a patient guide through the underside of UMNO politics
in the 1960s and 70s. Muhammad Shafee Abdullah, Rehman Rashid, Liew
Chin Tong, Chandra Muzaffar, Chandran Jeshurun, Karpal Singh, Tan Siok
Choo, Mustapa Kassim, Abdul Rahim Aziz and Austin Zecha assisted in other
ways. I thank Steven Gan for providing the sourcing for a number of *Malaysiakini* reports, and Perdana Leadership Foundation, Malaysia's Information
Department and Bernama for supplying photographs.

Several scholars with expertise in Malaysian affairs rendered assistance.
Greg Barton, Johan Saravanamuttu and Peter Searle read various sections
and made helpful suggestions. John Funston's support was invaluable. He
answered a string of questions and undertook a detailed critique that
significantly improved the manuscript. For the foreign policy chapter,
Marvin Ott plugged a sourcing gap and NUS Press made available in
advance a book on Dr. Mahathir's foreign policy.[4]

I am indebted to former colleagues at the *Asian Wall Street Journal*, renamed
the *Wall Street Journal Asia* in 2005, for their support. As editor, John Bussey
granted access to the paper's files, including memorable reports from Malaysia
in the early 1980s that were not available online. Celine Fernandez in Kuala
Lumpur and Judy Chan in Hong Kong acted as unpaid research assistants.
Crucially, Raphael "Rocky" Pura, the paper's Kuala Lumpur-based veteran
reporter and editor, some of whose compelling dispatches are reflected in this
volume, provided running advice on both structure and content.

At the Institute of Southeast Asian Studies in Singapore, the library staff were extremely helpful and ISEAS specialists generously shared their knowledge. Among them, Mustafa Izzuddin and R. Ramasamy assisted with translation, and Lee Hock Guan, Michael Montesano, Verghese Mathews, Ooi Kee Beng, Rod Severino and Ian Storey offered useful insights. The numerous individuals I interviewed over a period of two and a half years, including some of those mentioned above, are identified in the text and footnotes. While all these sources informed my understanding and were much appreciated, ultimately mine is very much an independent study, the product of observing Dr. Mahathir in action across more than 30 years.

Barry Wain
Singapore

N.B.

1. The protagonist's name, Mahathir bin Mohamad, which identifies him as Mahathir, son of Mohamad, is rendered Mahathir Mohamad. The "bin" is dropped in line with modern usage. Mahathir is pronounced ma–HAA–teer.
2. Although Mahathir held various honorific titles, reflecting his rising status – *datuk, datuk seri* and *tun* – I have chosen to call him "Dr." Mahathir throughout, or at least after his graduation from medical school in 1953. As he told me long ago when discussing titles, "I earned that one."[5] For convenience, the only other persons accorded titles in the book, apart from his wife, also a doctor, are members of royalty.
3. Although Malaysia has adopted a new way of spelling some place names in recent years – for example, Johor instead of Johore, Melaka for Malacca and Alor Setar rather than Alor Star – I have used the old style for consistency, since the book spans both periods.
4. Malaysia's currency, the ringgit, formerly known as the Malaysian dollar, and before that the Straits dollar, was loosely pegged to an American dollar-dominated basket of currencies during much of the Mahathir era. The ringgit fluctuated between an annual average of RM2.3033 and RM2.8132 to US$1 between 1981 and 1997, before falling to RM4.5450 when the peg was abandoned during the 1997–98 Asian economic crisis.[6] The government fixed the rate at RM3.80 when introducing currency controls in September 1998.

Notes

1   Khoo Boo Teik, *Paradoxes of Mahathirism: An Intellectual Biography of Mahathir Mohamad* (Kuala Lumpur: Oxford University Press, 1995).
2   Email correspondence with long-time acquaintance of Mahathir Mohamad, 2 September 2007.

3   Dr. Mahathir fingered print-outs of the chapters of his unfinished memoirs in early 2008 and explained why he had been unable to complete the job in more than five years. "Because I write and then I re-read and correct again. Sometimes I discard what I have written and rewrite the whole chapter again...and then sometimes while re-reading I remember something which should be in...". Interview with Mahathir Mohamad, 31 March 2008.

4   Kaminder Singh Dhillon, *Malaysian Foreign Policy in the Mahathir Era (1981–2003): Dilemmas of Development* (Singapore: NUS Press, 2009).

5. Barry Wain, "Enter Dr. M, Reaching for His Gun", *Asian Wall Street Journal*, 6 June 1981.

6   Bank Negara Malaysia's Monthly Statistical Bulletin, January 1998.

Part I

The Making of a Malay Champion

1
Politicized by War and Peace

Alor Star, the capital of Kedah state, might have been a sleepy backwater in the early years of last century, but the social distinctions were drawn as sharply there as anywhere in colonial Malaya. Malay royalty and the aristocracy lived in relative splendour in the northern outskirts around the palace. Senior civil servants and the wealthy occupied fine homes closer to the centre. The rest shared the rest, with the poorest finding shelter on the other side of the Kedah River that bisected the town. Mahathir Mohamad was born south of the river.

As Mahathir was to discover, inequality was not confined to owning a colonial house in the best neighbourhood. His father, founder of the government's first English-medium secondary school in Kedah and a passionate educationist, could not get his daughters into secondary school. Members of the elite were given priority, as they were in almost everything else, from university scholarships to coveted jobs in the Kedah civil service. Although Mahathir obtained the academic distinction that usually won a scholarship for someone with the right pedigree to study abroad and gain professional qualifications, none was forthcoming for him.

British elitism and a Malay sense of hierarchy combined to let people know their place in society. Tunku Abdul Rahman Putra, son of the Sultan of Kedah and the independent country's first prime minister, did better than most royals in socializing with fellow citizens, but he never forgot his regal origins. Explaining why he would not have known the young Mahathir, Tunku Abdul Rahman said, "He was a nobody. His father was a subordinate officer in Kedah. I did not mix with his father. We had a club in Kedah, a special club for civil servants, for royalty and so on. They had a subordinate club."[1]

The discrimination Mahathir's family suffered because it lacked the necessary socio-economic background and connections was general, not personal. It said much about Mahathir's strength of character, and the family support he received, that he did not allow it to obstruct a successful career in medicine and politics. Indeed, it made him more determined to succeed,

3

though memories of the inequities of the system permanently coloured his outlook.

Where the establishment was concerned, Mahathir was a maverick, an "outsider" in the words of Zainuddin Maidin, a journalist-turned-politician and supporter in Kedah.[2] Mahathir challenged the rules and conventions, whenever they appeared to make no sense, or got in his way. He revelled in being a contrarian, doing what was popularly forbidden. To many others, Mahathir's youthful experience manifested itself as an inferiority complex that made him fight harder, shout louder, build bigger and remain super-sensitive to any slight or criticism. "I prefer to say he has a big chip on his shoulder," commented Abdullah Ahmad, a long-time political ally.[3] Khalid Abdullah, an early business partner and friend for more than half a century, observed with a gentle laugh, "I think he has a little superiority complex." Khalid quoted an Arab proverb to explain Mahathir's mentality: "If you see me with one eye, I have no eyes to see you. If you see me with both eyes, I have all my eyes to see you."[4]

Eyes wide open, Mahathir focused on politics early. He got hooked while he was still in school and never deviated from his desire to become a polit-ician. Every step he took, including qualifying as a doctor, was meant to enhance his credentials for a political career. He entered the national polit-ical arena because he was unhappy with the state of the country and wanted to change it. Most of all, he set out to improve the status of fellow Malays, the country's predominant ethnic group who, despite their numerical superiority, lagged economically behind the Chinese. He would not become prime minis-ter until the age of 56, after overcoming several serious political obstacles, two potentially fatal. But then he would cling to the post for more than 22 years, almost as long as his three predecessors combined, unceasingly trying to shape a modern nation in his own image.

Although Mahathir was deeply embroiled in the contentious debates that preceded and followed Malaya's independence in 1957, he was not in the vanguard of the country's first-generation leaders. He was an early member of the United Malays National Organization (UMNO), formed to oppose a specific British colonial arrangement perceived to weaken the position of Malays, which emerged as the country's premier political party. But UMNO initially was led by members drawn from the traditional aristocracy such as Abdul Rahman, the first prime minister, who was a *tunku,* or *tengku,* prince. He was followed by Abdul Razak Hussein and Hussein Onn, both of royal lineage, who became brothers-in-law when they married into the royal family in the southern state of Johore. Mahathir, decidedly a commoner, was an outspoken critic of UMNO policies under Tunku Abdul Rahman, whom he blamed for accepting passively the plight of the Malays.

The youngest of nine children – a tenth had died at birth – Mahathir was born in the family home in Seberang Perak, a semi-rural slum in Alor Star, on 10 July 1925. His father, Mohamad Iskandar, a teacher, had been recruited from Penang by the Kedah state authorities to open a secondary school for the sons and daughters of the sultan and local elite. Left with three children after the death of his wife, he moved to Alor Star and married Mahathir's mother, Wan Tempawan Wan Hanafi, a local woman 14 years his junior, who also had been previously married. As indicated by the "Wan", she had links to state royalty, but too distant to provide any entrée into aristocratic circles.[5] With six surviving children of their own, Mohamad and Wan Tempawan raised all nine kids.

Although the family could be considered lower middle class, they set up home where they could afford to live, in ramshackle Seberang Perak. With cheap rental accommodation, it attracted new arrivals, among them Javanese and Sumatrans from Indonesia, Indian Muslims and poorer Chinese. They were known as *pendatang*, newcomers or immigrants, if only from other parts of the Malay Peninsula, accepted but still not integrated into the local community. The immigrant mentality, the desire to succeed, was in the air. Abdul Daim Zainuddin, who would become one of the country's longest-serving finance ministers, grew up nearby and went to school in Seberang Perak.

Mohamad Iskandar was a "Penang Malay", or more correctly, *Jawi per-anakan* – often shortened to *Jawi pekan* – meaning a locally born Muslim with Indian blood.[6] A forbear, most likely Mohamad's father Iskandar, had emigrated from southern India to begin a new life in British Malaya.[7] Some Indians, after marrying Malays, retained aspects of their culture, including language and links to their former homeland. Mohamad never looked back: He acknowledged no relatives in India and spoke no Indian language, according to Mahathir,[8] though one grandson said Mohamad's cousins in Penang were fluent in Tamil and he heard Mohamad scold a stranger with impeccable Tamil pronunciation.[9] While some other family members speculated that Iskandar hailed from Kerala, Mahathir said he was not even sure it was his grandfather who was the immigrant, since no records survived and his father had never mentioned the subject. "Frankly, we don't know which part of India we came from," he said. "Maybe this grandfather or great grandfather: One of them must have come from India."[10] Mahathir never met his grandfather Iskandar, who died before he was born, though he knew his grandmother, Iskandar's wife Siti Hawa, whom he identified also as a "Penang Malay".

Like his father, Mahathir did not discuss his Indian side publicly, and the matter was treated like a dirty family secret and not mentioned in polite company. After he became deputy prime minister, an official government publication described his father as the first "Malay" to become a secondary school headmaster. A genealogical chart displayed in Mahathir's old house, converted into a museum in 1992, traces his lineage through his Malay mother, but has almost nothing on his father's side. While he was active politically, Mahathir left the impression it was a sensitive subject, even with his immediate family,[11] though he was highly amused when people from India, Pakistan and Bangladesh all claimed him as a native son.[12] After he retired, he was more relaxed about it. "You know, what I resent most is that anything I do which appears to be successful, they attribute it to my Indian origin. If I fail, then it must be my Malay origin."[13]

The country has never had any trouble accepting leaders of mixed parentage. In that respect, Mahathir continued what had become almost a leadership tradition. Tunku Abdul Rahman's mother was Thai, Razak traced his ancestry to the Bugis from the Indonesian island of Sulawesi and Hussein Onn had Turkish blood. While Mahathir's political rivals occasionally tried to use his Indian background against him, the issue found little traction. For the Malay community, whose view is reflected in the nation's Constitution, the concept of being Malay is not ethnic as it is in being Chinese or Indian. Constitutionally, a "Malay" is defined as a person who professes the Muslim religion, habitually speaks the Malay language and conforms to Malay custom. Indians, Europeans or anyone else may be accepted as Malay if they adhere to those requirements.

Somehow, though, being part Indian was not quite as exotic as being Turkish or Thai, since the overall Indian community, the third-largest ethnic group, was bottom of the economic pile. And the Malays, for all their intermarrying with Indian and Arab Muslims, often vaguely yearned for an idealized leader who was "pure Malay", even though such a person hardly existed. For Mahathir, joining UMNO, whose membership was restricted to Malays, raised no questions. But he was easily riled over his sub-continental connections, complaining privately soon after serving a term in Parliament that Tunku Abdul Rahman would refer to him as "that Pakistani".[14]

Many of Mahathir's other defining characteristics were apparent in his early life, or can be traced to influences in those formative years. No factor was more important than his pipe-smoking father. Master Mohamad Iskandar, as he was called at school, imposed a similarly strict regimen at home as he famously did in the classroom. He supervised his children's homework, helping them with mathematics and English. Relatives sent their children to stay with the family, knowing he would insist that they study. His role was to inculcate in the children work habits and learning, having acquired his own education in Penang over the objections of his parents and lifted himself to a position of authority and respect in the community. As Mahathir recalled, "The sound of his cough as he approached the house was enough to send us boys flying back to our books."[15]

Wilful though not rebellious, Mahathir absorbed the workload and excelled at school. Quiet, studious and not much interested in sports – he once told a friend he played marbles[16] – he read voraciously and kept pretty much to himself. At home, Mahathir had his own ideas and stuck to them with precocious obstinacy. As his sisters said, they found no point in trying to stop him once he had made up his mind to do something because he knew exactly what he wanted. The whole family learned in the end that it was easiest to let stubborn little Mahathir do things his way.[17] In due course, the entire country went along with him. Adult Mahathir's theme song – suggested by others and readily embraced by him – was the one popularized by Frank Sinatra, *My Way*.

In later life, Mahathir was often judged to be "un-Malay" in his dominant personal values: discipline, hard work and self-improvement, the qualities acquired from his highly-motivated and upwardly mobile father. Realizing the rewards of striving for excellence, he believed other Malays could be successful too, if they were given half a chance and changed their attitudes. Providing that opportunity and trying to bring about an adjustment in the Malay mindset would remain a lifelong commitment.

If his father was emotionally distant, Mahathir found love and affection among the women in the household. While his sisters indulged the last born, his mother could be counted on to provide protection on those occasions that his father lost his temper with the boy.[18] They called him Che Det, the pet name by which he would always be known to relatives and close friends in Kedah. Che is a short form of *encik*, the Malay equivalent of mister, while Det is a popular shortening of the final syllable of Mahathir.

Living in a traditional wooden house on stilts with an *attap* roof of palm fronds, the kind found in every *kampung*, village, Mahathir was raised in a normal Malay environment. He attended the local Malay-medium primary school for boys – barefoot because his parents could not afford to buy him shoes[19] – and took Qur'an-reading classes after school. But Mahathir was obviously different from the other kids in the area. While they ran carefree in the fields, he and his siblings were confined to home in supervised study sessions, even during holidays. Whereas Mahathir could read, write and speak English, most of the neighbourhood kids could not. They sometimes teased him and called him *mamak*, a term for an Indian Muslim that can be derogatory, and to which Mahathir long remained sensitive.[20] "He was nothing like us," some of the former neighbours and old friends – all fans of the retired prime minister – who attended a reunion dinner for Mahathir in Alor Star in 2006, told organizers.[21]

After completing his primary education, Mahathir sailed through the entrance examination that would enable him to enter the Government English School, founded by his father in 1908, and later renamed the Sultan Abdul Hamid College. Established for the convenience of royalty and the rich, the school had become much more egalitarian, dropping the restriction on non-Malays and admitting Chinese, Indians, Thais and others. In fact, the entrance exam was a barrier for many Malays, who lived in rural areas and either could not afford to continue studying, or did not have sufficient command of English. Mahathir felt a twinge of pride at being a cut above his former schoolmates, but knew he owed it to his father's rigorous routine: All four of his brothers already had made it into secondary school.[22]

Much to Master Mohamad Iskandar's disgust, however, none of his four daughters could attend secondary school in Kedah, as all places in the girls' school were taken by children of the elite. He was shocked when the school rejected his first daughter after she had finished primary school. Said Mahathir, "He was very annoyed because he was a government officer, and he was invited to Kedah to start the school. And yet this girls' school, which was started later on, refused to accept my sister." None of the other three girls had any better luck when their time came.[23]

Just how galling that was to Mohamad Iskandar, who was obsessed with education as a means of getting ahead, can be gauged by one measure: He had falsified the birth dates of his sons to ensure they could start the first year of primary school without any of the usual arguments about having to wait until the following intake. Mahathir's birth certificate showed he was born on 20 December 1925, and it remained his official birthday, being chosen by the government, for example, as the day on which to open his old house as a museum. But, as Mahathir discovered from notes written by his father in the back of a dictionary, he was actually born five months earlier. His father had given all the boys arbitrary December birth dates, while recording the correct dates in the dictionary.[24]

If the authorities hoped to make amends later by naming a primary school, established within the Sultan Abdul Hamid College compound, after Mohamad, their efforts went awry. They called the school by mistake Iskandar, which of course was his father's name, not his.[25] Hundreds of uniformed students from the Iskandar school and the college, girls included, marched in Mohamad's funeral procession in 1961, recognition of his contribution to education, but also a reminder of his niggling unhappiness.

Mahathir's teenage innocence was shattered by two traumatic events, which thoroughly politicized him and changed the course of his life: the Japanese occupation of Malaya from 1941 to 1945 and Britain's return after World War II with radical plans for the future administration of the country. Mahathir watched arriving Japanese troops flush a British soldier out of the local courthouse, drag him to the riverbank and bayonet him to death. His lasting memory of the Japanese interlude, however, was the exposure of Malay "backwardness and incompetence".

With the schools shut, 16-year-old Mahathir found himself on the street and trying to earn a living. He joined two Malay friends and set up a coffee stall in the local market. They sold the shop for a small profit and graduated to selling bananas and more lucrative items before the war ended. But most Malays were not so savvy or adaptable. Many, including his own brothers, who were retrenched by the Japanese from their government jobs, found it hard to make ends meet. Mahathir described their lack of knowledge of even petty trading as "pitiful". He concluded that if Malays were ever to enjoy the same living standards as Chinese, they would need extra government help.

As it happened, the returning British proposed to form the Malayan Union, which would remove the advantages the Malays had long enjoyed, while extending citizenship freely to all races. As Mahathir and others saw it, if the Malays were behind when they already received preference in areas such as employment in the bureaucracy, land ownership and educational assistance, they would suffer grievously in the open competition being envisaged with the Chinese and Indians.

Introduced in 1946 over fervent Malay objections, the Malayan Union grouped the nine Malay states, where Britain ruled indirectly through monarchies headed by sultans, with the settlements of Penang and Malacca – which Britain administered directly, along with Singapore – turning the Malay Peninsula into a single colony. It stripped the sultans of their traditional powers and transferred jurisdiction to the King of England. Without consultation, the British withdrew their near-century-old recognition of the "special position" of the Malays, which was meant to protect their heritage and birthright.

The deep sense of betrayal felt by the Malays was matched only by their grave fear of the future. After all, it was British sponsorship of large-scale immigration to peninsular Malaya in the nineteenth century – Chinese to work in the tin mines, Indians to labour on the rubber estates – that had turned the Malays into a minority in their own land. More enterprising and sophisticated in business, the newcomers spread to the *kampungs,* where they became storekeepers and moneylenders. In time, they gained a monopoly in the industrial and commercial sectors and lived mostly in urban centres, while the Malays remained in coastal and rural settlements engaged in traditional subsistence agriculture and fishing. Having created what may have been the world's most complex society – three communities divided by religion, language, culture, value systems, place of residence, occupation and income – the British had made no attempt to integrate the immigrants, originally regarding them as guest workers. Now that they and other foreigners had control of the economy, Britain was intending to grant them citizenship.

As part of the Malay nationalist outrage that swept the country, Mahathir led school friends in organizing protests, mainly producing and distributing posters at night. He joined activist groups and attended, as an observer, a national congress of Malay organizations that gave birth to UMNO.[26] In the face of the fierce UMNO-led resistance, the British abandoned the Malayan Union in 1948, replacing it with a federation that allowed the sultans to retain certain powers, though under one overall government.

Although Mahathir had not previously thought much beyond becoming a government clerk, he lifted his aspirations as he imbibed and contributed to the new-found Malay nationalism:

...my interest in politics was stirred up actually during the Japanese period. You know, I read a lot of history, and I felt that the Malays seem

fated to live under the domination of other people...they used to be
under the Thais...and they had to pay tribute to China. They had to
submit to the British, the Portuguese...for 450 years...I read about the
thirteen colonies and how they struggled for independence and how the
United States emerged...this influenced me a lot.[27]

Back in school at the age of 20 to complete his final year, Mahathir
edited the school magazine, penning a front-page editorial for the single
issue produced in 1945. In it he welcomed victory in the war by the
"Powers of Right and Justice".

Mahathir calculated that two professions, law and medicine, would give
him the credibility in the Malay community he felt was necessary to pursue
a career in politics, "particularly among people older than me".[28] His
choice was law, the field chosen by the country's first three prime ministers, who studied in England. Having graduated in December 1946 with
excellent results for the Cambridge School Certificate – he obtained the top
grade for three subjects and the second-highest mark for his four other subjects – "I would have expected a state scholarship, of course," Mahathir
said. "But after the British returned, the British military administration
operated as if the whole country was under one government." In those
unsettled conditions, his application went unheeded. Ultimately, the federal government offered him financial assistance – "not a true scholarship,
but just support"[29] – to study at the King Edward VII College of Medicine
in Singapore, precursor to the University of Malaya. Making a virtue of
necessity, he would later position himself as the first home-grown leader,
untainted by close association with the former colonial power.

Money was an issue for Mahathir. None of his brothers got the chance to
attend university, though one made it into agricultural college. They all
became state civil servants, occupying modest positions. Mahathir's father,
who had quit teaching to remain in Kedah, after having been transferred
inter-state for several years, joined the Audit Department of the state administration. But he was compulsorily retired as a senior auditor at 53, when
Mahathir was still in primary school. His monthly salary of 230 dollars
was replaced by a 90-dollar pension, which dwindled in purchasing power
every year as it was not adjusted for inflation. "Well, it made us rather poor,"
Mahathir said. His father kept trying to earn money from other sources, at
times working as a clerk in an Arabic school and as a petition writer.[30]
Mahathir himself worked in the state government while awaiting his final
exam results, and he earned income from contributions to the nationally-
circulated, Singapore-based *Straits Times*. He began writing for the paper
after taking a correspondence course in journalism, using the pseudonym,
C.H.E. Det, a variation on his nickname. When college administrators learned
from a routine assessment that Mahathir's father was sending him 10 dollars a
month, they cut his allowance by 10 dollars.

Relocating in 1947 at 22 from the fringes of empire to the commercial centre of colonial Malaya, Mahathir encountered a completely different world in Singapore.[31] It opened his eyes to the possibilities of modernization and confirmed his worst fears about the Malays being dispossessed of their own country. The island settlement at the foot of the Malay Peninsula administered directly like Malacca and Penang previously, was British territory, having been acquired from the Sultan of Johore in the early nineteenth century, and anyone born there was a British subject. Mahathir recalled, "They were so very far ahead of us – huge urban community, very sophisticated and very rich people – whereas I came from Alor Star, where the Malays in particular were very poor."[32]

The dangers, though, were just as conspicuous. As Mahathir wrote, the "easy-going" Malays had been unable to compete with the "native diligence and business drive" of the immigrant Chinese, who had been encouraged by the British to settle in Singapore. Once the owners and rulers, Malays now were to be found only in the poorer quarters living in dilapidated *attap* and plank huts, "sometimes only a stone's throw from the palatial residences of Chinese millionaires". They worked as *syces, tukang kebun, tambies* – drivers, gardeners, office boys – and cooks. Most English schools were completely without Malay students. So unenviable was the position of the Malays in Singapore that "most of them have lost their self-respect and racial pride". If Malay interests were not safeguarded, there was no doubt what would happen: "...the prevailing condition in Singapore would invade the Peninsula".[33]

Malay under-representation in his college, where 630 of 700 students were non-Malay, reinforced the impression of their exclusion.[34] Against strong opposition, Mahathir argued for the retention of a 75 per cent quota in favour of Malays for government scholarships to the college.[35] While Mahathir did well in his medical studies, it worried him that other Malays, who numbered just seven of the intake of 75 students in his year, often struggled. Only four of them graduated as doctors, despite special coaching to which Mahathir contributed. One who had trouble with physics and chemistry and needed his help – she had not been able to study these subjects in her secondary school – was Siti Hasmah Mohamad Ali, the only female among the Malay students, who was from a respected family in Selangor state. Although Mahathir was shy and awkward in the presence of girls – meeting the opposite sex was a totally new experience for him – he soon became "possessive" and "jealous".[36] Dr. Mahathir, who graduated in 1953, married his first and only girlfriend in 1956, a union that was to last a lifetime.

Not surprisingly, Mahathir acquired a jaundiced view of the often unruly, poorly educated Chinese who jostled aggressively in the crossroads port. He knew from personal experience how the Malays were often brushed aside and their dignity flouted. He once asked a taxi driver to take him to the home of a woman friend, only to be delivered to the servants' quarters of the house.[37] Mahathir had a long memory, particularly when it came to insults and enemies. Invited to Singapore in 1978 by Prime Minister Lee Kuan Yew soon after becoming Malaysia's deputy prime minister, Dr. Mahathir did not try to hide his deep anti-Singapore feelings. He told his host that Singapore Chinese looked down upon the Malays.[38]

At a personal level, however, Mahathir had no trouble at all making friends with people of all ethnic backgrounds. In the Class of 47 – the students thoughtfully named it after their freshman year to include those who graduated late or dropped out – the bonds were especially warm and enduring. They had a deal that those who turned up for dull and dreary classes signed attendance for the absentees. "We shared our lecture notes and even our case write-ups in obstetrics," recalled Wong Hee Ong. "In all this, Mahathir was one of us."[39]

They held regular reunions, in Singapore or Malaysia, culminating in a 60th anniversary gathering in 2007, with Dr. Mahathir always making a supreme effort to attend. While he was prime minister, he would tell his bodyguards and minders to leave, exposing himself to the ragging of aging medicos reliving their youth, and dishing it out to them in return. At these intensely private, informal gatherings, Dr. Mahathir and Dr. Siti Hasmah, both considered to have good voices – hers somewhat better than his – were usually called upon for a duet. In 1997, Dr. Mahathir sang *My Way* solo, with lyrics written for the occasion by class members and featuring American investor George Soros, blamed by the Malaysian leader for aggravating the Asian economic crisis that year.[40]

Living away from home for the first time, Mahathir proved a true son of his father as he managed his time expertly. Socializing little beyond occasional visits to the cinema, he shunned campus politics, dismissing such activity as "playing games", and telling fellow students he preferred to participate in the real political drama unfolding on the Malay Peninsula.[41] Mahathir became president of the college Islamic Society, and edited and produced an issue of his medical school journal, the *Cauldron*. He continued writing articles regularly enough for the *Straits Times* and *Sunday Times* to help buy a motorcycle; Siti Hasmah rode pillion. His varied output, written in a "direct, didactic style", was a "remarkable accomplishment for a full-time student in a demanding discipline".[42] And it was appreciated, at least by the *Straits Times*. An editor called him to the paper's offices in Singapore and asked if he was interested in a job as a journalist. No, he was not.

Singapore gave birth to an urban myth, that Mahathir thought of himself as an Indian when he entered university. The story was retold in several gossipy versions, losing none of its appeal across the decades. Academics, diplomats and even a former cabinet colleague delighted in passing along the details, all completely untrue. Mahathir's father considered himself a Malay and he ensured that all his children were nothing else but Malay.

In his writings, which began before he went to Singapore, Mahathir identified totally with the Malays and showed he was intimately familiar with their customs, social life and problems, whether it was education, fishing or *padi* planting. His more overtly political contributions were polemical, and uncompromising in defence of Malay rights. Foreshadowing the nationalist stance that would make him a hero to many Malays when he entered Parliament, he criticized the colonial administration, called for the re-introduction of Malay as an official language, alongside English, and made the case for "retarding progress" sometimes in order to help the Malays advance. Well ahead of his time, he also advocated women's rights, arguing especially for women to be given opportunities in education and employment.[43] At the same time, Mahathir began to reveal critical opinions about the Malays themselves that would become another of his trademarks: for instance, their "low average intelligence quotient".[44]

After graduating, Dr. Mahathir spent only four years in government service in Penang and Kedah before resigning to open a private practice, while his wife was to work as a doctor for the government for 25 years. Although the immediate reason for his quitting was the failure of a superior to support his application for a posting to study in a teaching hospital in Penang to be a surgeon, he also wanted to remain near his aging parents. Borrowing money from a brother-in-law, he opened in Alor Star the MAHA Clinic – a name meaning "great" in Malay that combined the first two letters of Mahathir and Hasmah, his wife[45] – in 1957. As one of only five private doctors in the town and the first Malay, he came to be known as "Dr. UMNO", with his office often identified as the "UMNO Clinic".

Dr. Mahathir acquired the reputation of being a caring doctor, willing to make house calls at any hour and trudge across *padi* fields in the dark to treat patients. If they could not afford his fee, they settled by installment or paid what they had. But he never missed an opportunity to scold Malays when their performance fell short. Observing hard-working Chinese farmers next door producing more rice, he would ask idle Malays with more than a hint of sarcasm, "No rain this side?"[46]

While the sarcasm was never far away, Dr. Mahathir would carry much of his bedside manner into politics: Even his sharpest comments, which stung, cut and wounded, were usually delivered in dulcet tones, as if advising an ill farmer to take his pills three times a day. Mukhriz Mahathir saw his father lose his temper and curse only once: when it was discovered just in time that someone in Dr. Mahathir's re-election campaign office had incorrectly completed his nomination papers in an attempt to sabotage his candidacy. The expletive was mild, Mukhriz said. "In Kedah, especially that generation, they swear somewhat politely."[47]

Dexterous, Dr. Mahathir spent his spare time in a home workshop on carpentry, wood turning and metalwork. He built boats powered by outboard motors and used machinery to fashion wrought iron into name plates, lamps and chandeliers. "I like the feeling of building things, of working with wood or metal and creating something," he once told a British journalist. No one who witnessed him at his hobbies doubted he would have made a fine surgeon.

Dr. Mahathir and Dr. Siti Hasmah were also involved in welfare and public health activities. While he, as President of the Kedah Tuberculosis Association, visited Indian workers on rubber plantations to treat and give advice to TB sufferers,[48] she threw her weight behind the Kedah Family Planning Association. At Dr. Mahathir's request, Shaari Daud, a federal bureaucrat and friend, helped him establish a private education association to finance the studies of disadvantaged Malay children.[49]

The couple lost no time in starting what became a sizable and happy family: A daughter, Marina, arrived in June 1957, ten months after they were married. Altogether, the Mahathirs had seven children, five of whom joined the household in under nine years and lived for a while in Alor Star. Years later in Kuala Lumpur, when they had left home to study overseas or marry, Prime Minister Mahathir and his wife, finding it "a little bit lonely" as empty-nesters,[50] and "fed up" waiting for grand children,[51] started what amounted to a second family. Dr. Mahathir built on his father's "strange liking for the letter M", as he once put it.[52] Where Mohamad Iskandar gave all five sons names starting with M, Dr. Mahathir did the same for his three girls as well as the four boys.

Three of the kids were adopted in two different and unusual circumstances. The couple's third child, Melinda, actually chose Dr. Mahathir and his wife as her parents, rather than the other way around. They became her godparents in a traditional ceremony at the age of six months, after Dr. Mahathir cured her of a minor ailment. When he visited her house to treat her brother years later, she wanted to follow Dr. Mahathir home. He agreed, as did her parents, farmers who worked their own land at Tokai outside Alor Star. Siti Aisha Abdul Rahman joined the Mahathir family in 1960, aged six and with an M name, remaining until she married in 1982. She was treated the same as her brothers and sisters, except that she returned to the farm to spend school holidays with her real parents.[53]

Dr. Mahathir was inspired to expand the family again on a state visit to Pakistan in 1983. Invited to review a national day parade by President Zia ul-Haq, he was struck by the "very good-looking children" in national dress. "I thought, wow, they look very nice to me. I thought I would adopt Pakistani children".[54] Later, a close friend who also wanted to adopt, visited Pakistan and selected four babies from an orphanage, and returned to Malaysia with them. In October 1984, the Mahathirs got a fourth son, Mazhar, nine months, and a third daughter, Maizura, seven months. Dr. Mahathir was 59 and Dr. Siti Hasmah 58.

Growing up in Alor Star, the older children remember "an almost idyllic childhood", especially after they moved into a new, split-level brick home at Titi Gajah, 11 kilometres out of town – on the prestigious northern side.[55] Designed by Baharuddin Abu Kassim, the architect responsible for the National Mosque in Kuala Lumpur, the house featured modern conveniences unknown to most locals and sat in spacious grounds that backed onto a river and opened at the front to a vista of almost endless green fields. Both parents stressed the traditional and religious values that had been drummed into them: honesty, gratitude, respect for elders, hard work and discipline, along with the importance of education and the value of money. Dr. Mahathir laughed when the kids entered newspaper contests involving a certain amount of luck. He told them that nothing came easy, and there was no shortcut to success. The fast track to corporal punishment was to lie, steal or commit another of the offences that were not tolerated. Dr. Mahathir got out the cane and, with the other children assembled to absorb the lesson, administered the requisite number of whacks to the offender's backside.[56] Although the girls escaped the cane, Marina recalled being soundly spanked when small for poking out her tongue at the gardener.[57]

From the backblocks of Malaysia, the children learned about the wider world from their father. Marina was not allowed to have pen pals from South Africa or Israel because of apartheid and the Palestinian cause. Twice, an American teenager stayed with the family for a couple of months under a student exchange programme, which Dr. Mahathir "was really into", as Mukhriz Mahathir put it. The parents lost some of their enthusiasm, though, after Marina, at 16, returned from three months in California "quite influenced by the American way of life", in her mother's words. Marina had become "very forward, argumentative", Dr. Siti Hasmah said.[58] Marina later became a journalist, newspaper columnist and social activist, heading the non-governmental Malaysian AIDS Council for ten years.

Indulging an entrepreneurial streak that had been with him since childhood, Dr. Mahathir invested in various businesses. In primary school, he had peddled balloons to earn pocket money, buying them at two cents for three and selling them at two cents each. If he inherited the business bug, it surely came from his mother. Wan Tempawan had been resourceful in contributing to the family budget. She rented space under the house to itinerant hawkers, who slept there and moved around selling their wares during the day. She also grew jasmine, which the children collected and threaded on string made from dried grass, fashioning garlands for sale.[59] Mohamad Iskandar's only foray into business, on the other hand, had flopped. Against his youngest son's advice, he sold fruit-producing land to buy two trishaws, which he rented out. "We never saw the rent or the trishaws again," said Dr. Mahathir.[60]

Dr. Mahathir went into property development, tin mining, a franchised petrol station and a shop to do quick printing – sometimes to rescue Malay businessmen in financial trouble – though not all his ventures were profitable. Dr. Mahathir recalled that before the war there had been only two Malay shops in the whole of Alor Star.[61] He helped found the Malay Chamber of Commerce and later served as a director. "Mahathir was an inspiration," said locally-born Jaafar Ismail, who in 2007 was the executive director, infrastructure, of an Australian-listed international investment fund and asset management group. "I saw business as a thing to do."[62]

One of Dr. Mahathir's noteworthy investments began with his pitch to a sales representative, who distributed pharmaceuticals to doctors, to quit his Penang-based agency and join Dr. Mahathir in forming a rival company. Dr. Mahathir, with 30 per cent of the equity, was one of eight shareholders when MICO Farmasi Sdn. Bhd. was incorporated in 1964. He organized the financial side while the former salesman put together the management team and ran the company. It was called MICO, at Dr. Mahathir's suggestion, for Malaysian Indian Chinese Organization, because the owners were drawn from all three ethnic groups. In addition to distributing drugs wholesale throughout Kedah and Perlis states, the company operated a retail pharmacy in Alor Star. In 2008, 44 years later, MICO was humming along with a staff of ten, its original family shareholder structure still in place, including Dr. Mahathir's stake. The managing director was Haja Nasrudeen Abdul Kareem, 46, the physician son of the salesman-founder, who had taken over upon his father's death in 1992.[63]

While Dr. Mahathir told friends he was trying to make money to launch his political bid, he did not hesitate to flaunt his wealth. He bought one of the biggest and most imposing automobiles ever produced by Detroit, a blue Pontiac. His later explanation that he acquired the car from a friend, who was the agent, because he was having trouble selling the Pontiac and offered it cheap – "only 12,000" dollars – and on installments, was only part of the story. At a time when most people in Alor Star walked or pedaled bicycles along dusty streets lined with low wooden buildings and everyone knew who owned which car, Dr. Mahathir was making a statement: It was "a symbol of his aspiration to prove the capabilities of the Malays", as one admirer saw it.[64] Most immediately, it was a declaration that the boy from the wrong side of the tracks had arrived. "Maybe there's some element also of that," Dr. Mahathir conceded.

In case anyone missed the point, Dr. Mahathir employed a Chinese driver. His later contention, that "I never realized that I was doing something odd" and that he hired the man because he asked for the job and spoke Malay, should be taken with more than a grain of salt. His friends in Kuala Lumpur certainly let him know they found the arrangement "unusual". Remember that Dr. Mahathir had cited Malays working as drivers as evidence of their marginalization in Singapore. As he once told a friend, "A driver sits in the front of the car, but who is the *tuan*? The master sits in the back. Who opens the door? The driver."[65]

Nationally, the UMNO-led Malays, energized by the likes of Dr. Mahathir, secured arrangements for independence largely on their terms, following British re-recognition in 1948 that Malaya was essentially the land of the Malays. Independent Malaya, which materialized on 31 August 1957, was a "Malay" nation-state where the "special position" of the Malays was recognized in the Constitution. The sovereignty of the sultans in the nine Malay states was reaffirmed, and they were given powers to reserve government jobs, licences, services and scholarships for Malays, exercised in practice through political leaders.

But while the British conceded Malay political primacy among the various races, they insisted that UMNO work out a basis for inter-racial cooperation, unity and harmony. It took the form of an Alliance linking UMNO with political parties representing the Chinese and Indians. The three parties negotiated what came into focus later as an unwritten "social contract", which most Malays hoped would lead to economic improvement while most non-Malays hoped to gain political influence. Although Malay was the national language and Islam "the" religion, qualified non-Malay residents of Malaya would share citizenship with Malays, and they would enjoy freedom of worship. The terms of the agreement remained contentious, making the future nation-state subject to continuing racial pressures and challenges.[66] Just as some Malays always would be ready to press even harder for *ketuanan Melayu*, Malay supremacy, there would be non-Malays prepared to resist. Dr. Mahathir would be in the thick of the recurring wrangling.

Although Dr. Mahathir was well placed to plunge into national politics, trouble loomed in the form of his nagging disagreements with Prime Minister Tunku Abdul Rahman, who was acclaimed as *Bapa Merdeka*, Father of Independence. At one level, it might be considered an inherited clash: Master Mohamad Iskandar had found it necessary to get outside help to keep a young Tunku Abdul Rahman in check in his school. The first to admit in adulthood that he was naughty and in need of discipline as a child, the Tunku used to arrive every day on the shoulders of an aged palace attendant, resplendent in a gold-studded cap as part of his royal regalia. With the approval of the Tunku's mother, Mohamad Iskandar had put a stop to the fancy dress, in the interests of equality among the students, and he devised a quick solution to a teacher's complaint that the Tunku was disrupting his class. He sat him near the teacher's table.[67]

Differences between Dr. Mahathir and Tunku Abdul Rahman, however, were much deeper. The irritation and periodic ill-feeling, which would be a factor in Malaysian politics for 40 years, was mutual. The two came from vastly different backgrounds and generations, and saw the world through different eyes. It was hard to imagine two more opposite personalities, who happened to be born in the same state and engaged in the same endeavour at such a critical juncture in the country's history.

One of 45 children of the Sultan of Kedah, Tunku Abdul Rahman was an Anglophile, who readily admitted he had misspent his youth in England on slow horses and fast women. He earned his arts degree with the lowest possible marks for a pass and was 45 by the time be passed his final bar exam, having worked in the Kedah civil service. A confirmed bon vivant who continued to drink and gamble moderately, he was superstitious, charming and put a high store on being happy, though he had natural political instincts and developed a steely resolve. "The Tunku", or simply "Tunku", as he was affectionately known even though numerous others of royal birth bore the same title, became UMNO leader fortuitously. When the post opened up unexpectedly in 1951, Razak Hussein was asked to stand, but nominated his friend, the Tunku, because he considered himself too young.

Not only did Dr. Mahathir not smoke or gamble, he strongly disapproved of the lifestyles of senior civil servants and politicians who spent their leisure hours in bars and dance halls – and on the golf course, a game played by the first three prime ministers. He was incensed by feudal aspects of royalty and scathing about the hold that some traditions had on the Malays, exemplified by the proverb, "Let the child die, but let not the custom perish." He pointed out with dour logic that "if the child dies, then the custom dies along with it".[68]

As far as Tunku Abdul Rahman was concerned, Dr. Mahathir lacked respect for Malay custom known as *adat* and did not know his place. He was certain he recognized in Dr. Mahathir an inferiority complex occasioned by his part-Indian ancestry, because he himself had suffered from the same "disease" when looked down upon over his skin colour while studying in Cambridge. "To overcome this feeling of inferiority," said the Tunku, "I bought the most expensive, at that time, super sports car and I sped through town in it making quite a nuisance of myself. Just to be noticed."[69]

While Dr. Mahathir had his giant Pontiac, he wanted more than personal attention. He had a cause to sell as well. Although he and Tunku Abdul Rahman shared the opinion that the Malays were not very clever or demanding, they parted sharply over what should be done about it. The Tunku figured they would be content to control the machinery of state, heading government departments, the police and the army, and issuing licences and collecting taxes. He was quite open about leaving business to the Chinese because, he said, they were good at it and the Malays "have no idea how to make money". Dr. Mahathir wanted nothing less than to teach the Malays to compete and get their fair share of the nation's riches.

Dr. Mahathir and Tunku Abdul Rahman first clashed during the anti-Malayan Union campaign back in the 1940s. The Tunku was "very annoyed" when Mahathir, still a student, corrected grammatical mistakes in a letter drafted by the Tunku to be sent to the colonial secretary.[70] Dr. Mahathir emerged as an internal critic in 1954 after Tunku Abdul Rahman – named chief minister of a government that was granted home rule after leading the Alliance to victory in 51 of 52 contested seats in the country's first general election – negotiated with London for an end to the British presence. Dr. Mahathir objected to an agreement allowing British and other Commonwealth forces to remain in Malaya after independence in return for a commitment to the country's external defence. He sometimes found himself out of step with UMNO's leadership and sharing views with opposition parties. He also opposed the adoption of the folk tune *Terang Bulan*, repackaged as *Negaraku*, as the national anthem, on the grounds of its sentimentality. He lost that argument, too, but had the last say when he became prime minister much later.

Chairman of UMNO in Kedah and known nationally, Dr. Mahathir was expected to be a candidate in the 1959 general election, the first in independent Malaya. But he withdrew over a minor conflict, revealing another side of his personality and political style that would crop up periodically in his career: a deep sensitivity to the actions of others and, on occasions, an all-or-nothing response to political problems.[71] Dr. Mahathir had proposed that UMNO members chosen as candidates should have certain educational qualifications, alienating some members, who appealed to Tunku Abdul Rahman. Dr. Mahathir said that as "the party president backed them", he "withdrew from active participation in the party".[72]

Determined that when he made his entry it would be on his terms, Dr. Mahathir kept up the criticism. "There is no way that I will go to Kuala Lumpur just to tag along with the Tunku at the golf course in order to make a comeback," he said.[73] He did not have to. Nominated as the Alliance candidate for Kedah's Kota Star South parliamentary constituency in 1964, he romped home against a Persatuan Islam Sa Tanah Melayu (PAS) opponent.

Notes

1 Kua Kia Soong, ed., *K. Das & the Tunku Tapes* (Petaling Jaya: Strategic Info Research Development, 2002), pp. 131–132.
2 Zainuddin Maidin, *The Other Side of Mahathir* (Kuala Lumpur: Utusan Publications & Distributors Sdn. Bhd., 1994), p. 14.
3 Interview with Abdullah Ahmad, 30 May 2007.
4 Interview with Khalid Abdullah, 28 February 2007.
5 John Funston, "Political Careers of Mahathir Mohamad and Anwar Ibrahim: Parallel, Intersecting and Conflicting Lives", IKMAS Working Papers (Institute of Malaysian and International Studies, Universiti Kebangsaan Malaysia), no. 15 (July 1998): i–iv, 1–32.
6 Conflicting views exist on Dr. Mahathir's origins. Two prominent scholars have written that Dr. Mahathir's father was an immigrant from India. See John Funston, "The Legacy of Dr. Mahathir", *Australian Financial Review*, 30 July 2004; and Michael Leifer, *Dictionary of the Modern Politics of Southeast Asia* (London and New York: Routledge, 1996 edition), p. 158. Khoo Boo Teik, *Paradoxes of Mahathir-*

ism: An Intellectual Biography of Mahathir Mohamad (Kuala Lumpur: Oxford University Press, 1995), p. 15, suggested that Dr. Mahathir's father, Mohamad Iskandar, was born in Malaya by noting that he was "half Indian".

7   Dr. Mahathir denied – email correspondence 12 February 2009 – that his grandfather's full name was Iskandar Kutty, as reported in some newspaper articles and on the Internet. He said he had never heard the name Kutty in his family: email correspondence 18 February 2009.

8   Interview with Mahathir Mohamad, 14 August 2007.

9   Phone interview with Ahmad Mustapha Hassan, 31 May 2008.

10   Interview with Mahathir Mohamad, 20 March 2007.

11   Interview with Mukhriz Mahathir, 22 March 2007.

12   Email correspondence with Marina Mahathir, 24 January 2008.

13   Interview with Mahathir Mohamad, 14 August 2007.

14   Email correspondence with John Funston, 2 June 2006.

15   J. Victor Morais, *Mahathir: A Profile in Courage* (Petaling Jaya: Eastern Universities Press (M) Sdn. Bhd., 1982), p. 1.

16   Interview with Shaari Daud, 27 February 2007.

17   Robin Adshead, *Mahathir of Malaysia: Statesman and Leader* (London: Hibiscus Publishing Company, 1989), p. 27.

18   Interview with Mahathir Mohamad, 31 March 2008.

19   Ibid.

20   John Funston, "The Legacy of Dr. Mahathir".

21   Interview with Mustapa Kassim and Abdul Rahman Aziz, 26 February 2007.

22   Robin Adshead, *Mahathir of Malaysia*, p. 28.

23   Interview with Mahathir Mohamad, 20 March 2007.

24   Ibid.

25   Interview with Mahathir Mohamad, 31 March 2008.

26   Robin Adshead, *Mahathir of Malaysia*, p. 33.

27   Interview with Mahathir Mohamad, 20 March 2007.

28   Robin Adshead, *Mahathir of Malaysia*, p. 34.

29   Interview with Mahathir Mohamad, 31 March 2008.

30   Interviews with Mahathir Mohamad, 20 March, 14 August 2007.

31   John Funston, "Political Careers of Mahathir Mohamad and Anwar Ibrahim: Parallel, Intersecting and Conflicting Lives".

32   Interview with Mahathir Mohamad, 20 March 2007.

33   Dr. Mahathir Mohamad, "New Thoughts on Nationality", in *The Early Years: 1947–1972* (Kuala Lumpur: Berita Publishing Sdn. Bhd., 1995), pp. 85–87.

34   John Funston, "Political Careers of Mahathir Mohamad and Anwar Ibrahim: Parallel, Intersecting and Conflicting Lives".

35   Dr. Mahathir Mohamad, "Malay Progress and the University", in *The Early Years*, p. 70, cited in John Funston, "Political Careers of Mahathir Mohamad and Anwar Ibrahim: Parallel, Intersecting and Conflicting Lives".

36   Interview with Siti Hasmah Mohamad Ali, 17 January 2008.

37   Lee Kuan Yew, *From Third World to First: The Singapore Story: 1965–2000* (Singapore: Times Media Pte. Ltd., 2000), p. 276.

38   Ibid., p. 276.

39   Interview with Dr. Wong Hee Ong, 21 March 2007.

40   Interview with Dr. Wong Hee Ong, 21 March 2007; phone interview with Dr. James Murugasu, 23 June 2008.

41   Interview with Wang Gungwu, 6 October 2006.

42 John Funston, "Political Careers of Mahathir Mohamad and Anwar Ibrahim: Parallel, Intersecting and Conflicting Lives".
43 Ibid.
44 Dr. Mahathir Mohamad, "Malay Progress and the University", in *The Early Years*, p. 70.
45 Interview with Mahathir Mohamad, 14 August 2007.
46 Interview with Khalid Abdullah, 28 February 2007.
47 Interview with Mukhriz Mahathir, 22 March 2007.
48 Zainuddin Maidin, *The Other Side of Mahathir*, p. 6.
49 Interview with Shaari Daud, 27 February 2007.
50 Interview with Siti Hasmah Mohamad Ali, 17 January 2008.
51 Email correspondence with Marina Mahathir, 24 January 2008.
52 J. Victor Morais, *Mahathir*, p. 1.
53 Interview with Siti Hasmah Mohamad Ali, 17 January 2008.
54 Interview with Mahathir Mohamad, 20 March 2007.
55 Email correspondence with Marina Mahathir, 24 January 2008.
56 Interview with Mukhriz Mahathir, 22 March 2007.
57 Email correspondence with Marina Mahathir, 24 January 2008.
58 Interview with Siti Hasmah Mohamad Ali, 17 January 2008.
59 Interview with Mahathir Mohamad, 31 March 2008.
60 J. Victor Morais, *Mahathir*, p. 1.
61 Interview with Mahathir Mohamad, 20 March 2007.
62 Interview with M. Jaafar Ismail, 11 December 2007.
63 Interview with Haja Nasrudeen Abdul Kareem, 28 February 2007.
64 Zainuddin Maidin, *The Other Side of Mahathir*, p. 7.
65 Interview with Abdullah Ahmad, 23 March 2007.
66 Cheah Boon Kheng, *Malaysia: The Making of a Nation* (Singapore: Institute of Southeast Asian Studies, 2002), p. 6.
67 J. Victor Morais, *Mahathir*, pp. 4–5.
68 Zainuddin Maidin, *The Other Side of Mahathir*, p. 15.
69 Kua Kia Soong, ed., *K. Das & the Tunku Tapes*, p. 132.
70 Interview with Mahathir Mohamad, 20 March 2007.
71 John Funston, "Political Careers of Mahathir Mohamad and Anwar Ibrahim: Parallel, Intersecting and Conflicting Lives".
72 Interview with Mahathir Mohamad, 31 March 2008.
73 Zainuddin Maidin, *The Other Side of Mahathir*, p. 15.

2
An Early Introduction to Brutal Politics

Grabbing the political spotlight after his election, Dr. Mahathir established a reputation as an active and articulate parliamentarian in defence of the Malays. He became UMNO's main spokesman in the ruling party's conflict with Singapore, led by Lee Kuan Yew, over the kind of society they were trying to build.[1] Dr. Mahathir's first parliamentary term, from 1964 to 1969, was an extremely turbulent period in the country's political development, and one of the hottest issues was the presence of Singapore.

By the time Dr. Mahathir took his place in the House of Representatives, Malaya had become Malaysia, a new territorial configuration whose legitimacy was opposed by the Philippines and challenged by President Sukarno's Indonesia with armed incursions. Established on 16 September 1963, Malaysia had Malaya as the core, with three other former British colonial territories tacked on: self-governing Singapore, joined by a causeway to peninsular Malaya, and Sabah and Sarawak, several hundred kilometres away across the South China Sea in Borneo. Among the numerous calculations that went into the creation of Malaysia was the primary desire to offset Singapore's predominantly Chinese population in order to protect the peninsular Malays. While Indonesia's so-called Confrontation faded with the end of the Sukarno regime through internal turmoil, Singapore's inclusion turned Malaysia into a communal battleground that recalled the Malayan Union debate.

Lee Kuan Yew's People's Action Party advocated a "Malaysian Malaysia", meaning a multiracial nation in which everyone enjoyed political equality even if the Malays were accorded special economic and social rights. While Dr. Mahathir's more experienced colleagues were reluctant to do direct combat with Lee, acknowledged as a brilliant politician and debater, the country doctor was fearless. Referring to Lee, he dismissed "the mad ambition of one man to see himself as the first Chinese prime minister of Malaysia".[2]

Selected to give the formal "address of thanks" to the King, despite being a relatively raw backbencher, Dr. Mahathir delivered an emotional speech to Parliament on 26 May 1965. He attacked the "so-called non-communal parties", the People's Action Party and the Malayan Socialist Front, for being "pure Chinese chauvinists" and "the most communal and racialist in their attitudes". He discerned only one difference between them: "The Socialist Front is merely pro-Chinese and communist-oriented, while the PAP is pro-Chinese, communist-oriented and positively anti-Malay."[3] Dr. Mahathir contrasted some Chinese who "appreciate the need for all communities to be well-off" with "the insular, selfish and arrogant type, of which Mr. Lee is a good example". Most of them had never crossed the causeway, he said. "They have never known Malay rule and could not bear the idea that the people that they have so long kept under their heels should now be in a position to rule them."[4]

When Singapore was expelled from Malaysia less than three months later and became a nation in its own right, Dr. Mahathir cheered. "I felt Singapore was too big a mouthful for Malaysia," he said. "Singaporean Chinese were too aggressive" and lacked the understanding and sensitivity of most Malaysian Chinese.[5]

The Singaporeans may have lost their Malaysian Malaysia dream, but they left a mark on Dr. Mahathir that was to haunt him for a long time: the label of "ultra", or communal extremist, which was adopted enthusiastically by his Malaysian opponents as well. Certainly radical, Dr. Mahathir appealed emotionally to the Malays and often frightened the Chinese, who viewed him with suspicion. Yet he denied being an extremist and complained that he was misinterpreted and misunderstood, and that the tag made it hard to explain his stand in a rational manner.

Dr. Mahathir identified with a younger group in UMNO that began to develop different views from those of party leaders. They urged greater government assistance for Malays, closer alignment with Afro-Asian developing countries and opposition to foreign troops being based in Malaysia. Elected chairman of the Afro-Asian People's Solidarity Organization's committee for Malaysia in 1964, Dr. Mahathir represented the country overseas in a bid to weaken international support for Indonesia, then engaged in its anti-Malaysia Confrontation. Members of the group looked to Dr. Mahathir for leadership, light-heartedly calling him among themselves "Osagyefo", the title given to Kwame Nkrumah, the president of Ghana, the first black African country to shake off the chains of colonialism.[6] Osagyefo means "Redeemer" in Twi, a dialect of the Akan language.

Life in Kuala Lumpur for Dr. Mahathir was not all sweat and tears, however. For one of the few times in his life, he let his hair down occasionally in the company of another first-term UMNO parliamentarian, Tunku Abdullah Tuanku Abdul Rahman, a playboy prince from the Negri Sembilan royal family who went by the name of Charlie. An unlikely duo, they became firm friends, with Dr. Mahathir staying in Tunku Abdullah's house when Parliament was in session. "With him I could go to all the best places in Kuala Lumpur and not feel out of place," said Dr. Mahathir.[7] Urged by the absent Dr. Siti Hasmah to give her still-shy husband a "push" socially, Tunku Abdullah obliged by escorting him to the Selangor Club, the Lake Club and elsewhere, while persuading him to dance and have a glass of white wine. "I brought him down to my level," said Charlie. "Otherwise it would have been boring."[8]

In the company of Tunku Abdullah, who would later build a substantial business group, Dr. Mahathir's entrepreneurial sparks began to fly again. They went into partnership, starting a limousine service from the airport to the city, and acquiring a 20-room hotel in Sumatra, but neither venture took off. Lacking borrowing power, they had to sell out to a third partner after acquiring land and building Wisma Budiman, a high-rise commercial building, in the capital. "It was a good effort" and they made "some money", said Tunku Abdullah, though politics remained the priority for Dr. Mahathir.

With the various races represented by the Alliance, however imperfectly, and the economy ticking over, Malaysia was seen internationally as a developing-world success. The newly created country had survived expansion to include Singapore, Sabah and Sarawak, contraction with the withdrawal of Singapore, a China-backed communist insurgency that required a state of emergency from 1948 to 1960, and Sukarno's military provocations. So it was no surprise that Tunku Abdul Rahman was inclined to sit back, smile and periodically proclaim himself "the happiest prime minister in the world". Who could blame him? Answer: Dr. Mahathir. He warned that the Tunku's approach was misguided and would not last, and that behind the peaceful façade pressures were building dangerously.

Subsequent research would show Dr. Mahathir was right. The constitutional bias in favour of the Malays simply was not working in practice. Soon after Malaya obtained independence, the average annual income for an adult male was calculated at RM3,223 for Chinese, RM2,013 for Indians and RM1,463 for Malays.[9] Many assessments showed that the Malay share of national wealth declined over the next ten to 15 years.

While government spending was supposed to have been heavily skewed in favour of the countryside where 70 per cent of Malays toiled as rice farmers, fishermen and rubber small-holders, it was insufficient, or not guided by the appropriate policies, to promote meaningful change. Malay rural life, in fact, was stagnating, with farmers missing out on the growth being achieved by the overall economy. While the provision of roads, irrigation, electrification and technical advice helped, such infrastructure could not overcome institutional constraints such as landlessness, lack of reasonable credit and marketing monopolies.[10]

Looking back, political scientist John Funston found that the reason for the lack of Malay progress was that UMNO did not have control of the political system, despite what was almost universally believed. While UMNO fielded most candidates in elections and had a decisive majority of Cabinet slots, it was the Chinese partner, the Malaysian Chinese Association, that provided most of the Alliance funds and held the two key portfolios, Finance, and Commerce and Industry. And while it was true that power was concentrated in the hands of Tunku Abdul Rahman, he was no typical Malay and did not always represent their interests. In many ways, the Anglicized, mahjong-playing, horse race-loving Tunku had more in common with the leaders of the Alliance partner parties than with the rank and file of UMNO.[11]

Presciently, in a newspaper article published in 1968, Dr. Mahathir fore-saw a "pent-up reservoir of ill-feelings", with the potential for violence, behind the seemingly "harmonious relationship between the races". Noting that racial intolerance leading to riots had occurred in the United States, Britain, Africa and neighbouring Asian countries, he said preventive meas-ures were needed to avoid it happening in Malaysia. He was in touch with people on the ground, and "I know that the signs and symptoms are already there." Having given a similar warning in an article the previous month, Dr. Mahathir concluded, "If I may say so again, soon it may be too late."[12]

Just over a year later, on 13 May 1969, Dr. Mahathir's grim prediction came true. Three days after a general election result upset the precarious balance of hope and fear, following a campaign that aroused communal passions, Malays and Chinese indulged in an orgy of killing, looting and burning in Kuala Lumpur. Although the Alliance government retained a majority in Parlia-ment, UMNO lost 8 of its 59 seats, one of them Dr. Mahathir's. The oppos-ition won 14 urban seats, 13 of them at the expense of the Malaysian Chinese Association. Critically, the opposition captured half of the seats in the Selangor State Assembly, raising the possibility that a Malay state that included the nation's capital would pass into Chinese hands.

Chinese and Indian opposition supporters paraded through the streets of Kuala Lumpur in celebration, taunting and insulting the Malays. Fearful that they were losing their last refuge, political dominance, the Malays retal-iated. They slaughtered each other with an assortment of *parangs*, a type of machette with a wooden handle, knives, daggers, iron bars and other impro-vised weapons, while torching cars and buildings. By the time the army moved in and restored order, terrified Chinese and Malays were huddled behind makeshift barricades in a maze of fortified enclaves patrolled by armed vigilantes. The official toll was put at 196 dead and 439 wounded. Unofficial estimates ran much higher. "May 13" was seared in the young nation's soul: a date, a bloodbath, a tragedy.

The following day, the king proclaimed a State of Emergency, suspended Parliament and a National Operations Council took over, a serious setback for the fledgling democracy. It effectively marked the end of Tunku Abdul Rahman's reign, though he did not formally retire as prime minister until September 1970. Deputy Premier Razak, who was also defence minister and minister for home affairs, slipped easily into the chairmanship of the council, which governed by decree for the next 21 months.

In UMNO, young Malay nationalists associated with Dr. Mahathir, including Musa Hitam, an assistant minister, and Abdullah Ahmad, political secretary to Razak, reached a rough consensus on the electoral results. They felt the "social contract" had failed, that UMNO had conceded too much to the Chinese, and the country must be "returned" to the Malays. They held Tunku Abdul Rahman responsible and felt he should quit, but Ismail Abdul Rahman, recruited as home affairs minister by Razak, told a four-man delegation, which included Dr. Mahathir, that he would not tolerate any attempt to depose the Tunku. At the same time, though, Ismail said to give him and Razak a year, and if they failed to "arrange things" with the Tunku, they would openly back a putsch against him.[13] The anti-Tunku agitators were supposed to be patient.

Dr. Mahathir had other ideas. He sat down in Alor Star on 17 June and hammered out the most notorious letter in Malaysian politics. This was no *surat layang*, flying letter, an anonymous poisoned message designed to discredit an opponent, which is a common tactic. He addressed his missive to Tunku Abdul Rahman, and signed it. Having been reprimanded by the Tunku for commenting publicly on the delicate political situation, Dr. Mahathir sent a letter in Malay that political scientist Karl von Vorys called noteworthy not only because it was deliberately offensive but also because it represented the mood of many Malays.[14]

In it, Dr. Mahathir said Tunku Abdul Rahman's pro-Chinese policies were directly responsible for the "May 13" riots. Malays, whether UMNO or the opposition Persatuan Islam Sa Tanah Melayu (PAS), "really hate you...," he said. "I wish to convey what the community really thinks, which is that it is high time you resigned as prime minister and head of UMNO." Dr. Mahathir said he felt the responsibility to speak up, even if it meant he might be jailed. He accused the Tunku of continuing to play poker "with your Chinese friends" during the emergency, using police vehicles and escorts to find players.

On a sensitive, personal note, Dr. Mahathir wrote that he had heard that the Tunku had called him "Pakistani" – an allusion to his South Indian forebears – but he did not believe it. This was because Dr. Mahathir had always defended the Tunku when PAS called him "the son of Siam" – a reference to his Thai mother – which implied he was unfit to be the leader of the Malays. So, Dr. Mahathir said, he expected that the Tunku would have defended him, despite his having "two spoonfuls of Pakistani blood in my body".

Having withdrawn earlier at the merest hint of a brush with Tunku Abdul Rahman, Dr. Mahathir chose the extreme opposite tack this time: frontal assault. It was all or nothing again. And it was hugely risky for anyone hoping to climb the political ladder, though it was almost certainly carefully calculated. As would become clearer later, Dr. Mahathir rarely, if ever, made a political move without weighing the likely consequences.

More than most, he realized how deeply unpopular the Tunku had become among Malays.

The Tunku was doubly furious to find that Dr. Mahathir's letter was being read throughout the country. While student sympathizers passed on copies, the letter was systematically distributed by a group that included Razak's aide, Abdullah Ahmad. Members chipped in a total of RM1,500 to cover ink, envelopes and postage, copied the letter and mailed it to everyone on UMNO, universities and civil service invitation lists that they obtained.[15]

How and when the letter left Dr. Mahathir's hands remained disputed. "He gave it to the right people," said Abdullah, who maintained that he saw a copy before Dr. Mahathir sent it to Tunku Abdul Rahman. Abdullah said he showed the letter to Razak, who said, "I've read it. We've discussed it, but please understand that I haven't seen this letter."[16] Dr. Mahathir, however, denied circulating the letter in advance to anyone. "Later on, I gave copies to friends" as a "kind of insurance. If anything happens to me they will know I have done this".[17]

The one person Dr. Mahathir might have informed, considering he was jeopardizing his political career, was Dr. Siti Hasmah. But he told his wife nothing – "I was shocked," she said – establishing a pattern of behaviour that he was to observe throughout his political life.[18] Involved in some of the most tumultuous events in the nation's history, Dr. Mahathir declined to discuss them as they unfolded with his family. Returning home in the evening after upheavals in the government or party, he would usually remain tight-lipped. Like other Malaysians, his wife and children learned what happened from newspaper and TV reports. "We would never know about it, even if he had a big day," said Mukhriz Mahathir.[19]

Tunku Abdul Rahman's response to Dr. Mahathir was an ultimatum: Resign or be expelled from the party. Sensing high-level sympathy for Dr. Mahathir, even with the deputy prime minister, the Tunku also issued an ultimatum to Razak: It was either him or Mahathir.[20] With Razak presiding, Dr. Mahathir was evicted on 12 July 1969 from UMNO's Supreme Council, to which he had been elected on an annual basis since 1965. Aware of what the verdict would be, Dr. Mahathir still refused to apologize or back down when addressing fellow council members. The charge was breach of party discipline, that he had widely circulated correspondence containing "vitally important party matters" that should have been first discussed by the Supreme Council. He insisted then, as he would subsequently, that he had not abetted its dissemination. On 26 September, Dr. Mahathir was kicked out of the party altogether. Musa Hitam, one of his staunchest allies in the anti-Tunku campaign, was forced to resign as assistant minister to the deputy prime minister.

With Musa heading abroad to study and Dr. Mahathir beating a retreat to Kedah to resume full-time practice as a doctor, the crisis in UMNO was over, and Tunku Abdul Rahman appeared to have prevailed. But it was something of a last gasp for the Tunku. Students at institutions of higher learning were agitating for his removal, making it necessary for the National Operations Council to ban "any meeting, procession, demonstration or public utterance to get Tunku Abdul Rahman to step down from office". Dr. Mahathir's letter was also formally banned, with printing, selling or distributing it punishable by three years imprisonment and a fine of RM2,000. With this sort of protection, no outsiders could force the Tunku to quit, though just as surely he would no longer have the final say on matters of substance. New policies were on the way to ensure Malay political dominance, and the Tunku would be carried along with the tide, before being eased out.

Dr. Mahathir blamed Chinese voters for the surprising loss of his seat. Friends said he courted defeat with a loose comment in advance that he could win if all the Malays, who constituted 80 to 90 per cent of the Kota Star South constituency, voted for him. His remark was interpreted in a Chinese newspaper as an insult to mean he did not need Chinese support, and Chinese voters responded by deserting him in favour of his PAS opponent.[21] Dr. Mahathir agreed that the Chinese – who held what he called "the casting vote" since the Malays were fairly evenly split – had switched allegiance. But he said it was because "they thought I was a Malay ultra", the label given to him by Singapore. Defying national trends, "because I was known as a champion of the Malays," his Malay vote actually increased, he said.[22]

With the police still investigating his letter, Dr. Mahathir feared arrest. He learned from police friends that Tunku Abdul Rahman wanted to detain him, but they persuaded the Tunku it would only make a martyr of Dr. Mahathir.[23] Too late: He was already a hero in Malay eyes. The rapid sequence of shattering events – a traumatic election campaign, his defeat, the "May 13" violence, the Tunku letter, double expulsion – gave him an almost cult-like following in his community. As political scientist Khoo Boo Teik said, "It transformed him from being a failed electoral candidate into a living symbol of Malay nationalism."[24]

At no stage during his almost three years in the political wilderness did Dr. Mahathir lose interest in shaping the debate on Malaysia's future. In addition to running his clinic and investing, he stepped up his writing. In early 1970, he published his best known book, *The Malay Dilemma*,[25] which was promptly banned in Malaysia, remaining proscribed until he became prime minister in 1981. The ban added to Dr. Mahathir's maverick image without the contents of the book remaining secret, since it was available in Singapore and he accepted speaking invitations and discussed the substance of it. Two other publications that appeared a few years later were substantially written during this period. *Panduan Peniaga Kecil*, published in 1974, appeared in English in 1985 as *Guide for Small Businessmen*. It advised Malays how to get started in business and, in particular, how to succeed against Chinese competition.[26] The 14 essays published as *Menghadapi Cabaran* in 1976, and issued in 1986 as *The Challenge*, was a reflective work that emphasized the importance of spiritual values, education, discipline and organization. It was critical of corruption, destructive opposition to governments from pressure groups and allegedly decadent Western ways – resistance to hard work, untidiness, nudity and homosexuality.[27]

Contentiously, *The Malay Dilemma* argued that the Malays were the original or indigenous people of Malaya, and should be accepted as the "definitive race". It rejected non-Malay claims to political, linguistic and cultural parity with the Malays, but not on the grounds that the Malays were superior in any way. Just as countries such as the United States and Australia required a certain minimal assimilation of migrants to their own national culture, the Malays had a right to expect the non-Malays to do the same. The aim was "not designed to perpetuate the privileges of the original definitive race to the exclusion of the new immigrant races…settlers willing to conform to the characteristics of the definitive citizen will in fact become definitive citizens and will exercise the same rights and privileges". In practice, they would need to speak Malay and be educated in Malay, though they would not be required to adopt Islam.

The book defined its title: "The Malay dilemma is whether they should stop trying to help themselves in order that they should be proud to be the poor citizens of a prosperous country or whether they should try to get at some of the riches that this country boasts of, even if it blurs the economic picture of Malaysia a little." The answer was never in doubt: "The cup of Malay bitterness must be diluted. A solution must be found, an equitable solution which denies nothing to anyone and yet gives the Malay his place in the Malayan sun."

Dr. Mahathir's proffered solution was "constructive protection", a vague term implying a level of support somewhere in between leaving the Malays defenceless in the face of Chinese aggression and making their lives so comfortable that they would forget how to compete and progress. His concern about over-protecting the Malays was due to his belief in the then popular, later discredited, notion known as Social Darwinism to explain their inferiority and Chinese superiority. While he never used the term, Dr. Mahathir, like Social Darwinism's other adherents, applied the phrase "survival of the fittest" – first coined by the British economist, Herbert Spencer, after Charles Darwin's evolutionary theory of "natural selection" – to the competition for survival in human society. Dr. Mahathir even embraced the eugenics offshoot idea, that the unfit transmit their undesirable characteristics.

The book surmised that the early Malays, inhabiting a lush land with plenty of food, did not suffer starvation and even the weak in mind and body were able to survive and procreate. The hot, humid climate was not conducive to either vigorous work or mental activity, so they were content to spend most of their time resting or talking to each other. In-breeding, and the absence of inter-racial marriages in rural areas, together with certain social practices, sapped their enterprise and had a disastrous effect on the Malay community over the long term. The Chinese, by contrast, from a homeland littered with disasters and with a custom of "cross-breeding", were the fit survivors of a natural weeding out process.

If all protection for the Malays were removed, the book argued, "it would perhaps be possible to breed a hardy and resourceful race capable of competing against all comers. Unfortunately, we do not have four thousand years to play around with." So while Dr. Mahathir accepted the need for constructive protection immediately, in the end it would be "the people alone who make themselves equal". In other words, he concluded that the ultimate solution to Malay inequality was to remake the Malays, changing some of their "inherent traits and character acquired over the centuries", including their "fatalism", and "failure to value time" and "appreciate the real value of money and property". It was a task that would absorb much of his energy in the years ahead.[28]

From the political sidelines, Dr. Mahathir could watch with satisfaction as his like-minded allies in UMNO came to exercise decisive influence over party policies. The trend, which could easily have been following a Mahathir script, was to put Malay political predominance, whose reality was questioned in the election result, beyond dispute. By the time Parliament reopened in early 1971, Razak had succeeded Tunku Abdul Rahman as prime minister and Malaysia's Constitution and the Sedition Act were amended to make it illegal to question "sensitive issues": citizenship, the special position of the Malays and natives of Sabah and Sarawak, the national language and the status of the sultans. Not even elected members of parliament could question them.

The Razak government's major response to the May 13 riots was a far-reaching affirmative action programme called the New Economic Policy (NEP), to last for 20 years from its introduction in 1971. Just as Dr. Mahathir advised, it pinpointed Malay deprivation as the underlying cause of the unrest and set national unity as the long-term goal. The two main objectives of the NEP were the eradication of poverty for all Malaysians, and the restructuring of society so that race was no longer identified with economic function. As no ethnic group was to feel a sense of deprivation and the Malays had to make significant gains, the NEP was predicated on strong and sustained overall economic growth.

According to the official target, Malays and other indigenous people would own and manage at least 30 per cent of the "total commercial and industrial activities in all categories and scales of operations". The government also stipulated that the employment pattern, "at all levels and in all sectors", must reflect the racial composition of the population.[29] The share of national corporate equity held by Malays and other native races was to increase from 2.4 per cent in 1970 to 30 per cent in 1990. In practice, the wide application of the 30 per cent quota was broadly in line with Dr. Mahathir's argument that equality required that "each race is represented in every strata of society, in every field of work, in proportion more or less to their percentage of the population".[30] Although he played no part in formulating the economic blueprint, Dr. Mahathir was godfather to the NEP and would always be strongly identified with it in the public mind.

With Tunku Abdul Rahman in retirement, the way was open for Razak to rehabilitate Dr. Mahathir, which he did by readmitting him to UMNO on 7 March 1972. A Malay-language newspaper cartoon depicting his return as Superman, descending from the skies to be met by all members of UMNO's Supreme Council, arms outstretched in welcome, irritated some of them who did not want him back.[31] Among those who agreed to his re-admission only reluctantly was a fellow physician, Ismail Abdul Rahman, the highly principled deputy prime minister and home affairs minister, who felt Dr. Mahathir had gone too far in his criticism of the Tunku.[32]

After such a tumultuous, decade-long prelude – and partly because of it – Dr. Mahathir's ascent was meteoric. He re-entered Parliament in 1973, appointed to the Senate by Kedah state, and was returned to the House of Representatives in a general election the following year. Immediately made a full minister, bypassing the normal progression from a deputy position, he served in a coalition government that had been broadened by Prime Minister Razak beyond the original Alliance to become the multi-party National Front. As PAS had renamed itself Parti Islam Se-Malaysia and joined the administration, Dr. Mahathir could not contest his old seat, but moved instead to another Kedah constituency, Kubang Pasu, where he was unopposed. Significantly, his portfolio was education, a particular interest of his and a post that gave him the opportunity to entrench his support among schoolteachers, then the most important group in UMNO.[33] It was seen as a logical stepping stone to higher office. Dr. Mahathir formally abandoned medicine after 20 years of practice and relocated his family from Alor Star to Kuala Lumpur.

In UMNO, Dr. Mahathir was immediately embroiled in a vicious factional fight that convulsed the party in the aftermath of Tunku Abdul Rahman's induced retirement. While Dr. Mahathir's allies, the "development-oriented reformists", or leftists, aligned with Razak, were in control, the Tunku's "independence fighters", or conservatives, were mounting a serious rearguard action.[34] Separated mainly by generation and ideology, the two factions often referred to each other in abusive terms: The Old Guard called some of Razak's inner circle "communists", while the Young Turks reciprocated by referring to Tunku's men as "American stooges".[35]

Dr. Mahathir was elected to the UMNO Supreme Council with the highest vote only months after being accepted back into the party in 1972, though he failed in a simultaneous bid for the vice presidency. But with the decision to hold future UMNO elections triennially rather than annually, the real test of factional strength would come in 1975, and the outcome would shape Malaysian politics for a generation or more. Three years of intense politicking was heightened by the unexpected death in 1973, from a heart attack, of Deputy Prime Minister Ismail. Razak appointed Hussein Onn, his brother-in-law, to fill the vacancy, but it was generally understood that Hussein would be an interim deputy. Adding pressure was the fact that Razak himself was dying of leukemia, though only a few people knew that and they were sworn to secrecy. Diagnosed in 1969 and given four years at most to live, Razak was already on borrowed time. Ismail's death at 57 had robbed him of his logical successor as prime minister, and left him scrambling to assemble a future leadership for the country before he died.

As the UMNO General Assembly approached in 1975, Razak called in Abdullah Ahmad to discuss tactics for the election of three vice presidents. These posts were considered crucial, as one occupant before long would move up to deputy president and then party president, giving him the prime ministership. Abdullah, a former journalist, was a deputy minister in the Prime Minister's Department and a member of UMNO's Supreme Council, who functioned as Razak's de facto political adviser, confidant and hatchet man. Razak was specific. Of the eight candidates, he wanted elected, in order: Abdul Ghafar Baba, minister for national and rural development, and Tengku Razaleigh Hamzah, chairman of state-owned Bank Bumiputra, both incumbents; and Dr. Mahathir, the education minister. Ghafar and Dr. Mahathir were tightly aligned with Razak. Tengku Razaleigh, a businessman-banker who owed his rise in the party to Razak's sponsorship, positioned himself in the centre of the ideological struggle.[36]

Razak was equally adamant who was to be stopped: Syed Jaafar Albar, dubbed the Lion of UMNO, and Harun Idris, UMNO Youth leader and chief minister of Selangor state,[37] who were hard-core Tunku supporters; Muhammad Ghazali Shafie, the home affairs minister, regarded by the Razak camp as a political opportunist; and Hamzah Abu Samah, trade and industry minister and another brother-in-law of Razak. Harun, Syed Jaafar Albar and Ghazali were politically unacceptable, while Razak would face accusations of nepotism if Hamzah were elected. Razak told Abdullah to make sure the four did not win "in that order". He said the abrasive Abdullah could "use his big stick" and Razak's name because he did not want them to be elected "at any cost".[38]

Apart from working the ground at divisional level to get the votes and avoid last-minute defections, Abdullah planned to have Razak influence the outcome of the election by endorsing his three preferred candidates in his opening speech. Alert to that possibility, Tunku supporters on the Supreme Council, at its last meeting before the General Assembly, warned him not to mention personal preferences. As a ploy, Razak suggested that Senu Abdul Rahman, UMNO's secretary general and a known Tunku ally, check a draft of the speech, which Abdullah had prepared. Senu left the room and returned about half an hour later to report finding no mention of names. In fact, Razak's choice of Senu was deliberate, as he was the sort of person without the patience to comb his way line by line through a lengthy document. The names of Ghafar, Tengku Razaleigh and Dr. Mahathir were there, but he missed them. Breaking his promise to the Supreme Council, Razak read that speech, drawing audible objections from a few delegates.[39] The three were duly elected, and in Razak's preferred order.

Ghazali Shafie, who saw himself as a future prime minister, was particularly upset by his failure to win a vice president's slot. Indeed, the dynamic Ghazali, a former permanent secretary of the foreign ministry who rose to prominence with the National Operations Council during emergency rule, was humiliated to trail the field. Flamboyant and brimming with confidence, however, "King Ghaz" or simply "Ghaz", as he was known, never relinquished his ambition to lead the country, and plotted to make it a reality.

Ghazali actually found himself in contention when Razak died in January 1976 – unexpectedly, since most people did not know he was ill – and the leadership of Malaysia was thrown wide open. Razak was succeeded by Hussein Onn, who had suffered a heart attack the previous year and was unlikely to remain as prime minister for more than one term. Although party tradition indicated Hussein should choose one of the party's three elected vice presidents, he initially favoured Ghazali. Hussein told associates that Ghazali was familiar with international relations, had the most recognized name in the region and was popular with neighbours such as Indonesia and Singapore.[40]

In fact, the Indonesian government took the extraordinary step of urging Hussein to appoint Ghazali, rather than Dr. Mahathir, in the interests of enhancing Indonesia-Malaysia relations.[41] The Indonesians were familiar with Ghazali from Confrontation days, when he was Malaysia's prime interlocutor in bilateral ties. According to Dr. Mahathir, Indonesian intelligence chief Ali Murtopo visited Kuala Lumpur and spoke with Hussein, indicating a preference for Ghazali.[42]

When Hussein looked like he might bypass Ghafar, Tengku Razaleigh and Dr. Mahathir, they met several times among themselves and then called on him at his office and presented the case for maintaining tradition. He was left in no doubt that they would hesitate to serve in a government in which one of them was not deputy prime minister. Notoriously indecisive, Hussein agonized for more than six weeks over his choice. Ghafar, the most senior vice president, lacked higher education and social graces, and was not comfortable speaking English. Tengku Razaleigh was, in many ways, his ideal: royal, sophisticated and dependable. But, as Tengku Razaleigh himself volunteered, he had several strikes against him. Still under 40, he was on the young side, lacked cabinet experience and was not married, which did not sit well with some Malays. Dr. Mahathir, the most junior of the vice presidents, got the nod.

Not close to Hussein, Dr. Mahathir was as surprised as anybody. He speculated that Hussein could have relied on some advice an ill Razak gave him. Dr. Mahathir said that when he went to see Hussein, as Razak was being treated in London, Hussein "did tell me that Tun Razak told him if he had any problem to call me".[43] Hussein might also have been influenced by Tengku Razaleigh, who said Hussein had told him privately he was the best person for the job. "I said no," said Tengku Razaleigh, who ruled himself out on grounds of youth, inexperience and his single status. "So I suggested it is Dr. Mahathir."[44] Hussein could have relied, too, on the opinion of Musa Hitam, another cabinet member, who was asked by the prime minister to write an analysis of the merits of every potential deputy premier. "I strongly recommended Dr. Mahathir," Musa said.[45]

However he reached his decision, Hussein was deeply troubled by his choice of Dr. Mahathir as deputy party president and deputy prime minister. Before announcing it, Hussein called on Tunku Abdul Rahman, who would not have welcomed Dr. Mahathir's promotion. As the Tunku related the story, Hussein arrived at his house in Kuala Lumpur, kissed his hand in the normal greeting, sat down in a chair and stared at the floor. After half an hour, without saying a word, Hussein stood, begged to leave in the usual way, and departed. The Tunku told close friends it was all very strange, but he surmised that the extremely polite and gentlemanly Hussein wanted to explain why he was going to appoint Dr. Mahathir, but could not bring himself to utter the words.[46]

Ghafar Baba was also unhappy at being bypassed and refused to serve in Hussein's Cabinet, though he kept his senior vice president's post. The most disappointed, however, was Ghazali Shafie who, lacking grassroots appeal in UMNO, had missed what appeared to be a heaven-sent chance to be directly appointed prime minister-in-waiting. Undeterred, Ghazali pressed ahead with one of the most cynical power plays ever conducted in Malaysian politics, designed to stop Dr. Mahathir becoming prime minister and to claim the prize for himself.

His political cover was the factional fighting within UMNO, which flared anew after Razak's death. Conservatives, who already had been targeting left-leaning members of Razak's "palace guard", smelled blood once he was no longer around to protect them. With the Beijing-backed Malayan Communist Party still engaged in guerrilla warfare against the government, the Tunku's contemporaries criticized Razak's young advisers for his shift towards a non-aligned foreign policy, which included establishing diplomatic relations with China. On the domestic front, the conservatives, basically old-style laissez-faire capitalists, detected creeping socialism as official agencies in support of the NEP proliferated under Razak. While the rallying cry of the Old Guard was subversion at the heart of government, several issues, in reality, were being contested. Among them was an attempt to restore the political fortunes of the popular former chief minister of Selangor, Harun Idris, forced out by Razak for corruption.

Syed Jaafar Albar, who succeeded Harun as head of UMNO Youth, spear-headed the campaign to root out alleged communist sympathizers in senior government positions. He was joined by Tunku Abdul Rahman, who took revenge on the Razak staffers who had pushed him out in 1969 and ensured he received little coverage in the media in retirement. He found a vehicle in the form of a weekly column he began writing in the *Star*, owned by a friend's company that the Tunku chaired, which was later acquired by the Malaysian Chinese Association. "In my articles I started to pinpoint these fellows as enemies of the country, and that got the security people working on them," he said.[47] Among those he named were Abdul Samad Ismail, managing editor of the *New Straits Times* and a major literary figure, and two deputy ministers who had served on Razak's staff, Abdullah Ahmad and Abdullah Majid.

As home affairs minister in charge of internal security, Ghazali Shafie was only too willing to oblige. In addition to his towering ambition, he had no love for Abdullah Ahmad, who had helped engineer his failure in the vice presidential party stakes in 1975. Ghazali's weapon was the police Special Branch, a political-intelligence unit that kept tabs on enemies of UMNO and the government as religiously as it tracked enemies of the state, its formal mandate. Ghazali went one step further, deploying the Special Branch against his enemies within UMNO under the guise of a threat to national security.

In June 1976, just five weeks after being honoured by the prime minister with Malaysia's highest literary award, Samad Ismail was arrested as a sus-pected member of the outlawed Communist Party. He was detained without trial following the arrest of two journalists working for a Malay-language paper in Singapore, who said they were part of a communist scheme directed by Samad. After Samad confessed on TV – as political detainees were required to do if they hoped ever to be released – that he had worked for years to subvert the government on the orders of com-munist agents abroad, Ghazali returned to the forefront of politics. He was the star of UMNO's General Assembly that year, receiving a standing ovation as he assured fellow delegates that the battle against communism was being fought and won.[48]

Amid calls for Samad's communist network to be dismantled, Abdullah Ahmad came under pressure. He was effectively sidelined by Hussein, who made him deputy minister for science, technology and environ-ment. Summoned by the prime minister, Abdullah was informed that the Special Branch had identified him as a communist "agent of influence" behind the façade of a playboy. Hussein offered Abdullah an ambassadorial post if he agreed to go abroad and give up pol-itics, but later withdrew the offer. He said that while he did not believe Abdullah was a communist, he would have to be detained temporarily.[49]

In November 1976, Abdullah Ahmad, 36, and Abdullah Majid, 50, deputy minister for labour and manpower, who had worked as Razak's press secretary, were arrested, along with four others. Intimidated by Special Branch officers, the "two Dollahs", as they were known, duly appeared on TV and confessed to communist activity while they held office. As the witch hunt accelerated and widened, Deputy Prime Minister Mahathir and Musa Hitam, minister for primary industries – the ultimate targets – began to feel the heat. The arrest of the two deputy ministers "in itself was attacking us, indirectly," Musa said later.[50]

Ghazali was able to jail so many people with no real evidence because he had an unwitting accomplice in Prime Minister Hussein Onn. Upright, honest and ill-suited to the rough and tumble of Malay politics, Hussein did not effectively control the UMNO he unexpectedly inherited. Ghazali was one of two cabinet members Hussein relied heavily on for advice, the other being Finance Minister Tengku Razaleigh Hamzah. Naïvely, Hussein accepted Ghazali's reports at face value, as if unaware that the Special Branch used coercion where necessary to extract confessions from political detainees. Some of the detainees, such as Samad Ismail and Abdullah Majid, were easy prey because of their past involvement with the Communist Party during the anti-colonial struggle in Singapore. Had Hussein been alert to prevailing political currents, however, he might have noticed the weaknesses and inconsistencies in the cases against the accused. For a start, Abdullah Majid's confession that part of his work involved writing an article in 1974 praising China's progress sat oddly with the charge that he maintained close contact with Beijing's communist rival, the Soviet Union, through its embassy in Kuala Lumpur. Moreover, the article was published in a government sponsored magazine, which reported in the same issue that Razak intended to open diplomatic relations with China.

The extent of Hussein's naivete, not to mention the depth of his anti-Soviet paranoia, was apparent when he asked Abdullah Ahmad to understand he had no choice but to detain him. He said he would tell the police to hold Abdullah under house arrest for only six months. Placed in a detention camp and cut off from powerful friends, however, Abdullah was unable to defend himself against increasingly incriminating – and doctored – Special Branch reports. He spent most of the next five years locked away, two of which were in solitary confinement.[51]

Dr. Mahathir and Musa, who sat next to each other at weekly Cabinet meetings chaired by the prime minister, were aware of Ghazali's manoeuvrings. Said Musa: "When Hussein Onn says, 'This is from neutral sources', we'd nudge each other and say, 'Special Branch, Special Branch'. That's all. We knew what was going on, yes."[52] Musa said that "if Ghaz had his way, all of us would have been in" detention. It was to Hussein's credit, Musa said, that he had resisted Ghazali's recommendations that Dr. Mahathir and Musa join the others behind bars.

It was not for want of trying on Ghazali's part, though. Syed Husin Ali, a political prisoner for 19 months at a camp at Taiping in Perak state, was suddenly transferred without explanation to Kuala Lumpur in mid-1976 at the height of the anti-communist hysteria. An associate professor of anthropology and sociology at the University of Malaya, he had been detained since late 1974 for supporting protests by farmers at Baling in Kedah. Held at an unknown location in the capital, he was questioned, threatened, cursed, slapped, punched, kicked and deprived of sleep around the clock for nearly three days and nights, with only brief breaks, by teams of Special Branch officers who focused on his socialist leanings and possible communist links. One officer spat on his face repeatedly. Then, when his head ached and he was at his most vulnerable, a fresh interrogator switched subjects. "Syed," he said. "We know that you have connections with the underground. We know that you were the intermediary between underground elements with Dr. Mahathir and Musa Hitam. You must tell us about this."[53]

At the time, Syed Husin Ali was puzzled why the police wanted him to implicate Dr. Mahathir and Musa. Only much later, after he had spent six years in detention accused of helping the Communist Party and disseminating subversive ideas among students, did he figure it out. If he had been tempted to take the bait of an early release and falsely confirm their part in subversion, Ghazali Shafie would have been a giant step closer to the prime ministership.

Although the anti-communist campaign fizzled after the death in early 1977 of Syed Jaafar Albar, Dr. Mahathir lived in "constant fear of being arrested on the orders of his hidden enemies" and his succession "remained uncertain even when he was very nearly there", according to an associate.[54] Ghazali made one final attempt to discredit Dr. Mahathir. Three days before he was to be installed as prime minister, his political secretary for seven years, Siddiq Mohamed Ghouse, 43, was arrested for allegedly spying for the Soviet Union, and three Soviet diplomats were expelled from Malaysia. Ghazali said Siddiq, a journalist by training and head of an UMNO Youth branch, had sold secrets for money to KGB agents, who supplied him with cameras, bags with secret compartments and a radio they used to contact him. Siddiq had not damaged security because he did not have access to top-secret documents, Ghazali said. But Ghazali did not explain why Siddiq had been picked up only in 1981 when he had been suspected of spying since 1979. Long after, Dr. Mahathir agreed that the dramatic arrest could have been timed to stop him taking over as prime minister. "The action against Siddiq might have [had] that intention," he said. "So it would seem he was another agent of influence who has been placed in my office, and therefore I might be subject to this leftist influence."[55]

As his political allies and others were being rounded up, Dr. Mahathir had told journalist friends repeatedly he did not believe they were guilty.[56]

Two weeks after becoming prime minister, with Musa as his deputy and home affairs minister, Dr. Mahathir released 21 people being held under the Internal Security Act, including those sacrificed in Ghazali's desperate bid for power. Some were broken in health, spirit and financially by the time they were freed. Others who survived incarceration in better shape, notably Samad Ismail and Abdullah Ahmad, returned to prominent positions. Samad worked as editorial adviser to his old newspaper group, received an honorary doctorate from a university that lauded him as a "champion of the Malay language, and a political activist and genuine nationalist", and was knighted by Malaysia's king.[57] Abdullah resumed his political career as a member of parliament and later was appointed editor-in-chief of the New Straits Times publishing group.

Dr. Mahathir had a fairly miserable five years as deputy prime minister, quite apart from dodging Ghazali's bullets. Although Hussein Onn had chosen Dr. Mahathir as his deputy, he did not seem to like him personally and often ignored him. In Dr. Mahathir's assessment, Hussein treated Ghazali Shafie and Tengku Razaleigh Hamzah as de facto deputy premiers, consulting Ghazali on defence and security, and Tengku Razaleigh on economics, finance and party affairs.[58]

Theoretically the second most powerful man in Malaysia, Dr. Mahathir found his title counted for almost nothing with Number One. Under the impression that "I had influence with him", Dr. Mahathir went to see Hussein to persuade him not to proceed with the prosecution of Harun Idris for corruption. "He took out the file from his safe and banged it on the table," said Dr. Mahathir. "Then I realized that, although I may be the deputy prime minister, my standing is not that high." Hussein got just as angry when Dr. Mahathir tried to persuade him to re-examine Abdullah Ahmad's case.[59] At times, relations between Hussein and Dr. Mahathir almost broke down. Musa Hitam recalled visiting the deputy prime minister's office when Dr. Mahathir was complaining about Hussein. "I lifted the phone and said, 'Talk to him. You're the deputy. Talk to him'. No, no, no. He never did."[60]

It was extremely frustrating for Dr. Mahathir, who was already bursting with many of the ideas that would mark his leadership. He advocated a freeway to run the length of peninsular Malaysia, a single time zone for the country and the establishment of a heavy industries corporation.[61] Not only did Hussein dismiss most of Dr. Mahathir's proposals out of hand, he also considered some a joke, for instance, describing the suggestion for Japanese-style international trading houses, *sogo shosha*, as *sunggoh susah*, very difficult, in Malay.[62]

So close to the pinnacle, Dr. Mahathir was still treated as an outsider. Steeped in traditional values, Hussein appreciated the relationship with Tengku Razaleigh, because they were both royalty and had studied law together in London, and their late fathers were friends. At Dr. Mahathir's request, Tengku Razaleigh intervened with Hussein to ask that some of the deputy prime minister's proposals be allowed to go to the Cabinet for other ministerial opinions. "And, of course, he agreed, you know," Tengku Razaleigh said. "You go up to him and explain to him nicely, he'll accept it." That left Dr. Mahathir "very unhappy with me", Tengku Razaleigh said. "He thought that he being deputy prime minister couldn't get things through, but I could go and whisper to Hussein and everything was OK."[63]

Not only was there no personal chemistry between leader and deputy, they also had starkly contrasting styles. Whereas Dr. Mahathir was keen to remake the country from top to bottom, Hussein was cautious to the point of dithering. When reading a brief, he underlined key words three or four times. Loath to make a tough decision before consulting all parties, he would usually agree to "consider it" as a way of postponing an outcome. One of his favourite expressions was, "OK, I'll sleep over it."[64] He once advised Dr. Mahathir that "when you have a problem, just don't do anything"; it would go away, he said.[65]

Even when Hussein reached a decision, he might have second thoughts. For example, Dr. Mahathir persuaded him that Malaysia should strengthen its claim to part of the disputed Spratly Islands in the South China Sea by occupying Amboyna Cay. With the navy ready to move in, Hussein "changed his mind one week later", said Dr. Mahathir.[66] The Vietnamese beat the Malaysians to the punch and established a permanent presence on the cay.

In a cabinet shuffle in 1978, Dr. Mahathir relinquished the education portfolio and became minister for trade and industry, where he was happy to proceed with some of his plans that did not require government policy changes. He established a heavy industries corporation within his ministry, and minimized his unhappiness with Hussein by spending time abroad selling Malaysia. Dr. Mahathir's four years as education minister were remembered for the tough stand he had taken against student and academic protests. He forced scholarship holders to sign guarantees that they would not become involved in politics, and amended the Universities Act to give the government extensive disciplinary powers over staff and students who were politically active.[67]

Eventually, Hussein fell victim to his own philosophy. As the work piled up, elements in UMNO defied his weak leadership by forcing the readmission of Harun Idris to UMNO, after Hussein had insisted on his expulsion following his conviction on corruption charges. Although Harun's court appeals failed in early 1978 and he went to jail, Hussein was being pressed to pardon him. At the 1978 UMNO General Assembly, Hussein was humiliated by being challenged for the presidency of the party by Sulaiman Palestin, the UMNO publicity chief, who secured just over one-fifth of the votes. While Sulaiman was not a serious contender for national leadership, his candidacy was an act of defiance by Harun supporters. As a friend of

Sulaiman who opposed Harun's prosecution and felt thwarted under Hussein, Dr. Mahathir had reason to support the dissident challenge covertly, as rumoured, and dissuade the prime minister from being tempted to seek a second term. While Dr. Mahathir denied doing so,[68] as acting premier he sought a pardon for Harun from Malaysia's king during Hussein's absence in London for a heart bypass operation in early 1981.[69]

The pressure on Hussein built relentlessly, and after the operation he announced his retirement, citing ill health. Hussein told friends his memory began failing after the surgery.[70] But in any case he could not cope with the job. When Dr. Mahathir took over on 16 July 1981, he was handed not one but 18 red dispatch boxes, used to carry pending files between the office and home, which were awaiting attention.[71]

Notes

1 John Funston, "Political Careers of Mahathir Mohamad and Anwar Ibrahim: Parallel, Intersecting and Conflicting Lives", IKMAS Working Papers (Institute of Malaysian and International Studies, Universiti Kebangsaan Malaysia), no. 15 (July 1998): i–iv, 1–32.

2 Parliamentary Debates, Malaysia, 26 May 1965, cited in Khoo Boo Teik, *Paradoxes of Mahathirism: An Intellectual Biography of Mahathir Mohamad* (Kuala Lumpur: Oxford University Press, 1995), p. 20.

3 Ibid., p. 19.

4 Parliamentary Debates, Malaysia, 26 May 1965, cited in Lee Kuan Yew, *From Third World to First: The Singapore Story: 1965–2000* (Singapore: Times Media Pte. Ltd., 2000), pp. 274–275.

5 Robin Adshead, *Mahathir of Malaysia: Statesman and Leader* (London: Hibiscus Publishing Company, 1989), p. 54.

6 Interview with Musa Hitam, 3 January 2007.

7 Tunku Halim, *Tunku Abdullah: A Passion for Life* (Kuala Lumpur: All Media Publications Sdn. Bhd., 1998), "Foreword", unnumbered.

8 Interview with Tunku Abdullah Tuanku Abdul Rahman, 22 March 2007. Tunku Abdullah passed away on 20 August 2008.

9 John Funston, *Malay Politics in Malaysia: A Study of UMNO & PAS* (Kuala Lumpur: Heinemann Educational Books (Asia) Ltd., 1980), pp. 2–3.

10 Ibid., pp. 2–10.

11 Ibid., pp. 12–17.

12 Dr. Mahathir Mohamad, "Disparities: Helpful Suggestions Needed", in *The Early Years: 1947–1972* (Kuala Lumpur: Berita Publishing Sdn. Bhd., 1995), pp. 133–136.

13 Dato' Abdullah Ahmad, *Tengku Abdul Rahman and Malaysia's Foreign Policy 1963–1970* (Kuala Lumpur: Berita Publishing Sdn. Bhd., 1985), p. 105. Interview with Abdullah Ahmad, 1 August 2008. Dr. Mahathir confirmed Ismail's comments: email correspondence with Mahathir Mohamad, 20 August 2008.

14 Karl von Vorys, *Democracy without Consensus: Communalism and Political Stability in Malaysia* (Kuala Lumpur: Oxford University Press, 1976), p. 372.

15 Interview with Abdullah Ahmad, 23 March 2007.

16 Ibid.

17 Interview with Mahathir Mohamad, 14 August 2007.

18 Interview with Siti Hasmah Mohamad Ali, 17 January 2008.

19 Interview with Mukhriz Mahathir, 22 March 2007.
20 Dato' Abdullah Ahmad, *Tengku Abdul Rahman and Malaysia's Foreign Policy 1963–1970*, p. 19.
21 Interview with Shaari Daud, 27 February 2007.
22 Interview with Mahathir Mohamad, 31 March 2008.
23 Ibid.
24 Khoo Boo Teik, *Paradoxes of Mahathirism*, p. 23.
25 Mahathir bin Mohamad, *The Malay Dilemma* (Singapore: Times Books International, 1999 edition).
26 John Funston, "Political Careers of Mahathir Mohamad and Anwar Ibrahim: Parallel, Intersecting and Conflicting Lives".
27 Ibid.
28 Dr. Mahathir stood by his controversial views that Malays were disadvantaged by hereditary and environmental factors. Asked in retirement if he disowned his arguments in view of scientific evidence, he said, "No. I think there is a basis for that." Interview with Mahathir Mohamad, 14 August 2007. Only on one point, that the Malays lacked the ability and confidence to succeed, did he change his mind. "I admit that at the time I felt very disappointed. I spoke to many people my age then who did not have the confidence. I too was not confident that Malays could achieve success. Now I reverse my stand. I no longer believe what I had written in *The Malay Dilemma*," he said. "We Can Do It: Dr. M No Longer Holds to Views Expressed in 'Malay Dilemma'", *Star*, 12 May 1997.
29 Cited in John Funston, *Malay Politics in Malaysia*, p. 255.
30 Mahathir bin Mohamad, *The Malay Dilemma*, p. 79.
31 Zainuddin Maidin, *The Other Side of Mahathir* (Kuala Lumpur: Utusan Publications & Distributors Sdn. Bhd., 1994), p. 44.
32 Ooi Kee Beng, *The Reluctant Politician: Tun Dr. Ismail and his Time* (Singapore: Institute of Southeast Asian Studies, 2006), pp. 268–269.
33 John Funston, "Political Careers of Mahathir Mohamad and Anwar Ibrahim: Parallel, Intersecting and Conflicting Lives".
34 Shamsul A.B., "UMNO's Politics: Past and Present", in *Trends* no. 39, distributed in *Business Times*, 27–28 November 1993.
35 Interview with Abdullah Ahmad, 23 March 2007.
36 Interview with Abdullah Ahmad, 26 February 2007.
37 The chief minister of a Malay state formally is called the *mentri besar*.
38 Interview with Abdullah Ahmad, 26 February 2007.
39 Interviews with Abdullah Ahmad, 26 February, 23 March 2007.
40 Interview with Abdullah Ahmad, 30 May 2007.
41 Joseph Chinyong Liow, *The Politics of Indonesia-Malaysia Relations: One Kin, Two Nations* (London: Routledge, 2005), p. 132.
42 Interview with Mahathir Mohamad, 14 August 2007.
43 Ibid.
44 Interview with Tengku Razaleigh Hamzah, 21 March 2007.
45 Musa Hitam, "We Were Followers", *Far Eastern Economic Review*, 9 October 2003 <http://www.feer.com/articles/2003/0310_09/p024region.html> (accessed 19 January 2006).
46 Interview with Tengku Razaleigh Hamzah, 29 May 2007.
47 Barry Wain, "Malaysia Ex-Premier Still Keeps His Hand On the Nation's Pulse", *Asian Wall Street Journal*, 12 May 1977.
48 *Asia 1977 Yearbook*, Far Eastern Economic Review Ltd., p. 228.
49 Interview with Abdullah Ahmad, 23 March 2007.

50   Interview with Musa Hitam, 3 January 2007.
51   Interview with Abdullah Ahmad, 26 February 2007.
52   Interview with Musa Hitam, 3 January 2007.
53   S. Husin Ali, *Two Faces (Detention Without Trial)* (Petaling Jaya: INSAN, 1996), p. 109.
54   Zainuddin Maidin, *The Other Side of Mahathir*, pp. 73–74.
55   Interview with Mahathir Mohamad, 20 March 2007.
56   Zainuddin Maidin, *The Other Side of Mahathir*, p. 73.
57   Samad Ismail passed away on 4 September 2008, aged 84.
58   Interview with Abdullah Ahmad, 30 May 2007.
59   Interview with Mahathir Mohamad, 14 August 2007.
60   Interview with Musa Hitam, 3 January 2007.
61   Interview with Mahathir Mohamad, 14 August 2007.
62   Interview with Tengku Razaleigh Hamzah, 29 May 2007.
63   Ibid.
64   Interview with Musa Hitam, 3 January 2007.
65   Interview with Mahathir Mohamad, 31 March 2008.
66   Interview with Mahathir Mohamad, 14 August 2007.
67   John Funston, "Political Careers of Mahathir Mohamad and Anwar Ibrahim: Parallel, Intersecting and Conflicting Lives".
68   Interview with Mahathir Mohamad, 31 March 2008.
69   Zainuddin Maidin, *The Other Side of Mahathir*, p. 72.
70   Interview with Tengku Razaleigh Hamzah, 21 March 2007.
71   Interview with Mahathir Mohamad, 31 March 2008.

Before politics: The youngest of nine children, Mahathir learned the value of discipline, hard work and self-improvement from his father. He entered the national political arena to help fellow Malays claim their share of the nation's wealth.

Source: Perdana Leadership Foundation

Life-long union: Mahathir married Siti Hasmah, his first and only girlfriend, after they met as medical students at university. They celebrated their 52nd wedding anniversary in 2008.

Source: Perdana Leadership Foundation

A partnership: Although she steered clear of politics, Siti Hasmah was never far from her husband's side. She accompanied Mahathir to party gatherings, political rallies and social functions, often travelling abroad with him as well.

Source: Perdana Leadership Foundation

Hands on: After he became prime minister, Mahathir took a personal interest in nearly every aspect of Malaysian life. Here, he and Siti Hasmah inspect Malay textiles at a craft centre in Kuala Lumpur.

Source: Information Department, Malaysia

In tune: Mahathir and Siti Hasmah had good voices and enjoyed singing, entertaining guests with a duet on special occasions. His theme song was *My Way*, a title reflecting natural instincts that were obvious from childhood.

Source: Information Department, Malaysia

Off duty: Despite total immersion in politics, Mahathir effectively separated political activity from his professional, social and family life. He did not discuss current political events, no matter how momentous, with Siti Hasmah and their children.

Source: Perdana Leadership Foundation

Formal sitting: Siti Hasmah was described by a family friend as the "quintessence of gentleness and grace", an opinion widely shared. It was hard for anyone meeting her to believe Mahathir could be as ruthless as his record suggested.

Source: Perdana Leadership Foundation

Part II
Prime Minister for Life, Almost

3

From Outcast to Presidential Premier

Although he swept into office with the intensity of a typhoon, Dr. Mahathir moved cautiously to consolidate his position as leader of both UMNO and Malaysia. Taking command of the political party that had expelled him 12 years earlier, he had to contend with adversaries who regarded him as a usurper to be opportunistically deposed. While introducing activist domestic and foreign policies and managing a spate of financial scandals, he gave little indication initially that he would rewrite the political rulebook and become the longest-serving and most controversial premier in the nation's history.

As Dr. Mahathir imposed his forceful personality and priorities on the political system and the country, however, he engaged in bitter contests with UMNO pretenders, resulting in two major upheavals. After barely retaining the presidency in an election in 1987 that split the party in half, he drove out his enemies and rebuilt UMNO according to his requirements. Engineering procedures within the party so that he would never again be threatened, he turned annual meetings into orchestrated, made-for-TV productions that showcased his supremacy and presented an image of unity. His crude dismissal and persecution of his deputy, Anwar Ibrahim, in 1998 irrevocably tarnished Dr. Mahathir's credibility and created a crisis of legitimacy for UMNO among the Malays, but still he managed to retain his authority, select a successor and retire at a time of his own choosing.

Simultaneously, Dr. Mahathir weakened state and informal institutions and packed them with loyalists to facilitate his autocratic rule. In the most egregious case, he intervened to subdue the judiciary and ensure it would yield the results he sought when his political control was endangered. In the National Front government, the Malaysian Chinese Association and the Malaysian Indian Congress – stalwarts from the early days when they, with UMNO, constituted the ruling Alliance – found themselves downgraded. Across the years, Dr. Mahathir transformed the regime in Malaysia into a highly institutionalized party-state that he personally operated, manipulated and dominated. Dr. Mahathir and Malaysia not only had phonetic consonance,[1] but also shared an eerily similar eight-character identity, and were at times virtually synonymous.

Although Dr. Mahathir did not murder adversaries, as did some other Southeast Asian strongmen, he ruled in familiar authoritarian fashion. He selectively jailed without trial legitimate political opponents and civil society critics, as well as genuine terrorists and subversives. Impatient, he had no end of ideas about how to build Malaysia into a modern industrialized nation, but allowed nobody of stature to question his plans. The Malaysian media, run by his acolytes, functioned as an amen chorus, ever ready to lavish praise on the leader and ignore or discredit dissenting voices.

With a combination of ruthlessness and dexterity, Dr. Mahathir delivered social peace and sustained economic growth, introducing increasing numbers of Malaysians to middle-class comforts. Even if they were critical, few were willing to jeopardize their rising living standards, or risk ostracism and worse, to explore alternatives. Corporate Malaysia, hooked on constant economic expansion, lined up solidly behind Dr. Mahathir to keep the contracts – and profits – flowing. By the end of his 22-year tenure, Dr. Mahathir had remade the country in his own image and become Malaysia's "presidential premier".[2]

Far too late in the day, Dr. Mahathir's opponents realized that he played politics harder, faster and smarter than anyone they had encountered, making most of them look like rank amateurs. Although he became addicted to the job, Dr. Mahathir did not seek it for the perks or the pay-offs. He had a mission, to bring about an economic and social revolution that would turn Malaysia into a fully developed and respected nation within a generation, with the Malays playing a prominent part. As that required his personal attention and leadership, political longevity was essential, regardless of the cost. The price could always be rationalized in terms of his project, which was for the good of the country. There was no higher priority than staying in power.

For Dr. Mahathir, a political animal, the ends justified the means, though he specifically denied it was a guiding principle.[3] After his retirement, two of his great rivals in UMNO, Musa Hitam and Tengku Razaleigh Hamzah, used the same word to describe Dr. Mahathir: He was, they said, a "politician". The term contained a grudging admiration for Dr. Mahathir's willingness and ability to do what was necessary to survive, unhindered by ethical considerations or the harm it might do to others. Both acknowledged his decisive advantage – a killer instinct, a readiness to go for the jugular at critical moments and venture beyond what previously had been acceptable behaviour in Malaysian politics – attributes they were pleased to report they lacked. Musa, who served as Dr. Mahathir's first deputy prime minister before quitting in acrimony, but ended up on comfortable terms with Dr. Mahathir, said, "When it suits him, he says 'today I love you'. Tomorrow, if it suits him, he says 'I hate you'. 'Today you are a lovely man, tomorrow you are ugly'. That's Mahathir, the politician."[4]

Their judgment did not rule out Dr. Mahathir being a caring doctor, a loving father or a firm friend, provided that friend did not get in his political way. Dr. Mahathir was adept at separating politics from his professional, social and family life. Author Rehman Rashid, who dated Marina Mahathir and found her mother to be the "quintessence of gentleness and grace", would thereafter find himself "unable to believe that such a woman would countenance the sort of man Mahathir's bitterest enemies were convinced he was".[5] Dr. Mahathir did not take politics home. He put politics in a completely different compartment. As he once reassured Musa, who invited Dr. Mahathir to his daughter's wedding but worried he would not attend because they had been quarrelling, "That is politics; this is friendship."[6]

Malaysians had never seen a leader quite like Dr. Mahathir, who appeared to be in perpetual motion. In contrast with his cautious predecessor, Hussein Onn, who was invisible much of the time and committed to keeping the country on an even keel, Dr. Mahathir produced initiatives "a million a minute", as one colleague put it. And he maintained the pace, taking a personal interest in almost every aspect of Malaysian daily life. He conducted spot checks of public toilets and would shock officials by phoning them directly to complain about untidiness and other evidence of neglect in their work. To save public spending, he cut his own salary and that of his cabinet ministers, reduced the number of civil servants and abolished some of their privileges.[7] Indefatigable, dressed in trademark open-neck bush jacket, he gave the impression he wanted to micro-manage the entire country.

Wrote Rehman Rashid, "After the greyness of Hussein, here was an electrifying personality, as much a visionary as Razak, but with infinitely more popular appeal...In his first months as prime minister, Mahathir was clearly, completely, a man in his moment."[8]

Although he had less time for his hobbies, Dr. Mahathir re-assembled his workshop at the prime minister's official residence. In the first few years he invented an Islamic toilet – actually, a variation on European and Japanese paperless commodes – that went into commercial production.[9] And he still found time to cook the occasional Sunday lunch for the family, usually something simple like fried rice, after venturing out to buy the ingredients himself. He joked that his older children "always find some sudden prior engagement" when they learned he was duty chef. At 60, Dr. Mahathir took up horse riding after visiting Pakistan and being escorted and impressed by Pathan cavalry guards.[10] He also learned to fly a twin-engine Cessna belonging to the Royal Malaysian Air Force.[11]

With discipline that had become second nature, Dr. Mahathir adopted a working routine that he adhered to religiously. After morning prayers, he would begin writing an article or speech, with pen and paper, continuing to do so even in the toilet. Having eaten, he would arrive at his office at 8 o'clock sharp. His first task was to check the newspapers, spending 30 to

45 minutes on them, starting with the English-language *New Straits Times*, followed by the Malay-language *Utusan Malaysia*, before going on to the others. He had time only to scan the headlines, read articles of immediate interest and mark others to read later, in the car or at home. Dr. Mahathir usually went home to have lunch and dinner with his wife, leaving the office between 6 and 6:30 p.m. at the end of the day. If they did not have an evening function, he would read or write, rarely watching TV – "because I like to be doing things, not just sitting down" – before selecting his wardrobe for the next day, and retiring about 11 p.m. for six or seven hours sleep.

Dr. Mahathir did his best to inject his sense of purpose into his ministerial colleagues and the bureaucracy. In the office, as at home, he could be aggressive and demanding if there were delays in what he wanted done.[12] Civil servants were required to wear nametags for easy identification by the public in case of poor service, and they had to clock in and out for work. He also wore a nametag. It simply said "Mahathir". Everywhere Dr. Mahathir went he carried a notebook in which he recorded things that needed attention: from a meeting with a potential investor to dirty drains and poor street lighting. "Nothing was too small and nothing too big," said Daim Zainuddin, who twice served as finance minister.[13] Dr. Mahathir opened his weekly cabinet meeting by pulling out his notebook, reading his entries and calling for action by the relevant ministers. Sometimes he produced his own photos as evidence. He gave a similar pocket-sized notebook to each minister and encouraged them all to adopt his habit.

A technology buff, Dr. Mahathir realized the potential of information technology before his colleagues and told them it would revolutionize daily life and the way business was conducted. He ensured all ministers were given computers in the early 1980s, even though few knew how to use them.[14]

Fearful that he would run out of time to introduce his far-reaching reform agenda, Dr. Mahathir was always in a hurry. His greatest regret was that he "began late"; at 56, he was the oldest person to be sworn in as Malaysia's leader.[15] Just as he read books between customers as a teenage street vendor and between patients as a doctor, he shortened his signature as prime minister to a scrawled "M", in place of a flowing "Mahathir bin Mohamad", to save time.[16] He disdained golf, the game of Southeast Asian diplomacy, because it took too long to play. In 1996, at 71, after he had been premier for more than 15 years, Dr. Mahathir said, "I don't think I should waste time. I don't know how much longer I have."[17] In retirement, discussing his development record across two decades, he remarked, "I didn't have much time."[18]

One way Dr. Mahathir could have saved a lot of time was to let his staff draft his speeches, common practice everywhere. But he insisted on writing his own, leaving his press secretary, when he was deputy premier, with little to do except arrange media conferences and prepare short forewords for souvenir programmes.[19] While Dr. Mahathir could not possibly write all of his speeches as prime minister – he delivered thousands – his forceful, didactic style was recognizable in many of them.[20] Speeches written by others "do not reflect my thinking, or my way of putting the words into sentences", he said. Although he once could touch type, he chose to labour away on each speech in longhand. "I feel satisfied writing it myself," he said.[21]

Despite intense pressures, Dr. Mahathir had no trouble relaxing. He would nap most days for 15 minutes after lunch at home in a comfortable chair, in the car while being driven to an appointment, or on a flight, arriving refreshed.[22] Even as he aged, Dr. Mahathir showed little sign of flagging. For instance, in 2003 he conducted, alert and hands-on, the annual meeting of the International Advisory Panel of Malaysia's Multimedia Super Corridor. From 8 a.m. to 6 p.m., he asked and answered thoughtful questions, received members in his house for dinner at 8 p.m. and personally saw them off at 11 p.m. "That is a clear fifteen hours," observed Narayana N.R. Murthy, an Indian businessman and panel member. "I am sure there are not many 78-year-old people who can exhibit that kind of mental and physical energy."[23]

One reason Dr. Mahathir could rest easy was that he never made mistakes, or at least none that he admitted. He rebuked Musa Hitam as deputy prime minister for listening to critics and conceding that some things done by the government were wrong. "The biggest raging debate I had with him was simply that he said admitting mistakes is showing weakness, whereas I argued the other way around," said Musa. "I said admitting your mistake is a courageous act."[24]

Another great asset was Dr. Mahathir's ability to meet a crisis calmly and not succumb to panic. On those occasions when he suffered inner turmoil, he was able to keep it hidden behind what his wife, Dr. Siti Hasmah, called a "poker face". For the most part, though, he shrugged and uttered a favourite comment, "The world will not come to an end", maintaining a serenity that sometimes infuriated her.[25]

One day in 1989, Dr. Mahathir informed his wife without fuss that he had persistent shoulder pains and wanted to be examined by a physician. He was unfazed when an electro-cardiogram indicated he had to be hospitalized immediately. Left in no doubt a week later that the next step was a coronary bypass, in measured fashion he called Malaysia's top cardiac surgeon and directed him to perform the operation.[26] Dr. Mahathir's decision to trust Malaysian doctors and equipment with his life, instead of seeking treatment abroad as the elite routinely did, won him popular respect but alarmed some people. Finance Minister Daim Zainuddin helped locate an American heart specialist travelling in Asia and directed him to Kuala Lumpur.[27] Singapore Prime Minister Lee Kuan Yew, explaining the added risks with less-experienced surgeons, offered to send in, at Singapore's expense, renowned Australian heart specialist Victor Chang.[28]

But Dr. Mahathir went ahead, turning his personal ordeal into a national triumph.

One of the few times Dr. Mahathir appeared vulnerable was when confronted by flowers on which pollen was visible, which caused him to have asthmatic attacks. He was also allergic to feathers and dust, once suffering severely on Laying Laying, a Malaysia-claimed outpost in the disputed Spratly Islands, after encountering migratory birds. And, for all his self-control and gruff demeanour, Dr. Mahathir could become emotional in public, periodically breaking down in tears. While some cynics offered him acting awards, Dr. Siti Hasmah had no doubt it was genuine and heart-felt. She said, "Every time this happens, he comes back and says 'I've done something shameful. I was emotional and cried'. I said that's not shameful, it's human."[29]

In the Malaysia that Dr. Mahathir inherited, nerves of steel were necessary as political crises and confrontation became common under his stewardship. While Malaysia was modeled on the British parliamentary system, it had moved away from liberal democracy. Opposition political parties seriously contended for power in regular elections, but the obstacles they faced made it almost impossible to defeat the National Front government. The real political contest took place inside the hothouse of UMNO, given its centrality in the ruling coalition after 1969, rather than in general elections. UMNO delegates chose a president – the party met in General Assembly annually, but voted for office holders every third year – who automatically became prime minister. He would then select his cabinet ministers and appoint the chief minister of each state. By tradition, the party's deputy president was regarded as the heir apparent for the top job.

For inspiration in how to ensure he remained in power, Dr. Mahathir looked no further than the man he criticized for dictatorial traits, Malaysia's first prime minister, Tunku Abdul Rahman. Out of office in 1971, Dr. Mahathir had analysed the Tunku's modus operandi in an academic article. In office, he proceeded down the same path, only more deliberately, systematically and effectively. Dr. Mahathir said the Tunku's first action, on taking over UMNO:

> ...was to seek amendments to the party's constitution giving the president the right to choose his own secretary-general and nominate six other members of the executive council. These amendments decisively gave the president complete control of the party...[They] marked the beginning of the end of democratic practices within the party, and by extension within the governments that were dominated by the party... To ensure the president will not be challenged the 11 state branches of the UMNO were broken up into numerous small divisions which dealt with the headquarters directly...the president arrogated to himself the right to choose all the candidates for elections, his position thus became

completely immune to challenge. The drift back to feudalism culminated in the president naming his successor in true feudal fashion.[30]

While Dr. Mahathir appeared to assume the leadership of UMNO smoothly on Hussein Onn's retirement in 1981, his manoeuvrings sowed the seeds of virulent factionalism that surfaced later. Tengku Razaleigh was left feeling he had been double-crossed twice and deprived of his rightful place as deputy president of the party. Tengku Razaleigh concluded that Dr. Mahathir "cannot be trusted",[31] but it was the young Kelantan prince who lost out. Although he almost unseated Dr. Mahathir when he later challenged him for the leadership of UMNO, Tengku Razaleigh was forced from the government altogether, a crushing blow for a man who had been talent spotted for national leadership in his 30s.

Dr. Mahathir had outfoxed Tengku Razaleigh when Hussein Onn summoned them both to a meeting at the prime minister's official residence in Kuala Lumpur and told them he was quitting because of ill health. There was no question he would be succeeded by Dr. Mahathir, who was deputy UMNO president and deputy prime minister. Tengku Razaleigh was finance minister and a party vice president. Hussein "implored the two of us to work together, which Mahathir acknowledged during that meeting", said Tengku Razaleigh. "I thought there was an understanding that we can work together."[32]

Assuming he would be unchallenged for the deputy presidency as part of the tacit agreement, Tengku Razaleigh told "all my chaps" to support Dr. Mahathir for president. But after Dr. Mahathir was nominated unopposed, Tengku Razaleigh found himself in a clash with Musa Hitam, the education minister, for the deputy's slot. Mindful of the need to strengthen his hold on the party, Dr. Mahathir did not openly endorse either, which would have alienated one of the powerful contestants and a legion of followers. Instead, he made a democratic virtue of leaving the choice to the UMNO General Assembly. Behind his publicly neutral stance, however, Dr. Mahathir supported Musa, with whom he had closer personal ties. Dr. Mahathir was wary of the ambitious and popular Tengku Razaleigh, whose royal status was another strike against him in Dr. Mahathir's eyes.[33] By secretly backing Musa's candidacy, Dr. Mahathir hoped to check Tengku Razaleigh's rapid rise, while recognizing that Musa, behind his easy smile, also coveted the top spot.

Tengku Razaleigh said that Dr. Mahathir, once on top, should have behaved "like a father" and not taken sides. "I could easily have become the deputy prime minister" in 1976, he said, by persuading Prime Minister Hussein Onn, a close family friend, to let Tengku Razaleigh challenge Dr. Mahathir for the deputy presidency of the party. At the time, said Tengku Razaleigh, Hussein "was not sure Mahathir should be the man, because Hussein never trusted Mahathir, never liked Mahathir". Instead, Tengku Razaleigh said, he had recommended that Hussein choose Dr. Mahathir. "I could have played to win also," Tengku Razaleigh said, "but I was being too fair – because it's in the same party, you know. We're not fighting another party."[34]

In a rancorous race with Musa, Tengku Razaleigh was the early favourite, but his declaration that he could not lose and would leave the Cabinet if he did so worked against him in a community that valued compromise and politeness.[35] Musa won by a vote of 722 to 517. When Tengku Razaleigh nominated again and challenged Musa for the deputy presidency in 1984, Dr. Mahathir was much more confident of his own leadership, having steered UMNO to an impressive victory in a general election in 1982. He openly backed his deputy this time, helping Musa weather another roiling contest to retain his post by a slightly wider margin.

After using Musa to dampen the threat from Tengku Razaleigh, Dr. Mahathir reversed their roles to ensure Musa did not build too strong a power base in UMNO. Musa wanted Tengku Razaleigh out of the government altogether, on the grounds that his presence would perpetuate a growing split within the party. Indeed, Musa was under the impression he had an "unwritten agreement" with Dr. Mahathir that Tengku Razaleigh would be purged from the Cabinet and denied any nominated post in UMNO if he contested again in 1984 and lost.[36] Instead, Dr. Mahathir shifted Tengku Razaleigh to the Ministry of Trade and Industry, while replacing him as UMNO treasurer. Like Tengku Razaleigh earlier, Musa and his backers considered that Dr. Mahathir had broken his promise, or at least half of it.

Although trade and industry was less prestigious than the treasury, it was deeply involved in the implementation of the New Economic Policy and offered just as many possibilities to distribute benefits and gather supporters. In a confidential letter of protest to Dr. Mahathir that was leaked, Musa listed all the patronage points available to Tengku Razaleigh, including granting import permits, recommending local partners for foreign investors and nominating individuals for the distribution of shares. Musa said Tengku Razaleigh would have "the greatest opportunity ever to prepare himself for his political future, even better than [in] Finance".[37] In truth, Dr. Mahathir kept Tengku Razaleigh's candidacy alive for a third clash in 1987, just in case the prime minister needed to cut Musa off at the knees.

While Dr. Mahathir did not invent the informal system of checks and balances to restrain rivals and remind others they were in constant competition for the prime minister's favour, he embraced it with a Machiavellian touch. One technique he copied from predecessors was to ensure that in the politically more important Malaysian states a particularly powerful UMNO figure was offset by another prominent politician.[38] The chief minister, for example, often had to look over his shoulder at the head of an UMNO state liaison committee or a cabinet minister.

Dr. Mahathir used the 1982 general election, called more than a year before it was due, to promote a new generation of Malay leaders, who would start to balance some of the old-line, entrenched politicians. Almost half of the existing members of parliament and state assemblies, among them three ministers, were dropped in favour of fresh candidates, younger and better educated, who might share Dr. Mahathir's outlook.[39] In a campaign that lacked compelling issues, it became a referendum on his first nine months in office, characterized by vigorous attempts to shake up the bureaucracy, denunciations of corruption and promises to push ahead with heavy industrial and infrastructure projects despite a slowing economy.

Dr. Mahathir personally co-opted star candidate Anwar Ibrahim, the charismatic president of the Malaysian Islamic Youth Movement and a fierce government critic, who had positioned the movement as independent of both UMNO and the opposition Parti Islam Se-Malaysia (PAS). After Anwar easily captured a PAS constituency and took his place in Parliament, Dr. Mahathir immediately made him a deputy minister, promoting him to a full minister the following year. Attending his first UMNO General Assembly in 1982, Anwar aggressively contested the leadership of the party's youth wing as Dr. Mahathir's man, defeating the stodgy incumbent, who was also a deputy minister. As head of UMNO Youth, Anwar automatically became an ex-officio vice president – all within a year or so of joining the party. His rapid ascent was resented by younger aspirants who had toiled long and loyally for UMNO, only to find their further advancement blocked by a man who spent those years denouncing the party. His arrival also spelled more uncertainty for Musa and Tengku Razaleigh over their leadership ambitions.

With Dr. Mahathir at the helm for the first time, the 11-party National Front took all 13 states in the election. It won 132 of the 154 seats in Parliament compared with 131 in 1978, and it could count on backing from five nominally independents in Sabah. Peninsular Malaysia delivered an even broader mandate for Dr. Mahathir, with the pattern of voting showing he had overcome his reputation as a Malay extremist and won the trust of Chinese Malaysians.

Within UMNO, however, unhappiness over the way Dr. Mahathir was handling the party boiled over at the 1983 General Assembly, after he declared his faith in Musa a year ahead of party elections. Dr. Mahathir's explanation that he spoke not so much to support Musa as to squash malicious rumours that they were drifting apart politically, which hampered the administration of the country, was rejected by many of the more tradition-minded delegates. They said a how-to-vote directive from the president violated convention and opened the way to dictatorial action in future.[40]

While Dr. Mahathir's political acumen kept him in power, his actions in fending off rivals and encouraging them to fight among themselves contributed to unprecedented open factionalism in UMNO. As he gradually strengthened his position, opposing factions also became better organized and more defined. UMNO's direct and deepening involvement in business with the implementation of the New Economic Policy raised the economic stakes and sharpened competition for government contracts, privatization awards and other benefits.

Musa Hitam's abrupt resignation as deputy premier and home affairs minister in early 1986 opened more fissures within UMNO, and confirmed three years of rumours of trouble inside what was dubbed the 2-M administration. Dr. Mahathir had never liked the label, bestowed by the local press, grumbling that it should have been understood to mean Mahathir Mohamad rather than Mahathir-Musa. Sure enough, when the breach came, at the heart of the friction was Dr. Mahathir's conviction that Musa saw himself as nearly equal and wanted his job prematurely.

Admittedly, the two had sharply contrasting political styles. While Dr. Mahathir was assertive and brooked little criticism, Musa tended to be more personable and moderate. And they differed sometimes over policies, with Musa decidedly unenthusiastic about some of Dr. Mahathir's plans for heavy industry. But it was Dr. Mahathir's belief that Musa was disloyal and trying to topple him from the premier's perch that caused the breach. "Your accusations toward me are a terrible blow to my dignity and credibility," Musa wrote in a seven-page resignation letter that was reported by the foreign press but not by domestic news outlets.

For a replacement deputy premier, Dr. Mahathir turned to Ghafar Baba, the wealthy businessman who had quit Hussein Onn's Cabinet ten years earlier in protest at Dr. Mahathir's selection for the same post. He was a sound bet for Dr. Mahathir, who had his eye on UMNO's next triennial election. Experienced in government, Ghafar had been a vice president since 1962, proving his consistent party appeal. At 61 and dependent on the government for business, he was unlikely to risk it all for a shot at the prime minister's office. Even at this stage, 60-year-old Dr. Mahathir's choice to succeed him – eventually – was Anwar Ibrahim, but he was not about to let Anwar, 38, get too near too soon.

As the Malaysian economy began to contract and patronage available to keep followers on board dwindled, even deeper factional alignments coalesced around Musa and Tengku Razaleigh. Sharing a common desire to curb Dr. Mahathir's growing strength, they joined forces to oust him. As the 1987 UMNO General Assembly approached, it was decided that Tengku Razaleigh would oppose Dr. Mahathir while Musa would defend his deputy president's position against Ghafar. The clash between the two sides, dubbed Team A and Team B by the Malaysian press, compelled almost all aspirants for party posts to declare their allegiance openly.

Dr. Mahathir used a general election in August 1986, which he called a year before his five-year term expired, to narrow subtly the options open to Tengku Razaleigh and Musa. While the election was little more than a sideshow, Dr. Mahathir risked weakening his hold on the UMNO presidency if the National Front polled poorly. At the same time, he left his UMNO rivals no choice but to close ranks and campaign against the opposition on some of the same issues they sought to use against him in the intra-party feud. Despite a sagging economy, disunity in the Malaysian Chinese Association as well as UMNO, and scandals over state-owned Bank Bumiputra and Malaysia's attempts to rig the international tin price, the government won easily. The National Front took 148 seats in an expanded 177-seat Parliament, and retained control of all states. And while the Malaysian Chinese Association paid a heavy price for its internal bickering, UMNO performed exceptionally well. Completing a minor cabinet reorganization he began three months earlier when naming Ghafar deputy premier, Dr. Mahathir moved his people into more strategic positions and demoted some of Musa's allies.

With the battle lines drawn publicly in early 1987, the contest for UMNO represented a radical departure in Malay politics, which traditionally eschewed confrontation and made a virtue of unity, consensus and loyalty to leaders. Team A enjoyed many of the benefits of incumbency that the National Front took for granted in a general election. The press gave members more favourable coverage, the police cooperated in issuing permits for meetings, and the tax authorities harassed some Team B supporters. Team A was able to draw on UMNO assets and generate additional funds by allocating government contracts.

Dr. Mahathir lined up pledges of support from leaders of the other National Front component parties and from state chief ministers. But five cabinet ministers and four deputy ministers defected. Team B also received both a moral and a morale boost from the support of the country's two surviving former prime ministers, Tunku Abdul Rahman and Hussein Onn. Hussein told close friends he had made a colossal mistake in selecting Dr. Mahathir as his deputy. "The fellow was behaving himself at the time," Hussein confided to one intimate. "I didn't know he was going to turn out like this."[41] As for the normally genial Tunku, he volunteered his distaste for Dr. Mahathir, repeatedly calling him "scum" in private conversations.[42]

Team B members made much of Dr. Mahathir's pursuit of showcase projects in heavy industry and public works, claiming they were poorly conceived and would be a long-term drain on the state. They also alleged mismanagement, corruption and cronyism, pointing to huge losses at Bank Bumiputra and in the prime minister's secret intervention in the world tin market. They further claimed a few of his friends were benefiting disproportionately from state munificence, identifying Finance Minister Daim Zainuddin as the principal offender in mixing private business with public office.

Characteristically, Dr. Mahathir sought to cultivate among UMNO delegates the fear that a vote against Team A would usher in a period of uncertainty in which the most unlikely or outrageous turn of events – in brief, instability – was possible. He said that if Ghafar lost to Musa for the deputy presidency, Ghafar would stay as his deputy premier. He also said that technically he could remain prime minister if he lost the presidency, and that only a vote of no-confidence in Parliament would remove him. Malaysia's Constitution was silent on both points. Since Dr. Mahathir was unpredictable and was acquiring a reputation for making his own rules, nobody could be sure how he would react if the vote went against him. His own supporters were apprehensive. As one of them said, Dr. Mahathir "has been flouting the laws of the tribe. He's been acting un-Malay by saying he might not accept the wishes of the party."[43]

The 1,479 delegates who voted secretly at the UMNO General Assembly on 24 April 1987 returned Team A with the slimmest of margins. Dr. Mahathir defeated Tengku Razaleigh 761–718, a majority of just 43. Ghafar beat Musa 739–699, a majority of 40, with 41 spoiled ballots that observers assumed was the work of Tengku Razaleigh diehards taking revenge on Musa. Defence Minister Abdullah Ahmad Badawi captured Team B's only vice presidency, scoring second in the vote, while fellow team members filled eight of 25 elective positions on the Supreme Council. Dr. Mahathir might have won, but his legitimacy as a leader of UMNO and Malaysia had been dented.[44]

With a bare 51.45 per cent of UMNO behind him, Dr. Mahathir faced a formidable task if he chose the customary route and tried to rebuild party unity. In the new political environment, open dissent in UMNO was a reality and a challenge to the leadership was no longer considered taboo. Tengku Razaleigh, 50, confident that he and 52-year-old Musa commanded almost half the party, said he was willing to assist in healing the rift, "provided the hand of cooperation is extended". Otherwise, he indicated, they would repeat their leadership bid in 1990. "We have the bases – Musa's base, my base," he said. "It's still there. It will be there in three years."

Back in 1981 when he became president, Dr. Mahathir had appealed for unity after the first bruising Tengku Razaleigh-Musa encounter, urging the party faithful to forget the harsh exchanges from the heat of battle and accept the outcome in a democratic spirit. "There are no winners or losers in an UMNO contest," he told the General Assembly. Having repulsed the combined might of Tengku Razaleigh and Musa in 1987, however, Dr. Mahathir ignored his own advice. He decided to eliminate rather than accommodate his rivals, dropping from the Cabinet Team B's nine ministers and deputies. In sacking Abdullah Badawi, Dr. Mahathir trashed the tradition that senior positions in Cabinet should go to those who performed strongly in UMNO elections.

Dr. Mahathir's purge also found victims in the civil service and corporate ranks, extending his tough new line of direct domination of UMNO to critical points in society. Later in the year, Dr. Mahathir used racial tensions as a screen to jail a wide spectrum of government critics. He also encouraged a court to declare UMNO an illegal organization so he could form a new party that would assume UMNO's identity without the presence of the dissidents. In the process, he undermined the judiciary, a move that would plague the Malaysian justice system for decades. All the steps were inter-locked, part of a strategy to eliminate sources of resistance and give Dr. Mahathir unfettered control of the country.

Even after Dr. Mahathir sacked his ministerial foes and decided to play hardball, his grip on the party and country was far from assured. As he waited for the High Court to hear a suit filed by 11 Tengku Razaleigh sup-porters seeking to invalidate the UMNO General Assembly leadership vote, a second year of recession meant more bankruptcies, worsening unemploy-ment and further belt-tightening all round. Predictably, relations between Malaysia's main ethnic groups began to fray as insecurity took hold and politicians looked for scapegoats.

With the competing UMNO camps continuing to clash at all levels, threat-ening the coherence of the party, some leaders resorted to naked communal politics. Portraying themselves as champions of the Malays inevitably meant encroaching on Chinese emotional territory. For their own reasons, the Chinese political parties also adopted sharpening communal attitudes. Trying to recover ground lost in the previous year's general election, the Malaysian Chinese Association was under pressure to reassert itself as the community's representative in the government. Determined to protect its electoral gains, the opposition predominantly Chinese Democratic Action Party was not about to give an inch. Several issues connected with the emotive subjects of language and education, which reopened a sensitive debate over the contents of Malaysian culture, drew in the Indians as well.

After the Malaysian Chinese Association and Parti Gerakan Rakyat Malaysia, another predominantly Chinese party in the National Front, joined the Democratic Action Party in a protest over the appointment of non-Mandarin speaking teachers as administrators in Chinese primary schools, UMNO Youth seized the chance to organize the Malays in response. Acting leader Mohamed Najib Razak, keen to claim permanent leadership of the youth movement, led a huge rally in October near where the 1969 strife erupted. Demonstrators carried provocative banners and posters bearing anti-Chinese slogans. The fol-lowing day an army deserter, Adam Jaafar, went on a shooting rampage nearby, killing one person and wounding others, reviving memories of the racial riots 18 years earlier. Although unrelated to political events, the incident caused panic, with shops closing early and people rushing to stock food.

When Dr. Mahathir returned from abroad a few days later, UMNO leaders were making preparations for an even bigger rally in Kuala Lumpur to demon-strate Malay resolve and unity, hoping to attract 500,000 people. He called it off and ordered the biggest crackdown on political dissent Malaysia had ever seen. Between October and December, police arrested 119 people, 106 of them in the first three weeks, in what was called Operation Lalang. *Lalang* is Malay for useless grass, suggesting the prime minister was "weeding out" his critics. They were held under the feared Internal Security Act (ISA), which permits indefinite detention without trial. Three newspapers were closed.

The round-up profoundly shocked the nation because Dr. Mahathir had cultivated a favourable image over the ISA, encouraging the hope that it might lapse into disuse eventually. In his first six years as premier, hundreds of people held without trial had been released, leaving only suspected hard-core subversives still in jail. Moreover, Dr. Mahathir told lawyers how he had feared arrest under the ISA after being expelled from UMNO in 1969.[45] And, as deputy premier, he had narrowly escaped being implicated in UMNO factional fighting that saw innocent allies incarcerated.

Dr. Mahathir, however, maintained that the 119 detainees were fanning the flames of racial unrest and religious zealotry. "Preventive action must be taken now to save the country from disastrous riots," he told Parliament.[46] Residents of the capital undoubtedly were relieved that the situation had been defused, though they noted that UMNO was a major contributor to escalating tensions and that the government waited far too long before clamping down. While no doubt some of the participants in the ugly communal debates were behind bars, none of the high-profile UMNO organizers and instigators, most conspicuously Najib, had been arrested.

In fact, most of the detainees had no connection with recent developments in Kuala Lumpur. A more common feature was that they had opposed government policies or offended the UMNO leadership's sensibilities. Many were prominent academics and activists who worked for non-governmental organizations that were concerned with issues of importance to all ethnic communities. While they sometimes highlighted corruption and misuse of government power, they were usually considered no more than irritants. But with UMNO divided, they were providing ammunition for Dr. Mahathir's factional rivals.[47]

Chandra Muzaffar, 40, a political scientist who founded and led the multiracial reform movement Aliran – small but influential and based in Penang – was probably the most successful in stirring broader awareness and scrutiny of public affairs. Chandra's detention was brutally ironic since he actually had rebuked both government and opposition politicians, in a letter to a local paper, for playing a dangerous game of brinkmanship over race. Another detainee, Chee Heng Leng, 32, was a university lecturer and member of the Institute of Social Analysis, a social-reformist organization. Chee, who obtained a master's degree from Harvard University's School of Public Health, had been completing her doctoral thesis on health problems among Malaysia's poor. Others included Meenakshi Raman, 29, a legal adviser to the Consumers Association of Penang, who worked on behalf of squatter farmers being evicted by a developer; Harrison Ngau, 29, the representative of a local affiliate of the international environmental outfit Friends of the Earth, who led the Penan tribe in anti-logging protests in Sarawak; and Tan Ka Kheng, 35, a university lecturer and member of the Environmental Protection Society of Malaysia, who was an ardent critic of a radioactive waste dump in Perak state.

Their detention chilled for a decade or more Malaysia's budding middle class, where liberal views and social activism were spreading beyond urban Chinese and Indians to growing numbers of Malays. As the police net widened, some Malaysians who were temporarily abroad refused to return home immediately, having heard whispers they were "on the list". Others took to sleeping at different places at night and notifying friends and family of their whereabouts at all times. Critics accused the police of staggering the detentions over many weeks and nabbing people at all hours of the day and night deliberately to spread fear among activists.

Reports of grim conditions in prison added to the anxiety. Political prisoners were known to be held initially in solitary confinement in concrete cells, badly lit and ventilated and infested with bugs and mosquitoes, and deprived of bed and blankets and other basic comforts. Families hesitated to discuss the detentions in case they jeopardized the chances of early release, or provoked harsher treatment, of their relatives. Special Branch officers broke up a gathering in Kuala Lumpur of those who dared to organize a detainees support group, photographing participants and recording their names.

The government had silenced its most effective critics. Among the 16 detained members of the Democratic Action Party – ten of them parliamentarians – were the official leader of the opposition, Lim Kit Siang, and V. David, secretary general of the Malaysian Trade Union Congress. Eight members of the Malaysian Chinese Association and five members of Gerakan were also detained. Only four UMNO members were jailed, three of them Team B supporters. Dr. Mahathir explained the communal imbalance in the detentions by saying he had to take action against "the people who have been provoking the Malays", as a trade-off for cancelling the giant UMNO rally.

Lim had worked doggedly to expose the financial scandals that characterized the early years of Dr. Mahathir's rule. Lim and Karpal Singh, a lawyer and the party's deputy chairman, temporarily stopped the government proceeding with Malaysia's biggest public works project, a RM3.42 billion contract to complete the north-south highway. With Karpal acting for Lim in a civil suit, they obtained an injunction to prevent the government and a company controlled by UMNO closing the deal. They claimed it was unlawful and tainted by conflict of interest because it involved senior government officials who were also UMNO leaders. Although a majority of the detainees were released after a few months, 49 were served with two-year detention orders. Lim and Karpal, as well as five other Democratic Action Party legislators, were among them.[48]

The closure of the newspapers – the English-language *Star*, the Chinese-language *Sin Chew Jit Poh* and the Malay-language *Watan* – provided more evidence that the government was acting not only to avoid racial unrest. They were the only domestic papers that regularly covered the activities of the public-interest groups and reported the comments of their leaders. The revocation of their publishing licences by the home affairs ministry, though restored the following year, left Malaysia for the time being without a major paper not controlled by UMNO. Although the *Star*, which carried a weekly column by the paper's publisher and the country's first prime minister, Tunku Abdul Rahman, had been the most outspoken, its criticism of the government was fairly mild. That cautious line was understandable, as the *Star* had been owned since 1977 by a government party, the Malaysian Chinese Association. The paper's disappearance meant the UMNO-owned *New Straits Times* had almost no competition for English-language readers. "We are on the road to dictatorship," said the Tunku, a comment not carried by surviving Malaysian papers.

In his address to Parliament, Dr. Mahathir suggested that his administration's openness and liberalism in the first six years had invited the rise of political hostility and criticism, and he would tolerate it no longer.[49] He developed this theme as he shifted into authoritarian gear in the months ahead. In reality, Dr. Mahathir had always held a dim view of democracy, with a particular dislike for pressure groups, the press and other un-elected bodies. As education minister in the late 1970s, he had supported the suppression of the student movement and introduced legislation that ended university autonomy. As deputy prime minister in 1979, he had no hesitation in using the ISA to detain unionists in a dispute with state-owned Malaysian Airlines System.

The record showed that the "growing authoritarianism" of Dr. Mahathir's leadership actually began almost the day he took over as prime minister.[50] Constitutional amendments in 1981 empowered the king – in practice, the executive – to proclaim a state of emergency even "before the actual occurrence of the event" that might threaten security, economic life or public order. And his proclamation could not be questioned in court. It was a drastic departure from the 1957 Constitution, which stipulated that Parliament should decide when an emergency existed.

Dr. Mahathir also tightened regulations affecting press freedom several times between 1984 and 1987, strengthened the Official Secrets Act in 1984 and moved to head off any possible political challenge, especially from civil society groups, outside the political party system. Under an amendment to the Societies Act, an organization had to register as a "political society" to comment on the policies or activities of the government. Otherwise, the Registrar of Societies, a civil servant under the Home Ministry, could interpret any comment as "political" and deregister a society. While compromises were accepted in 1982 and 1983 to accommodate increasing opposition to the act, most of the repressive provisions remained intact.[51]

If there was a liberal gloss to the 2-M administration it was provided by Musa, and his departure left Dr. Mahathir free to indulge his autocratic instincts. Having taken over the Home Ministry from Musa in 1986, Dr. Mahathir would keep it firmly in his grasp for 13 years, using the ISA more freely than any of his predecessors. Soon after Ghafar replaced Musa, Dr. Mahathir pushed another Official Secrets Act amendment through Parliament in defiance of a nine-month campaign by Malaysian lawyers, journalists, labour unions, reform groups and the political opposition. It enhanced the "intimidating effect" by broadening the definition of an official secret and, for the first time, prescribed a mandatory jail sentence for violators.[52]

Hardly had the prison gates slammed shut on the Operation Lalang detainees than Dr. Mahathir moved again to limit the space available to anyone else who might disagree with him. In December 1987, he introduced two pieces of legislation on the same day that imposed additional restrictions on publications, and granted broader powers to the police to curb public gatherings. An amendment to the Police Act made it easier to prosecute organizers and participants of ostensibly private meetings that turned into public forums, while the Printing Presses and Publications Act was amended again in a way that would "further bind an already cowed, pro-establishment media".[53] Dr. Mahathir said the amendments were aimed at individuals and groups who abused the government's liberal attitude. "Being liberal to them is like offering a flower to a monkey," he said. "The monkey would rather tear the flower apart than appreciate its beauty."

Just when it appeared that Dr. Mahathir had cleared all obstacles to his rule, he found a new target in another un-elected body, the judiciary. Stung by several court decisions, he set out to wrest discretionary power from the judges and place it where he felt it belonged, in the hands of the executive. The irony was that as Dr. Mahathir limited political and civil rights, fellow Malaysians increasingly turned to the courts for the redress of grievances, or at least to score points against the government. By late 1987, Dr. Mahathir had the country's legal establishment on edge with his repeated attacks on judges, and the disclosure that he was drafting legislation to define the boundaries of the executive, legislative and judicial branches of government.

Again, Dr. Mahathir's frontal assault was surprising since Malaysia's judiciary previously had not been the source of controversy. The courts had an international reputation for independence and integrity, though they were fairly conservative and had never held any act of parliament unconstitutional. Malaysia's first three premiers, lawyers all, coexisted comfortably with the judiciary, and Dr. Mahathir seemed to share their appreciation of the institution. "I will always respect the independence of the judiciary," he had told the Asean Law Association General Assembly in October 1982. While the legislature must retain the right to make laws, he said the judiciary should be free to judge the government's alleged trespasses without fear or favour, in accordance with the Constitution, the law and the law of evidence and procedure, as well as justly and fairly. "We shall always respect their judgments."[54]

Having been thwarted at times by the courts, however, an aggrieved and aggressive Dr. Mahathir felt differently. In private, one of his favourite slogans became, "Hang the lawyers, hang the judges."[55] Deep in his heart, Dr. Mahathir found it hard to respect legal practitioners. He had no doubt he was trained in a more noble profession. As he noted, "I ask questions of my patients to get at the truth. The lawyer asks questions of his client in order to find out how to defend his client even if he is wrong."[56]

One case that annoyed him was the government's attempt in 1986 to ban the Hong Kong-based *Asian Wall Street Journal* for three months and expel its two Kuala Lumpur-based staff correspondents. The Supreme Court, the country's highest legal tribunal, ruled that reporter John Berthelsen was denied his right to a hearing when his work permit was cancelled. Dr. Mahathir was also deeply unhappy that Lim Kit Siang had been able to obtain an injunction, before his detention, delaying the north-south highway contract. It further irked Dr. Mahathir that the High Court ruled in 1987 that his Home Ministry did not have the right to stop Chandra Muzaffar's 263-member Aliran organization from publishing a Malay-language version of its English monthly magazine.

Dr. Mahathir said the laws in the Berthelsen case clearly stated that the minister could decide how long a foreigner could stay in the country and that this decision was final. "But the judge overruled this," he said. "...The person was allowed to stay here and the minister could not do anything." Dr. Mahathir either failed to appreciate the nature of the judicial function, or he no longer accepted there was a place for it in his Malaysia. The judge was simply pointing out that the principles of natural justice, well established in the English common law world, required that the minister let the accused tell his side of the story before being thrown out.

In truth, Dr. Mahathir was familiar with these principles, having invoked them himself two years earlier when he criticized former auditor general Ahmad Noordin Zakaria for failing to give certain individuals named in his report on a bank scandal the right to be heard. "You have created doubts and suspicions about them without their being able to clear themselves," Dr. Mahathir had written to Noordin. "It is elementary justice that people must be allowed to give their side of the story."

That was then. Now, Dr. Mahathir told Parliament that natural justice was an alien British concept that should not apply in Malaysia. He complained that the judiciary used precedents from other countries and that the common law they relied on was unwritten. If judicial review persisted, he said, "the government is no longer the executive. Another group has taken over the role".

Unwilling to accept curial constraints imposed upon the exercise of ministerial powers, Dr. Mahathir took to modifying legislation so that a minister's decree was set in concrete. Typically, the amendments to the Printing Presses and Publications Act gave the home affairs minister "absolute discretion" in granting publishing licences and printing permits. His decision could not be "called in question by any court on any ground whatsoever".

Amendments to the Constitution whisked through Parliament in March 1988 tackled the problem, as Dr. Mahathir saw it, head on: They virtually emasculated the judiciary. The judiciary's powers were removed from the Constitution and transferred to Parliament. Specifically, the High Courts were denied the constitutional right to judicial review. Also, the attorney general assumed responsibility for deciding which court should try a particular criminal case. Almost overnight, the judiciary was stripped of much of its independence and authority, undermining the separation of powers envisaged in the Constitution.[57]

With Lim Kit Siang still in jail in early 1988, the Supreme Court dismissed his legal challenge blocking the government from awarding the huge north-south highway contract to United Engineers (Malaysia) Bhd., a company ultimately controlled by UMNO. It was a significant victory for the government and a setback for public-interest litigation, though the three-two split judgment was a reminder of the executive's vulnerability before an independent judiciary. A High Court judge ordered the release of Karpal Singh, Lim's lawyer, ruling that his two-year detention order – approved by Dr. Mahathir as home affairs minister – was "made without care, caution and a proper sense of responsibility". Shamelessly, as one critic commented, the police re-arrested Karpal under the ISA a couple of hours after he was freed.

The Tengku Razaleigh supporters seeking to overturn Dr. Mahathir's election got more than they bargained for when the High Court in February declared UMNO, the backbone of Malaysian politics since 1946, an illegal organization. While the ruling created considerable confusion and appeared to be a blow to Dr. Mahathir, in reality it was what he sought and anticipated. The last thing he wanted was a re-run of his showdown with Tengku Razaleigh. He had committed himself to the formation of a new party free of the troublemakers.

The UMNO 11, as they were called, were seeking a fresh party election on the grounds that the poll held in April 1987 was flawed. They argued that some delegates who voted were from party branches not approved by Malaysia's Registrar of Societies. A total of 45 delegates selected at the branch level were unacceptable under party rules and Malaysian law, they contended, which could have affected the outcome. Not only was their point uncontested in court, but Dr. Mahathir's lawyers also opted for what was called a "kamikaze defence". They relied on another provision of the Societies Act, that if any branch was unregistered, UMNO itself was an unlawful society. And that was the way Judge Harun Mahmud Hashim ruled.

Amidst the confusion, the competing factions scrambled to register a successor organization that might inherit the former party's 1.4 million members spread over about 800 branches, with its vast assets and even bigger liabilities. Although a premier without a party, Dr. Mahathir could still afford to smile at the ill-fated efforts of his rivals since the Registrar of Societies came under his Home Ministry. When followers of Tengku Razaleigh, under the nominal leadership of ex-premiers Tunku Abdul Rahman and Hussein Onn, tried to register UMNO Malaysia, they were refused. The registrar told them that UMNO, though illegal, had not yet been deleted from the list of societies. A little later, Dr. Mahathir's group had no such trouble registering UMNO Baru, or New UMNO, which before long was referred to as simply UMNO. Dr. Mahathir became member number 0000001, and subsequently would refer to it as "my" party.[58]

By registering a new party before waiting to see if the UMNO 11 would appeal within the 30 days allowed, Dr. Mahathir had painted himself into a corner. A successful appeal would restore the legality of UMNO from which Dr. Mahathir and his followers would be excluded under UMNO's constitution, because they now belonged to another political party. The UMNO 11 had not planned to appeal, but decided to do so on the recommendation of their lawyer, Muhammad Shafee Abdullah, who realized the implications late in the day. Shafee's notice of appeal, filed on day 29, caused panic in the Mahathir camp.

In response to the appeal, Mohamed Salleh Abas, Lord President of the Supreme Court, scheduled an unprecedented hearing by a full bench of nine judges on 13 June 1988. The full court was to sit for the first time, for nothing less than Dr. Mahathir's political survival was at stake. His fate was to be decided not in the rough and tumble of politics where he could be confident of outsmarting and out-slugging most players, but in the rarefied atmosphere of a courtroom in the sway of a majority of judges who were independent enough not to be intimidated by the executive.

If Salleh had convened the court as planned, the hearing "would have been all over in less than an hour", according to one respected former Supreme Court judge,[59] whose opinion was widely shared. The panel would have followed a binding precedent set in Malaysia's Supreme Court in 1983 and allowed the appeal, he said, declaring the election of the UMNO president null and avoid.

Malaysian political history took a dramatically different course, however. Salleh was summoned to the prime minister's office on 27 May, where he was informed that he was being suspended as head of Malaysia's judiciary on the instructions of the king. Dr. Mahathir told Salleh that the king was displeased by a letter the lord president had written to the king two months earlier complaining about the executive's persistent criticism of the judiciary, and copied to the other sultans. The letter was written on behalf of "all the judges of the country" after 20 of them based in Kuala Lumpur held a meeting and decided on this quiet move, "with the hope that all of those unfounded accusations will be stopped". Salleh, who enjoyed a sound reputation as a competent, independent and somewhat conservative judge, was to face impeachment before a specially constituted tribunal. On the day that Salleh met the prime minister, the acting lord president, Abdul Hamid Omar, postponed the hearing of the UMNO 11 appeal.

What Dr. Mahathir did not tell Salleh, or the rest of the country, was why King Mahmood Iskandar might want to cooperate with the prime minister in decapitating the judiciary. The king owed Dr. Mahathir an incalculable debt, for the prime minister had chosen not to reveal that the king, who had a record of violent conduct before he ascended the throne, had killed his caddy with a golf club, in a fit of temper, the previous year. In retirement, Dr. Mahathir defended his inaction on the grounds that the king and his fellow rulers had legal immunity at the time. As there was no legal provision, "I couldn't just go and tell him resign or something like that...So it was a very difficult situation for me," he said.[60]

Malaysia's Constitution, however, gives the hereditary rulers of the country's nine Malay states, meeting as the Conference of Rulers, the power to remove the king by a majority vote. A compelling case could be made that Dr. Mahathir was under a strong moral obligation to inform the Conference of Rulers, with whom he met regularly, that the sultan they elected for a five-year term as head of state, had taken the life of an innocent man. Indeed, a small group of Malaysian lawyers made an unpublicized private attempt to persuade the rulers to remove the king, not over the killing but because of his role in the action against Salleh Abas. According to one of the lawyers involved in the initiative, four rulers agreed but a fifth, needed for a majority, backed out at a meeting in Kuala Lumpur.[61]

When he learned of the caddy's death, Dr. Mahathir informed the Cabinet. He mentioned it "in his notes and not for discussion, just to say, 'look, we have to handle this carefully. Let me handle it'".[62] The news was never published in Malaysia, though word circulated in elite circles and was alluded to obliquely. For instance, Tunku Abdul Rahman told a conference on the Constitution he was "concerned" that the king and rulers "are free to commit crime", and he suggested that a special court be established to try them "in order to protect the fundamental rights" of all Malaysians.[63]

Any publicity about the caddy's death probably would have made the king's continued occupation of the throne, until his term expired in 1989, untenable. By remaining silent, Dr. Mahathir placed the king under a heavy personal obligation, a situation the prime minister deftly exploited when it involved politicians and officials indebted to him, or vulnerable in some other way. And, indeed, the king showed early signs of gratitude: Although he was supposed to be above politics, he had ignored constitutional propriety and endorsed Dr. Mahathir's Team A the previous year. Karpal Singh, the opposition lawyer-legislator detained twice under the ISA, suggested years later that Dr. Mahathir's silence concealed an ulterior motive. Speaking in Parliament, he asked rhetorically "why didn't the prime minister do anything" when the Sultan of Johore, as king, killed the caddy. He added, "That time, the prime minister wanted to use him...he used him to fire the Lord President, Tun Salleh Abas, and some other things. That's the reason".[64]

Dr. Mahathir's contention that he was carrying out the king's instruction that Salleh be sacked sat oddly with established practice and the prime minister's own fiercely held view that the monarchy had no place in political affairs. Under the Constitution, the king acted on the advice of the prime minister, not the other way around. When he was no longer king, the Sultan of Johore apologized to Salleh for his role in Salleh's dismissal, saying he was "made use of" in 1988.[65] The sultan invited Salleh to his palace and expressed regret over what had happened more than four years earlier. "In the meeting, the Johore Sultan openly asked for my forgiveness because of his involvement in the move to dismiss me as the lord president in 1988," Salleh said.[66]

After he left politics, Dr. Mahathir said the king also had been upset by another letter from Salleh, sent earlier, in which Salleh complained about noise during repair work at the king's palace, near Salleh's house.[67] When the charges against Salleh were published, however, royal displeasure over renovations was not one of them. Rather, many stemmed from speeches and interviews Salleh had given, and some even related to his behaviour after suspension.

In essence, Salleh was accused of being biased against the government. The proceedings against him were considered by independent legal experts to be highly improper in several respects. For a start, Dr. Mahathir, as his accuser, got to name the six-member tribunal. Only one judge met the principle of being of superior rank to Salleh, despite the availability of suitable candidates, while the inclusion of the speaker of the House of Representatives was inappropriate under Malaysia's separation of powers doctrine. The tribunal refused Salleh's application for the hearings to be open, and declined to adjourn to give his British counsel time to appear for him.

The participation of Hamid Omar "made a mockery of the whole process".[68] As acting lord president, Hamid stood to be confirmed in that position if Salleh was convicted, and as chairman he would cast the deciding vote if the panel was deadlocked. Worse, Hamid was an interested party as one of the 20 judges who approved the letter written by Salleh to the king.

Although the public did not know, Hamid, too, was vulnerable to pressure, having lost a considerable amount of money investing in a company that subsequently performed poorly. His financial losses, as well as social indiscretions, were known to the government, having been circulated in a *surat layang*, the contents of which he confirmed, in a private interview, to be accurate.[69] Hamid told a Bar Council delegation that urged him not to accept a role in the tribunal he feared he would be dismissed if he refused. "If I am sacked, will you or the Bar Council compensate my losses of remuneration," he said.[70]

Convinced he could not get a fair hearing, Salleh withdrew and sought an order from the High Court to halt the tribunal for being allegedly unconstitutional and illegal. Failing to get a response and fearing the tribunal was within days of submitting its report to the king, Salleh's counsel sought a temporary ban from the Supreme Court. The most senior judge – considering that the lord president was suspended and that the acting lord president was involved in the hearing – took the initiative and convened a five-member panel that issued the stay order. Soon after, those five judges were also suspended, after a complaint by Hamid that they conspired to hold a special session of the court without his approval. A second tribunal was established to hear charges of gross misbehaviour against the five.

The first tribunal's report, described by an eminent Queen's Counsel in Britain as "the most despicable document in modern legal history", found Salleh guilty of misconduct and recommended his removal.[71] He was sacked as lord president with effect from 8 May 1988. On the same day, the appeal by the UMNO 11 was heard by a mixed panel of five Supreme and High Court judges, presided over by Hamid, and dismissed the following day. Dr. Mahathir had survived. As Salleh wrote later, "I have no doubt – and few would now disagree – that it was the UMNO saga that led to my destruction as a judge."[72]

The second tribunal's report – the work of "young colonels [who] were appointed to sit in judgment against generals", since three of the five members were relatively junior judges of the High Court and the accused were all Supreme Court judges[73] – recommended in a split vote that two be dismissed and the three others reinstated. When Hamid subsequently was confirmed as Lord President of the Supreme Court of Malaysia, one constitutional scholar wrote, "This elevation of a man, who many believe had violated the fundamental rules of natural justice, underscored the irregularity of the whole episode."[74] The Malaysian Bar, representing all the country's lawyers, passed a resolution of no confidence in Hamid by a vote of 1,002 to 0. All the High Court judges who were involved in the affair were promoted to the Supreme Court in due course.

The assault on the judiciary, as it was ever after known, though motivated by political factors, opened the way for money to seep into the system. Some of the judges who played ball with the Mahathir administration rose rapidly and could not resist the temptation of bribes. They came to occupy some of the most senior positions in the judiciary, seemingly untouchable as long as they cooperated with their political masters. The integrity of at least three heads of the judiciary was "called into question".[75]

Indications surfaced in the mid-1990s that litigants in several civil and commercial cases had manoeuvred to have their cases heard before judges of their choice.[76] According to one judge, where lawyers once took books, law reports and legal authorities to court, they now carried cash so the judges could reach a decision "with complete disregard for facts and the law!".[77]

The judge anonymously circulated a 33-page document listing 112 allegations of impropriety: 39 charges of corruption, 21 of abuse of power, and 52 of misconduct, immorality or other indiscretions.[78] The government forced the judge, Syed Ahmad Idid Syed Abdullah Aidid, to resign, but did not prosecute him, even though it declared his allegations baseless and said all the dozen judges questioned by investigators were clean.

What many regarded as the "final nail hammered into the coffin of judicial independence" was another constitutional amendment in 1994.[79] Apart from restructuring Malaysia's judicial hierarchy, it allowed a judge to be dismissed for breaching a proposed, government prescribed code of ethics. Although the restructuring, to create an appeal court at home following the abolition of appeals to the Privy Council in Britain in 1985, was necessary, the adoption of new nomenclature aroused suspicion. The Supreme Court reverted to its original name, the Federal Court, and the lord president became the chief justice. Seemingly innocent, the renaming exercise could be perceived as further subtle diminution of the prestige of the judiciary.[80]

Later, Dr. Mahathir said it would have made no difference if a full panel of the Supreme Court had considered the appeal against the judgment outlawing UMNO. He said UMNO "wanted nothing more than the validation of the election results making me president and Ghafar Baba deputy president".[81] Without explaining how he would have dealt with two UMNOs, had the appeal by the UMNO 11 been successful, Dr. Mahathir said that even if the full bench had heard the appeal, "I'm quite sure that I'll somehow or other manage to stay on as leader of UMNO."[82] As it was, Hamid, Dr. Mahathir's choice for lord president, handed him a clear-cut victory.

In March 1988, before the final court decision on the legality of UMNO, the government had amended the Societies Act to facilitate the transfer of the old party's assets to New UMNO. All New UMNO had to do was adopt a constitution that closely resembled the old one and admit a majority of UMNO's members. The amendments contained disincentives for dissidents tempted to cause trouble. If those who did not join the new party objected formally to the assets transfer, they could be held liable for their share of the old party's debt. Dr. Mahathir made sure his most committed opponents, especially those associated with the attempt to form UMNO Malaysia, were not admitted to New UMNO. The rest he courted in a nation-wide membership drive, backed with the full armory of government patronage, as well as the usual coercive measures to discourage intransigence.

Tengku Razaleigh formed a new party but was not permitted to use the name UMNO. He settled for Semangat '46, or Spirit of '46, in the hope that it would evoke the Malay community fervour of UMNO's founding year. A dissident strategy to stage rolling by-elections got off to a promising start in mid-1988 when a Musa ally, former welfare minister Shahrir Abdul Samad, resigned to re-contest his seat in Johore as an independent. He whipped the

New UMNO candidate backed by the National Front machine, on a platform of rebuking Dr. Mahathir over the sacking of Salleh Abas. But any hope of spurring disaffection and building momentum dissipated when the New UMNO candidate pipped the Spirit of '46 standard bearer in an overwhelmingly Malay Johore state constituency five months later. After the National Front easily retained a Malay-majority parliamentary seat in the suburbs of Kuala Lumpur in January 1989 – with a Malaysian Chinese Association novice against an old-style, tainted Spirit of '46 candidate – the rebel offensive was effectively dead.

Although Dr. Mahathir suffered a heart attack in January and required immediate surgery, he had emerged as the undisputed victor from the UMNO power struggle. Musa and many of his followers were enticed to join Dr. Mahathir's UMNO without any promise of reward, leaving Tengku Razaleigh commanding only 12 seats in the House of Representatives, and with narrowing prospects. Dr. Mahathir continued to discard anyone whose loyalty was suspect, demanding fidelity to his leadership above other qualities. "I don't need intelligent, honest, hard-working people in Parliament," he told Mohamed Tawfik Ismail, a first-term parliamentarian and Musa ally from Johore he was about to axe. Urging Tawfik to go into business, he said, "My members of parliament should stand when I enter the chamber, thump the table and shout, 'Long Live Mahathir'."[83] As political scientist Gordon Means observed, after a couple of years of turmoil, "For political friend and foe alike, Dr. Mahathir had become the epicenter of politics."[84]

Despite the instillation in him of five coronary bypass arteries, Dr. Mahathir returned to the scene after several months convalescing with no erosion of his authority. With winner's disdain, he continued to enhance the power of the executive branch. Parliament passed amendments to the ISA and other laws on emergency powers, crime and drug prevention to remove judicial review. In the 1990 election, Dr. Mahathir led the National Front to another comfortable victory, winning 127 of the 180 seats, against Spirit of '46 in separate alliances with both PAS and the Democratic Action Party. Although the National Front was floored in Tengku Razaleigh's home state of Kelantan, losing all state and federal seats, Dr. Mahathir retained his two-thirds majority in Parliament. After Dr. Mahathir scored his greatest electoral triumph in 1995, capturing 162 of 192 parliamentary seats, a demoralized Tengku Razaleigh and supporters disbanded Spirit of '46 and drifted back to UMNO. According to a joke doing the rounds, UMNO stood for Under Mahathir No Opposition.

Similarly, Dr. Mahathir concentrated power at the top of UMNO, particularly in the presidency. His display of "brute strength" in routing the dissidents – as Musa Hitam described it – marked Dr. Mahathir as not only a superior leader and strategist, but also an unforgiving one. Seeped into the psyche of every UMNO ladder-climber was the gnawing fear that to make what could be construed as a move against Dr. Mahathir invited political oblivion. If he could destroy Musa and Tengku Razaleigh, he would not hesitate to snuff out their own political careers – and the good life enjoyed by them and their friends. Musa called it "a political Mahathir thing": the prime minister's "ability to create this worry, because if you are so powerful nobody dares challenge you. And he managed to create that impression. And nobody dared, indeed."[85]

Still, Dr. Mahathir took no chances. After his narrow squeak in 1987, New UMNO's constitution was changed to make it almost impossible for anyone to challenge him and his deputy by arranging so-called bonus votes for the number of nominations that candidates received. Every nomination received from party divisions for the posts of president and deputy president carried with it ten bonus votes. The number of votes that could be gathered through nominations almost equaled the number of ballots cast by delegates in the actual election. If that was not enough to dissuade rivals, the rules were altered again so that presidential candidates had to be nominated by at least 30 per cent of UMNO's divisions. Dr. Mahathir was allowed to appoint the head of the party's youth and women's wings, a temporary expedient that was reversed a few years later to allow elections again for both posts.[86] Amendments in 1998 allowing the triennial party elections to be postponed for up to 18 months gave Dr. Mahathir even more room to re-order adverse circumstances to his liking. And there would be no recourse to the courts again over voting irregularities: Legislation passed in late 1989 gave political parties the final say over the interpretation of their constitutions.

According to political scientist John Funston, "under a Malaysian version of 'guided democracy', Dr. Mahathir frequently asked for, and was granted, full power to make decisions on contentious party issues".[87] By the time the General Assembly arrived each year, everything of note had been settled, right down to the detail of Dr. Mahathir's telling key delegates what was expected in pre-assembly, closed-door sessions. What the public saw was a staged performance designed to reinforce the image of unity behind Dr. Mahathir's leadership, with his presidential and summary addresses broadcast live to the nation.[88]

By continuing to permit rivalries in UMNO one level below him, Dr. Mahathir countered pressures for a generational shift in the party's leadership and kept the focus of succession away from himself. As Finance Minister Anwar Ibrahim, 46, prepared to dislodge Ghafar Baba, 68, from the deputy presidency in 1993, Dr. Mahathir shifted from a plea for no contest, to a neutral stance, to a comment that was interpreted as an endorsement of Anwar, his obvious choice to succeed him. Anwar marshalled such a show of strength before the General Assembly that Ghafar had no choice but to step down. Anwar not only became vice president unopposed; he also brought to power a slate of three vice presidents known as the Vision Team, while other followers captured most seats on the Supreme Council.

The results signalled danger for Dr. Mahathir, though also a warning for anyone tempted to try and exploit the situation, for Dr. Mahathir had shown he was politically astute, even lethal, when seemingly cornered. Analysts calculated that Anwar probably had enough control of the party to force Dr. Mahathir into early retirement before long, if he so chose. Dr. Mahathir was testy when asked by journalists if he was losing his grip on UMNO. "Would you like to bet?" he retorted. He made his point about still being boss by waiting a month before officially making Anwar deputy prime minister. In another move to circumvent Anwar's advancement, he appointed Muhyiddin Yassin, who topped the vice presidential poll for Anwar's team, to a junior portfolio. Clearly not confident, though, Dr. Mahathir invoked party unity as a higher cause than democracy and insisted on a "no contest" agreement with Anwar for their positions before 1999.

Although their relations were strained at times, Anwar was still on track to succeed Dr. Mahathir as of early 1998, but complications that arose over the deepening effects of the Asian economic crisis wrecked transition plans. On 2 September, a day after introducing capital controls, Dr. Mahathir sacked Anwar as deputy premier and finance minister, claiming he was morally unfit. The real reason was that he believed Anwar was trying to take advantage of the economic upheaval to unseat him. On 3 September, the UMNO Supreme Council complied with Dr. Mahathir's demand that Anwar be stripped of his deputy presidency and party membership. On 20 September, Anwar was arrested under the ISA and held without access to a lawyer or his family. When he appeared in court at the end of the month, charged with abuse of power and sodomy, he had a black eye, the result of being bashed in custody.

Dr. Mahathir had learned from 1987, when the ruling political elite fractured over the Tengku Razaleigh-Musa challenge. By removing immediately any possibility that Anwar could make a return to UMNO politics, Dr. Mahathir was able to carry the party's top leadership with him. But lower level leaders and the party rank and file, as with Malay society and the country at large, were numbed, disbelieving and alienated. Several hundred thousand members abandoned UMNO in protest to join PAS or Keadilan, a new party established by Anwar's wife.

In making Abdullah Badawi deputy premier, Dr. Mahathir implicitly drew attention to the toll that his prolonged, iron rule had taken on UMNO. As one study noted, he had defeated in masterful fashion every threat to his rule, burying in succession the dynamic and talented Musa, Tengku Razaleigh and Anwar.[89] In doing so, he had eliminated from the party just about any possible successor approaching their calibre. Almost no younger leaders had been promoted, apart from Anwar, not even through UMNO Youth. With the leadership pipeline clogged for so long by Dr. Mahathir, he turned to Abdullah, an experienced but bland former civil servant, who had sided against Dr. Mahathir in the 1987 split.

Abdullah was 59, scarcely representing the hope of regeneration in a party in deep trouble.

Appalled by the humiliation of Anwar, the Malays routed UMNO in the 1999 general election. While the National Front secured its two-thirds majority in Parliament, winning 148 of 193 seats, UMNO had its worst result ever. Its representation fell from 94 seats to 72, with four ministers and five deputies being defeated.

UMNO's problem went beyond numbers. No longer able to claim confidently majority Malay support, the party's very legitimacy was in doubt. The best estimates put UMNO's share of the Malay vote at between 40 and 50 per cent. While most UMNO leaders advocated reforms to both party and government policies to meet public demands for improved governance that focused on Anwar's persecution, Dr. Mahathir objected to any concessions. He cracked down hard again on his political opponents, particularly PAS and Keadilan, prosecuting and jailing several leaders and restricting their attempts to mobilize. The measures included withdrawing petroleum royalty payments, amounting to more than RM800 million a year, from opposition-held Trengganu state, even though they were legally guaranteed. Dr. Mahathir was able to win stronger support from non-Malays worried about Islamic extremism after the "September 11" terrorist attacks in the United States. As prime minister, he was secure.

Yet UMNO leaders and followers alike knew in their hearts that only Dr. Mahathir's departure would assuage Malay anger, as much of it was directed at him personally. Mindful of Anwar's fate, though, nobody who hoped for a future in the party was about to ask him to go. What they really needed was a Dr. Mahathir of three decades earlier, the one who dared speak bluntly to Tunku Abdul Rahman, to accept responsibility for the 1999 debacle and quit. Since acquiescing under pressure, even if it was unspoken, was anathema to Dr. Mahathir, party insiders tended to agree with hostile Internet analysts, who predicted he would die with his boots on. Anwar supporters began deriding him as "prime minister for life".

Dr. Mahathir shattered the irresolution in his closing address to the UMNO General Assembly in June 2002, abruptly departing from his text to say he was resigning "from UMNO and all positions in the National Front". As he broke into sobs, supporters mobbed him at the podium, some of them also in tears, imploring him to remain – all live on TV. Dr. Mahathir was taken to a back room, and his deputy, Abdullah Badawi, appeared after an hour to say he had been persuaded to stay on. Later, it was announced that he would retire at the end of October 2003.

For 16 months Dr. Mahathir stayed on in the position he had vowed to avoid, as a lame duck prime minister, making arrangements so that Malaysia would be run for the foreseeable future by his anointed leaders. He ensured that Abdullah faced no contest in UMNO elections before he became prime minister. Abdullah, in fact, was the first deputy president never elected to the post by the party, though he was "approved" under an arrangement that saw no challenge to the president or his deputy. Dr. Mahathir also extracted a public promise from the party's three vice presidents that they would accept Abdullah's future choice for deputy premier, and support that person unopposed in party elections. Dr. Mahathir made known his preference for Najib Razak as deputy, a choice confirmed by Abdullah in due course.

As promised, Dr. Mahathir stepped down on 31 October 2003 in an atmosphere of near disbelief that his era was finally ending. By voluntarily surrendering power, he once more confounded his critics. While Dr. Mahathir did not retain any official government or party office, he said he would play an active role as an "ordinary" UMNO member, as if a person with his record could ever be considered ordinary. Rather, it was the new leadership that appeared less than life size. Recall that Abdullah was once a member of the Tengku Razaleigh-Musa Team B, and Najib had belonged to Anwar's Vision Team. "That...must make one wonder", observed political scientist Khoo Boo Teik, "if the going gets rough, whether history will repeat itself as tragedy or farce".[90] As it happened, it was a bit of both.

Notes

1   Clive S. Kessler, "The Mark of the Man: Mahathir's Malaysia after Dr. Mahathir", in Bridget Welsh, ed., *Reflections: The Mahathir Years* (Washington: Southeast Asia Studies Program, The Paul H. Nitze School of Advanced International Studies, Johns Hopkins University, 2004), p. 16.
2   In-Won Hwang, "Malaysia's 'Presidential Premier': Explaining Mahathir's Dominance", in *Reflections*, p. 67.
3   Frank-Jurgen Richter and Thang D. Nguyen, eds, *The Malaysian Journey: Progress in Diversity* (Singapore: Times Editions-Marshall Cavendish, 2004), p. x.
4   Interview with Musa Hitam, 3 January 2007.
5   Rehman Rashid, *A Malaysian Journey* (Petaling Jaya: Rehman Rashid, 1993), pp. 172–173.
6   Eddin Khoo and Jason Tan, "Transitional Times", *Off the Edge*, November 2005, p. 23.
7   Zainuddin Maidin, *The Other Side of Mahathir* (Kuala Lumpur: Utusan Publications & Distributors Sdn. Bhd., 1994), pp. 224–225.
8   Rehman Rashid, *A Malaysian Journey*, pp. 171–172.
9   John Berthelsen, "Malaysian Prime Minister Invents an 'Islamic Toilet'", *Asian Wall Street Journal* (hereafter *AWSJ*), 18 October 1984.
10   Email correspondence with Mahathir Mohamad, 25 June 2008.
11   Ibid.
12   Interview with Siti Hasmah Mohamad Ali, 17 January 2008.
13   Interview with Daim Zainuddin, 18 October 2007.
14   Musa Hitam, "We Were Followers", *Far Eastern Economic Review* (hereafter *FEER*), 9 October 2003 <http://www.feer.com/articles/2003/0310_09/p024region.html> (accessed 19 January 2006).
15   V.G. Kulkarni, S. Jayasankaran and Murray Hiebert, "Dr. Feelgood", *FEER*, 24 October 1996, p. 18.

16 Interview with Mahathir Mohamad, 14 August 2007.
17 "Mahathir on Race, the West and His Successor", *Time Asia*, 9 December 1996 <http://www.time.com/time/asia/2003/mahathir/mahathir961209_intvu.html> (accessed 27 January 2006).
18 Interview with Mahathir Mohamad, 20 March 2007.
19 Ahmad Mustapha Hassan, *The Unmaking of Malaysia: Insider's Reminiscences of UMNO, Razak and Mahathir* (Petaling Jaya: Strategic Information and Research Development Centre, 2007), p. 65.
20 John Funston, "Political Careers of Mahathir Mohamad and Anwar Ibrahim: Parallel, Intersecting and Conflicting Lives", IKMAS Working Papers (Institute of Malaysian and International Studies, Universiti Kebangsaan Malaysia), no. 15 (July 1998): i–iv, 1–32.
21 Interview with Mahathir Mohamad, 31 March 2008.
22 Mahathir Mohamad, *Reflections on Asia* (Subang Jaya: Pelanduk Publications (M) Sdn. Bhd., 2002), p. 113.
23 Narayana N.R. Murthy, "A Hands-On Leader", *FEER*, 9 October 2003 <http://www.feer.com/articles/2003/0310_09/p024region.html> (accessed 19 January 2006).
24 Interview with Musa Hitam, 1 April 2008.
25 Interview with Siti Hasmah Mohamad Ali, 17 January 2008.
26 Robin Adshead, *Mahathir of Malaysia: Statesman and Leader* (London: Hibiscus Publishing Company, 1989), p. 113.
27 Cheong Mei Sui and Adibah Amin, *Daim: The Man Behind the Enigma* (Petaling Jaya: Pelanduk Publications (M) Sdn. Bhd., 1995), p. 140.
28 Ibid., pp. 140–141.
29 Interview with Siti Hasmah Mohamad Ali, 17 January 2008.
30 Mahathir B. Mohamad, "Problems of Democratic Nation-Building in Malaysia", *Solidarity* (Philippines), October 1971.
31 Interview with Tengku Razaleigh Hamzah, 29 May 2007.
32 Interview with Tengku Razaleigh Hamzah, 21 March 2007.
33 Cheong Mei Sui and Adibah Amin, *Daim: The Man Behind the Enigma*, p. 30.
34 Interview with Tengku Razaleigh Hamzah, 21 March 2007.
35 *Asia 1982 Yearbook*, Far Eastern Economic Review Ltd., p. 194.
36 In-Won Hwang, *Personalized Politics: The Malaysian State Under Mahathir* (Singapore: Institute of Southeast Asian Studies, 2003), p. 129.
37 Harold Crouch, *Government & Society in Malaysia* (Sydney: Allen & Unwin, 1996), p. 38.
38 R.S. Milne and Diane K. Mauzy, *Malaysian Politics Under Mahathir* (London: Routledge, 1999), p. 160.
39 In-Won Hwang, "Malaysia's 'Presidential Premier': Explaining Mahathir's Dominance", in *Reflections*, p. 68.
40 *Asia 1984 Yearbook*, Far Eastern Economic Review Ltd., p. 212.
41 Interview with Param Cumaraswamy, 3 April 2008.
42 Ibid.
43 Stephen Duthie, "Poll Proves Bruising for Malaysian Party", *AWSJ*, 22 April 1987.
44 Stephen Duthie, "Mahathir Faces Hard Job on Party Unity", *AWSJ*, 27 April 1987.
45 Param Coomaraswamy [sic], "Injustice for All", *FEER*, 9 October 2003 <http://www.feer.com/articles/2003/0310_09/p024region.html> (accessed 19 January 2006).
46 Stephen Duthie, "New Detentions Net Malaysia's Chief Dissidents", *AWSJ*, 29 October 1987.

47 Harold Crouch, *Government & Society in Malaysia*, p. 112.
48 The last to be released, Lim Kit Siang and his son, Lim Guan Eng, spent 18 months in detention.
49 Stephen Duthie, "New Detentions Net Malaysia's Chief Dissidents".
50 In-Won Hwang, *Personalized Politics*, p. 125.
51 Ibid., p. 126.
52 Ibid., p. 123.
53 *Asia 1988 Yearbook*, Far Eastern Economic Review Ltd., p. 180.
54 Stephen Duthie, "Mahathir's Rift with Judiciary Worsens", *AWSJ*, 30 December 1987. Mahathir Mohamad, speech at the Asean Law Association General Assembly, University of Malaya, 26 October 1982.
55 K. Das, *Questionable Conduct* (Kuala Lumpur: K. Das, 1990), p. 6.
56 V.G. Kulkarni, Murray Hiebert and S. Jayasankaran, "Tough Talk: Mahathir Thrives on No-Nonsense Policies", *FEER*, 24 October 1996, p. 23.
57 R.S. Milne and Diane K. Mauzy, *Malaysian Politics Under Mahathir*, p. 47.
58 Alan Friedman and Jonathan Gage, "Malaysia's Currency Controls will be Eased, Mahathir Promises", *International Herald Tribune*, 30 January 1999 <http://www.iht.com/articles/1999/01/30/maha.t.php> (accessed 14 December 2006).
59 Dato Sri George Seah, "If UMNO-11 Appeal Had Been Heard...", *Aliran Monthly*, 2003: 11, p. 35.
60 Interview with Mahathir Mohamad, 31 March 2008.
61 Interview with Param Cumaraswamy, 19 October 2007.
62 Interview with Anwar Ibrahim, 15 August 2007.
63 *Reflections on the Malaysian Constitution* (Penang: Persatuan Aliran Kesedaran Negara, 1987), p. 20.
64 Parliamentary debates, House of Representatives, Malaysia, 8 December 1992, p. 11311.
65 Phone interview with Salleh Abas, 24 August 2008.
66 "Johor Sultan Seeks Forgivenes", *Aliran Monthly*, 1995: 4, p. 27, an English translation of a report in *Harakah*, 21 April 1995, p. 32.
67 Dr. Mahathir Mohamad, "The Tun Salleh Saga", 6 June 2008 <http://test.chedet.com/cgi-bin/mt/mt-search.cgi?search=salleh&IncludeBlogs=1> (accessed 28 August 2008).
68 H.P. Lee, *Constitutional Conflicts in Contemporary Malaysia* (Kuala Lumpur: Oxford University Press, 1995), p. 60.
69 Interview with Param Cumaraswamy, 19 October 2007.
70 Beh Lih Yi, "If I don't Accept, I'll be Sacked", 1 October 2007 <http://www.malaysiakini.com/news/73038> (accessed 1 October 2007).
71 Geoffrey Robertson, "Justice Hangs in the Balance", *Observer*, 28 August 1988.
72 Tun Salleh Abas with K. Das, *May Day for Justice* (Kuala Lumpur: Magnus Books, 1989), p. xx.
73 George Seah, "Lessons to be Learnt from the 1988 Judicial Crisis", *Aliran Monthly*, 2004: 8, p. 40.
74 H.P. Lee, *Constitutional Conflicts in Contemporary Malaysia*, p. 57.
75 Param Cumaraswamy, "Judicial Reforms Must Meet the Test of Constitutionality", *Sun*, 30 December 2008.
76 Raphael Pura, "Rulings Spark Controversy in Malaysia", *AWSJ*, 25 August 1995.
77 Untitled, undated anonymous 33-page document circulated in 1996, which High Court judge Syed Ahmad Idid Syed Abdullah Aidid later admitted writing, p. 1.
78 Roger Mitton, "Courting Controversy", *Asiaweek.com*, 26 July 1996 <http://www.asiaweek.com/asiaweek/96/0726/nat3.html> (accessed 16 February 2006).

79 H.P. Lee, *Constitutional Conflicts in Contemporary Malaysia*, p. 127.
80 Ibid., p. 128.
81 Dr. Mahathir Mohamad, "The Tun Salleh Saga".
82 Interview with Mahathir Mohamad, 20 March 2007.
83 Interview with Mohamed Tawfik Ismail, 23 September 2006. Tawfik is the oldest son of a former deputy prime minister, the late Ismail Abdul Rahman. Dr. Mahathir later denied making the comment. He said Tawfik was dropped because of his "lacklustre performance". Dr. Mahathir Mohamad, "Fitnah", 15 February 2009 <http://chedet.co.cc/chedetblog/2009/02/fitnah.html> (accessed 20 March 2009).
84 Gordon P. Means, "Malaysia in 1989: Forging a Plan for the Future", *Southeast Asian Affairs 1990*, p. 186.
85 Eddin Khoo and Jason Tan, "Transitional Times", p. 25.
86 In-Won Hwang, *Personalized Politics*, pp. 173, 203, fn 110.
87 John Funston, "UMNO: What Legacy Will Mahathir Leave?", in *Reflections*, p. 135.
88 Ibid., p. 135.
89 R.S. Milne and Diane K. Mauzy, *Malaysian Politics Under Mahathir*, p. 186.
90 Khoo Boo Teik, "Who Will Succeed the Successor?", *Aliran Monthly*, 2003: 5, p. 6.

4
The Vision of a Modern Nation

Dr. Mahathir wasted no time in transforming Malaysia in line with his vision of a modern, industrialized nation, setting the goal of becoming fully developed by 2020. Once dominant primary commodities, already receding, gave way to the production of manufactured goods and the embrace of a high-tech future. With the economy expanding at an annual average rate of 6.1 per cent for the 22 years he was prime minister,[1] Malaysia was one of the developing world's most successful countries. It was all the more impressive for being a Muslim-majority nation, indicating that Islam could be compatible with representative government and modernization. That it was achieved while a comprehensive affirmative action programme was being applied to such an ethnically diverse population added lustre to Malaysia's internationally acclaimed success.

As the government poured money into highways, airports, skyscrapers, bridges and container ports, Malaysians ditched their bicycles and motorbikes for cars and more cars. With manufacturing growing from about 30 per cent to more than 70 per cent of exports, Malaysia became an economic dynamo and one of the world's top 20 exporters. It even became an exporter of capital, investing in regions as diverse and distant as Eastern Europe, South Africa and China. The World Bank declared Malaysia, along with neighbours Singapore, Thailand and Indonesia, part of East Asia's "economic miracle".[2]

Actually, high growth rates in Malaysia were not new. Throughout the 1970s, the decade before Dr. Mahathir came to power, the country averaged an outstanding 8 per cent a year.[3] Under the tech-savvy and driven Dr. Mahathir, however, it was the transformation of the economy, with its modernizing effects, that was more palpable than the increase in gross domestic product (GDP), and more resonant in the public mind.[4] The expansion of industry, construction and finance changed the face of the economy and society and fuelled what political economist Lee Hwok Aun called "a nationalistic fervour towards the development project".[5]

With per capita GDP almost quadrupling to about US$9,000 in purchasing-power parity terms, poverty was reduced dramatically. Malaysia experienced accelerated urbanization, and saw the emergence of a growing middle class that included a significant number of Malays. Change was most visible in Kuala Lumpur, where gleaming steel and glass towers sprouted, while mansions appeared alongside luxurious condominium blocks in residential areas to accommodate the newly rich and ostentatiously wealthy.

Yet Malaysia's development under Dr. Mahathir was far from smooth. In seeking to industrialize, he directed Malaysians not to emulate the West but to "look east" and become a powerhouse like Japan, with their own steel mills, cement plants and a national car to clog the roads. Almost ten years of unprecedented prosperity, when Malaysia was the darling of international investors, opened and closed with severe recessions. To deal with the second contraction, the 1997–98 Asian economic crisis, Dr. Mahathir defied International Monetary Fund (IMF) orthodoxy and introduced capital controls.

Amid overall progress, signs of increasing inequality at the lower end of society were a cause for concern. While reducing the gap between the Malays and Chinese, the affirmative action New Economic Policy (NEP) was leaving the poorest Malaysians behind. The evidence suggested the NEP was being used – and abused – to channel benefits to better-off Malays, especially those closely connected with UMNO. No element was more controversial or politicized than privatization, where contracts were awarded to help build a Malay industrial and commercial class that was internationally competitive. Although a number of Malay entrepreneurs became household names, their companies faltered during the regional economic crisis, indicating they had failed to overcome their dependence on government support.

The NEP itself, originally meant to last for 20 years, morphed into a semipermanent policy and was regarded by most beneficiaries as an entitlement. Deeply resented by other Malays, as well as non-Malays, it posed an obstacle to national integration. It also hindered the country's external performance, just when Malaysia needed to sharpen its game to participate in a more competitive international environment.

Although the NEP had been running for ten years and was half completed when Dr. Mahathir took over in 1981, it fell short in his eyes. In urbanizing many Malays and helping them acquire new skills, in free-trade zone factories and in universities at home and abroad, the NEP was meeting some of his earlier demands. But Dr. Mahathir aimed for nothing less than the creation of a "new Malay". It would take a mental revolution[6] and a cultural transformation to rescue the Malays from their economic backwardness, which amounted to a "millstone around the nation's neck".

In his writings, Dr. Mahathir identified what he called Malay traits, such as passivity and laziness, as well as negative attitudes to money, property and time, as impediments to progress. He sought to instill in Malays a competitive spirit to replace fatalistic tendencies and low aspirations. The new Malay would possess "a culture suitable to the modern period, capable of meeting all challenges, able to compete without assistance, learned and knowledgeable, sophisticated, honest, disciplined, trustworthy and competent".[7]

Dr. Mahathir's endeavour to modify Malay culture and remove barriers to advancement invites comparison with Turkey's Mustafa Kemal Ataturk, whose national revolution in the 1920s and 30s influenced the independence generation of Malay intellectuals. Ideologically, Dr. Mahathir can be described as an Ataturk-reformer, particularly in terms of development.[8] After victory in a nationalist war, Ataturk secularized Turkey by abolishing the sultanate and the caliphate, "disestablishing" Islam and replacing sharia with European laws. Emphasizing education, he opened modern schools in place of madrassahs, outlawed polygamy and granted women equal rights with men. His abrupt, top-down, total cultural restructuring aimed to lift Turkey from the depths of ignorance – the literacy rate was a bare 10 per cent – into the age of modern civilization.

In response to Islam, however, Dr. Mahathir and Ataturk differed fundamentally. Where Ataturk boldly chose secularism, Dr. Mahathir adopted an Islamization policy, leading UMNO to abandon its secular character as it tried to outbid the opposition Parti Islam Se-Malaysia (PAS) on religion. The two countries ended up strikingly different. In Turkey, with a population 99 per cent Muslim, citizens readily identified themselves by their Turkish nationality, not the religion. By contrast, in 60 per cent-Muslim Malaysia, Islam became the most important identity marker for the Malays. Most Malays thought of themselves as Muslim first, Malaysian next, then Malay.[9] Turkey eventually applied to join the European Union, while Dr. Mahathir's Malaysia proclaimed itself an Islamic state, though it lacked the attributes of one.

While that might be considered a huge disappointment for Dr. Mahathir, regarded as the foremost Malay nationalist of his time,[10] he breezily declared that "Ataturk was wrong" to blame religion for the downfall of the Ottoman empire. Since Islam "is a way of life" and "includes everything that you do", church and state cannot "really" be separated, he said.[11]

On the job, Dr. Mahathir felt the imperative, as did his predecessors, to represent all Malaysians and not just a single ethnic community. The NEP recipients were bumiputras, a term coined from Sanskrit meaning "sons of the soil", covering not only Malays but those judged to be "other native races". They included the Orang Asli, original inhabitants, in peninsular Malaysia, the Dusuns, Kadazans, Bajans and many smaller tribes in Sabah, and the Ibans, Bidayuhs, Melanaus and others in Sarawak. Non-Malay bumiputras, a substantial number of them Christian, formed a majority in both East Malaysian states, though official figures showed a Muslim majority in Sabah from 1980.

Without lessening his commitment to the Malays, Dr. Mahathir subsumed his most cherished goal within a wider one, that of a rapidly modernizing Malaysia able to compete and stand proudly with other economically successful nations. Dr. Mahathir, the Malay champion, assumed the mantle of a Malaysian nationalist, adjusting the country's sights away from Malay versus Chinese to Malaysians against the rest – usually the West. As one analyst put it, Dr. Mahathir, at his most imaginative, looked decades ahead and envisaged a society "in which the races stop looking inwards with prejudice but rather outwards with pride".[12]

Dr. Mahathir set his sights on:

> ...creating a psychologically liberated, secure and developed Malaysian society with faith and confidence in itself, justifiably proud of what it is, of what it has accomplished, robust enough to face all manner of adversity. This Malaysian society must be distinguished by the pursuit of excellence, fully aware of all its potentials, psychologically subservient to none, and respected by the peoples of other nations.[13]

Over the years, Dr. Mahathir reformulated, repackaged and refined his vision, but never wavered in his commitment to it. He relentlessly badgered, berated and browbeat Malaysians, especially the Malays, to shape up and convert his dreams into reality. If necessary, he would crucify opponents, sacrifice allies and tolerate monumental institutional and social abuses to advance his project. Much of what he did, or did not do, could be explained by devotion to this cause.

When Dr. Mahathir became prime minister, Malaysia was growing at a lively clip, with a focus on the export of light industrial products. Foreign companies, responding to a range of incentives, were producing toys, air conditioners and electronic components for sale overseas in free-trade zones and providing jobs for tens of thousands of young women drawn from rural homes. Malaysia's switch to the export-oriented, employment generating industrialization that was to characterize East Asia's dynamic economies had taken place in the late 1960s. It was a step towards recognizing that without structural change, the patterns established by colonialism would persist and fail to deliver the dividends most Malaysians expected from independence.

Producing greater quantities of tin and rubber than anywhere else, Malaya had been Britain's most profitable colony, integrated into the world economy through the trade in both commodities. While the British left Malaya with one of the highest living standards in Asia, much of the economy was in foreign hands. The small local business community was mostly Chinese. And the main ethnic groups lived separately, the Chinese around the urban tin mines and the Indians on semi-rural rubber plantations, leaving the peasant Malays to their traditional farming and fishing in more remote areas. Conscious that tin deposits were running out while rubber products might be replaced by synthetics, and also trying to guard against commodity price fluctuations, Malaysia pursued crop diversification. Cocoa and pepper were added, and the country became the world's biggest producer and exporter of palm oil. The production of oil and the discovery of natural gas significantly boosted exports from the second half of the 1970s.

The neglect of Malay interests contributed to the "May 13" riots in 1969 and resulted in the redistributive NEP, which required the government to abandon the hands-off approach followed since colonial times and intervene deeply in the economy. In practice, the government gave priority to restructuring to end the identification of race with economic function, ahead of the other main objective, eliminating poverty. The basic focus was on raising bumiputra corporate ownership from 2.4 per cent in 1970 to 30 per cent in 1990. Other Malaysians would be allowed to own 40 per cent, while the foreign stake would be reduced to 30 per cent. A 30 per cent quota became the minimum bumiputra requirement for many things, including company ownership, government contracts, public share listings, employment and new private housing plans.

As individual bumiputras lacked capital and expertise, the government established state-owned enterprises to enter business on their behalf. All 13 states set up development corporations, which registered companies that were given bumiputra status and fed with resources, such as timber and minerals. The central government also established corporations to hold in trust the shares issued to bumiputras when a company expanded or initially listed. To distribute the shares to individual bumiputras, the government formed the National Equity Corporation, which also bought shares and took over blue-chip companies on the open market and channeled its portfolio into unit trusts. The number of state-owned enterprises in Malaysia rose dramatically, from 54 in 1965, to 656 in 1980 and 1,010 in 1985. Overall, they performed poorly, losing RM6.8 billion in 1984.[14]

Dr. Mahathir brought strong and idiosyncratic ideas to the economy. "We run development as if we are executing a war," he said,[15] a comment that recalled former premier Razak's "operations room" for rural development a couple of decades earlier. Long before he read an economics textbook, Dr. Mahathir believed governments should spend generously, not just Keynesian-style with borrowed money in economic downturns, but at all times. "I had this crazy idea" that if the government outlays money, "it stimulates the economy....usually it generates a lot of economic activity, and people make money, and of course they have to pay taxes, so the government gets back its money".[16] Conversely, "if you don't spend money, then the country will not grow".[17] It went back to what a teacher had told him in primary school, that when the Malayan government built the railway line from Penang to Padang Besar on the border with Thailand, settlements sprang up along the tracks.[18] Although he was personally frugal, Dr. Mahathir spent freely and Malaysia's economy grew fast along the lines he decreed, unhindered by such concepts as cost-benefit analysis and seemingly unconcerned about a future without oil and gas.

With a poor opinion of the civil service and determined not to be hamstrung by resistance, red tape and incompetence, Dr. Mahathir devised alternative ways to speed up decision making and build momentum for his initiatives. As he centralized authority within the executive branch, he increasingly bypassed the bureaucracy in favour of special planning bodies answerable to him, as well as independent state agencies and corporations.[19] The Prime Minister's Department was more influential than any of the regular ministries, containing national oil and gas company Petronas and the Economic Planning Unit, as well as the politically powerful Attorney General Chambers, Anti-Corruption Agency, Public Service Commission, Election Commission and others.

Dr. Mahathir's partner on the economy for much of the time was lawyer-turned-businessman Daim Zainuddin. Serving twice as finance minister, from 1984 to 1991 and from 1998 to 2001, Daim was at other times a government economic adviser. When the Asian financial crisis spread to Malaysia in 1997, Dr. Mahathir brought Daim back to head an emergency task force that undercut Bank Negara and the finance ministry. Daim was made minister with special functions in early 1998, before becoming finance minister for the second time later that year. He was UMNO treasurer throughout this entire period, from 1984 to 2001.

Both from Kedah, Dr. Mahathir and Daim enjoyed a friendship that contributed to the image and tone of the Mahathir administration. By his actions, Daim made it clear he was not going to let conventional notions of conflict of interest interfere with the way he ran his private business empire, the economy, or UMNO's financial affairs. They became deeply entangled. Daim's provocative stance added to the perception that the government was conducting its business first and foremost for the benefit of insiders. Although they remained on talking terms, Dr. Mahathir and Daim fell out politically and parted ways in 2001, with Dr. Mahathir making the extraordinary comment that he was tired of defending Daim against allegations of corruption, "trying to whitewash him, literally".[20] The same accusations had not unduly troubled Dr. Mahathir for the preceding 17 years.

The duo dovetailed in practical ways. With his heart in the business world, Daim was content to try to make Dr. Mahathir's policies work, even after registering his disagreement with some of them.[21] As Dr. Mahathir said of Daim, "he knows the nitty gritty, the way to carry out" a mandate. "For example, if I say privatization, his job is to find the means of privatizing. He showed how it should be done and all that."[22]

Lacking political ambition, Daim was never a threat to Dr. Mahathir, as were Musa Hitam and Tengku Razaleigh Hamzah. Daim declined to seek elected office in UMNO so that he did not have to worry about making friends, or perhaps, face the public and the media to explain his wealth. As he put it, "I was not prepared to be blackmailed with votes."[23] He even resented having to campaign for Dr. Mahathir's faction when UMNO split in 1987, despite Daim's handling of the economy and the party's finances being hot issues. His usual reaction to the severest and most pertinent criticism was to ignore it, regarding it as "a waste of time" to respond. More than anyone else in the administration, Daim had a fairly free hand, because everyone who mattered knew he had Dr. Mahathir's ear and steadfast backing. In return, he was loyal.

Known to his friends as "Muscles", the soft-spoken and diminutive Daim, who usually shunned the press and often conducted business dressed in jeans, a casual batik shirt and sandals without socks, saw no reason to change his ways because he was in the Cabinet. He dismissed concerns about his overlapping public and private interests. An accelerated acquisition spree, in which Daim bought significant stakes in food, property and building-materials companies, culminated in his biggest and potentially most lucrative deal a week before he was named finance minister. He swapped his 51 per cent interest in Malaysian French Bank and RM125 million in cash for a co-dominant, 40.7 per cent stake in the much bigger United Malayan Banking Corporation. The timing was most convenient, as allowing a serving finance minister to assume shared control of the country's third-largest bank would have given the government a political headache.

Although Daim pledged to put his businesses in a blind trust, out of sight two of his family-owned companies did not complete their purchase of the bank stake until five months after he joined the Cabinet. More seriously, the two companies took outright control of the bank the following year in a move that was not publicly disclosed. On top of that, Bank Negara two months later announced sweeping policy changes that may have pre-empted the takeover by the Daim companies. New guidelines, which had been drawn up and awaiting implementation for some time, forbid individuals or family-owned companies from owning more than 10 per cent of the equity of a local bank. Crucially, the guidelines were not made retroactive.[24]

Once they surfaced, the transactions raised legal and ethical issues as well as thorny political problems. Malaysia's Banking Act of 1973 required the approval of the finance minister for any "agreement or arrangement" for the sale or disposal of shares in a Malaysian bank or affecting management and other matters "which will result in a change in the control or management of the bank". The minister's approval was also required for any "reconstruction" of the bank that transferred any part of the bank to another corporation. While Bank Negara said the Cabinet had approved Daim's purchase of the bank shares and he "was never at any stage involved", the explanation left the question of legality unsettled, since the Banking Act made no specific provision for the minister to delegate authority for such approvals. And neither did it provide for the Cabinet to play any role in the approval process.

After Dr. Mahathir announced in 1986 that ministers, deputy ministers and their immediate family would no longer be able to buy shares in companies and would be required to reduce any existing holdings, Daim's planned sale of his controlling interest in United Malayan Banking Corporation proved every bit as contentious as its purchase. He sold out to state-owned Perbadanan Nasional Bhd., the previously co-dominant shareholder that had not subscribed to a preferentially priced rights issue in 1985, which had allowed Daim to take outright control of the bank. A year later, the state enterprise was paying at least RM27 million more for those shares, bankers estimated, though the price was not disclosed.[25]

Announcing his Look East policy in late 1981, Dr. Mahathir sought a paradigm shift in the mentality of Malaysians, especially in the Malay-dominated bureaucracy, which had defied all previous efforts to eliminate the influence of the long-gone British. Declaring that the West was in decline and had lost the values that made it great, he urged Malaysia to consider Japan, South Korea and Taiwan – and, publicly unstated, Singapore – as models for economic development. While the West itself was awestruck at the time over Japan's seemingly inexorable rise, Southeast Asia's bitter wartime memories precluded any spontaneous inclination to look northward with affection.

As Dr. Mahathir understood from his visits to Japan, a competent political and bureaucratic establishment was guiding the country to an economic miracle. With the government and business cooperating closely, industrial action was rare and economic performance did not come at the expense of national solidarity and social stability.[26] If Malaysia could similarly blend economic achievement with local values and nationalistic pride, it would facilitate Dr. Mahathir's aim of transforming the Malay community.[27]

In practice, however, Look East remained a confusing concept. With Dr. Mahathir closing meetings by intoning *domo arigato gozaimashita* and politely bowing his head in place of the usual "thank you", the government dispatched thousands of students and skilled workers to Japan to learn its secrets.[28] Among them was a disappointed Mukhriz Mahathir, who had obtained a scholarship to study in the United States, but was directed to Japan for five years instead by his father. "I didn't like it at first, but now I have no regrets," he said later.[29] The Japanese view of themselves as culturally unique, and more aligned with the industrial West than developing Asia, made it difficult to transfer some of their practices to Malaysia. With English the widely spoken foreign language in Malaysia, plans to teach Japanese and Korean to workers, and make Japanese an optional language in secondary schools, made little headway.

In a memo to senior government officials in mid-1983, Dr. Mahathir said, "Looking East does not mean begging from the East or shifting responsibility for developing Malaysia" to the East. Nor did it mean "buying all goods from, or granting all contracts to, companies of the East, unless their offer is best".[30] Yet the idea persisted that Malaysia would be doing more business with Japan and South Korea and expected something concrete in return, especially for being such an ardent admirer and willing student of their winning ways. Hoping flattery would soften the hearts of the Japanese, who had built the world's second-largest economy with practices so predatory they were sometimes depicted as "economic animals", was more than a little naive.

Japanese and South Korean construction companies swooped on Malaysia and bagged about RM5 billion in major contracts within three years, frustrating and angering local builders.[31] Making use of official assistance in the form of cheap finance from Tokyo and Seoul, they won not only private contracts but also jobs for Malaysian government-linked agencies. Their prizes included an office block and convention centre for UMNO, a new headquarters for the National Equity Corporation, and a 55-storey tower for state-controlled Malayan Banking Bhd.

None caused more offence than the RM313 million contract awarded by the government to two Japanese companies to build the sprawling Dayabumi complex in Kuala Lumpur, then Malaysia's most expensive building, even though a local company bid RM71 million less. Dr. Mahathir's defence, that the Japanese would introduce new management skills and modern building techniques, proved hollow. The bumiputra engineering company that the Japanese were required to work with subsequently complained that its Japanese partners were using it merely to maintain good relations with the government, and said that no technology transfer was taking place.[32]

Complaints that Malaysia was reaping few tangible benefits from Look East extended into trade, investment, management and shipping. After nearly three years, Malaysia's trade deficit with Japan had widened sharply, and the Malaysians had little success in persuading the Japanese to buy more of their manufactured goods. Japanese companies were slow to invest in skill-intensive industries in Malaysia, and even slower to transfer new technology to their Malaysian units and establish research and development facilities in the country. They also tended to bypass local contractors and suppliers and acquire components, materials and services from Japan. Japanese manufacturing companies employed more expatriate managers and staff than most other foreign investors, locking Malaysians out of decision-making functions and inhibiting their career development. With appeals to Japan to use more Malaysian vessels for their bilateral trade going unheeded, the shipping imbalance contributed to a large and widening deficit in their invisible trade as well.[33]

In a hard-hitting speech in August 1984 that reeked of embarrassment, Dr. Mahathir registered his unhappiness over the way Malaysia's relations with Japan had failed to evolve. Accusing Tokyo of conducting a colonial economic relationship, he said the Japanese economy was extremely pro-tectionist, and the Japanese were guilty of "improper behaviour" over air rights while engaging in "the dishonest and tension-generating" practice of transfer pricing, by which companies show minimal profit, or even losses, to avoid taxes. "We cannot and will not remain merely as hewers of wood and drawers of water," he said. Not for the last time, Dr. Mahathir called on Tokyo to exercise the "duties" of leadership: "I ask the Japanese to look not only at what they can take but also at what they can give."[34]

Malaysia's attempt to duplicate the Japanese-style trading companies known as *sogo shoshas* – at least six were formed in the early and mid-eighties – also went nowhere. Malaysia lacked the close connections between the banks, government and industry that were needed to facilitate their trading operations. When they did get going, the Malaysian *sogo shoshas* found themselves competing with the real thing: Many countries preferred to use the services of the Japanese, who provided better marketing information, offered more competitive prices, made loans and opened letters of credit on their behalf.[35] After a few years – in some cases a few months – the imit-ation *sogo shoshas* closed down after losing a great deal of money.[36]

Nevertheless, Dr. Mahathir remained enamoured with Japan, basing two of his other major development policy innovations on the Japanese experi-ence: Malaysia Incorporated and heavy industry. His concept of Malaysia Inc., modeled on Japan Inc., was simple: Government and private business must cooperate closely to enable companies to flourish. He said Malaysia should be viewed as a company, in which "the government and the private sector are both owners and workers together". More efficient and prompt government services would increase prospects for company profits, he said, creating more jobs and related enterprises, paying more taxes and spread-ing income to people who would in turn purchase goods, some of which would also be taxed. His administration also encouraged the formation of docile in-house unions, as in Japan, which "appeared intended to further weaken the already weak trade union movement in the country".[37]

No undertaking gave Malaysians a better understanding of what Dr. Maha-thir was all about than the country's head-long crash into heavy industry. With almost all commodity prices dipping on world markets simultaneously in the early 1980s, the weakness of Kuala Lumpur's diversification strategy was exposed. After a threefold increase in export earnings between 1975 and 1980, the country's economic planners had forecast exports to top RM63 billion by 1985. They failed to reach RM38 billion. Dr. Mahathir blamed rapidly advanc-ing technology as well as manipulation by the developed countries for the collapse, and declared that "there is no future in commodities".

As trade and industry minister as well as deputy premier from 1978 to 1981, Dr. Mahathir had sold Malaysia to American, European and Japanese multinationals as a platform on which to manufacture industrial products for overseas markets. But as prime minister he argued that export-oriented manufacturing was insufficient. "We do not want to be grounded in the mediocrity of mere assembly operations," he said.

Although the world was entering a recession that would inevitably affect Malaysia, Dr. Mahathir pushed ahead with plans for a Malaysian car, steel and cement industries, motorcycle-engine factories, an oil refinery and a pulp and paper mill. The vehicle was the Heavy Industries Corporation of Malaysia (HICOM) that he had established in 1980 and taken with him to the prime minister's office. In quick order, HICOM negotiated joint ventures mostly with Japanese and South Korean companies, usually taking 70 per cent of the equity. By 1983, heavy industry plans were expected to require more than RM8 billion in investments.[38]

The arguments against the programme were formidable, though few businessmen, academics and officials expressed their doubts publicly for fear of offending the prime minister. Heavy industries would require massive amounts of capital and foreign borrowings over long gestation periods, diverting investments from other projects. Given Malaysia's small population – 14 million in 1983 – cars and steel especially were unlikely to be profitable in the domestic market unless sheltered behind protectionist walls or subsidized. Either way, it would be a burden on local consumers, who enjoyed easy access to imported manufactured goods. If Malaysia tried to export its output, it would find itself competing with established producers in fields already threatened by global over-capacity.

Dr. Mahathir would have none of it. He regarded heavy industries as an expression of nationalism that would show how Malays could advance beyond the economic limits previously set for them.[39] He was thinking beyond individual products, prices and market share to the next stage of industrialization, as in South Korea. Seoul had ignored conventional advice and refused the temptation to continue buying steel cheaply from Japan, Dr. Mahathir said, and now the South Koreans were selling steel to Japan. He was certain heavy industry would bring similar substantial benefits to the Malaysian economy through technology, skills and numerous spin-offs. Large manufacturing enterprises needed supporting industries and services, which must be provided mainly by locals. "The spillover is literally tremendous," Dr. Mahathir said, echoing his primary school teacher's message. "Whole new towns spring up where industries are located...new services and trades spring up."[40]

Dr. Mahathir conceded that cars, for example, could be imported cheaper, but insisted the capacity to produce vehicles was a necessary component of Malaysia's industrialization. He was frustrated that many Malaysians did not share his enthusiasm about building a great nation and, worse, some did not even believe it was possible. He urged them to "overcome the mental block which condemns us to being the producers of primary commodities to fuel the growth of the industrialized countries".[41] Just as "everybody" had said South Korea was "stupid", Dr. Mahathir disparaged his own critics, predominantly economists. "These people don't have the faintest notion of what they are talking about", because "what they say is purely academic based on theories learnt in universities".[42]

One theory that kept cropping up was economies of scale. Dr. Mahathir had a typically novel solution: Malaysia should increase its population by 400 per cent to 70 million by 2100 to create its own market. He recommended five children in a family. His pronouncements jolted the family planning authorities, who had been trying to hold down population growth, as was standard practice in most developing countries, to increase the per capita benefits of economic expansion. So the official target was set at 70 million people by the end of the twenty-first century, even though no serious thought was given to how they would be productively absorbed.

From Dr. Mahathir's standpoint, the government's lead in the heavy industry charge would also help it meet its NEP targets, by giving bumiputras the chance to train as industrial managers and skilled blue-collar workers. But in bypassing the Chinese who dominated domestic manufacturing, the government was forced to rely "almost exclusively on mostly inexperienced, often inept and sometimes corrupt elements from the Malay-dominated government apparatus" – and foreign companies.[43] Most of the business went to large Japanese and South Korean companies without any open, competitive tendering. Particularly lucrative were turnkey contracts that gave them total control over design, material and construction. The Malaysians found out later they had been ripped off by some of the foreign outfits, which overpriced imported technology and supplies.[44] Altogether, it was "a helluva expensive way to transfer technology to a few workers".[45]

Launched as the global recession gripped Malaysia, with projects run by bureaucrat-managers lacking appropriate training, Dr. Mahathir's heavy industrialization programme floundered. Saddled with huge foreign debts and high interest rates, ventures that were commercially unviable generated few jobs and failed to spark an economic take-off. Two cement plants, one in Perak state and the other on Langkawi Island, doubled Malaysian capacity but did not justify their combined cost of more than RM2 billion. HICOM's three motorbike engine joint ventures – one each with Honda, Suzuki and Yamaha – found themselves in disastrous competition with each other. A steel complex, Perwaja Trengganu Sdn. Bhd, swallowed billions and never worked properly, crossing the line from ill-conceived and executed to financially improper.

Malaysia's most visible foray into heavy industry was in pursuit of a goal dearest to Dr. Mahathir's heart, a national car. It became a reality and a point of considerable pride for many Malaysians before succumbing to the laws of economics. Having commissioned a feasibility study as early as

1980, Dr. Mahathir nursed the venture for two decades, glorying in its many milestones and stubbornly resisting its numerous setbacks, before railing against its inevitable decline. With Dr. Mahathir in retirement after 2003 and no longer able to protect it against foreign rivals, Malaysia's car simply ran out of competitive gas.

HICOM and two Mitsubishi companies formed a 70 per cent-Malaysian owned joint venture in 1983, Perusahaan Otomobil Nasional, known as Proton, and promised to have a car on the road "in record time". The prime minister was fed up with the slow pace at which local assemblers of foreign vehicles were increasing their Malaysian content. He also was prepared to write off private-sector attempts to establish complementary car industries in the then five-member Association of Southeast Asian Nations (ASEAN), where parts produced in one country might qualify as local content in the others.

Although the first Proton Saga was essentially a Mitsubishi Lancer Fiore, imported in crates and assembled in Malaysia, Dr. Mahathir drove it off the assembly line in September 1985 in a burst of ribbons, balloons and nationalistic hoopla. He had a stretch version made as his official car. Proton's logo initially featured the crest from Malaysia's coat of arms, and subsequent models followed the Saga, meaning a kind of seed from the saga tree, in bearing patriotic Malay names: Wira (hero) and Putra (prince). And the Proton assembly line was depicted on the country's 100-ringgit note.

In contrast to South Korea, Taiwan and elsewhere, Proton did not seek to export, even as worldwide auto trends made economic nationalism a precarious adventure. Proton took aim squarely at the domestic market, where Malaysians had developed a love affair with the car in the buoyant 1970s. In Asia in the early 1980s, per capita auto ownership in Malaysia trailed only Japan and Singapore, with sales of about 90,000 cars a year. By offering a four-door sedan with a choice of 1300 c.c. or 1500 c.c. engines, Proton targeted the segment of the market accounting for the bulk of sales. Proton expected demand to keep increasing by leaps and bounds, and figured the company could capture 60 per cent of it in the first year.

But those easy assumptions evaporated as the Malaysian economy stagnated and passenger-car sales dropped to fewer than 70,000 in 1985 and 40,000 in 1986.[46] At the same time, Proton's costs soared, reflecting the price of yen-denominated loans and parts imported from Japan. As the yen continued to appreciate, Proton was forced to raise its prices, further dampening sales, though the company also had to absorb mounting losses to hold its position as Malaysia's cheapest auto. By the end of 1986, the Proton plant was working only three days a week. It produced about 24,000 cars during the year, less than a third of the 80,000-unit capacity under a two-shift schedule, and the outlook was no better for 1987.[47] Each sale was costing Proton an estimated RM35,000. In desperation, the company turned to export markets.

Highly protected at home and not designed for sale abroad, Proton predictably flopped. Exports accounted for only about 10 per cent of production in the mid-1990s, and declined later. Small numbers of vehicles were shipped to Bangladesh and other Asian and Middle Eastern countries with low emission and safety standards. They proved more popular in Britain, where they required more than 400 costly modifications to meet British standards,[48] but could not escape their stodgy image. Despite being given catchier names later, such as Gen-2 and Savvy, they appealed mostly to elderly drivers and car rental companies that were offered generous buy-back arrangements.

Nonetheless, Proton on paper became one of Malaysia's most successful and financially sound companies. It soon dominated the Malaysian car market, the biggest in Southeast Asia, capturing more than 70 per cent at its peak in 1988. After four straight years of losses, the company announced a modest profit in 1989. Earnings over the next year wiped out accumulated losses, and Proton Holdings Bhd. was listed on the stock exchange in 1992, where it became a favourite of institutional investors. By 2003, the company had cash reserves of RM4 billion and projected profitability.

But Proton's success came at a heavy cost to Malaysian consumers: taxes ranging from 140 per cent to 300 per cent on imported vehicles, and up to 40 per cent on cars locally assembled from imported kits. Built in to the protection, and little known to the motoring public being slugged, was an opaque import-licensing system for foreign cars. Introduced in the mid-1970s to encourage bumiputras to enter the vehicle distribution business, then dominated by foreign companies and business groups owned by Chinese Malaysians, the system covered trucks and motorbikes as well as cars. With the creation of Proton, the licensing system was blended with tariffs to protect the national car. Licensees were granted permits, which every vehicle manufactured or assembled outside Malaysia had to secure before it could be imported and sold locally. The Ministry of International Trade and Industry issued the permits to companies controlled by bumiputra investors. They did not have to bid openly, and nor did they have to pay a single cent for a permit, making permits, in effect, a licence to print money. Licensees typically sold the use of their rights to distributorships for between RM10,000 and RM50,000 per vehicle, depending on the make and model. This classic tollgate operation put more than RM1 billion a year into the pockets of the well-connected permit holders and yielded no benefit to the government.[49]

"You can buy a house in Malaysia cheaper than you can buy a car," one analyst wrote in 1989.[50] Malaysian car owners were generally paying three times the price of a similar model in the United States. Not only were rivals Honda, Toyota, Nissan and Mazda priced out of the market, but their once-established local assemblers, all Chinese-owned, were decimated in the "ethnic bypass" exercise and forced to shed thousands of skilled workers. The cost of Proton to Malaysian taxpayers, in the form of subsidies, totaled between RM11 billion and RM12 billion by the mid-1990s, according to a government study.[51] The full cost remained unknown.

Mitsubishi bailed out of Proton in 2004, ending a two-decade partnership that proved extremely lucrative for the Japanese group. When Mitsubishi was selected by Dr. Mahathir for the project without any competitive bidding, it had trailed its main Japanese competitors in Malaysia, with a passenger-car market share of less than 10 per cent. Mitsubish Corporation and its associate Mitsubishi Motors Corporation, which each held 15 per cent of Proton, were guaranteed handsome returns regardless of the venture's profitability. They were paid to provide the technology, components and training, as well as collecting patent, design and other fees. Dissatisfied with Proton's performance in 1988, the Malaysian government replaced the company's bumiputra management with Mitsubishi executives. Mitsubishi's withdrawal from Proton, through the sale of shares to other investors, reflected the Japanese companies' diminished role in Malaysia.[52] Over the previous decade, Proton had cut its dependence on Mitsubishi by acquiring auto-engineering companies such as Britain's Lotus Group International. Proton also started making its own engines, which it previously purchased from Mitsubishi and its Japanese suppliers. But it was not easy for Proton to strike out on its own.

Proton's day of reckoning neared as Malaysia met its obligations under an ASEAN Free Trade Area pact, which required tariffs on all manufactured goods in the most developed member countries to be reduced to no more than 5 per cent by 2002. Kuala Lumpur obtained an exemption for cars and components: 20 per cent by 2005 on the way to the 5 per cent cap by 2008. As Proton gradually became exposed, its share of Malaysia's 430,000 a year passenger-car market tumbled from 60 per cent in 2002 to 41 per cent in 2005 – and the company slipped back into the red. The entire Malaysian motor industry, employing a total workforce of more than 100,000, was vulnerable, including Proton's two factories built at a cost of RM2 billion and producing a range of cars from 1300 c.c. to 2000 c.c.; another Malaysia-Japan joint venture, which began producing a second "national car" in 1994, the tiny 660-c.c. Kancil (mousedeer) based on Daihatsu Motor Company's Mira model; a third "national car", a Citroen with 1100 c.c. to 1500 c.c. versions, assembled by Malaysian interests with technology and equipment supplied by France's Automobiles Citroen SA; and dozens of uncompetitive local auto-parts makers and vendors. The biggest threat emanated from Thailand, which had pursued the opposite strategy to Malaysia in the 1990s. Thailand turned itself into the "Detroit of the East" by eschewing a national car and instead luring major auto makers by offering itself as a global production base.

One possible way to save Proton was for it to forge an alliance with a major foreign automaker. But the Malaysian government, which retained control of the company through state investment vehicle Khazanah Nasional Bhd., was reluctant to sell a major stake or allow management control to pass into the hands of foreigners. Yet that seemed to be the only way to attract a suitable partner, which naturally would want to protect its technology and completely upgrade Proton. The company's future became one of the first serious points of contention between Dr. Mahathir and his successor, Abdullah Badawi.

To revive Malaysia's flagging economy, which had been punctured by global recession and further burdened by the government's heavy industry commitments, the Mahathir administration in the early 1980s drastically altered the country's development strategy. It reduced the government's role in the economy and gave a bigger stake once again to private business. To switch from state-spurred to private sector-led growth, Malaysia encouraged foreign investment and adopted a policy of privatization, which Dr. Mahathir unveiled in 1983. Privatization was novel, as the worldwide wave that was to become identified with British Prime Minister Margaret Thatcher and U.S. President Ronald Reagan was just getting started. It was also radical, since it promised to reverse the method chosen by Dr. Mahathir's predecessors in pursuing the NEP: creating public enterprises to redistribute wealth and generate jobs.

Trying to spend its way out of recession, Malaysia had sunk into economic malaise. Its expansionary fiscal policies, funded by heavy borrowing at home and abroad, led to serious budget deficits and rapidly rising debt-service charges. Between 1970 and 1982, government consumption and investment as a share of GDP had jumped almost 50 per cent as the bureaucracy quadrupled. Counting investments in Petronas, the public sector share of GDP was about 38 per cent in 1982, one of the highest levels in the non-communist world.[53] After three straight years of large budget deficits – the shortfall reached a staggering 19 per cent of GDP in 1982, financed by foreign borrowing that tripled in three years – the government concluded that, as one senior finance official put it, "We bit off more than we can chew."[54]

As Dr. Mahathir's finance minister at the time, "I did try to contain his obsession with big spending," said Tengku Razaleigh Hamzah. Projects spearheaded by the prime minister that contributed to Malaysia's soaring debt – Perwaja steel, Proton, the Dayabumi building and a bridge from the mainland to Penang island – "were to be completed in a short time and were not provided for in the country's Five-Year Plan", he said.[55]

Having cut public spending and borrowing as part of an austerity regime, Dr. Mahathir framed privatization largely in terms of the financial squeeze: Since the government could not foot the bill for the infrastructure the country needed, the task was being assigned to the private sector. Yet he almost certainly would have turned to privatization anyway. As he recorded in *The Malay Dilemma*, Dr. Mahathir believed strongly in the ability of profit-motivated private companies to deliver the goods. In the 1960s, he had persuaded the Alor Star Town Council to partially privatize night-soil collection to overcome the problem of recalcitrant workers, who showed their displeasure with houses and shops that did not give them a tip by spilling and scattering waste.[56]

Privatization was a crucial element in Dr. Mahathir's vision to mould Malaysia into a nation of innovative entrepreneurs and skilled, disciplined workers. He would sponsor the nascent Malay business class, which in time could take its place alongside successful, non-Malays and be internationally competitive. Privatized ventures had to meet the NEP target of at least 30 per cent bumiputra equity and employment participation. The close connection between privatization and affirmative action goals made Malaysian privatization unique.[57]

Privatization Malaysian-style was as much a political as an economic exercise. Characterized by Lim Kit Siang, the opposition leader, as "piratization", it usually operated on a first-come, first-served basis, without any open bidding. A company that submitted a proposal ahead of rivals got the contract, as long as it had the right connections: an inside track to the UMNO leadership. The winners were almost all well-connected and influential businessmen, or relatives of politicians.

In 1984, a year after it was introduced, privatization received a huge boost when Dr. Mahathir recruited Daim Zainuddin directly from the private sector to replace Tengku Razaleigh as finance minister and UMNO treasurer. Under Daim, the scope of privatization broadened and the pace quickened, especially as Malaysia's economic recession deepened into crisis in 1985–86. While Dr. Mahathir defined privatization as simply the opposite of nationalization and thought in terms of "just a few" projects, Daim "identified so many it went beyond my expectation," the prime minister said.[58] Privatization covered everything from the complete or partial sale of state concerns, the lease of government property, joint ventures such as Proton, management buy-outs, private financing of construction projects, contracting out public services, and allowing outside competition in fields previously restricted to the state.

Nearly 500 enterprises and services were injected with private capital or management over the next 22 years.[59] They included ports, utilities and highways, and some of the generally poorly performing state-owned enterprises formed mostly in the 15 years since the introduction of the NEP. Select government departments were corporatized and listed on the stock exchange, such as Tenaga Nasional Bhd., the power company, and Telekom Malaysia Bhd., the telecommunications utility. Both remained majority state-owned, and the government held a "golden share" that allowed it to veto company decisions deemed to be against the national interest. As state governments and municipal authorities joined the trend, dockyards, hotels, garbage disposal, water supply and city bus operations were privatized.

The main beneficiaries of privatization, though denounced as cronies by critics, were fledgling entrepreneurs as far as the government was concerned.

They bought official assets at discounted prices, obtained soft credit and enjoyed state-backed guarantees for loans. Dr. Mahathir was happy to defend the creation of corporate empires built through personal contacts with the UMNO elite. He argued that they were more capable of using state patronage resources than the broad mass of bumiputras. They also performed "national service" by undertaking less profitable projects in the country's interest, he said.

While some high-profile non-Malay tycoons benefited from privatization, most lucrative contracts were directed at Malay businessmen associated with one of Malaysia's three top political leaders: Dr. Mahathir, Daim and Anwar Ibrahim, the deputy prime minister who took over from Daim as finance minister in 1991. Each of the politicians seemed to have different aims: Dr. Mahathir thought he had the ability to pick future winners for his globally competitive bumiputra class; Daim used business protégés as proxies for his own commercial interests, with most of them sitting on the boards of his family companies; Anwar, by contrast, created a group of business associates to develop a political base in UMNO.[60]

The most successful were "Daim's boys", the best and brightest of the young executives he had nurtured at Peremba Bhd., a state-owned commercial property corporation, before joining the government. They became high profile multi-millionaires and enjoyed celebrity status in the late 1980s and 1990s, the best known being Halim Saad of the Renong Group, Tajudin Ramli of Technology Resources Bhd. and Wan Azmi Wan Hamzah of Land and General Bhd. They were the new role models for the Malays, "a position previously filled by political figures, especially those who had fought for the country's independence".[61]

The government declared privatization a resounding success. It said it gained about RM23 billion from the sale of equity and nearly RM13 billion from the sale of assets, and pointed to savings of at least RM122 billion for not having to build infrastructure. New revenue was amassed from lease payments and corporate taxes, and substantial debt was transferred to the private sector. Privatization was also credited with improving efficiency and service, and with trimming the bureaucracy by more than 114,000 employees.[62]

While there was no doubt that privatized entities considerably deepened and broadened Malaysia's stock market and made it the biggest in Southeast Asia, privatization itself remained extremely contentious. That it concentrated wealth and opportunity in a privileged handful of Malays at the expense of the vast majority was a sore point. Public monopolies sometimes became private monopolies with a noticeable deterioration in performance. A hidden cost to taxpayers, potentially devastating, was what economists call contingent liabilities: The government sometimes guaranteed a certain rate of return to recipients, stretching over decades, so that profits but not risks were privatized; details were not disclosed to the public and not reflected in the national budget. By 2004, the Malaysian government's total contingent liability stood at roughly RM80 billion.[63]

Much of the debate about privatization ceased after the Asian financial crisis engulfed Malaysia in 1997–98 and devastated the celebrated bumi-putra companies. They were too indebted and lacked managerial competence. The government either bailed them out or effectively re-nationalized them, converting private debt into public burden, with no one held responsible for the losses.[64] In five years, the government spent RM11 billion rescuing seven privatized enterprises, including RM7.73 billion for two light rail systems in the capital.[65]

Although the NEP officially expired in 1990 as originally envisaged, it continued as Malaysia's defining development framework in other guises – the National Development Policy until 2000 and the National Vision Policy until 2010. Colloquially, it was still called the NEP. The twin objectives – the eradication of poverty irrespective of race and the restructuring of society to end the identification of race with economic function – were to be pursued in the name of national unity, however long it took.

Dr. Mahathir's proposal for Malaysia to be fully developed within 30 years, outlined in a speech in early 1991, was promoted as Vision 2020. Although most of the elements were familiar, drawn from existing plans and programmes, the package caught the public imagination and was the subject of numerous studies, seminars and conferences. It would require the country to grow at 7 per cent annually on average, from 1990 to 2020, doubling GDP every ten years. GDP would be eight times larger in 2020 than in 1990, and Malaysians would be four times richer in real terms.

Dr. Mahathir's idea of a fully developed nation went beyond the material. He outlined nine "central strategic challenges" that must be met to achieve all-round and well-balanced development – politically, socially, spiritually, psychologically and culturally, as well as economically. His single reference to the goal of "one *Bangsa Malaysia*", usually translated as "Malaysian race" or "Malaysian people", raised the hope for an end eventually to race-based politics. Although Dr. Mahathir probably meant nothing more than a united Malaysian nation bound together by prosperity, non-Malays, especially, saw him as the leader most likely to narrow ethnic divisions.

Although privatization generated lots of buzz around the Malaysian stock market, it was the more dynamic foreign-dominated, export-oriented manufacturing sector that would ease Malaysia out of its prolonged slump and power it to glory. With unemployment at a record high and the economy contracting by 1.1 per cent in 1985 and growing by a feeble 1.2 per cent in 1986, Dr. Mahathir pragmatically liberalized Malaysia's investment climate. He took practical steps to loosen the NEP guidelines for both foreign investors and wary Chinese Malaysians, who had been transferring their assets abroad rather than build factories at home. As early as 1984, Dr. Mahathir signalled a change in attitude by announcing that foreign investors in capital-intensive and resource-based export industries might be allowed to keep majority control. When the Swiss food and drink maker Nestle S.A. restructured its Malaysian operations in line with the NEP, it was able to retain a 51 per cent stake, rather than sell 70 per cent to local investors.

A raft of other measures culminated in Dr. Mahathir's announcement that the bumiputra equity requirements would be suspended for certain new foreign investments and foreign-owned expansions made between 1 October 1986 and 31 December 1990, when the NEP was supposed to end. Such investments committed in that period would not be required to restructure their equity "at any time". Dr. Mahathir's stand took courage, since there was no more sensitive topic than the NEP. He simply told the Malays that distributing jobs was as important as distributing equity. "Obviously, if there is no growth there will be nothing to distribute," he said.

Another near simultaneous structural adjustment a world away held profound implications for Malaysia. Worried by the strength of the dollar, the finance ministers of the five largest industrial countries, then known as the G-5, met at the Plaza Hotel in New York in 1985 and agreed on concerted action to reduce its value. As the Plaza Accord took hold, the sustained appreciation of the yen triggered a rolling change in the international division of labour. To remain competitive, Japanese companies moved up the technological ladder and relocated their older factories to countries with cheaper land and labour. As South Korea, Taiwan and Hong Kong prospered anew from the influx of Japanese investment, their own currencies appreciated and their production costs rose. They in turn relocated their manufacturing operations to China and Southeast Asia, taking the Japanese with them. Foreign investment flooded into Thailand first, then Malaysia and Indonesia, spreading the "economic miracle" southward.

With Malaysia cutting corporate tax rates, the country quickly climbed out of the doldrums and entered an extended period of phenomenal growth. GDP expanded annually by an average of 9.3 per cent for the nine years from 1988 to 1997,[66] with manufacturing replacing agriculture as the leading segment of the economy by the late 1980s, and mining becoming more important.[67] By 1980, crude petroleum exports had taken over the historical position of rubber as the chief foreign exchange earner, and petroleum was contributing 25 per cent of government revenue by 1985.[68] Hundreds of thousands of foreign workers streamed into Malaysia, often illegally and working out of sight on plantations, as unemployment turned into a labour shortfall. Malaysia was among the world's fastest growing economies.

Kuala Lumpur also liberalized the domestic financial sector to welcome portfolio investment, giving little thought to its being the most mobile form of capital, relentlessly profit-seeking and prone to depart as quickly as it arrived. The government sought to take advantage of this "hot money" to expand Malaysia's capital market and transform the country into a regional financial centre. Official statements hinted that Kuala Lumpur aspired to overtake Singapore or displace Hong Kong after the British colony's return to China in 1997.[69] With Malaysia one of the world's "emerging markets" then in vogue with foreign fund managers, portfolio investment deluged the Kuala Lumpur Stock Exchange, later renamed Bursa Malaysia. Foreign funds invested in shares and corporate securities increased by more than nine-fold from 1991 to 1996.[70]

Big or small, other countries were impressed with Malaysia's performance. Sometimes-smug Singapore was jolted by Kuala Lumpur's investment in container ports, a "super" airport and an enlarged financial centre. "This made us re-examine our competitiveness, improve our infrastructure and work smarter to increase our productivity," said former Singapore prime minister Lee Kuan Yew.[71] Stunned by Malaysia's visible progress since a visit 16 years earlier, Indian Prime Minister V.P. Singh in 1990 asked his economic adviser to prepare a paper that would help New Delhi emulate Kuala Lumpur's "spectacular success".[72]

The only economic problems in the mid-1990s seemed to be the stresses and strains of success. Demand for power began to outstrip supply. A growing shortage of skilled and semi-skilled workers drove up wages, eroding Malaysia's competitive edge in labour-intensive manufacturing. But the government dismissed suggestions that the economy was overheating and should be allowed to take a breather.

Despite Vision 2020's lofty rhetoric about balanced development, "acquisitive, profiteering, short-termist behaviour proliferated" as the good times rolled. "It was a regime of accumulation and speculation....Rapid growth became entrenched as a desirable objective for its own material ends..."[73] Many Malaysians "saw nothing else but wealth".[74] With higher incomes, lifestyles changed. The wealthy adopted fetishes that "followed the footsteps of the rich and famous of the world", while members of the middle-class nouveau riche competed with one another over status symbols: blue-chip stocks, expensive houses, imported cars, golf club memberships and the latest cell phones.[75] "We are developing our unique Malaysian Dream," economist-banker and former official Ramon V. Navaratnam told a reporter for a U.S.-owned newspaper, "just as you have your American Dream."[76]

The dream turned into a nightmare in 1997, the tenth year of Malaysia's boom. As Thailand capitulated to market pressure and allowed the baht to float on 2 July, other Southeast Asian currencies pegged to the dollar also came under speculative attack. They were targets because, like the baht, they were overvalued, and these countries had long maintained large current account deficits. The pegs, which made the economies more competitive as the dollar declined for a decade after the Plaza Accord, became a growing liability from the mid-1990s as the yen began depreciating again.[77] Almost no one, however, could have predicted that the baht's collapse would reverberate throughout East Asia, devastating Malaysia, Indonesia and South Korea as well as Thailand.

Herd-like panic by currency traders and inexperienced fund managers based in London and New York, treating the region as one instead of a series of quite distinct economies, created a contagion that spread rapidly. As investors abruptly withdrew their funds, share and property market bubbles in Malaysia burst, undermining the country's heavily exposed banking system. Having traded as high as RM2.493 to US$1 in April 1997, the ringgit crumbled to RM4.595 in January 1998, as the Malaysian authorities abandoned its loose peg to a dollar-dominated basket of currencies. The Kuala Lumpur Stock Exchange's market capitalization plunged from RM806.77 billion in 1996 to RM375.8 billion in 1997. The exchange's composite index, which stood at 1300 in February 1997, touched a low of 262 in September 1998.

Dr. Mahathir's Vision 2020 was imperiled as more than RM30 billion net in portfolio investments fled Malaysia in the last nine months of 1997, much more than net inflows since 1995.[78] Elaborate symbols of the vision then under construction – among them Putrajaya, a new administrative capital for the country, the Bakun hydroelectric dam in Sarawak and the high-tech Multimedia Super Corridor – would have to be postponed, downsized, or abandoned with the end of the high-growth era. More seriously, international financial forces that had intruded so dramatically would almost certainly require the sort of structural and market reforms in Malaysia that might compel Dr. Mahathir to dismantle his entire development project.

Initially, Malaysia followed Thailand's example in trying to defend its currency, with similar results. Bank Negara intervened in the market, wasting more than RM9 billion in foreign exchange vainly attempting to maintain the value of the ringgit.[79] Government spending was cut drastically, interest rates were raised and the definition of non-performing loans was tightened to three months in arrears from six months. All this was conventional wisdom, standard prescriptions urged by the IMF – and it aggravated the situation. Such contractionary measures helped turn what began as a currency and financial crisis into a more general economic crisis for the country.[80]

In August 1997, Malaysian authorities banned the short selling of 100 indexed-linked stocks, but rather than arrest the slide in share prices it sent them skidding further. Similarly, the creation of a RM60 billion fund in early September, to buy stocks selectively from Malaysian companies or shareholders, was interpreted negatively, as a move to bail out cronies. Although the use of the special fund was never fully explained or implemented, government-controlled public funds were deployed to begin rescuing some of the most influential groups.

Particularly vulnerable were the UMNO-connected conglomerates, formed around privatized projects and nurtured by government policies and patronage, which had found it easy to fund their often frenzied expansion by raising capital in the local stock market, or by borrowing abroad. They had evolved into politically protected market leaders, oozing wealth and power, but not distinguished by productivity or innovation and were completely untested in export markets. With the onset of the crisis, they seemed to be "living on borrowed time and not just borrowed money".[81]

The most damaging case, in terms of loss of investor confidence, was the protracted RM2.34 billion bailout, from November 1997, of Renong Bhd., UMNO's own holding company. After takeover rules were bent in January 1998 to permit United Engineers (Malaysia) Bhd. to acquire 32.6 per cent of Renong, its parent company, at the expense of minority shareholders, the stock exchange lost RM70 billion in market capitalization over the next three days.[82] In another noteworthy case, Petronas took control of Malaysian International Shipping Corporation, after MISC acquired the shipping assets and debts of Konsortium Perkapalan Bhd., which was 51 per cent owed by Dr. Mahathir's son, Mirzan Mahathir. When further plans were announced to save well-connected debt-ridden banks and companies, "capital flight hardened into a capital strike: the market would not return if the state, under Mahathir, could not be disciplined".[83]

Investors were unnerved just as much by Dr. Mahathir's vitriolic attacks on the foreigners he held responsible for Malaysia's pain. Assuming a more direct role in policy-making as the crisis deepened, Dr. Mahathir branded foreign currency traders as "international criminals" led by American financier George Soros, a "moron...with a lot of money".[84] He accused the IMF of wanting to "subvert" Malaysia's economy after an IMF official suggested the government go easy on its giant infrastructure projects. The more he insinuated a Western conspiracy to sabotage Southeast Asia, hinted at a Jewish plot against Muslim Malaysia and railed against "an international dictatorship of manipulators", the faster capital departed Malaysia and neighbouring countries. His remarks "continued to undermine confidence and to exacerbate the situation until he was finally reined in by other government leaders in the region", and no doubt by some of his own advisers.[85]

Another aggravating factor was the perception that Dr. Mahathir and Daim had taken over economic policy making from Finance Minister Anwar Ibrahim, who had endeared himself over the years to the international financial community.[86] Daim reappeared on the scene in late 1997, being named executive director of the National Economic Action Council, chaired by Dr. Mahathir, which was established to manage the crisis. When Dr. Mahathir announced the commitment of state funds to defend the stock market, Anwar was nowhere in sight. Dr. Mahathir felt compelled to quash rumours of policy differences with Anwar and to deny that he had taken over Malaysia's economic management. "I am responsible because I am the head of government," he told reporters. "I can't let just everybody carry on their responsibility without myself helping."[87]

Malaysia's lower exposure to private bank borrowings, serious though it was, meant it did not have to run to the IMF for emergency credit facilities, a humiliation suffered by Thailand, Indonesia and South Korea. A typical IMF package, which involved submitting to deflationary "conditionalities", would have crippled Dr. Mahathir's grand plans. Still, Malaysia had to contend with an increasingly shrill international clamour for reform, including transparency, good governance and allowing foreign investors to buy into and even control local corporations. Domestically, Dr. Mahathir faced what he considered an even more urgent threat. He was convinced that Anwar, his deputy and heir apparent, was plotting amidst the economic dislocation to topple him. Dr. Mahathir's solution, which put him at the centre of a worldwide controversy, was selective capital controls, introduced on 1 September 1998, 14 months after the crisis hit. He sacked Anwar the next day, declaring him morally unfit to hold office.

In an effort to further loosen credit and increase government spending to boost the economy while keeping the currency steady – the easing of monetary and fiscal policy began earlier – Dr. Mahathir banned the trading of the ringgit abroad. Holders of offshore deposits, including currency traders and stock market investors, were given a month to repatriate ringgit to Malaysia. With the country's external account frozen, currency traders were no longer able to short-sell the ringgit, by borrowing it offshore to finance dollar purchases in anticipation of a crash in the ringgit's value. The government fixed the exchange rate at RM3.8 to US$1. Portfolio investment – only the principal, not interest or dividends – had to remain in Malaysia for a year. The offshore market in Malaysian shares, conducted in Singapore, was shut down. Longer-term foreign direct investment was unaffected, as was international trade.

Behind what officials viewed as an economic shield, which itself was a defiance of the IMF, the Malaysian government carried out a programme of recapitalization, rescue and reflation that was also at odds with IMF and international money market thinking. Bank Negara lowered interest rates further, redefined non-performing loans at six months instead of three, set targets for loan growth and directed more credit to the property market, auto industry and other key sectors. The government established three institutions to deal with the financial system. Danaharta removed non-performing loans from the balance sheets of financial institutions, allowing debt-strapped banks to resume lending. Danamodal recapitalized the banks, while the Corporate Debt Restructuring Committee did as it was titled.

Contrary to many forecasts, Malaysia did not commit economic suicide by resorting to a fixed exchange rate and capital controls. The currency turmoil in most of the region, with the exception of Indonesia, subsided by the end of 1998, due mainly to external factors. Thailand and South Korea, subjected to onerous IMF conditionality, showed signs of recovery from the final quarter of 1998, while Malaysia's turnaround began early in 1999.

Malaysia rebounded more strongly in 1999 and 2000 than Thailand and Indonesia, though not as impressively as South Korea. In addition to proving wrong the pundits who predicted Malaysia's demise, Dr. Mahathir could take satisfaction in the tarnished reputation of the IMF. He helped discredit the IMF's austerity fix, the one-sized-fits-all solution that the fund misguidedly – and arrogantly – tried to impose in East Asia.

Eminent economists continued to argue inconclusively about the efficacy of Malaysia's action, which was entangled in a global debate about the timing of full-scale capital account liberalization for emerging market economies. But in practice Kuala Lumpur's example meant little. No other country subsequently opted for capital controls, until the military-installed government in Thailand was tempted to intervene to curb the rapid appreciation of the baht in late 2006. The measure – requiring foreign investors to deposit 30 per cent of the funds sent into Thailand to buy shares or bonds in a non-interest bearing account with the central bank – triggered a stock market meltdown in Bangkok and rattled other Asian markets. Just 24 hours after being imposed, the provision applying to the purchase of shares was lifted, though the controls remained on bonds and other debt instruments. The lesson from the botched exercise was that the use of capital controls continued to carry enormous risks.

By focusing on defects in the international system, however, Dr. Mahathir succeeded in diverting attention from domestic flaws and his problems with Anwar. Almost desperate by his own later admission, he was forced to contemplate the elimination of the state-supported conglomerates, the heart of his cherished vision for the Malays and Malaysia. Capital controls for him were both a political and economic solution. As political scientist Khoo Boo Teik observed, "He had no orthodoxy to defend, only interests to protect. He had no theories to prove, only a project to preserve. And, if it needed saying at all, he had his career and reputation to save."[88]

By locking in foreign funds for a year, Dr. Mahathir prevented any fresh flight of capital that might be unsettled by the shock of Anwar's dismissal. The restriction was eased after six months to allow funds to leave on payment of a graduated exit tax, before expiring on 1 September 1999. Dr. Mahathir's insistence on blaming greedy currency traders and stock market manipulators alone for the regional crisis strained credulity. The government tried to hold Anwar responsible for all inappropriate Malaysian responses, when clearly they were mostly collective decisions until his ouster. Dr. Mahathir and Daim were primarily responsible for the nepotism and other types of cronyism, involving the use of public funds to resuscitate local business, which undermined investor confidence in Malaysia.

The personalized way business and politics intertwined under the Mahathir administration was highlighted when Daim abruptly resigned from the government and as UMNO treasurer in June 2001. Although nothing was said officially, it was known that a rupture had occurred between him and

Dr. Mahathir.[89] Daim's protégés came under immediate financial pressure, just as did those owing allegiance to Anwar Ibrahim when he was sacked in 1998. With Daim's departure, Dr. Mahathir "exercised the political will to tackle the problem of corporate debt" among formerly protected companies. In quick succession, three of Daim's closest associates lost control of their conglomerates, which were taken over at public expense and restructured. "The targets, timing and remarkable haste of the takeovers" implied that Dr. Mahathir "was politically rather than economically motivated".[90]

Affirmative action in combination with Dr. Mahathir's distinctive economic policies, including breakneck growth, had a profound affect on Malaysia and Malaysians. The results were mixed, although a growing band of critics argued that the NEP should be modified or scrapped altogether. During the general election in 2008, the opposition led by Anwar Ibrahim made unprecedented gains, drawing support from all communities by proposing a Malaysian Economic Agenda that focused on needs, rather than ethnicity, to replace the NEP.

Absolute poverty, which claimed half the population in 1970, was reduced enormously, plunging to 5.1 per cent in 2002. Rural poverty fell to 11.4 per cent while urban poverty shrank to 2 per cent. Malay poverty, much of it in rural areas, dropped from 64.8 per cent to 7.3 per cent in the same period. The incidence of poverty among Chinese and Indians also declined markedly.[91] Altogether, it was an outstanding achievement for one of the NEP's two main aims, even though the income threshold used for the poverty line was unrealistically low and underestimated the residual problem.

Considerable progress was also recorded in another key objective, to enhance bumiputra participation in the economy and reduce the gap between the Malay and Chinese communities. The ethnic income disparity ratio in peninsular Malaysia narrowed from 2.29 in 1970 to 1.74 in 1999, though it widened again during the boom years before resuming its positive trend. By its own reckoning, the government failed to boost bumiputra ownership of share capital, just 2.4 per cent in 1970, to the 30 per cent target by 1990. Officially, it rose to 19.2 per cent in 1990, before dipping slightly to 19.1 per cent in 1999. But the government's methodology underestimated the amount – for example, by using the par rather than market value of shares and excluding stakes held in trust for bumiputras – which made it easier to argue for a continuation of affirmative action. According to one independent academic assessment, the 30 per cent bumiputra equity target was achieved as early as 1997.[92] The 30 per cent figure had become so politically charged that a serious study showing the bumiputra corporate share was about 45 per cent in 2004, rather than the official 18.7 per cent, caused a national uproar and prompted the resignation of the director of the group that produced the figure.[93]

Affirmative action, however, also sharpened inequality in Malaysian society, and risked a backlash the longer it stayed in place. As the gap between bumiputras and others was closing, fissures were opening within indigenous ranks. As one analyst put it, bumiputra gains "have not been widely shared", and inequality had "reared its ugly head again".[94] In 1999, the average monthly income of the bottom 40 per cent of bumiputra households was RM742, with the corresponding figure for rural areas RM670, compared with RM865 for the bottom 40 per cent of all Malaysian households.[95] Individual inequality in Malaysia, as measured by the World Bank using the common Gini Coefficient, was the worst in Southeast Asia,[96] widening from 0.452 in 1999 to 0.462 in 2004.[97]

Malay dissatisfaction was starting to build as better-off and better-connected Malays benefited disproportionately. The majority resented the use of public funds to rescue wealthy Malay cronies during the regional economic crisis. It was also a source of anger that Malay millionaires, for example, could take advantage of a 5 per cent housing discount for bumiputras. Small-scale, mostly Malay farmers and fishermen, who did not fit into Dr. Mahathir's idea of a modernized economy, were being comparatively marginalized in a countryside where pockets persisted without water and electricity.[98] And the children of newly minted middle-class Malays were best placed to capitalize on ethnic preferences in future, leaving their country cousins and poorer city relatives further behind.

Non-Malay bumiputras, predominantly in Borneo, were also being left in the dust, along with lower-class Indians. They constituted the new poor. Although other bumiputras were supposed to be accorded the same preferential treatment as Malays, in fact they suffered a higher incidence of poverty and lagged in equity ownership and enrolment in higher education.[99] Several studies indicated that the overall plight of the Orang Asli had worsened over the years, despite their status as bumiputras.[100] Significant numbers of Indian labourers, displaced by the influx of foreign workers and the development of plantations for industrial and residential use, joined the ranks of the unemployed in urban squatter areas. Not being bumiputras, they lacked the support needed to acquire skills and obtain jobs.

Ethnic preferential policies in education and employment went a long way towards ending identification of race with job. Where more than 62 per cent of Malays had been employed in agriculture in 1970, most found work in manufacturing. More Malays had jobs even in services, if government agencies were included, than on the farm. With all public universities reserving a majority of places for bumiputras until 2001,[101] Malays joined Chinese and Indians in the professions and filled the ranks of Malaysia's burgeoning middle class. Measured by jobs and income levels, the middle class more than doubled to encompass 26.3 per cent of the population.[102] By 2000, about one in three dentists, doctors and lawyers and one in four architects and engineers, along with a sprinkling of accountants, were Malay, whereas there had been few 30 years earlier.[103] More than one-third of the entire Malay community was in middle-class occupations – professionals, technicians, teachers, nurses, administrators, managers and clerks.[104]

With the high-flying Malay champions chosen for privatized projects top-pling during the Asian economic crisis, attempts to create a credible bumi-putra commercial and industrial community all but collapsed. By 2000, the government had majority ownership of seven of the ten largest companies listed on Bursa Malaysia, "an indication of the failure of privatization". Among them were the two largest local banks, two privatized utility com-panies, a shipping line and a gas producer. The three other companies were Chinese owned. None was owned by a Malay.[105] The one Malay who made the top ten in *Forbes's* first Malaysian rich list in 2006, Syed Mokhtar Albuk-hary, was a relative late-comer, a businessman who had dallied with Anwar and in whom Dr. Mahathir invested heavily after becoming disillusioned with Daim Zainuddin's protégés.[106]

Some economists argued that affirmative action as a means to redistribute wealth more equitably hindered growth and competitiveness, citing Malay-sia's relative decline in the East Asian region: When the NEP was introduced in 1971, Malaysia ranked third only to Japan and Singapore in terms of GDP per capita; by 1990, it had fallen behind South Korea, Taiwan and Hong Kong as well.[107] And the gap continued to widen, despite Dr. Mahathir's denials, leaving Malaysia scrambling to compete in a globalized world, where China and India were setting a sizzling pace.

Malaysia's population, at more than 23 million in 2003, had almost doubled since 1981 while simultaneously being urbanized and ethnically reconfigured. The portion designated urban swelled from just over one-third to almost two-thirds. Responding to incentives offered when Dr. Mahathir set his 70-million goal, the birthrate defied established international patterns and did not decline as prosperity increased. Malaysia became one of the youngest countries in the region, the envy of others saddled with geriatric liabilities. The Malay birthrate was double that of Chinese and Indians, for Malay fam-ilies could count on scholarships and jobs for their children as well as tax breaks for more than two kids.[108] Constituting less than half the population in 1981, Malays became a clear and growing majority, without the need to be grouped among bumiputras to achieve national majority status.[109] For non-Malays, minorities lacking political power and shrinking further, the prospect of being demographically marginalized at some point, however distant, fostered a degree of unease.[110]

Although the rest of the country had learned to live with affirmative action, there were clear limits as to how much the NEP and its subsequent variants could help ensure stability and foster national integration. Prosperity con-tributed to a general satisfaction that crossed ethnic lines. New urban residen-tial developments were ethnically diverse, in contrast with the old racially homogeneous suburbs. The rows of trendy restaurants in Kuala Lumpur's Bangsar neighbourhood, along with the ubiquitous McDonalds, Pizza Hut and KFC fast-food outlets, dispensed officially certified *halal* fare, acceptable to

Muslims, as the eateries catered to every race. A mass consumption culture, common to all groups, appeared to be "the most Malaysianizing of all forces".[111]

Yet ethnic cleavages could not be wholly suppressed by rampant consumerism and rising class consciousness alone. While there was no repeat of the 1969 savagery, small-scale violence, mostly directed against Indians, occurred near the turn of the century. In the worst incident, in March 2001, six people were killed and 37 injured in Kampung Medan, a crowded squatter area near Kuala Lumpur plagued by poverty, crime and substance abuse.

Disturbingly, ethnicity became entrenched as the basis for public assistance, even as it inadvertently promoted inequality within the favoured community and disenfranchised outsiders. Critics worried, too, that what was originally intended as a temporary measure was, over time, creating a culture of dependency that would defeat the very purpose of affirmative action: making the Malays competitive. Dr. Mahathir joined the chorus warning against a "crutch mentality".

Contradictions abounded in the idea of assisting one ethnic group while trying to build unity and a national identity. Official policies produced unintended results, such as the formation of ethnic enclaves in Malaysian society. In the most glaring example, preferential hiring converted the civil service, reasonably ethnically diverse previously, into a wholly Malay preserve.[112] At the time of Dr. Mahathir's retirement, the country generally enjoyed peace, stability and unprecedented affluence, but his *Bangsa Malaysia*, a "fully united and ethnically integrated Malaysian nation", remained elusive.

Notes

1 Bank Negara Malaysia, percentage GDP growth: 1982, 6.0; 1983, 6.2; 1984, 7.8; 1985, –1.1; 1986, 1.2; 1987, 5.4; 1988, 9.9; 1989, 9.1; 1990, 9.0; 1991, 9.5; 1992, 8.9; 1993, 9.9; 1994, 9.2; 1995, 9.8; 1996, 10.0; 1997, 7.5; 1998, –7.5; 1999, 6.1; 2000, 8.5; 2001, 0.3; 2002, 4.1; 2003, 5.2.

2 *The East Asian Miracle: Economic Growth and Public Policy* (New York: Oxford University Press, 1993).

3 Bank Negara Malaysia, percentage GDP growth: 1970, 5.0; 1971, 10; 1972, 9.4; 1973, 11.7; 1974, 8.3; 1975, 0.8; 1976, 11.6; 1977, 7.8; 1978, 6.7; 1979, 9.3.

4 Lee Hwok Aun, "The NEP, Vision 2020, and Dr. Mahathir: Continuing Dilemmas", in Bridget Welsh, ed., *Reflections: The Mahathir Years* (Washington: Southeast Asia Studies Program, The Paul H. Nitze School of Advanced International Studies, Johns Hopkins University, 2004), p. 274.

5 Ibid., p. 274.

6 The idea of a *mental revolusi*, mental revolution, dates to the late 1960s, and is identified with Senu Abdul Rahman, a former cabinet minister and UMNO strategist.

7 Mahathir Mohamad, speech at UMNO General Assembly, 8 November 1991.

8 Ozay Mehmet, "Mahathir, Ataturk and Development", in *The Mahathir Era* (Subang Jaya: International Investment Consultants, undated), p. 38.

9 Carolyn Hong, "Muslims First, Malaysians Second", *Straits Times*, 21 August 2006.

10 Khoo Boo Teik, *Paradoxes of Mahathirism: An Intellectual Biography of Mahathir Mohamad* (Kuala Lumpur: Oxford University Press, 1995), p. 17.

11 Interview with Mahathir Mohamad, 20 March 2007.

12 K. Das, "Mahathir's 'Restoration'", *Far Eastern Economic Review* (hereafter *FEER*), 11 June 1982, p. 38.

13 Dr. Mahathir Mohamad, "Malaysia: The Way Forward", in Ahmad Sarji Abdul Hamid, ed., *Malaysia's Vision 2020: Understanding the Concept, Implications and Challenges* (Petaling Jaya: Pelanduk Publications (M) Sdn. Bhd., 1997 edition), p. 404.

14 Lorraine Carlos Salazar, "'First Come, First Served': Privatization Under Mahathir", in *Reflections*, p. 283, citing Radin Soenarno Al Haj and Zainal Aznam Yusof, "The Experience of Malaysia", in "Privatization: Policies, Methods and Procedures" (Manila: Asian Development Bank, 1985).

15 Excerpts from transcript of the dialogue with members of parliament, cabinet ministers and scholars in Syria in August 2003, published in *New Straits Times*, 20 August 2003, pp. 12, 14 cited in Patricia Martinez, "Perhaps He Deserved Better: The Disjuncture between Vision and Reality in Mahathir's Islam", in *Reflections*, p. 29.

16 "Dr M on Current Issues in Malaysian Politics", 11 May 2006 <http://www.malaysiakini.com/news/50970> (accessed 27 May 2006).

17 Fauwaz Abdul Aziz, "Mahathir Vents Frustration on DVD", 11 May 2006 <http://www.malaysiakini.com/news/50965> (accessed 27 May 2006).

18 Interview with Mahathir Mohamad, 20 March 2007.

19 Greg Felker, "Mahathir and the Politics of Economic Policy in Malaysia", in *Reflections*, p. 264.

20 Interview with Mahathir Mohamad, 20 March 2007.

21 Interview with Daim Zainuddin, 18 October 2007.

22 Interview with Mahathir Mohamad, 14 August 2007.

23 Cheong Mei Sui and Adibah Amin, *Daim: The Man Behind the Enigma* (Petaling Jaya: Pelanduk Publications (M) Sdn. Bhd., 1995), p. 84.

24 Raphael Pura, "Malaysia's Daim Tied to Private Bank Deal", *Asian Wall Street Journal* (hereafter *AWSJ*), 30 April 1986.

25 Raphael Pura, "Pernas Will Buy Daim Stake in Malaysian Bank", *AWSJ*, 6 October 1986.

26 Lee Poh Ping, "The Look East Policy, the Japanese Model, and Malaysia", in *Reflections*, p. 321.

27 Khadijah Md. Khalid, "Malaysia-Japan Relations under Mahathir: 'Turning Japanese'?", in *Reflections*, p. 328.

28 Raphael Pura, "Malaysia's Vague Campaign to Learn from Japan", *AWSJ*, 13 July 1982.

29 Interview with Mukhriz Mahathir, 22 March 2007.

30 Jomo K.S., *M Way: Mahathir's Economic Legacy* (Kuala Lumpur: Forum, 2003), p. 34.

31 Raphael Pura, "Malaysia Builders Hit Japan Dominance", *AWSJ*, 8 March 1984.

32 Jomo K.S., *M Way*, p. 43.

33 Raphael Pura, "Malaysia's 'Look East' Policy Fails to Solve Some Disputes with Japan", *AWSJ*, 8 March 1984.

34 Mahathir Mohamad, "The Second Opening of Japan", in *M Way*, p. 52.

35 Jomo K.S., *M Way*, p. 50.

36 Ibid., p. 51.
37 Ibid., p. 60.
38 Ibid., p. 70.
39 R.S. Milne and Diane K. Mauzy, *Malaysian Politics Under Mahathir* (London: Routledge, 1999), pp. 64–65.
40 Mahathir Mohamad, speech at the Seminar on Transnational Corporations and National Development, 2 October 1979, cited in Khoo Boo Teik, *Paradoxes of Mahathirism*, p. 119.
41 Mahathir Mohamad, speech at the Top Leaders Conference on National Economic Development, 18 May 1984, cited in Khoo Boo Teik, *Paradoxes of Mahathirism*, pp. 119–120.
42 *Star*, 2 February 1982, cited in Khoo Boo Teik, *Paradoxes of Mahathirism*, p. 120.
43 Jomo K.S., *M Way*, p. 70.
44 Ibid., p. 71.
45 Raphael Pura, "New Doubts Arise Over Mahathir's Industrial Brainchild", *AWSJ*, 10 June 1983.
46 Raphael Pura, "Malaysia Gambles in Exporting Saga Car", *AWSJ*, 14 January 1987.
47 Ibid.
48 Jomo, K.S., *M Way*, p. 85.
49 Leslie Lopez, "Malaysia to Lower Car-Import Tariffs", *AWSJ*, 10 November 2004.
50 Halinah Todd, "The Proton Saga Saga", *New Internationalist*, No. 195 (May 1989), pp. 14–15.
51 Anwar Ibrahim, speaking to journalists in Singapore, 21 May 2008.
52 Leslie Lopez, "Mitsubishi Sells Proton Shares", *AWSJ*, 9 March 2004.
53 Raphael Pura, "Malaysia Still Will Cut Government Role", *AWSJ*, 30 August 1983.
54 Ibid.
55 "Tengku Razaleigh Responds to Dr Mahathir's Allegations against Him", *Aliran Monthly*, 1994: 11, p. 36.
56 Zainuddin Maidin, *The Other Side of Mahathir* (Kuala Lumpur: Utusan Publications & Distributors Sdn. Bhd., 1994), pp. 6–7.
57 Lorraine Carlos Salazar, "'First Come, First Served': Privatization Under Mahathir", in *Reflections*, p. 284.
58 Interview with Mahathir Mohamad, 14 August 2007.
59 Agence France-Presse, Reuters, "KL Spent $4.8b on Bailouts of Companies in Past 5 Years", *Straits Times*, 15 December 2006.
60 Lorraine Carlos Salazar, "'First Come, First Served': Privatization Under Mahathir", p. 287.
61 Mohamed Ariff and Syarisa Yanti Abubakar, "Strengthening Entrepreneurship in Malaysia", Malaysian Institute of Economic Research, 2003, p. 4.
62 Jeff Tan, *Privatization in Malaysia: Regulation, Rent-seeking and Policy Failure* (London: Routledge, 2008), pp. 58–60.
63 Leslie Lopez, "A Bit Stretched", *FEER*, 1 July 2004 <http://www.feer.com/articles/2004/0407_01/henry.html> (accessed 19 January 2006).
64 Lorraine Carlos Salazar, "'First Come, First Served': Privatization Under Mahathir", p. 288.
65 Agence France-Presse, Reuters, "KL Spent $4.8b on Bailouts of Companies in Past 5 Years".
66 Bank Negara Malaysia.

67 Edmund Terence Gomez and Jomo K.S., *Malaysia's Political Economy: Politics, Patronage and Profits* (Cambridge: Cambridge University Press, 1999 edition), p. 41.

68 Peter Searle, *The Riddle of Malaysian Capitalism: Rent-seekers or Real Capitalists?* (Sydney: Asian Studies Association of Australia with Allen & Unwin and University of Hawai'i Press, 1999), p. 59.

69 Khoo Boo Teik, *Beyond Mahathir: Malaysian Politics and its Discontents* (London: Zed Books Ltd., 2003), p. 42.

70 Ibid., p. 45.

71 Lee Kuan Yew, *From Third World to First: The Singapore Story: 1965–2000* (Singapore: Times Media Pte. Ltd., 2000), p. 289.

72 Jairam Ramesh, "Mahathir's Mantra", *India Today on the Net*, 21 May 2001 <http://www.india-today.com/itoday/20010521/jairam.shtml> (accessed 1 June 2006).

73 Lee Hwok Aun, "The NEP, Vision 2020, and Dr. Mahathir: Continuing Dilemmas", p. 273.

74 Halim Salleh, "Development and the Politics of Social Stability in Malaysia", *Southeast Asian Affairs 1999*, p. 189.

75 Ibid., p. 190.

76 Stephen Duthie, "The Asian Economist", *AWSJ*, 12 November 1992.

77 Jomo K.S., *M Way*, p. 180.

78 Ibid., p. 183.

79 Ibid., p. 182.

80 Ibid., p. 188.

81 Khoo Boo Teik, *Beyond Mahathir*, p. 47.

82 Jomo K.S., *M Way*, p. 187.

83 Khoo Boo Teik, *Beyond Mahathir*, p. 49.

84 Maggie Farley, "Malaysian Leader, Soros Trade Barbs", *Los Angeles Times*, 22 September 1997 <http://articles.latimes.com/p/1997/sep/22/business/fi-34969> (accessed 24 March 2009). After he retired, Dr. Mahathir met with Soros in Kuala Lumpur and accepted that the financier was not responsible for the Asian financial crisis. "Malaysia's Former Leader Mahathir Buries the Hatchet with Financier George Soros", *China Post*, 15 December 2006 <http://www.chinapost.com.tw/headlines/print/43088.htm> (accessed 24 March 2009).

85 Jomo K.S., *M Way*, p. 186.

86 Ibid., p. 187.

87 Raphael Pura, "Confidence Crisis: Tough Talk by Mahathir Rattles Overseas Investors", *AWSJ*, 2 September 1997.

88 Khoo Boo Teik, *Beyond Mahathir*, p. 64.

89 In separate interviews, they gave conflicting accounts of Daim's departure. Dr. Mahathir said he tired of defending Daim against accusations of corruption, "And I decided that, I told him, look, it's better if he resigns" (20 March 2007). Daim said he resigned because he had told Dr. Mahathir at the outset he was taking the post for a limited time. His resignation, he said, left Dr. Mahathir without his closest political ally after the uproar over Anwar's dismissal and the setbacks in the 1999 election. "If I left...he would be alone. But he has to explain why I leave" (18 October 2007).

90 Lorraine Carlos Salazar, "'First Come, First Served': Privatization Under Mahathir", p. 289.

91 Poverty figures are official, cited in Ragayah Mat Zin, "Malaysia: Poverty and Income Inequality – Prospects and Challenges Under the Ninth Malaysia Plan",

paper delivered to conference on the Malaysian economy, organized by the Institute of Southeast Asian Studies, Singapore, 25–26 January 2007.

92   Beh Lih Yi, "Bumi Equity Hit NEP Target 10 Years Ago", 1 November 2006 <http://www.malaysiakini.com/news/58885> (accessed 31 August 2008).

93   Koon Yew Yin, "What is Wrong with the NEP", *Aliran Monthly*, 2006: 9, pp. 34, 40.

94   Ragayah Mat Zin, "Malaysia: Poverty and Income Inequality – Prospects and Challenges Under the Ninth Malaysia Plan".

95   Lee Hwok Aun, "The NEP, Vision 2020, and Dr. Mahathir: Continuing Dilemmas", p. 276.

96   G. Lin, "Debating an Equitable Malaysia: Towards an Alternative Economic Agenda", *Aliran Monthly*, 2005: 8, pp. 7–10.

97   Figures from the Ninth Malaysia Plan cited by Lim Guan Eng, secretary general of the Democratic Action Party, in a speech to the DAP Economic Forum, "NEP vs. Vision 2020: Where Has All the Money Gone?", 26 September 2006.

98   Bridget Welsh, "Mahathir's Legacy: A New Society?", in *Reflections*, p. 361.

99   Lee Hock Guan, "Affirmative Action in Malaysia", *Southeast Asian Affairs 2005*, p. 221.

100 Ibid., p. 221.

101 Although the ethnic admission quota system for local public universities was dropped in favour of a merit-based system in 2001, non-bumiputras remained skeptical of the new policy since Chinese and Indian student intakes fell sharply.

102 Abdul Rahman Embong, *State-led Modernization and the New Middle Class in Malaysia* (New York: Palgrave, 2002), p. 41.

103 Lee Hock Guan, "Affirmative Action in Malaysia", p. 214.

104 Abdul Rahman Embong, *State-led Modernization and the New Middle Class in Malaysia*, p. 56.

105 Edmund Terence Gomez, "The Perils of Pro-Malay Policies", *FEER*, September 2005, p. 39.

106 Justin Doebele, "Malaysia's 40 Richest", *Forbes Asia*, 5 June 2006, pp. 35–38.

107 Christopher Adam and William Cavendish, "Background", in Jomo K.S., ed., *Privatizing Malaysia: Rents, Rhetoric, Realities* (Boulder and London: Westview Press, 1995), p. 15.

108 Bridget Welsh, "Mahathir's Legacy: A New Society?", p. 363.

109 Ibid., p. 363.

110 Ibid., p. 364.

111 Halim Salleh, "Development and the Politics of Social Stability in Malaysia", *Southeast Asian Affairs 1999*, p. 188.

112 Lee Hock Guan, "Affirmative Action in Malaysia", p. 216.

Precious moments: Mahathir adhered to a rigid routine to get the most out of each day. He used his defeat in the 1969 election to work on several books while practising medicine, reading between patients to save time.

Source: Perdana Leadership Foundation

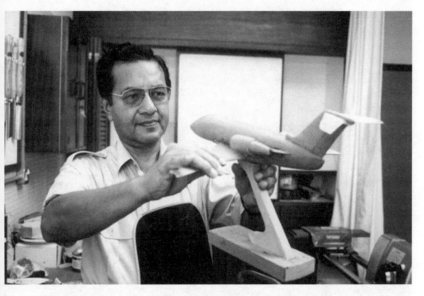

Deft touch: Dexterous, Mahathir enjoyed carpentry, wood turning and metalwork, making boats, wrought iron lamps and model aircraft. He shifted his workshop from Alor Star to Kuala Lumpur on joining the government, but ran out of time for his hobbies.

Source: Perdana Leadership Foundation

A vision: Mahathir's overwhelming priority was to turn Malaysia into a modern, internationally respected, fully developed nation by 2020. He allowed no one to question his plans or challenge his power.

Source: Perdana Leadership Foundation

Lighter moment: Usually stern, Mahathir badgered fellow Malays to overcome traits he identified as impediments to progress, such as passivity, laziness and sub-servience. Ultimately, he expressed disappointment over his efforts to alter their mindset.

Source: Perdana Leadership Foundation

Familiar face: Malaysian supporters promoted a Mahathir personality cult. Institutes of higher learning were urged to introduce a course on his thoughts, attempts were made to nominate him for a Nobel Prize, and he accepted an award as Man of the Millennium.

Source: Perdana Leadership Foundation

On parade: Mahathir inspected Malaysian troops at the National Monument in Kuala Lumpur on Warriors Day, 31 July 2002. As a backbencher, he opposed the presence of foreign forces in Malaysia, but as prime minister he did not seek their removal.

Source: Information Department, Malaysia

5
A Volatile Mix of Business and Politics

Before Dr. Mahathir became president of UMNO, the party dabbled in business to keep the media in friendly hands and generate income to cover operating expenses. Dr. Mahathir plunged UMNO deep into the corporate world, in partnership with Daim Zainuddin, his wealthy and most trusted business operative, whom he made UMNO treasurer. They turned the party into a vast conglomerate, with investments that spanned almost the entire economy, inducing a profound change in the nature and role of UMNO.

The key to UMNO's transformation was Malaysia's affirmative action programme to eliminate poverty and assist bumiputras. While devised to reduce inequality, it was often applied by the Mahathir administration in a way that enriched a political elite, whose common attribute was an intimate relationship with UMNO. The mandatory 30 per cent of share allocation for bumiputras during a company's public listing, or restructuring, was usually channeled to UMNO-owned or -linked corporate entities and other party allies. With privatization, too, UMNO was used as a vehicle to transfer government holdings to private or semi-private ownership, mostly for the benefit of the same clique.

With UMNO an active corporate player, the party at times was in competition or collaboration with state-owned agencies and private companies. Some valuable state assets passed into UMNO hands. The fusion – and often confusion – of party, state and private roles went far beyond the government-corporate cooperation implied in the Malaysia Inc. concept. Business and politics, ideally kept separate in the name of good governance, were inextricably mixed in what Lim Kit Siang, the opposition leader, called an "incestuous relationship".[1]

With UMNO membership an avenue to riches, ever larger amounts of money were poured into party and general elections to secure positions with access to tenders, licences and subsidies, while party leaders in turn channeled benefits back to their supporters to maintain their posts. Across the country, thousands of companies were set up by UMNO divisions, branches and members to collect shares and other forms of patronage allocated to bumiputra enterprises. Malays joined UMNO not so much to do community service anymore, but to make the contacts and get the contracts that would bring easy profits. The phenomenon was known as "money politics", and it dictated behaviour as much as, or more than, the official party rules and regulations that prohibited it. On more than one occasion Dr. Mahathir shed tears in public about vote-buying in UMNO party elections, but he failed to stop it. His presidency saw the final culmination of a transition from an UMNO of humble and self-sacrificing peasants and schoolteachers to a party of self-serving corporate chieftains and dealmakers.

Although the money-making opportunities through UMNO were known, the extent of the party's investments was not so obvious. As a political party registered under the Societies Act 1966, UMNO was not permitted to be in business. To conceal its assets, the party used the common practice of nominee companies or executives, or alternatively, trusted individuals, prominent businessmen who surreptitiously held stakes in various companies on UMNO's behalf. The trail could lead through a bewildering maze of transactions, involving shell companies capitalized at the legal minimum of RM2 and companies that were repeatedly reorganized and renamed. Another convenience for UMNO was that a private Malaysian concern whose shares were held by fewer than 20 individuals had "exempt private company" status, which meant it did not have to file financial statements with the Registrar of Companies. Documents filed by companies with government or political ties often were not available to the public for scrutiny at the registry, anyway.

After UMNO ventured directly into business under Dr. Mahathir and Daim and some of its trustees were publicly known, the party faced financial oblivion when it was declared illegal in 1988. Its assets were required to be placed with a government agent and sold off. But in a process that was never made clear, most of those assets ended up in the hands of many of the same people who were holding and managing them for UMNO before. The arrangement enabled Dr. Mahathir and Daim to maintain that the party, reconstituted as New UMNO, was no longer in business, which was only technically true.

While UMNO, as a political party, was required to submit its accounts each year to the Registrar of Societies, and it tabled a balance sheet at the party's annual General Assembly, the party did not disclose the real state of its financial affairs. Not even the party's Supreme Council, the highest policy-making body, could peek at the "UMNO Political Fund", whose very existence was never disclosed. The council entrusted the party's financial secrets to the top leadership: While he was supposed to keep Dr. Mahathir informed, Daim alone knew the details.[2] Two other official UMNO trustees, the party deputy president and secretary general, were not informed. So, along with the general public, UMNO's millions of members remained in the dark about the party's multi-million dollar enterprises, even though the assets theoretically belonged to them.

UMNO's strategic role in the distribution of patronage contributed to the severe factionalism that convulsed the party in Dr. Mahathir's time. In former finance minister Tengku Razaleigh Hamzah's challenge to Dr. Mahathir's leadership in 1987, the party dissidents directed much of their ire at Daim, who was accused of stripping UMNO for personal gain. Because of the way he mixed his private investments with state and party business, it would be a recurring theme for as long as Daim remained as party treasurer. After he quit in 2001, significant sections of UMNO were convinced he had pocketed billions that belonged to the party. Daim denied it, as did Dr. Mahathir, the only other person with access to the books, who then took over as treasurer for two years. When he stepped down in 2003, Dr. Mahathir handed his successor, Abdullah Badawi, the prime ministership and UMNO assets of RM1.4 billion, in property, shares and cash.[3]

Although the form differs, links between politics and business are widespread and growing in almost all East Asian countries.[4] In Japan, major corporations fund particular factions within the ruling Liberal Democratic Party.[5] Thaksin Shinawatra, who became prime minister of Thailand in 2001, brought with him representatives of some 15 major business groupings who were able to seize control of the state and contrive business-friendly policies.[6] Under Dr. Mahathir and Daim, Malaysia followed the example set by Chiang Kai-shek's Nationalist Party, which ruled Taiwan for 55 years until 2000 – and returned to power in 2008 – in taking direct or indirect control over a vast array of corporate assets.

Their enterprise was light years removed from UMNO's early days, after its formation in 1946, when founding members used their own money to fund party activities. So tight was the budget in 1954 that Tunku Abdul Rahman, as president of UMNO and representing the Alliance, had to share a bed with a member of his delegation when they visited London to discuss pre-independence constitutional arrangements with the British.[7] The Tunku recalled that in those days he drove and cleaned his own car because he could not afford a driver. At one point he sold 14 shophouses – two- or three-storey buildings with businesses on the ground floor and residences above – and donated the proceeds to UMNO. After independence, he realized he had disposed of almost all his personal property to contribute to the party, and others had done the same.[8]

As the Tunku's successor, Razak Hussein was keen to end UMNO's financial dependence on non-Malay supporters – its coalition partner, the Malaysian Chinese Association, as well as Chinese businessmen and companies – for election campaign expenses, emergencies and, embarrassingly, even for routine activity. At times, an UMNO official at headquarters could not afford transport to keep an appointment – say, to talk to villagers. He would have to wait for the Malaysian Chinese Association to send over a cheque, which then had to be cashed, before summoning a taxi to get to the meeting.[9]

Razak was also under pressure from UMNO's youth wing to take control of the foreign-owned, Singapore-based media company that published Malaysia's main English-language daily, the *Straits Times*. To buy it would require funds, and UMNO's decision in 1971 to build an elaborate new headquarters for itself meant the party would need access to even more substantial resources.

Appointed party treasurer by Razak in 1972, Tengku Razaleigh Hamzah established the UMNO Political Fund to give the party a stable financial base, replacing the informal "special fund" Razak had been operating covertly since 1959, when he was deputy party president.[10] As the Political Fund was to be secret, the Supreme Council authorized the party's leadership, effectively the president, to operate it at his discretion. The arrangement was intended to bypass UMNO's trustees, who normally held assets for the party, as the Political Fund was not to be presented to the party's annual General Assembly.

It was agreed among Razak, his deputy, Ismail Abdul Rahman, who was a stickler for ethics and honesty, and Tengku Razaleigh that the fund should not be linked to major businessmen who dealt with the government; nor should it have anything to do with government contracts. They established an elaborate procedure to avoid any suspicion that donations could be siphoned off for personal use. Every cheque donated to the Political Fund had to be accepted by at least two of the three, photocopied and circulated to all three. A receipt would be issued immediately. The fund was audited annually and the results reviewed by the three of them. While some of the money in the Political Fund was transferred to an administration fund to finance the party's daily operations, the contents of the Political Fund were never disclosed to the UMNO Supreme Council.[11]

With Razak's approval, Tengku Razaleigh began investing UMNO funds in the stock market. By the time of the 1974 general election, UMNO for the first time was able to not only meet its own electoral expenses but also help finance candidates for three of the main National Front components, the Malaysian Indian Congress and Gerakan Rakyat Malaysia, as well as the Malaysian Chinese Association.[12] The UMNO Political Fund built up a modest portfolio. "We bought shares on the open market purely as an investment," said Tengku Razaleigh. "We did not run any organization as a business or a going concern."[13]

At Razak's request, Tengku Razaleigh bought 80 per cent of Singapore's Straits Times Press's operations in Kuala Lumpur in late 1972 and repackaged them as the New Straits Times Press (Malaysia) Bhd. The shares were held by Fleet Holdings Sdn. Bhd., a company that Tengku Razaleigh established in 1972 for UMNO, but which did not have any formal links to the party. Fleet listed New Straits Times on the stock market in early 1973, retaining 51 per cent control and realizing an immediate profit of RM7 million on the sale of the shares it offered to the public.

It was not the first time UMNO had acquired a newspaper. In 1961, Prime Minister Tunku Abdul Rahman had taken over Utusan Melayu Press Bhd., publisher of the leading Malay-language paper, provoking a bitter strike by staff, who objected to the loss of independence. As the voice of the Malays, the paper was an important propaganda weapon for UMNO and the government, and was never considered a business proposition. With the shares held by individuals, who had no written arrangements with UMNO, the company was not part of the party's investments controlled by the treasurer. Razak took over most of the shares from the Tunku and put an aide, Abdullah Ahmad, on the board, starting what became almost a tradition for the prime minister to hold a majority of the shares in Utusan Melayu Press.[14]

In the case of the New Straits Times Press, although it came directly under Tengku Razaleigh's charge, he left it in the hands of professional management. An accountant, Junus Sudin, was recruited from a British multinational to run Fleet as chairman. The company expanded steadily under Junus, who was content to allow Fleet to be sustained by the dividends it received. Profit was reinvested primarily in three sectors: newspapers and publishing, banking, finance and insurance, and telecommunications.

UMNO acquired Bian Chiang, a small bank in Sarawak state, almost by accident. Tengku Razaleigh bought 80 per cent of the bank's equity for just under RM5 million to help a friend, the late Wee Hood Teck, urgently settle a gambling debt. When Razak learned of the purchase, he worried that Tengku Razaleigh would leave his fulltime job at state-owned Bank Bumiputra, where he was chief executive, to run his own bank. Razak insisted that Tengku Razaleigh stay in his post and sell his Bian Chiang Bank shares to UMNO, at the same price for which they had been acquired. The entire bank – Wee's stepbrother also decided to sell his 20 per cent stake – was transferred in 1974 to Fleet Holdings, which was able to pay cash for it.[15] Bian Chiang was renamed Bank of Commerce. It ended up part of CIMB Group – headed by Razak's youngest son, Nazir Razak – whose state-controlled, listed holding company, Bumiputra-Commerce Holdings Bhd., had a market value of RM36 billion at the end of 2007.[16]

Apart from the New Straits Times Press, its subsidiaries and the Bank of Commerce, the only known significant purchase made by Fleet under Junus Sudin and Tengku Razaleigh was in insurance. In 1980, Fleet Group entered into a joint venture with United States-based AFIA Worldwide Insurance to form American Malaysian Insurance.[17]

Fleet Holdings all but disappeared from public view in 1974, when it qualified as an "exempt private company" and no longer had to file financial statements with the government. Fleet Group Sdn. Bhd. was formed in 1976 as a wholly owned subsidiary and operating arm. Public records show that its profit grew strongly, from RM327,443 in 1977 to RM15.7 million in 1982.[18]

Daim Zainuddin, with a penchant for secrecy and distaste for convention, took over Fleet that year, displacing Junus Sudin. Although he would not become UMNO treasurer formally until 1984, Daim effectively exercised some of that authority immediately – "de facto treasurer", as he called himself[19] – since he controlled Fleet and its associated companies. As prime minister, Dr. Mahathir was keen to reduce the political influence of the ambitious Tengku Razaleigh, who twice challenged Musa Hitam for the deputy premier's slot. Although almost unknown to the Malaysian public then, Daim was a close friend of Dr. Mahathir and one of Malaysia's most successful bumiputra businessmen. He would be primarily responsible for integrating politics and business in Malaysia,[20] though philosophically the connection was made by Dr. Mahathir, who was consumed by the ambition to transform Malaysia into a modern industrialized society.[21]

The youngest of 13 children of a Kedah government clerk, Daim had made it big in property development after studying law in Britain and returning home to work both as a government magistrate and prosecutor, and as a private lawyer. Abandoning in 1969 the law firm he opened only the year before, Daim failed in his early business ventures, in plastics and salt making. He got his break in 1973 when he used his political connections to obtain a large tract of land in Kuala Lumpur – then in Selangor state, but soon to become federal territory – which he and two partners turned into a residential community named Taman Maluri. While forced to sell the first houses at cost, they cashed in when property prices soared in 1976. Declared Daim's friendly biographers, "With the housing boom, Daim made his fortune. He owned one square mile [2.6 square kilometres] of the federal territory…he also had land in other places…Daim's dream of becoming a millionaire had come true".[22]

The accumulation of so much wealth so quickly was a source of wonder that marked Daim as an audacious and deft operator in the new, pro-bumiputra business environment. He declared he was the first Malay to donate RM100,000 to UMNO.[23] By 1977, still not 40, Daim had made enough money to "retire", taking himself off to Berkeley in the United States for two years to study urban planning at the University of California.

On his return home, Daim accepted a position as the non-salaried chairman of Peremba Bhd., a subsidiary of the government's bureaucratic and poorly run Urban Development Authority, an agency to promote bumiputra investment in the property market. At Peremba, formed at his suggestion to group commercial real-estate holdings, he gathered around him a coterie of bright young Malay executives, many trained in accountancy and engineering, who would become household names as major corporate and UMNO players. Known as Daim's protégés, or the Peremba boys, most of them maintained close ties with him across the deals and years.

Daim's rapid ascendancy coincided with Dr. Mahathir's assumption of the prime ministership in 1981. Although he held no official position,

behind the scenes Daim acted as a troubleshooter for Dr. Mahathir, travelling to the United States to lobby for a change in tin reserves policy and
discussing bilateral problems with the British in London. While Daim was
13 years younger than Dr. Mahathir and they did not get to know each
other until adulthood, they were from the same poor neighbourhood
in Alor Star, and hit if off. Daim seemed to embody the new breed of
dynamic bumiputra that Dr. Mahathir was trying to create. As Daim told
local reporters, "I went into business to prove one thing: that a Malay can
also succeed in business. Before now, Malays have only been company
directors, mainly figureheads on display."[24]

Operating mostly below the radar screen, Daim in 1982 won control of
a bank, the established path to serious wealth in Malaysia. His successful
bid again raised eyebrows because he prevailed over several bumiputra-
controlled companies, some of them government affiliated, which were at
least as well qualified. Also, in approving his 51 per cent stake, Bank
Negara, the central bank, ignored its usual insistence that majority control
of a commercial bank be held by a corporate entity rather than an individual, especially one with little experience in banking and finance. The
decisive factor: Dr. Mahathir gave the transaction his blessing.[25]

Neither Daim's move to Fleet to manage UMNO's finances, nor the simultaneous restructuring of the French-owned Banque de L'Indochine & de Suez
that gave him control of its replacement, locally incorporated Malaysian
French Bank Bhd., were publicly announced at the time. The sensitivity of
Daim's close association with Dr. Mahathir and his undercover role at Fleet
was reflected in undeclared sanctions against the Hong Kong-based *Asian Wall
Street Journal*, which reported both developments. After the paper carried
an article on Daim's expected acquisition of Indosuez, the government – on
Dr. Mahathir's orders – began systematically to delay distribution of the daily
to subscribers in Malaysia. The government also blocked for a month a subsequent edition of the paper that described Daim's appointment to head
Fleet.[26]

When Dr. Mahathir appointed Daim, 46, to his Cabinet in 1984, it capped a
three-year rise from near obscurity to one of Malaysia's most powerful figures,
during which he assembled a private empire that included major stakes in a
number of publicly listed companies. His preferred style was to make extensive use of the stock market, with rights issues and share swaps, often pledging
the shares he was buying to secure loans for the transaction. Along the way he
forged close links with some of the best-connected Malaysian Chinese businessmen, and shrewdly exploited the cozy, often loosely regulated business
environment. Having been persuaded by Dr. Mahathir to contest a parliamentary seat two years earlier, Daim replaced Tengku Razaleigh Hamzah as
finance minister as well as treasurer of UMNO.

The state of UMNO's finances, when Dr. Mahathir came to power and
Daim took control of the purse strings, is strongly disputed. As UMNO split

a few years later and polarized around factions led by Dr. Mahathir and Tengku Razaleigh, the matter was bitterly debated. It was the genesis of gossip and speculation in UMNO circles about the party eventually being looted of RM5 billion or RM6 billion. Dr. Mahathir and Daim insisted that Tengku Razaleigh left UMNO's finances thoroughly depleted. Dr. Mahathir directed his criticism not just at Fleet's bottom line, but at the system by which various people held the shares in trust for UMNO. He said the departing Tengku Razaleigh:

> ...told us that there was no money left with UMNO, not a single cent. So after that I had to go around tracing the shares, which were held by different people. You see, in those days they gave shares for people to hold on because they didn't have any system of trustees, or anything like that. And when these people died, their children claimed that their father's money didn't belong to UMNO. So I had a tough time gathering information on who had the money. And twice I had to do that.[27]

Dr. Mahathir said the assets were recovered on both occasions by tracking and approaching individuals believed to be holding party-owned shares and persuading them to return the scrip. "Eventually, I collected practically all the money that belonged to UMNO," he said.[28] According to Daim, Tengku Razaleigh and others, the missing shares were in Utusan Melayu Press, which Tunku Abdul Rahman had taken over for the party in 1961. Most of the shares, though not all, were recovered, they confirmed.

Daim affirmed that UMNO was completely broke when he took over management control of the Fleet group in 1982. In fact, he said the group was actually RM500 million in debt as a result of a poor business and investment strategy.[29] His statement was surprising, since an independent study later by Terence Gomez found that Fleet under Tengku Razaleigh had proceeded cautiously and made few major purchases, and there was little evidence of debt.[30] UMNO borrowed heavily for its new headquarters, but that was through Khidmat Bersatu Sdn. Bhd., a company set up to handle the building project, and the first of two major bank loans was obtained only in 1983.[31] It was public information that Fleet Group, with holdings in 23 companies, showed a profit of RM15.7 million in 1982. Daim said the problem was in Fleet Holdings, whose financial results were not published because it was an exempt private company. Although it had paid-up capital of only RM1 million, he said, Fleet Holdings had borrowed hundreds of millions of ringgit from banks only too eager to lend to UMNO. Daim contended it was almost impossible to make a profit: With so little capital, the company had to borrow heavily to acquire assets and use all its earnings to service debt and repay loans.[32]

Tengku Razaleigh scoffed at Daim's claim. Fleet had borrowed from a bank only once for investment, to purchase the Straits Times shares from

Singapore, and had repaid the loan within two years from the profit on floating 49 per cent of the shares, he said. "What is that RM500 million needed for?" said Tengku Razaleigh. "Fleet Holdings was making money," he said, and held shares in only two companies, New Straits Times Press and Bian Chiang Bank.[33]

Confidential UMNO financial accounts, professionally audited and obtained by the author in the course of his research, cast grave doubts on the version propagated by Dr. Mahathir and Daim.[34] The accounts, which did not include Fleet's operations, confirmed that Daim inherited a party in sound financial condition when he became treasurer in 1984. The top secret UMNO Political Fund – which both Dr. Mahathir and Daim specifically said was empty[35] – at 31 December 1983, actually had assets of RM88.6 million and no liabilities, including RM39.8 million on fixed deposit and RM6.8 million cash in the bank. Investments in nine publicly listed and three unquoted companies, Fleet Holdings among them, totalled RM5.9 million. That figure seriously understated their worth since the investments were declared at cost. For example, the stakes in the public companies, purchased for a collective RM4.5 million, had a current market value of RM28.5 million. The UMNO Political Fund contributed RM25 million towards the construction of the new party headquarters in 1983, in the form of an interest-free loan. After receiving dividends, interest and donations, the fund finished the year RM3.5 million in the black, according to the accounts certified as "true and fair" by a local auditing firm.

Regardless of the controversy, Fleet under Daim abandoned Tengku Razaleigh's passive approach to investing. With instructions from Dr. Mahathir to shake up the group by tightening management and financial control and getting the companies "really moving",[36] Daim sought to turn a profit in a hurry. "My role was to build up the Political Fund, as well as make sure the business activities generated income," he said.[37] Fleet adopted an aggressive growth strategy that saw it quickly add companies in diverse and unrelated fields. Fleet snapped up stakes in TV3, the country's first private television station, the hotel and real-estate group, Faber Merlin Malaysia Bhd., and food retailer Cold Storage (Malaysia) Bhd., all publicly listed, and Commercial International Merchant Bankers Bhd. By the mid-1980s, the number of companies had almost doubled, extending the Fleet group's reach into construction, plantations and management services as well as print and electronic media, telecommunications, banking, insurance, retailing, property and hotels.[38]

Typically, holdings were acquired "by a torrent of rights issues and share swaps and rarely involved cash outlays by companies associated with UMNO".[39] At the same time, many of the companies acquired during Tengku Razaleigh's tenure were spun off in a series of share swaps to the subsidiary New Straits Times Press. Inter-group sales created a convoluted web of highly-leveraged concerns. In the case of the acquisitions, Fleet's holdings in listed and unlisted companies were often pledged as collateral, and assets were shuffled among different listed companies held by the entire group. Although Daim denied it,[40] critics contended that in many cases the stakes purchased by Fleet were either overvalued or the shares offered were undervalued, allowing some individuals associated with UMNO to make large profits.[41]

Apart from what has been called Daim's "paper entrepreneurism", defined as the relentless pursuit of restructuring opportunities in search of a quick profit at the expense of actual production, there were other distinctive features of Fleet's acquisitions. Many of them were connected with Daim's family companies, or with his responsibilities as head of Peremba, and they were in his favoured property development.[42]

From 1982 to 1984, Daim's obligations were split three ways. He was building his own conglomerate at a rate that would make him the richest Malay in the country. As chairman of Peremba, he was serving the government while also acting as an unofficial adviser to Prime Minister Mahathir. And as chairman of the Fleet group, he was UMNO's trustee. "I am a man who can do many things at the same time," Daim once said. "I can put every one of them in separate compartments."[43] But in an academic study of Daim's "triple capacity", Terence Gomez concluded that Daim did precisely the opposite: He "apparently had no qualms about mixing his personal business interests with those of the companies entrusted to him".[44]

Interlocking directorships indicated that Daim had a few common nominees, who were assigned by him to manage the companies under his control. Mohamed Desa Pachi and Abdullah Mohamed Yusof, the most prominent, were appointed by Daim as directors of Fleet Holdings and Fleet Group. Desa was also a director of Fleet Group's main publicly listed companies and most of Fleet Group's other private limited subsidiaries. He was also a director of Peremba, and sat on the board of two of Daim's family companies, apart from being a director of publicly listed companies in which Daim had a significant stake. He was a director of several major government-owned companies as well. Abdullah, a lawyer, was also a director of Peremba, and a director of some of Fleet's listed and private companies. Younger associates, Daim's boys, also served as nominees: Halim Saad, Mohamed Razali Abdul Rahman, Wan Azmi Wan Hamzah and Tajudin Ramli.[45]

Daim stoutly defended his business methods:

> If I think the government can make money with me, why not? I mean, there's transparency, particularly as these are listed companies in which I was involved, or where Peremba was involved. Where some group want to sell, and Peremba doesn't want to buy, since I have the details

of the company and I think it is a good investment for my family, why not? If everybody is going to make money, why not? So I see no reason why it is a conflict, so long as everybody declares their interest.[46]

One of the government's first privatizations, the granting of a licence in 1983 for TV3, showed Daim's juggling act. The licence was given to Fleet Group, which took 40 per cent of the equity, while 10 per cent went to two of Daim's companies and 10 per cent to the holding company of the Malaysian Indian Congress, a partner in the ruling coalition. Another example was the use of a Daim-owned company, Daza Sdn. Bhd., to purchase the outstanding, Singapore-owned 20 per cent of New Straits Times Press for Fleet, with the negotiations, including bank loan commitments, conducted by the general manager of Peremba.[47] In another case, Fleet-invested Faber Merlin, in which Daim had a major equity stake, bought subdivided land from his main publicly listed company, while he was in control of both companies. Only a month earlier, Fleet had been allocated all the special bumiputra convertible unsecured loan stock in Faber Merlin by the government. Later, Fleet acquired Daim's stake in Faber Merlin.[48]

Daim mired himself deeper in controversy when he became finance minister in 1984 and accelerated Dr. Mahathir's privatization programme. Although he quit Peremba and pledged to put his businesses in a blind trust, "Daim brought to government a view that no longer saw the spheres of government, party or private interests as distinct entities", wrote Peter Searle, an academic specialist in Malaysian business. "For Daim national, political and private interests might be pursued simultaneously or in tandem...".[49] Daim himself described the situation as "commonness" rather than a "conflict" of interests.[50]

As the economy slumped in the mid-1980s, property prices sagged, leaving Fleet with a large quantity of overvalued real estate and shares that had lost a significant percentage of their market value. Fleet Group, which recorded a RM27.3 million profit in 1984, plunged into the red, losing RM20.3 million in 1985.[51] The company's financial statement for the year ended 31 August revealed a "shocking state of affairs".[52] The auditors qualified the accounts on the grounds that the ability of the company and the group to continue operating depended on the success of various steps taken by the directors. The balance sheet indicated that current liabilities exceeded current assets by about RM222.3 million. A significant portion of the company's investments – in listed and unlisted subsidiaries, amounting to RM178.4 million – had been pledged to financial institutions to secure bank facilities for Fleet Holdings. The company also owed Fleet Holdings about RM235.6 million. And Fleet Holdings itself had incurred losses, though as an exempt private company it did not report the details.[53]

By 1987, Fleet's debt had grown – or diminished, if one accepted Daim's figure of RM500 million debt in 1982 – to RM343.5 million.[54] To stay afloat, Fleet Group was forced to sell some of its best assets to New Straits Times Press, in which Fleet was the major shareholder. In other words, the most profitable arm of Fleet Group was used to purchase its holding company's major subsidiaries.[55]

UMNO was also seriously over-extended on another front. In 1981, the party had gone ahead with the construction of its 42-storey headquarters, together with a convention and exhibition facility, at a cost of more than RM300 million. It was built on a 3.6 hectare site on which Tengku Razaleigh once had an option, which he had been persuaded to relinquish to UMNO at cost.[56] Originally, UMNO planned to finance the Putra World Trade Centre, as it was called, with a RM200 million bank loan secured against the land. According to projections presented to UMNO's Supreme Council, which cleared the investment, cash flow from office and hall rentals would pay off the debt within 17 years.[57] But after drawing down the first portion of the loan in 1983, UMNO's vehicle, Khidmat Bersatu, defaulted, failing to pay interest or principal after 1984, until at least July 1988, when court records revealed the dire state of affairs. By then, according to the records, UMNO owed Bank Bumiputra nearly RM300 million and other banks about RM86 million, while incurring RM61,000 a day in additional interest.[58] In the absence of any plausible explanation, analysts suspected the rental income was diverted to other UMNO investments, or to service debt.

UMNO's lifeline, shrouded in the usual secrecy, took the form of financially beleaguered, publicly quoted United Engineers (Malaysia) Bhd, an engineering and construction company. Although it had suffered five straight years of losses, had never built a major road or bridge and was nearly insolvent, United Engineers was tentatively awarded a RM3.42 billion government contract in late 1986 to complete 494 kilometres of the north-south highway stretching from Thailand to Singapore. A consortium led by the company – Projek Lebuhraya Utara Selatan Bhd., known as PLUS – would operate the privatized road network and collect tolls for 30 years along the entire highway. With tolls to be increased regularly, revenue across the life of the concession would total RM17 billion, United Engineers estimated, though the political opposition put it at RM54 billion. In addition, the government provided RM1.65 billion in "supportive construction loans", as well as financial safeguards against exchange rate fluctuations on foreign commercial loans, or a shortfall in toll collections. In brief, PLUS was guaranteed profitability, securing UMNO's financial base. Later, toll roads were expanded to cover much of the country, becoming highly unpopular in many cases.

The initially-unpublicized connection with UMNO was through the controlling shareholder in United Engineers, an equally obscure concern with a money-losing record called Hatibudi Sdn. Bhd. Formed in 1984 with a registered address in Daim's office, Hatibudi at one stage listed two of Daim's protégés, Halim Saad and Mohamed Razali Abdul Rahman, as directors and shareholders. After initiating a financial restructuring package that paved the way for Hatibudi to take over United Engineers, Razali resigned from the board. His shareholding in Hatibudi was transferred to Halim, who was also appointed chief executive officer of United Engineers. Public records showed that all but one of Hatibudi's shares were held by Halim.[59]

The UMNO link remained hidden until Works Minister S. Samy Vellu, under fire in Parliament over the contract, apparently inadvertently identified Hatibudi as an UMNO-owned company. He said Hatibudi's "trustees", by virtue of their standing in the party, were Prime Minister Mahathir, president of UMNO; Deputy Prime Minister Ghafar Baba, deputy president; Finance Minister Daim, treasurer; and Agriculture Minister Sanusi Junid, secretary general. In an affidavit submitted in a subsequent court case, Halim said he held his Hatibudi shares "in trust for the ultimate beneficial owner, UMNO".[60]

Exposed, UMNO political leaders acknowledged that United Engineers was being used to pay for the Putra World Trade Centre. "In the case of the north-south highway project, it is a means of UMNO solving its problems by repaying loans taken for the new UMNO headquarters building", said Najib Razak, minister of culture, youth and sports. In response to critics who questioned the probity of the case, Dr. Mahathir said, "We agree...but who is going to pay the RM360 million for the UMNO complex?"[61]

Lim Kit Siang, the opposition leader, delayed the formal awarding of the contract through a series of legal actions and a report to the police alleging corruption. He portrayed the choice of United Engineers as political favouritism that amounted to yet another financial scandal in a series that had plagued the Mahathir administration. Lim said the participation of the four UMNO trustees in a cabinet meeting that decided to privatize the highway was a criminal offence under the Emergency (Essential Powers) Ordinance, which prohibited any elected or public official from using "his public position or office for his pecuniary or other advantage".[62] By the time the Supreme Court ruled narrowly against him in early 1988, however, the hapless Lim and his lawyer, Karpal Singh, another opposition legislator, were behind bars, rounded up with dozens of other alleged trouble-makers in Operation Lalang the previous year.

But before UMNO could secure its fresh source of funds, political turmoil within its own ranks put the coveted prize temporarily beyond reach. A High Court declaration on 4 February 1988 that UMNO was an illegal organization triggered a confused scramble by the competing Mahathir and Razaleigh factions to reconstitute the party and claim its assets. After Dr. Mahathir out-manoeuvred his rival and registered New UMNO, the government went ahead and signed the contract with United Engineers in March, despite uncertainty over the legal status of UMNO's 33.3 per cent stake in the company.[63]

The trouble was that with UMNO outlawed, the party was required by the Societies Act to place all its assets with the government's Official

Assignee, for safekeeping or eventual liquidation. Dr. Mahathir's followers were able to counter legal moves that would have required them to disclose details of UMNO's many businesses, not the least embarrassing aspect of which was their bleak financial position. Liabilities were "massive", Daim admitted later, with RM600 million in borrowings, and interest at 10 per cent amounting to RM60 million a year.[64] Bank Bumiputra had received High Court approval to auction the Putra World Trade Centre and the land on which it stood, though the sale was postponed while UMNO tried to renegotiate a refinancing plan with its creditors. It was a magnanimous gesture, considering that UMNO had failed to make any payments for years, though not surprising, since UMNO effectively controlled Bank Bumiputra; in Daim's words, "As long as UMNO is the government, the bank will not disturb you."[65] The need to recover the assets gained added urgency with the approach of a general election. It had to be held by mid-1991, and would require a bigger campaign war chest than usual if Tengku Razaleigh's camp, as expected, joined the opposition ranks.

Dr. Mahathir exploited the same crucial advantage that had enabled him to register a successor party to UMNO with a similar name ahead of his opponents. The Official Assignee's office, like the Registrar of Societies, was part of his home affairs ministry. Operating in secrecy, the Official Assignee sold UMNO's Hatibudi interest in United Engineers in June 1989, though it remained publicly unknown until the following month, when relatively small, publicly listed Time Engineering Bhd. made an announcement to the stock exchange. Time Engineering revealed it had acquired RM37.5 million of convertible unsecured loan stock in United Engineers from the company that obviously got it from the Official Assignee: Hatibudi Nominees Sdn. Bhd, created in 1987. Not only did the company's name closely resemble that of the former trustee of UMNO's holdings in United Engineers, but its two shareholders, Halim Saad and Anuar Othman, were also directors of the original Hatibudi, and of United Engineers. In a complex share-swapping arrangement, Hatibudi Nominees, the controlling shareholder in United Engineers, took over Time Engineering, which was given a RM400 million contract to provide electrical and communications equipment and steel guardrails for the north-south highway project. The bottom line was that the Mahathir faction had regained UMNO's coveted source of recurrent earnings – its "golden goose", as one party legislator called it – while also adding another company to the stable.[66]

With the highway contract as its bedrock, United Engineers, which had voluntarily suspended trading in its shares for five years until 1988, prepared for a phoenix-like rise. Toll revenue and management fees alone would guarantee the company about a 17 per cent return on its outlay. In addition to the basic contract, revised from RM3.42 billion to RM5.7 billion, rising eventually to RM7 billion, there were multiple spin-offs, such as roadside advertising, service stations, rest areas, restaurants, towing concessions and cable-communication lines. With a 60-metre right-of-way on both sides of the highway, United Engineers effectively had become one of Malaysia's largest landholders.[67]

The Time Engineering deal was a model for the rapid expansion that followed. By entering a series of financial and partial-ownership arrangements with major subcontractors, United Engineers and UMNO tried to ensure quick returns from work finished, rather than waiting several years for toll revenue to grow as stretches of the highway were completed. The acquisition of controlling stakes in listed companies and the creation of affiliated joint-venture construction concerns required little cash and generated ready income. Largely by swapping sharply appreciating United Engineers shares for those stakes, the company moved easily into the cement industry, electrical contracting, manufacturing and property. United Engineers also landed a host of other government contracts and privatization deals, ranging from land reclamation to a second road link with Singapore, and manufacturing drugs and distributing medical and dental products to state-run hospitals.[68]

By early 1990 UMNO, through proxies working on its behalf, principally Halim Saad and Anuar Othman, had regained control of most of the party's assets.[69] And, largely through United Engineers, those proxies had also built Hatibudi Nominees into another large business group that was ultimately beholden to the UMNO leadership.[70] One significant chunk of shares in Utusan Melayu Press, however, remained beyond the reach of the leadership. They were registered in the name of Tengku Razaleigh, the former party treasurer. He signed a public declaration that the shares belonged to UMNO and authorized the company to pay any dividends to the party, but refused to sign them over to a proxy, "afraid that somebody may hijack them".[71]

To consolidate what was threatening to become an unwieldy corporate sprawl and to get a grip on its runaway debt, UMNO in April 1990 restructured its businesses in one of the largest financial arrangements in Malaysia's history. It was valued at RM1.23 billion, though no cash was involved.[72] UMNO designated Renong Bhd., a modest-sized property company, in which to merge the party's controlling interests in eight publicly listed companies and dozens of its unlisted concerns, converting it into one of the biggest holding companies in Southeast Asia. The stakes included those in United Engineers and the bulk of the profitable communications and financial operations of Fleet Group. Renong swapped a controlling block of its shares for the party's corporate stakes, giving UMNO a commanding interest in Renong. To generate nearly RM440 million in cash for UMNO, Fleet Holdings sold some of its new Renong shares to existing Renong shareholders and reduced its stake in the company to 28.5 per cent. UMNO was in no danger of losing control of Renong, because Halim Saad also held, directly and indirectly, a substantial stake.[73]

Also subsumed under the Renong corporate umbrella were the ever-evolving companies in Halimtan Sdn. Bhd., another UMNO-linked conglomerate in which Daim figured prominently. Halimtan, an exempt private company whose activities spanned gambling, gold mining, manufacturing, food retailing and financial services, was an example of how common directorships were used to shift assets from the government to private, UMNO or party-related business groups.[74] A number of publicly listed former tin mining companies were separated from state-owned Malaysia Mining Corporation Bhd., becoming the core of Halimtan later, via a web of minority shareholdings and common or sympathetic directors.[75] The intricate manoeuvres showed "the increasingly symbiotic relationship between the government and the party".[76] In one "extraordinary passage" tracked by analysts, Daim's stake in Cold Storage was fed through three UMNO-linked, cash-rich companies within two years, earning substantial profit at each stage.[77] Commented Peter Searle, the academic business specialist, "Although it was difficult to determine at what points the individuals concerned were acting for the party or their private corporate interests, ultimately it appeared that both were served by the relationship."[78]

In early 1991, only nine months after the dramatic reverse takeover of Renong, UMNO again restructured what had become its flagship holding company. A RM1.95 billion package of measures sought to consolidate Renong's control over group companies, expand its operations and bolster cash flow. Renong increased its stakes in United Engineers and TV3, the two companies that were expected to contribute most to profit. In addition, Faber Group Bhd., the party's once-faltering hotel and property concern formerly known as Faber Merlin, was brought into the Renong fold. It had been left out earlier because of its heavy debts, which had since been cleared through a huge cash injection by Fleet Holdings.[79]

Capitalized at RM6 billion to RM7 billion, Renong in its new form was one of the top three companies on the Kuala Lumpur Stock Exchange.[80] By one estimate, the total value of UMNO's shares, including those held by nominees at party headquarters and at state branches, was RM4 billion. By that calculation, about half, RM2 billion worth, were listed shares, comprising 2 per cent of the Malaysian stock market's overall capitalization. In addition, UMNO's property holdings were believed to total billions of ringgit.[81]

Yet UMNO continued to adopt the formal position that the party was no longer in business. The official line was that all of UMNO's assets had been surrendered to the Official Assignee, and with their sale the party had effectively exited the corporate arena. That was the stand Dr. Mahathir took in Parliament. Daim went so far as to boast that his greatest achievement as UMNO treasurer was to get the party "out of business".[82] But the failure to disclose which assets had been held by the Official Assignee, by what process they were sold, and to whom and for how much, undermined UMNO's credibility. In the absence of evidence to the contrary, the blockbuster deal was regarded as merely "a new face on old practices".[83]

Actually, UMNO still owned a majority stake in Utusan Melayu Press, the now-listed Malay-language newspaper publisher, while the party's cooperative, Koperasi Usaha Bersatu, retained a huge interest in Sime Bank Bhd.[84] These investments, however, were exceptions in the new order in which UMNO withdrew from direct party ownership of companies. Instead, control of party assets was transferred to private individuals, who were accountable only to a few senior party leaders.[85] By this legal technicality, UMNO sought to deflect growing criticism of the party for doling out contracts to its holding companies, as well as avoiding the risk of being financially ruined again.

If, as Daim later claimed, UMNO received a "very good" price for the companies the Official Assignee supposedly sold to their previous managers,[86] the party should have been not only debt-free but flush with cash. As it was, UMNO remained in financial difficulty. In mid-1994, the High Court ordered that all the assets and liabilities of the old UMNO be turned over to Dr. Mahathir's New UMNO, which of course did not include the corporate empire. The court order reinstated UMNO's legal title to the party's headquarters, on which the party still owed about RM500 million, and to its many branch and divisional offices throughout the country.[87] Public corporate and legal documents indicated the party's remaining assets totalled about RM1.5 billion, while its total retained debt was more than RM1 billion. One of UMNO's lawyers estimated that the party's assets, minus its bank debt and other liabilities, amounted to about RM348 million.[88]

There was no doubt, however, that UMNO leaders continued to control the party's dispersed assets; Daim's boys got most of them. Apart from Halim Saad's taking over most of Fleet Holdings' investments, Tajudin Ramli and Samsudin Abu Hassan obtained control of the listed companies in the Waspavest group, as Halimtan was renamed.[89] While a few Chinese businessmen with close ties to the ruling party ended up with companies once directly owned by UMNO, they appeared to be assigned the task of bailing out well-connected Malays.[90]

The Renong-linked companies were required to contribute monthly to UMNO's operational expenses. Payments, in the form of cheques signed by two of the four UMNO trustees authorized to act on behalf of Hartibudi Nominees, were for varying amounts specified each month by Daim. At general election time, Daim simply told each company how much was needed, and the companies had to "figure out how to get it".[91]

With Halim Saad as its executive chairman and controlling shareholder, Renong lost none of the exalted status it enjoyed earlier as a declared UMNO company, being awarded eight of the government's 13 large national projects in the 1990s.[92] United Engineers agreed to build a national sports centre for the government, in time for the Commonwealth Games in 1998, in exchange for prime property in the capital. A subsidiary of United Engineers, the single largest beneficiary of Malaysia's accelerated privatization programme, took over the operation of the Penang toll bridge. Renong group companies were involved in the design and construction of a passenger terminal for the futuristic Kuala Lumpur International Airport, and a Renong subsidiary held the rights to develop more than 100 square kilometres of valuable land in Johore. The company also had the only national fibre optic network, and won the contract to build one of the light rail systems in Kuala Lumpur.

But there were clear limits to Halim's independence, mirroring the power plays in Malay politics and the aspirations of particular UMNO leaders. For example, in 1993 he had to relinquish Renong's interest in two major media companies, TV3 and New Straits Times Press, to businessmen aligned with Anwar Ibrahim.[93] To aid his bid for the deputy presidency of UMNO, Anwar wanted control of the country's only private TV network and the publisher of English-, Malay- and Chinese-language papers. Halim also responded to Malaysian government overtures to perform "national service" by taking over the Philippine government's ailing National Steel Corporation, after President Fidel Ramos sought help from Dr. Mahathir. The cost: US$800 million, no questions asked.[94]

The Malay political leadership did not hesitate to intervene when Halim's embarrassing marital troubles threatened to fracture the company in 1995. His wife responded to his divorce petition with a claim for RM500 million "compensation" in cash and 50 per cent of his assets, which she estimated at RM5 billion to RM7 billion. The sharia court drama, involving custody and visiting rights for their three children, was studded with allegations of intimidation, detention, wiretapping, adultery and black magic.[95] The police arrested and banished to internal exile without trial a part-time *bomoh*, a practitioner of Malay traditional medicine, whom Halim's wife had asked to cast a spell on him. Halim also had the help of immigration officers, who intercepted his children on a school outing and put their thumbprints on documents for use in making duplicate international passports. Two different lawyers representing his wife quit after being threatened, one physically, the other by phone. "It's difficult to say whether the problems I'm having are political or personal," she observed.[96]

As indicated by the acquisition of electronic and print media by Anwar's backers, the dispersal of UMNO's investments encouraged individual party leaders to cultivate their own business followings. Although Anwar had been a strident critic of entrenched political-business relationships, he ran into the harsh reality that control of resources was necessary to build a power base. Despite Anwar's disavowal of the links, executives identified with him secured more and more listed companies as he prepared to challenge Deputy Premier Ghafar at the 1993 party elections.[97] "Anwar's men", ambitious, younger and long frustrated by the domination of the Malay corporate scene by Daim's crowd, played a vital part as he staked his claim to be Dr. Mahathir's successor.[98]

With politicians cultivating personal ties with corporate captains and assuming control over major companies, factionalism within UMNO sharpened and the scramble for benefits intensified. Elected party posts became passports to wealth and status for which candidates and their supporting networks were prepared to pay on a scale according to potential returns. Businessmen who once shunned politics sought key posts in the UMNO hierarchy. By 1995, the teachers and farmers who once dominated UMNO ranks had long given way to civil servants, technocrats and opportunists; almost 20 per cent of UMNO's 165 divisional chairmen were millionaire businessmen-cum-politicians.[99] The rapid descent on rural areas by urban politicians to cultivate a grassroots base, usually by buying support, led to the further "monetization of politics".[100]

But it was hardly a case of innocent country folk being seduced by city slickers. With the plethora of development projects delivered at village and district level under bumiputra programmes, local UMNO politicians had already captured control of local administrations from bureaucrats. The biggest beneficiaries of policies aimed at alleviating the plight of impoverished peasants were, in fact, UMNO parliamentarians and state assemblymen, with their Malay and Chinese associates. They set up companies and awarded them contracts, persuading themselves they were fulfilling the 30 per cent quota for bumiputra ownership in business and management, even as they became wealthy and used their cash to buy continued support.[101] The internal clash over the spoils was fiercest in the pre-selection of general election candidates, leading to rising violence at UMNO branch and divisional meetings.[102] In the most notorious case, a member of Dr. Mahathir's Cabinet, Culture, Youth and Sports Minister Mokhtar Hashim, murdered a rival in Negeri Sembilan state eight days before the 1982 general election.

Although top party leaders repeatedly warned against the evils of "money politics", it spread exponentially in line with general affluence and became institutionalized in UMNO. What had been little more than a free-lunch-and-junket habit escalated dramatically with the 1984 clash for the deputy presidency between Musa Hitam and Tengku Razaleigh. An estimated RM20 million was spent on that contest, setting an example that was followed in all subsequent elections and for all positions, from branch leaders to party president. In the divisive 1993 party elections, in which Anwar deposed Ghafar and Anwar's team of vice presidents outpolled opponents, RM500 million to RM600 million was distributed. The pay-off rate had increased nearly 30-fold in less than a decade.

Among numerous abuses associated with the money ethos were insider trading and the manipulation of share prices to raise funds for political campaigns. Amidst speculation about a snap general election in the second half of 1989, for example, the share price of several UMNO-linked companies rose spectacularly for no other apparent reason. Kinta Kellas PLC, Time Engineering and United Engineers soared between almost three- and eight-fold within six months.[103] As Anwar marshalled his forces to drive Ghafar into reluctant retirement in November 1993, the Malaysian stock market was gripped by a familiar frenzy. Between 4 January and 9 June, daily trading on both the exchange's first and second boards averaged 356 million units valued at RM892.3 million, up from 77.7 million units valued at RM207 million for the entire 1992. Again, stock prices of three UMNO-linked companies, Renong, Idris Hydraulic (Malaysia) Bhd. and Granite Industries Bhd., surged nearly three-fold in just over a month.[104] With UMNO also exercising influence over regulatory and investigative agencies, official inquiries into insider trading went nowhere.

Dr. Mahathir was among the earliest and loudest to decry the use of money to win party votes, declaring in 1984 that if the trend continued "one day only millionaires will lead UMNO".[105] At the General Assembly the following year, he denounced members who distributed cash to be elected divisional chairmen and others who bought votes with overseas trips.[106] After Ghafar revealed that one aspirant was willing to spend up to RM600,000 in a bid for office, delegates "liberally amended the party constitution to deter money politics".[107] The constitution was rewritten again at a special General Assembly convened for the specific purpose in 1994. It banned the giving or receiving of "rewards, gifts or valuable returns in any way or in any form", and armed the Supreme Council with powers to curb corruption.

While tightening the rules might have looked like a reasonable response to the unprecedented display of "money politics" the previous year, in reality it was a public cover for inaction. Delegates had been embarrassed by news reports that Bank Negara ran out of RM1,000 and RM5,000 notes at the height of the campaign leading to the 1993 General Assembly.[108] At the convention itself, participants declared that they had received gifts ranging from pens, radios and watches to foreign travel and cash. Some delegates handed out their bank account numbers to contesting candidates.[109] When the call for reform went up, the worst offenders joined the chorus, feigning innocence. Zainuddin Maidin, a former newspaper executive who later became an UMNO minister, called it "a most amusing piece of political farce".[110] Zainuddin, who was close to the prime minister, said it was "impossible" that Dr. Mahathir did not know which people were involved in "money politics' and the amounts that had changed hands.[111] The head of an UMNO committee appointed to examine the money question declared in 1995, "We've put an end to vote-buying in UMNO." [112] But nothing changed except the size of the bribes. Dr. Mahathir wept in 1996 as he implored colleagues "not to let bribery destroy the Malay race, religion and nation".[113] In 2001, he said "filthy rich" businessmen would not be allowed to vie for UMNO positions.[114] Near retirement, he was still lamenting the lack of "clear evidence" that would enable him to clean up the party.[115]

Indeed, Dr. Mahathir bore responsibility for the money culture well beyond that of a leader who failed to treat a virulent cancer repeatedly diagnosed in the UMNO body. He actively contributed to the problem by increasingly centralizing power in the hands of the party president from the early 1980s.[116] By tightening his grip he ensured rivals would coalesce into stronger factions in an effort to get a share of the contracts, privatization opportunities and special bumiputra allocations of publicly-listed stocks.

When the Asian economic crisis struck in late 1997, the government lost no time in bailing out Renong and other political favourites. Renong by then was the country's largest conglomerate with debts of more than RM25 billion, about 5 per cent of the total loans in the banking system.[117] State support was widely assumed to be an attempt to rescue major Renong shareholders, specifically Halim Saad – and by extension UMNO – at the expense of minorities.

The government also bailed out UMNO over the Putra World Trade Centre, persuading state-owned banks to forgive Khidmat Bersatu at least RM140 million in accumulated interest.[118] According to a confidential accountants' report commissioned by UMNO in late 1985 after the UMNO complex was completed, it cost almost RM360 million and was financed primarily by loans of RM199.5 million from Bank Bumiputra and RM64.9 million from Malayan Banking Bhd. As of March 1986, Khidmat Bersatu had paid just RM51,570 in interest, and the report – obtained, again, by the author in the course of his research – made it clear the company would pay no more.[119] Malaysian taxpayers had subsidized the construction of UMNO's landmark headquarters, which became a cash cow for the party.

After Anwar was sacked in late 1998, Dr. Mahathir and Daim consolidated their power and sidelined Anwar-aligned companies and businessmen, who quickly faded away. Similarly, the sensational Mahathir-Daim split in June 2001, through devoid of any public explanation or recrimination, spelled the end for Halim and other Daim protégés. Halim was summoned within two weeks by a Mahathir aide and told the government intended to take control of Renong, which would be broken up and eventually sold to new investors.[120]

Where that left UMNO's finances was anybody's and everybody's guess. It was easy to believe but impossible to prove that vast sums had been skimmed off UMNO investments on Daim's watch. As the Democratic Action Party's Lim Kit Siang said, "Once he became financial czar, you could never tell where UMNO companies ended and Daim companies began."[121] For 17 years, only Daim knew how much was in the UMNO Political Fund, since, as Dr. Mahathir said, "Yes, he informs me, but…I don't look at the books".[122] In the absence of any public accounting, word circulated inside the party that billions of dollars were missing. Dr. Mahathir gently demurred after his own retirement. "I don't think so," he said. "UMNO never had billions of dollars."[123] Daim also begged to differ, at least as far as he personally was concerned. In a comment directed at UMNO and its leaders, he said, "They don't owe me any money and I don't owe them anything."[124]

Notes

1 Interview with Lim Kit Siang, 31 May 2007.
2 Interview with Daim Zainuddin, 18 October 2007.
3 Interview with Mahathir Mohamad, 14 August 2007.
4 Edmund Terence Gomez, "Introduction: Political Business in East Asia", in Edmund Terence Gomez, ed., *Political Business in East Asia* (London: Routlege, 2002), p. 6.
5 Ibid., p. 6.
6 Pasuk Phongpaichit, "Thailand under Thaksin: Another Malaysia?", Working Paper No. 109, September 2004, Asia Research Centre, Murdoch University, p. 7.
7 Tunku Abdul Rahman, *Viewpoints* (Kuala Lumpur: Heinemann Educational Books (Asia) Ltd., 1978), p. 53.
8 Stephen Duthie, "Mahathir Rivals Ask Court to Halt New UMNO Drive", *Asian Wall Street Journal* (hereafter *AWSJ*), 4 April 1988.
9 Interview with Tengku Razaleigh Hamzah, 29 May 2007.
10 Ibid.
11 Ibid.
12 Interview with Tengku Razaleigh Hamzah, 17 January 2008.
13 Interview with Tengku Razaleigh Hamzah, 21 March 2007.
14 Interview with Abdullah Ahmad, 1 August 2008. UMNO's direct majority stake in Utusan Melayu was disclosed when the company was publicly listed in 1994. Edmund Terence Gomez and Jomo K.S., *Malaysia's Political Economy: Politics, Patronage and Profits* (Cambridge: Cambridge University Press, 1999 edition), p. 96.
15 Interviews with Tengku Razaleigh Hamzah, 17 January, 11 August, 2008.
16 Yoolim Lee, "Malaysia's Banking Magnate", *Bloomberg Markets*, January 2008, p. 100.
17 Edmund Terence Gomez, *Politics in Business: UMNO's Corporate Investments*, (Petaling Jaya: Fortune Enterprise, 1990), p. 58.
18 Ibid., p. 58.
19 Interview with Daim Zainuddin, 18 October 2007.
20 Edmund Terence Gomez, "Political Business in Malaysia", in *Political Business in East Asia*, p. 101.
21 Peter Searle, *The Riddle of Malaysian Capitalism: Rent-seekers or Real Capitalists?* (Sydney: Asian Studies Association of Australia with Allen & Unwin and University of Hawai'i Press, 1999), p. 46.
22 Cheong Mei Sui and Adibah Amin, *Daim: The Man Behind the Enigma* (Petaling Jaya: Pelanduk Publications (M) Sdn. Bhd., 1995), p. 15.
23 Ibid., p. 15.
24 Raphael Pura, "Malaysia's Daim Charts Path to Power", *AWSJ*, 24 August 1984.
25 Ibid.
26 Raphael Pura, "Indosuez Unit Control Shifts to Malaysians", *AWSJ*, 15 October 1982.
27 Interview with Mahathir Mohamad, 20 March 2007.

28 Ibid.
29 Interview with Daim Zainuddin, 18 October 2007.
30 Edmund Terence Gomez, *Politics in Business: UMNO's Corporate Investments*, p. 58.
31 "Khidmat Bersatu Sdn. Bhd.: Accountants' Report for the Period from 1st June 1981 to 31st March 1986", Hanafiah Raslan & Mohamad, Kuala Lumpur.
32 Interview with Daim Zainuddin, 18 October 2007.
33 Interview with Tengku Razaleigh Hamzah, 17 January 2008.
34 "UMNO Political Fund: Accounts, 31st December 1983", Anuarul, Azizan & Company.
35 Interview with Mahathir Mohamad, 14 August 2007; interview with Daim Zainuddin, 18 October 2007.
36 Raphael Pura, "Fleet Group of Malaysia Has New Chief", *AWSJ*, 9 August 1982.
37 Interview with Daim Zainuddin, 18 October 2007.
38 Peter Searle, *The Riddle of Malaysian Capitalism*, p. 106.
39 Doug Tsuruoka, "Fleet's Stormy Voyage", *Far Eastern Economic Review* (hereafter *FEER*), 5 July 1990, p. 52.
40 Interview with Daim Zainuddin, 18 October 2007.
41 Doug Tsuruoka, "Fleet's Stormy Voyage", p. 52.
42 Peter Searle, *The Riddle of Malaysian Capitalism*, p. 106.
43 Nick Seaward, "Malaysia's Controversial Finance Minister Proves an Able Economic Manager: The Daim Stewardship", *FEER*, 1 September 1988, p. 52.
44 Edmund Terence Gomez, *Politics in Business: UMNO's Corporate Investments*, p. 43.
45 Ibid., p. 43.
46 Interview with Daim Zainuddin, 18 October 2007.
47 Edmund Terence Gomez, *Politics in Business: UMNO's Corporate Investments*, pp. 40–41; Cheong Mei Sui and Adibah Amin, *Daim*, pp. 58–59.
48 Edmund Terence Gomez, *Politics in Business: UMNO's Corporate Investments*, p. 38.
49 Peter Searle, *The Riddle of Malaysian Capitalism*, p. 104.
50 Hardev Kaur, "Daim: Person Behind the Name", *New Straits Times*, 21 July 1984, cited in Peter Searle, *The Riddle of Malaysian Capitalism*, p. 104.
51 Edmund Terence Gomez, *Politics in Business: UMNO's Corporate Investments*, p. 60.
52 Ibid., p. 61.
53 Ibid., p. 61.
54 Peter Searle, *The Riddle of Malaysian Capitalism*, p. 106.
55 Ibid., p. 106.
56 Interviews with Tengku Razaleigh Hamzah, 29 May 2007, 17 January 2008.
57 Interview with Tengku Razaleigh Hamzah, 29 May 2007.
58 Stephen Duthie, "Court Allows Auction of Land Held by UMNO", *AWSJ*, 11 January 1989; Stephen Duthie, "Consultant, Ministry Differ on UMNO Property Value", *AWSJ*, 22 February 1989; Stephen Duthie, "Effort to Auction Property Owned By UMNO Stalls", *AWSJ*, 17 April 1989.
59 Raphael Pura and Stephen Duthie, "Malaysian Court Allows Highway Award: Government Can Give Rich Project to Firm Owned by Ruling Party", *AWSJ*, 18 January 1988.
60 Ibid.
61 Edmund Terence Gomez, *Politics in Business: UMNO's Corporate Investments*, p. 129, citing the *Star*, 29 August 1987.

62　Stephen Duthie, "Lim Files Police Report Accusing Malaysian Cabinet of Corruption", *AWSJ*, 7 October 1987.

63　Stephen Duthie, "Malaysia Signs Disputed Highway Pact", *AWSJ*, 21 March 1988.

64　Cheong Mei Sui and Adibah Amin, *Daim*, p. 125.

65　Interview with Daim Zainuddin, 18 October 2007.

66　Stephen Duthie, "UMNO Regains Party Assets, Adds Holdings", *AWSJ*, 26 July 1989.

67　Stephen Duthie, "United Engineers Expands at Rapid Pace", *AWSJ*, 14 February 1990.

68　Ibid.

69　Peter Searle, *The Riddle of Malaysian Capitalism*, p. 110.

70　Ibid., p. 110.

71　Interview with Tengku Razaleigh Hamzah, 17 January 2008.

72　Stephen Duthie, "Mahathir's Party to Consolidate Business Assets: Transactions to Create Huge Holding Firm, Bolster Political Base", *AWSJ*, 2 May 1990.

73　Stephen Duthie, "UMNO's Asset Transaction to Yield Large Windfall", *AWSJ*, 3 May 1990.

74　Peter Searle, *The Riddle of Malaysian Capitalism*, p. 124.

75　Ibid., p. 121.

76　Ibid., p. 126.

77　Ibid., 123–124.

78　Ibid., 124.

79　Stephen Duthie, "UMNO Flagship Seeks Huge Restructuring", *AWSJ*, 4 February 1991.

80　Doug Tsuruoka, "Fleet Group to Benefit from Renong's Reorganization: The UMNO Shuffle", *FEER*, 17 May 1990, p. 70.

81　Doug Tsuruoka, "UMNO's Money Machine", *FEER*, 5 July 1990, p. 48.

82　Cheong Mei Sui and Adibah Amin, *Daim*, p. 130.

83　Doug Tsuruoka, "UMNO's Money Machine", p. 50.

84　Edmund Terence Gomez, "Political Business in Malaysia", in *Political Business in East Asia*, p. 97.

85　Ibid., p. 97.

86　Cheong Mei Sui and Adibah Amin, *Daim*, p. 125.

87　Stephen Duthie, "Mahathir Party to Sell Tower, Slashing Debt", *AWSJ*, 25 March 1994.

88　Stephen Duthie, "Ruling Lets Mahathir Party Regain Assets", *AWSJ*, 16 August 1994.

89　Edmund Terence Gomez, "Political Business in Malaysia", in *Political Business in East Asia*, p. 97.

90　Ibid., pp. 97–98.

91　Interview with former Renong executive, 19 October 2007.

92　Zafer Achi, et al., "Conglomerates in Emerging Markets: Tigers or Dinosaurs?", *Strategy & Business*, Booz-Allen & Hamilton, Second Quarter, 1998. Reprint No. 98206.

93　Edmund Terence Gomez, *Political Business: Corporate Involvement of Malaysian Political Parties* (Townsville: James Cook University of North Queensland, 1994), p. 291.

94　Raphael Pura, "Ties That Bind: Renong's Asset, Its History, Reveals Its Liability Side", *AWSJ*, 19 January 1996.

95　Raphael Pura, "Chairman's Family Feud Rattles Renong", *AWSJ*, 19 March 1996.

96   Raphael Pura, "A Malaysian Morality Tale for the 1990s: Control of Renong Could Be Up for Grabs in Spellbinding Divorce Battle", *AWSJ*, 30 July 1996.
97   Stephen Duthie, "Anwar's Ascent Creates New Clique of Businessmen", *AWSJ*, 13 March 1991.
98   Edmund Terence Gomez, "Political Business in Malaysia", in *Political Business in East Asia*, p. 98.
99   Ibid., p. 98.
100   Ibid., p. 98.
101   Shamsul A. Baharuddin, "Political Change and Economic Development at the Grassroots in Contemporary Rural Malaysia", in Manning Nash, ed., *Economic Performance in Malaysia: The Insiders View* (New York: Professors World Peace Academy, 1988), pp. 87–90.
102   Ibid., p. 90.
103   Edmund Terence Gomez, *Political Business*, p. 159.
104   Ibid., p. 160.
105   Harold Crouch, "Money Politics in Malaysia", in *Mahathir's Economic Policies* (Kuala Lumpur: INSAN, 1989), p. 87.
106   Edmund Terence Gomez, *Political Business*, p. 59.
107   Suhaini Aznam, "No Ruffled Feathers", *FEER*, 10 October 1985, p. 16.
108   Lee Kuan Yew, *From Third World to First: The Singapore Story 1965–2000* (Singapore: Times Media Pte. Ltd., 2000), p. 191.
109   Zainuddin Maidin, *The Other Side of Mahathir* (Kuala Lumpur: Utusan Publications & Distributors Sdn. Bhd., 1994), p. 167.
110   Ibid., p. 167.
111   Ibid., p. 173.
112   R.S. Milne and Diane K. Mauzy, *Malaysian Politics Under Mahathir* (London: Routledge, 1999), p. 26, citing *New Straits Times*, 3 May 1995.
113   Lee Kuan Yew, *From Third World to First*, p. 191.
114   *Asia 2002 Yearbook,* Far Eastern Economic Review Ltd.,, p. 153.
115   Mahathir Mohamad, "The UMNO Saga", in *Reflections on Asia* (Subang Jaya: Pelanduk Publications (M) Sdn. Bhd., 2002), pp. 120–121.
116   Edmund Terence Gomez, *Political Business*, p. 155.
117   Leslie Lopez, "Steelmaker's Demise Roils Malaysian Banks, Taxpayers", *AWSJ*, 19 September 2000.
118   Interview with Daim Zainuddin, 18 October 2007.
119   "Khidmat Bersatu Sdn. Bhd.: Accountants' Report for the Period from 1st June 1981 to 31st March 1986", Hanafiah Raslan & Mohamad, Kuala Lumpur.
120   Leslie Lopez, "At Malaysia's Renong, Change is About Perceptions", *AWSJ*, 26 July 2001.
121   Interview with Lim Kit Siang, 31 May 2007.
122   Interview with Mahathir Mohamad, 14 August 2007.
123   Interview with Mahathir Mohamad, 20 March 2007.
124   Michael Vatikiotis, "Daim's Expanding Empire", *FEER,* 25 March 2004, p. 42.

6
Scandal, What Scandal?

Dr. Mahathir's administration took office in 1981 with the slogan *bersih, cekap, amanah* – clean, efficient, trustworthy. Almost immediately, however, it became embroiled in financial scandals that exploded with startling regularity, some of them truly spectacular. A few were of an order of magnitude that would have bankrupted most developing nations. But tropical Malaysia was generously endowed with natural resources, notably offshore hydrocarbon deposits, and commanded by a leader committed to rapid development. The expanding economy absorbed the shock of much of the dissipated wealth and, where necessary, the gaps left by the missing billions were plugged with the proceeds of oil and gas exports.

Almost all the scandals involved the government directly, or senior officials and businessmen closely connected to UMNO. In some cases, impropriety – whether illegal or merely ill-advised – was officially authorized or condoned for an allegedly higher purpose. Public funds were stolen in various ways, or simply poured into a big black hole in the name of ventures that bordered on the reckless, improbable, or criminal. The extent of the losses – and in some cases the way the money disappeared – was never fully documented. Dr. Mahathir's administration generally did not hold Malaysians accountable for the financial disasters, and often laid the blame on others. By the early 1990s, cynics remarked that it had been a good decade for bad behaviour, or a bad decade for good behaviour.[1]

Although he initiated, promoted or at least approved some of the undertakings that turned into outright scams, Dr. Mahathir was remarkably blasé about the massive wastage and far from embarrassed that another government slogan was "leadership by example". His eyes fixed on the bigger picture, his vision of a modern Malaysia, Dr. Mahathir was more concerned to minimize publicity about mistakes and misdeeds than to punish those responsible for egregious offences. Two visiting academics, who interviewed him in the late 1990s, were taken aback to find him shrugging off the bad experiences and uninterested in studying what happened in order to avoid a repeat. Noting that Dr. Mahathir on special occasions could be persuaded to sing his favourite song, *My Way*, they suggested that an appropriate encore would be the anthem of the late French chanteuse, Edith Piaf, *Je ne regrette rien*, I have no regrets.[2]

Dr. Mahathir's ultimate protection was his government's large majority in Parliament and its control of the press and investigating agencies. With a revolt by backbench members of the ruling coalition almost unthinkable, it invariably fell to the small opposition Democratic Action Party and its harried leader, Lim Kit Siang, to try and expose malfeasance. His was a thankless task as the perpetrators or beneficiaries were often "Umno-putras", as Lim dubbed the UMNO elite and cronies. While he could usually count on support from a few non-governmental organizations, their clout was limited by their inability to get their message across in the mainstream media, or interest the police in investigating allegations of corruption and other wrongdoing.

Political scientists R.S. Milne and Diane K. Mauzy, commenting that Malaysia's financial scandals "reached almost endemic proportions" in the mid-1980s, concluded they might have been generated as a result of a "get-rich-quick mentality" that was encouraged by the policy of promoting bumiputras in business. And that, they suggested, may have "led to the pursuit of wealth, untempered by ethics, or even fear of the law".[3] Their observations largely are borne out in the following case studies.

The tin caper

David Zaidner, a fast-talking Egyptian metal trader who travelled on a Swiss passport, packed his bags with a clever idea and headed for Jakarta in 1980. Representing the large commodity broker, Swiss-based Marc Rich & Company, Zaidner wanted to handle sales of tin for Indonesia, the world's second-biggest producer. More than that, he had some unorthodox notions to offer about how the international price of tin could be raised.

Indonesian Minister of Mines and Energy Subroto and officials of the state tin company turned him down flat. They knew Zaidner was smart and experienced enough, but he did not always play by the rules. Back in the 1970s, when he worked for Amalgamated Metals Corporation, he had been fired after company executives raided his office in Zug, Switzerland, and found a troubling paper trail. The evidence suggested he may have bribed an Indonesian official and his Bolivian assistant, who both worked for the International Tin Council in London. There was also evidence of other irregularities intended to gain an edge in the tin market. Although the episode was hushed up to save embarrassment to the Tin Council, the Indonesians knew about it since it was their man who was involved with Zaidner. Subroto was a like-minded ally of the "Berkeley mafia", the team of acclaimed technocrats nicknamed after their alma mater in the United States and appointed by President Suharto, who were committed to restoring the country's reputation after the ruinous Sukarno years.

Undeterred, Zaidner took his proposal to Malaysia, the biggest tin producer, and found a more receptive audience. From his tin-trading activities, he had contacts at Malaysia Mining Corporation Bhd., the world's largest tin concern known as MMC, which was controlled by state-owned investment companies and worked closely with the government to implement tin policies. Through the company officials he already knew, Zaidner got acquainted with Abdul Rahim Aki, MMC's group chief executive, who was politically well connected. The higher Zaidner went, the easier it became to sell his idea. As an acquaintance of the chief executive told Raphael "Rocky" Pura, the investigative reporter who unravelled the escapade for the *Asian Wall Street Journal*, Abdul Rahim "knew as much about tin as could be contained on one-half of a ten-cent postage stamp".[4] Over the objections of some MMC advisers who knew of Zaidner's tainted past, Marc Rich was appointed as the company's tin-trading agent.

Another essential piece of the picture was Dr. Mahathir's presence at the top of the government. Hussein Onn was still prime minister when the Cabinet approved a clandestine plan to support sagging tin prices, but he was ill and Deputy Prime Minister Mahathir was effectively running the country, and would soon take over formally from him. The prospect of outwitting the West appealed strongly to the nationalistic Dr. Mahathir. He often complained that commodity producers such as Malaysia got a raw deal when trading their goods in international markets, which he felt were controlled by the industrialized nations.[5] Looking back much later, Dr. Mahathir acknowledged being conned by Zaidner. "He spun a very attractive story", suggesting "it would be possible for us to keep the price of tin high and in the process make a lot of money for ourselves," Dr. Mahathir said. "I must admit I was very new to all this. I didn't understand."[6]

Although the International Tin Agreement was one of the few successful global commodity agreements, Malaysia was becoming disenchanted with the pact's ability to deliver adequate returns on what was once the country's major foreign exchange earner. All 30 member countries, both producers and consumers, were required to contribute metal or cash to an International Tin Council buffer stock, where a manager was empowered to buy tin when the price fell below a specified level and sell when it rose above a certain point. A weakness from Malaysia's standpoint was that any increase in the price band had to win the backing of a majority of both producing and consuming members. When consumers led by the United States denied producers' demands for higher prices in July 1981, as Dr. Mahathir officially assumed the premiership, the Malaysian government instituted the Zaidner-inspired scheme.

In preparation for its covert attempts to prop up tin prices, the government involved ranking civil servants in the Ministry of Finance, the Ministry of Primary Industries and Bank Negara Malaysia, the central bank, as well as tin industry officials. To hide Malaysia's tracks, MMC executives incorporated a local company called Maminco Sdn. Bhd. with paid-up capital of just RM2, which became the government's secret vehicle to carry out the tin-buying plan. Abdul Rahim and an MMC accountant held one share each and served as directors. Nordin Ismail, a leading trader at MMC and Zaidner's friend, became general manager. The finance ministry directed state-owned Bank Bumiputra Malaysia Bhd. to extend credit to Maminco through its offshore branches to pay for the tin. Bank Bumiputra's coffers in turn were topped up with funds held offshore by the national oil and gas company, Petroliam Nasional Bhd., known as Petronas.

Maminco, which began buying tin in large quantities on the London Metal Exchange in July 1981, continued with the purchases through most of November. They were mainly for three-month forward delivery. Maminco traded through Zaidner and Marc Rich, who placed their orders through member firms of the exchange. Maminco also bought physical tin on the Penang market in Malaysia. The heavy buying forced up three-month futures prices by 20 per cent to about 8,600 pounds a tonne. The appearance of what the international press dubbed a mystery buyer was particularly conspicuous in the industry, since actual demand for tin was fairly slack as the developed world headed for recession. Experienced industry hands suspected Malaysia, but Dr. Mahathir's government consistently denied it.

The Malaysian-induced price rise helped producers obtain an increase of almost 6.9 per cent in the Tin Council's price-support range in October.[7] And it was not costing the Malaysians much, as buyers of three-month forward contracts had to pay only a 10 per cent deposit. But after four months the market began acting – well, like a market. The higher prices started to stimulate extra production, and when the United States announced it would sell some of its 170,000-tonne strategic stockpile of tin, Kuala Lumpur howled in protest.[8] Worse for the Malaysians, many London Metal Exchange traders, betting that the mystery buyer would not have deep enough pockets to sustain the operation, began to sell tin short three months forward, expecting prices to collapse.

As Pura reported in the *Journal*, these developments prompted an important switch in tactics by Zaidner and his Malaysian clients, "one that effectively changed the Malaysian plan from a price-support operation to an attempt to corner the tin market".[9] In late November, Malaysia switched from buying three-month futures to spot purchases of physical tin for cash. The tactic, provided Malaysia could maintain its spot buying, set up short-sellers for a squeeze. It meant that traders holding contracts to sell tin three months later, in February, might find no physical tin available to meet their obligations. They would have to buy tin from the mystery buyer at a higher price than that at which they contracted to sell, or default on their contracts.

The Malaysian move sent spot prices soaring to a peak of 8,970 pounds a tonne, and set off a global scramble by short-sellers to get tin into London Metal Exchange warehouses by late February 1982. While the Malaysians

looked like they were going to make a killing, the stakes were soaring dramatically and Maminco became dangerously exposed. It needed to borrow huge
sums, as much as RM1.5 billion at one point, at interest rates of around 20 per
cent, and pay storage and insurance on bulging tin stocks that eventually
reached 40,000 to 50,000 tonnes. Maminco had to bite the bullet and pay the
cost of holding the hoard in order to keep prices high, because its most recent
purchases were made at fairly high levels. The thinking was to sell 15,000
or 20,000 tonnes to the short-sellers at a huge profit to pay for the entire
exercise, and hang on to 20,000 to 30,000 tonnes indefinitely.

Alas, ever-rising prices attracted more releases from the U.S. stockpile and
supplies from other sources that had to be absorbed. At the same time, end
users of tin began reducing their inventories as the economic recession deepened. With the tin market braced for an expected squeeze on short-sellers, the
London Metal Exchange changed its rules and let trader-members off the
hook. It permitted short-sellers to pay a fine and avoid having to purchase tin
from the mystery buyer at steep premiums. The move helped sink the
Malaysian plan, but it was likely to fail anyway. After taking a close look at
Zaidner's books, Marc Rich fired him and began to dump its tin, sending the
spot price tumbling by 1,700 pounds a tonne in a single week.

The fallout was a disaster for the tin industry worldwide.[10] Compelled to
intervene to defend the artificially high floor price set when Malaysia was
driving up the market, the Tin Council buffer stock manager also had to sop
up the additional tin attracted by the higher prices. Although producer
members agreed to restrict exports according to a quota system, they and
consumers were forced repeatedly to kick in additional funds to support
the buffer-stock operations. When the money finally ran out in 1985, the
manager controlled a stockpile valued at about US$700 million. As the Inter-
national Tin Agreement disintegrated, the market collapsed completely and
prices hit record lows.[11]

In Malaysia, dozens of mines closed with heavy job losses.[12] Maminco
held thousands of tons of expensively acquired tin it could sell only at a
loss, and it was unable to repay Bank Bumiputra. Dr. Mahathir said later
the Malaysians had to honour Zaidner's purchases, even though he had
exceeded his "limited" authority when buying.[13]

Unwilling to acknowledge its part in the catastrophe, the Malaysian government devised a way of making money available to Maminco, so that
the large losses would not show up as bad debts on the bank's books
for lending made at the government's request. The novel solution was to
create another shadowy company, Makuwasa Securities Sdn. Bhd., which
again was ostensibly private but held by nominee shareholders on behalf
of the government. For two years, Makuwasa was allocated new issues of
shares in public companies normally reserved for bumiputras at preferential
prices. The transfers were made through Malaysia's Employees Provident
Fund, a national pension plan, at no profit.[14] Makuwasa was then free to

sell the shares at a profit on the Kuala Lumpur Stock Exchange to repay tin losses. In his investigations for the *Journal*, Pura uncovered another likely back-door channel to help Maminco settle with Bank Bumiputra: a "secret service vote" in the country's annual budget. Usually used for security and intelligence-related activity the government tried to shield from public view, this item contained funds that could be spent at the discretion of the finance ministry. By effectively transferring Maminco's losses to the national budget deficit, the government made it almost impossible to detect them.[15]

Dr. Mahathir's admission in 1986 of the government's role, after five years of denials or deliberate silence, staggered the business world. He almost certainly went public at the UMNO General Assembly because the Democratic Action Party had served notice that it intended to pursue the matter in Parliament. Dr. Mahathir disclosed the parts played by both Maminco and Makuwasa, but he was far from contrite. Rather, he defended the government's actions and blamed "massive cheating" by the London Metal Exchange – allowing the short-sellers to escape – for depriving Malaysia of trading profits. "If not for the cheating by the LME, changing the rules to protect its members, the government would not have lost and the question of the government's involvement in maintaining the tin price would not have been raised at all," he said. No government official had profited, he added. "What was done by the government was aimed at saving the tin industry."[16]

Dr. Mahathir's new primary industries minister, Lim Keng Yaik, tallied up the damage a few months later. He said Maminco had ended up about RM660.5 million in the red, consisting of actual trading losses, interest paid to Bank Bumiputra, foreign-exchange losses and administrative costs.[17]

But the cost to Malaysia's reputation was incalculable, not least for having repeatedly lied. Indonesia, Thailand and other members of the Association of Tin Producing Countries, formed on Kuala Lumpur's initiative in 1983, privately thought the Malaysians brazen and hypocritical to turn up to the next meeting after Dr. Mahathir's disclosures talking about reform. Among other things, Malaysia advocated the worldwide use of the new Kuala Lumpur Tin Market as "a natural corollary of the London collapse".[18] As a non-producer of tin, Singapore had reason to feel especially aggrieved by Malaysia's shenanigans. Before Kuala Lumpur's plotting was known, the Malaysian government had persuaded the producers' group to take the moral high ground and criticize Singapore for allegedly undermining their export-control programme, by exporting tin refined from ore smuggled out of neighbouring countries.[19]

The BMF affair

Bank Bumiputra and Petronas, glimpsed in contact on the edges of the tin saga, proved a highly combustible combination during the Mahathir era.

When they were brought together by the dictates of domestic politics, it was not always a comfortable or happy association.

Incorporated in 1965, Bank Bumiputra was assigned a central role in Malaysia's affirmative action programme. Specifically, the bank was to channel credit and financial services to the countryside, where the vast majority of Malays lived and worked in traditional pursuits such as farming and fishing. Bank Bumiputra was also to familiarize Malays with banking and train some of them to become bankers. A preferred repository of state funds, the bank grew rapidly, though its socio-political function inevitably caused its profitability, in terms of return on shareholders funds, to lag behind rivals. Some loss of commercial competitiveness resulting from forgone lending to non-bumiputra customers was implicitly accepted. To operate and keep watch on such a politically sensitive institution, the government usually appointed ranking UMNO officials or civil servants closely linked to the party, rather than professional managers. That left Bank Bumiputra a sitting target for well-connected business interests looking for cheap loans, the cheapest of which more accurately could be described as handouts or donations. The bank found it hard to say "no", ending up dispensing a constant flow of funds to favoured recipients in the Malay establishment.

As for Petronas, established under the Petroleum Development Act of 1974, it fared considerably better. It became Malaysia's largest and richest corporation, and the country's biggest source of tax revenue and foreign exchange, with an international reputation for being a savvy industry operator. But with an assured income stream and an accumulating pile of profits, including large cash deposits with banks around the world, Petronas, too, was sometimes called upon to do duty above and beyond its original charter. Not required to disclose its financial accounts, Petronas reported by law to the prime minister, rather than the finance minister as might be expected. It was Dr. Mahathir's favourite piggy bank, to be raided in emergencies and on other special occasions.

While Bank Bumiputra was being used to buy tin on a grand scale in London, a wholly owned subsidiary of the bank was being abused in even more breathtaking fashion for personal gain in colonial Hong Kong. Bumiputra Malaysia Finance Ltd. (BMF), a deposit-taking company, got involved in what a Hong Kong prosecutor called one of the biggest fraud cases in history. It was a remarkable tale of murder and suicide, false accounting, illusory profits and bankruptcy of an order not previously seen in Hong Kong. The mastermind was a Singaporean named George Tan, whose Carrian group rode a Hong Kong property boom to dizzying heights between 1980 and 1982. Bursting on the scene, Carrian diversified rapidly into transport, shipping, tourism, insurance, finance, catering, hotels and entertainment, spreading its tentacles to Taiwan, Singapore, Malaysia, Thailand, the Philippines, Japan, Australia, New Zealand and the United States. Almost overnight, it counted more than 200 interlocking companies in the group.

Previously unknown in business circles, Tan wrapped himself in mystery and assumed a façade of respectability by hiring prominent advisers and industry professionals. He was the centre of Asia-wide speculation as investors, analysts and journalists tried to figure out the source of his apparently bottomless wealth. The answer: He was a bankrupt civil engineer living illegally in Hong Kong and had no money, but bluffed major banks into lining up to lend to him after persuading neophyte BMF to provide Carrian with free-flowing funds. In early 1980, BMF loaned the then-obscure Carrian about RM310 million without collateral to buy a landmark building in Hong Kong's Central business district, a purchase that put the company on the map as an aggressive property player.[20]

Prime Minister Mahathir inherited the BMF affair and could have chosen to step in and clean it up. No doubt it would have been a severe embarrassment for UMNO and the government, but Malaysians surely would have appreciated a strong statement that the new premier was not prepared to tolerate blatant misuse of public funds. Instead, he opted to try to conceal the mess while endorsing a barely-legal secret plan by Bank Bumiputra to recover loan losses at the expense of other stranded creditors. With the benefit of hindsight, Dr. Mahathir said the bank was mismanaged by people who did not understand banking – "not always crooks, but quite incompetent" – who thought having a branch in Hong Kong was a status symbol. "But trying to find out who actually mismanaged it is not easy, you see."[21]

Dr. Mahathir's priority with government-controlled banks, after taking office in July 1981, was to put his appointees in charge. In the shuffle, Nawawi Mat Amin, a senior partner in an accounting firm and a member of UMNO's Supreme Council, took over as executive chairman of Bank Bumiputra in April 1982. He replaced Kamarul Ariffin Mohamed Yassin, a lawyer by training and one of Malaysia's best known bankers, who had steered the bank through six years of rapid growth. Kamarul also had excellent UMNO affiliations, having served as the party's legal adviser and headed its investment unit, but he was removed because he was close to Finance Minister Tengku Razaleigh Hamzah, a political rival of Dr. Mahathir and Deputy Prime Minister Musa Hitam. Dr. Mahathir wanted his own man running a major financial arm of the government.[22]

The details of BMF's deepening troubles were disclosed piecemeal by the regional press, digging and reporting from Hong Kong, from late 1982.[23] It emerged that BMF had not only played the property market in betrayal of its mandate, but concentrated its lending to just three borrowers, each of which ran into difficulties and could not repay. By the final accounting, BMF had loaned US$800 million to George Tan's Carrian empire, about US$123 million to companies controlled by speculator Kevin Hsu, and US$40 million to Eda Investments Ltd. and associated concerns.

This was dynamite in Malaysia. Bank Bumiputra was considered the flagship of the Malaysian financial system and a source of ethnic Malay and national pride after overtaking Thailand's Bangkok Bank in 1981 as the largest bank in Southeast Asia. Almost everyone wanted to know why an institution set up expressly to help Malaysia's bumiputras was lending extravagantly to ethnic Chinese real-estate developers in Hong Kong. Why was BMF in property at all? When the subsidiary was licensed in 1977, executives had said it aimed to complement Bank Bumiputra's participation in internationally syndicated loans, engage in foreign-exchange trading, and finance Malaysia's trade with Hong Kong and China.

A closer look revealed more cause for concern. BMF had persisted in a lending blitz as the Hong Kong property boom turned to bust, tripling its long-term loan portfolio. Moreover, BMF's lending for the most part was not from deposits or loans generated in Hong Kong. The money had been obtained from Bank Bumiputra in Malaysia and from other international branches, and included Petronas funds on deposit overseas. The market value of property and shares used to secure loans, when they were secured at all, was being eroded seriously by the downturn, exposing BMF to such large losses that the financial health of Bank Bumiputra itself might be at risk. With BMF operating almost autonomously, the lines of responsibility led back to Kuala Lumpur.[24] BMF's lending decisions were made by its own two-man board: Chairman Lorrain Esme Osman and Mohamed Hashim Shamsudin were both prominent directors of the parent bank. Lorrain was a member of Dr. Mahathir's panel of economic advisers, while Hashim was Bank Bumiputra's executive director, a post that ranked second in the bank's hierarchy. Ibrahim Jaafar, who ran BMF's day-to-day operations in Hong Kong as general manager, reported directly to Lorrain and Hashim.

In an incriminating turn, the Hong Kong-based press discovered that two of these three executives, who had controlled BMF from its inception, had outside business connections with customers. Ibrahim held large personal overdraft facilities in Hong Kong banks that were guaranteed by Carrian. Hashim became a director of a small company three days before it received a cheque for RM1.1 million from the wife of the chairman of Eda, just as BMF loaned the group US$40 million.[25]

As the controversy swirled through Southeast Asia with each fresh round of revelations in Hong Kong, the Malaysian authorities remained tight-lipped except to deny Bank Bumiputra faced a crisis. The dual nature of the bank blurred ministerial responsibility. Nobody at cabinet level admitted knowing anything about BMF's operations. As a commercial bank, Bank Bumiputra was subject to monitoring by Bank Negara, which came under the finance ministry. The public identified the bank with Tengku Razaleigh as he had been chairman from 1969 until he became finance minister in 1976. But Tengku Razaleigh said the bank was one of several government agencies answerable directly to the Prime Minister's Department. As finance minister, he ordered Bank Negara to conduct an inquiry into BMF after reading about its troubles in the regional press towards the end of 1982.[26] Bank Negara Governor Abdul Aziz Taha, in his first comments to reporters in April 1983, characterized the problem as a "situation of what you call an over-exposure of loans, which I would regard as exceeding…usual banking prudence". Bank Bumiputra's senior executives as well as the bank's external auditor were examining the subsidiary, he said, and "nobody should be alarmed" about the loans because "the government is fully behind" Bank Bumiputra.[27]

In their annual reports for the year ended 31 March 1983,[28] Bank Bumiputra and BMF maintained the same line, minimizing problems in Hong Kong, emphasizing that the parent would give full support to its offspring, and offering no explanation for the lending spree. But figures in the reports indicated that it would be impossible to keep the lid on much longer. BMF had doubled its lending in Hong Kong in 1982, when other banks were running for cover, and it was funded entirely by head office, Bank Bumiputra.[29] After a couple of years of modest growth, BMF's total lending, including short-term money-market deposits and inter-bank loans, had ballooned 285 per cent in 1981 and 1982 to RM1.55 billion. Bank Bumiputra made only small provisions for losses that might arise from its Hong Kong loans. At the same time, though, it increased its paid-up capital by RM600 million – 126 per cent – which suggested it was preparing to cover extensive bad debts, even though the bank denied it.[30]

Dr. Mahathir publicly addressed the issue of BMF's doubtful loans for the first time at a press conference in July 1983, on the completion of his second year as premier. It was eight months after the damaging disclosures began to surface, and Malaysia's normally cautious and respectful press was demanding answers. After all, the two government shareholders in Bank Bumiputra already had been required to kick in an extra RM600 million to increase the bank's capitalization in proportion to their holdings. That meant 70 per cent of the burden fell on the National Equity Corporation, which was established to hold blue-chip Malaysian corporate equity on behalf of bumiputras by selling them shares in its investment portfolio through a unit trust plan. The remaining 30 per cent was held by the Minister of Finance Inc., the ministry's holding unit. Also, there was no indication of how BMF could repay the RM1.2 billion it owed Bank Bumiputra. Whether BMF was paying interest on its debt, which would amount to RM93 million to RM124 million a year at prevailing rates, was also crucial. If the bank was not charging interest, it was tying up a huge amount in assets to subsidize the Hong Kong operation and act as a de facto reserve against BMF's possible bad debts.[31]

Answering Malaysian reporters' questions, Dr. Mahathir was sanguine. He acknowledged that BMF erred by lending too heavily in the real-estate market, but suggested the collapse of property values was the primary cause of the problems. "Almost all" the banks in Hong Kong were similarly affected, he said. He agreed it had not been wise to provide the bulk of loans to only three groups. "It is not prudent, but you must remember the atmosphere in Hong Kong at that time. Banks were anxious to lend money simply because the economy was booming, and when somebody who is established comes to you to borrow money, you don't look too closely, although by rights you should," he said. "This was their mistake." Dr. Mahathir sidestepped the question of accountability, promising that Malaysia would "take action" if malpractices were uncovered, but said the emphasis was on trying to salvage overdue debts, not on "witch hunting". He said that "how you deal with the mistake that has been made in Hong Kong depends also on how much we can recover. The priority at the moment is on recovery and not on punishment yet".[32]

What Dr. Mahathir did not tell the reporters was that in late 1982 he had approved a secret plan hatched by Nawawi Mat Amin, the man he installed as executive chairman of Bank Bumiputra, to maximize those recovery efforts. Much later, Dr. Mahathir admitted he was briefed by Nawawi about the plan to retrieve "as much money as possible", though he was not informed of the details and did not get involved in their implementation. "I agreed with this action," he said.[33] The most controversial part of the plan was to buy Carrian assets in the United States through an intricate web of dummy companies without informing other creditors, after Carrian declared financial difficulties. The idea was to prop up Carrian and at the same time get back some of the money it owed BMF.

The elaborate transaction to acquire several parcels of Carrian property in California and Florida was disguised as a loan by Bank Bumiputra to a third party. It began with the bank extending an US$85 million loan to a newly established Liberian company created by the bank. Called Marmel Inc., the Liberian company in turn loaned the money to a Channel Islands-based company called Trans Pacific Trust. From there, the funds were loaned yet again to another Liberian-incorporated outfit called Darton Ltd. Darton and Dragon Base Company in Hong Kong used the US$85 million to purchase the U.S. assets. Darton appeared to belong to Yap Lim Sen, the purported third-party buyer, who had his own property development company in Malaysia. But Darton was ultimately owned and controlled by the bank, and Yap was Nawawi's friend and agreed to hold the U.S. assets as a "national service".[34]

In 1986, a committee of inquiry appointed by the Malaysian government concluded that Bank Bumiputra's convoluted exercise was "clumsy, unprofessional, unethical and amounted to a fraud" on Carrian's shareholders and other creditors. The panel recommended that evidence and documents related to the property acquisition be turned over to the Malaysian police for further investigation. But no legal action was ever taken in Malaysia against those involved in the arrangement.[35]

In 1991, a minority shareholder in the defunct Carrian group, Bahamas-based Capri Trading Corporation, filed a lawsuit in the United States claiming it was denied a fair share of the proceeds from the sale of the property.[36] The suit alleged that Bank Bumiputra and its senior officers at the time acted "in concert and in conspiracy...to fraudulently conceal the looting" of the property from Carrian's minority shareholders and creditors. It claimed they engaged "in a pattern of racketeering" by paying less than one-third of the property's market value, depriving minority shareholders of adequate compensation and "significantly diminishing" the value of Capri's stake in Carrian.[37] After several hearings extending over 14 months, a U.S. Federal Court judge dismissed the suit on a technicality, that Hong Kong would be the most appropriate venue for such a case.[38]

News of the suit being filed in California, first reported in early 1992 by Bernama, Malaysia's national news agency, buffeted stock markets in Malaysia and Singapore. They were unsettled by the prospect, however remote, that Bank Bumiputra might have to cough up the US$3 billion being sought in damages.[39] The government immediately imposed a domestic news blackout on the story. Bernama was ordered to delete the report from its electronic news system and editors of the country's newspapers were told not to publish it.[40] Although the suit essentially repeated allegations made by the committee of inquiry five years earlier, it was an unacceptable reminder of Malay outrage and Mahathir administration culpability.

The practical flaw in Nawawi's 1982 secret rescue plan, in which Dr. Mahathir invested so much hope, was that it left in place the executives at BMF who were responsible for its predicament. Directors Lorrain Esme Osman and Mohamed Hashim Shamsudin in Kuala Lumpur, and General Manager Ibrahim Jaafar in Hong Kong were, at the very least, guilty of reckless lending that almost defied belief. As it turned out, press investigations showing that two of them had improper dealings with borrowers were not only accurate but merely the tip of the iceberg. Nawawi had taken the precaution of setting up a special supervisory committee to monitor BMF's lending in Hong Kong when he took over Bank Bumiputra in 1982. But Lorrain, Hashim, Ibrahim, and an alternate director of BMF, Rais Saniman, effortlessly circumvented the committee and continued lending to George Tan and Carrian. To avoid detection on one occasion, they arranged for China-owned Bank of Communications (Nominee) Company Ltd. to make a US$40 million loan on BMF's behalf.[41]

All the double dealing, back-room scheming and obfuscation began to fall apart days after Dr. Mahathir's press comments, when a BMF executive, Jalil Ibrahim, was murdered in Hong Kong.[42] Bank Bumiputra's head office had secretly dispatched Jalil, an internal auditor, specifically to inspect BMF's books covertly while occupying the post of assistant general manager.[43] Lured to Hong Kong's five-star Regent Hotel,[44] he was later found strangled in a remote banana grove in the New Territories. Mak Foon Than, 32, a little-known Malaysian businessman, was soon arrested, convicted and jailed for his murder. At the trial, the prosecution linked the crime to an attempt to bail out Carrian.[45]

With Hong Kong homicide detectives joining investigations by the police fraud squad, the securities commission and the anti-corruption agency, events moved swiftly. Police raided Carrian's offices on suspicion that someone was siphoning off assets from the group. Carrian and George Tan companies were found to owe BMF much more than either side had disclosed, effectively sinking a ten-month effort to rescue the conglomerate.[46] Tan and his principal assistant were arrested and charged with making false and misleading statements in their roles as company directors.

It was a different Dr. Mahathir who faced the press again three months later, in October 1983. Now he called BMF's lending "a heinous crime" and "a betrayal of trust". He identified five men responsible for the fiasco, said they had accepted consultancy fees from BMF that were "morally wrong" but not illegal, and indicated the four still in their jobs would be asked to leave.[47] But he made no mention of the reported financial transactions between some BMF executives and their Hong Kong customers, which had been reported in the press. Lorrain, Hashim and Rais duly quit their posts at both BMF and Bank Bumiputra. Ibrahim followed. The surprise was not that they were forced out, but that they had been retained so long as part of Bank Bumiputra's strategy of using the people responsible for the bad loans to try and salvage the debts.[48]

As the government tried to parry increasingly strident calls for a full account of what happened in Hong Kong, BMF sued George Tan for failing to repay seven loans for which he stood as guarantor. The banking industry interpreted the move as a shallow and belated effort by Bank Bumiputra to show it was serious about recovering its loans and to dispel rumours of a separate recovery effort.[49]

The three-man committee of inquiry announced by Dr. Mahathir in early 1984 was headed by Malaysia's Auditor General, Ahmad Noordin Zakaria, a veteran civil servant known for his thorough and often critical audits of state agencies. He was joined by a lawyer and an accountant. Dr. Mahathir said they would have a broad mandate to probe all aspects of BMF's lending, including any possible wrongdoing, and the findings would be presented to Malaysia's Parliament. But his decision to have the committee operate within the framework of Bank Bumiputra gave the impression that it was more in-house inquiry than independent investigation. It lacked the legal powers of a royal commission to secure evidence, call witnesses and cite for contempt those who did not appear. Dr. Mahathir saw no difficulties in getting former bank executives and others to cooperate. "The government is interested in getting to the bottom of this," he said.[50]

As the committee embarked on a two-year paper chase to reconstruct tangled records, however, the government continued to give the impression it was still reluctant to see the sordid details exposed. Noordin, the chairman, complained that he and his colleagues received better cooperation from Hong Kong authorities than they got at home in Malaysia.[51] After the committee delivered a series of interim reports detailing irregularities by BMF's former senior executives, Bank Bumiputra filed complaints with the Malaysian police and initiated legal action against some of the ex-staff. By now, most of the suspect bankers were living abroad. Malaysia's attorney general said his decision on whether to prosecute the case would not depend on the committee's findings, indicating the police criminal investigation was starting from scratch and would ignore the voluminous evidence already gathered by the committee.[52]

In a characteristic move, Dr. Mahathir discovered enemies abroad plotting to take advantage of the situation to blacken Malaysia's name, a familiar ploy to gather public support and deflect attention from domestic difficulties. He said Hong Kong police improperly passed BMF documents, obtained during the Jalil murder inquiry, to the colony's securities commission, and he refused to discount suggestions that Hong Kong or British officials might have manipulated the investigations to embarrass Malaysia.[53] But former premier Hussein Onn, for one, was not impressed. He joined some other members of UMNO, the Malaysian press, opposition parliamentarians, intellectuals, labour unions and consumer groups clamouring for the truth, many persuaded that responsibility reached deep into the political establishment.

The committee's final report, which consisted of two volumes and totalled 1,075 pages, was eventually published in early 1986, but not before a rancorous exchange between the committee and the government. Committee members applied maximum political pressure by addressing a press conference and calling on the Mahathir administration to keep its promise to make the findings public. While they declined to discuss their conclusions, they tantalized the public with the statement that the Malaysian authorities could have saved at least US$150 million if they had taken resolute action when Carrian declared its liquidity crisis in October 1982.[54] Dr. Mahathir accused the committee of acting "beyond its authority" in seeking publication of the report. Citing legal concerns, he told Noordin that "you don't care what happens to others so long as you satisfy your righteousness".[55] There was little doubt how taxpayers felt. The extensively documented allegations made the three committee members instant folk heroes. After praise for them poured in from readers, the *Star*, an English-language daily owned by the Malaysian Chinese Association, a senior partner in the National Front government, named them Men of the Year in 1984.[56]

Nobody connected with BMF was brought to trial in Malaysia, contributing to the belief among many Malaysians that the politics of the story remained untold. It was left to the Hong Kong government to extradite Rais from France, and Lorrain and Hashim from Britain, and to prosecute them successfully. They were all jailed for short periods, along with George Tan and several others.

Bank Bumiputra's 1983 results, announced in 1984 later than usual while the government arranged the bank's resuscitation, set records for all the wrong reasons. The loss of RM973.6 million for the year was the biggest in the history of the Malaysian banking system. It was Bank Bumiputra's first loss since opening its doors 19 years earlier. A RM1 billion write-off on the Hong Kong loans exceeded by far the total of all after-tax profits ever earned by the bank.[57] A decision to transfer almost all BMF's Hong Kong loan portfolio to Bank Bumiputra on the last day of 1983 proved controversial, since it masked the subsidiary's 1983 lending to Carrian, and enabled the bank to stretch out the write-offs so it was harder to link them with Hong Kong. Just the same, the absorption of the heap of bad debt was devastating, wiping out Bank Bumiputra's paid-up capital almost twice over.[58]

To avoid a financially difficult and politically embarrassing direct bailout, the government chose to use Petronas, the only state-owned institution that packed enough financial punch to do it. Under the complex RM2.49 billion arrangement, Petronas bought the bank from its major shareholder, National Equity Corporation, injected fresh capital, and acquired RM1.26 billion of problem Hong Kong loans from the bank. Petronas ended up with about 90 per cent of the equity, with the balance in the hands of the Minister of Finance Inc. Analysts calculated that Malaysia eventually would lose a total of about RM2.26 billion in bad loans, plus millions of dollars on forgone earnings on government funds diverted to the rescue.[59] Rather than impose an onerous financial burden on the treasury, the Malaysian government, in effect, decided to pay for the losses with accumulated and future earnings from the oil and gas industry.

Petronas's acquisition of Bank Bumiputra was almost certainly illegal. The Petroleum Development Act prevented the company from getting into the banking business. Dr. Mahathir, though, was unfazed, and defended the legality and logic of the takeover. "Petronas has excess funds and is the only organization capable of absorbing such things," he said.[60] But when a lawyer representing the Democratic Action Party filed suit in the Kuala Lumpur High Court challenging the transaction, the government pushed a retrospective amendment to the act through Parliament clearing Petronas's participation in any non-oil venture. While the government succeeded in legislating the litigation "out of the window", as the Malaysian Bar Council said, the High Court imposed a price for the government's lack of respect for the rule of law: It ordered Petronas and the government to pay the lawyer's legal costs.[61]

Unrepentant as ever, Dr. Mahathir claimed victim status on behalf of bumiputras when he addressed the UMNO General Assembly in 1986. In the same speech as he admitted Malaysia's involvement in the tin drama, he said, "Why is there only a fuss about Bank Bumiputra? Because it is a scandal, or because it is bumiputra?" The collapse of Singapore's Pan-Electric Industries Ltd., he said, caused the loss of RM16 billion in stock market capitalization, but it did not elicit the same reaction. "Why was it not raised by the scandal-mongers from the opposition parties? Could it be because it was not committed by bumiputras?"[62]

The comparison was spurious and contained ethnic overtones – what former deputy premier Anwar Ibrahim called, after he had been discarded by Dr. Mahathir, "subtle racist innuendos" – to suit the Malay audience. Pan-Electric, one of Singapore's biggest conglomerates, rocked the Singapore and Kuala Lumpur stock exchanges and triggered an unprecedented three-day halt in trading when it suddenly went into receivership in late 1985. It brought down affiliated companies, sent share prices crashing across the board and exposed a tangled web of precarious stock-contract agreements. But no public funds were involved, and the paper losses could conceivably be retrieved as the markets recovered. Furthermore, Tan Koon Swan, Pan-Electric's influential shareholder – who also headed the governing Malaysian Chinese Association and was a member of parliament – was held responsible. He was jailed in both Singapore and Malaysia for his role in the company's financial demise.

Hussein Onn, the former premier whose integrity was unquestioned, took the opposite stance to Dr. Mahathir over Bank Bumiputra's brush with oblivion. "We are asking for trouble if the matter is played down," he told local reporters. "It will happen again if we don't learn our lessons...".[63] Appalled by the skullduggery and upset by the government's weak and reluctant response, Hussein maintained a critical profile as events unfolded. As an adviser to Petronas with access to Bank Bumiputra's accounts, Hussein said in early 1985 that questionable loans in Malaysia, given out to all kinds of people, could match those in Hong Kong.[64]

His warnings were as prophetic as they were ignored. Five unhappy years later, in October 1989, Petronas had to save Bank Bumiputra again. The bank announced a loss of RM1.06 billion for the year ended 31 March 1989, after making RM1.23 billion in provisions for interest payments from loans previously recorded as revenue but never actually received by the bank. Once more shareholders funds were wiped out – RM949 million this time.[65] Petronas injected another RM982.4 million, giving the energy company almost 100 per cent ownership of the bank. The restructuring package included an extra RM450 million in provisions made in earlier years but never reflected in the bank's paid-up capital, in addition to the RM1.23 billion already noted.[66]

This time around Bank Bumiputra blamed heavy lending for real-estate and property development in Malaysia, not Hong Kong. Mohamed Basir Ismail, the new executive chairman who had brushed aside Hussein's comments with the assurance that Bank Bumiputra's bad loans were no different from those of other Malaysian banks, now admitted that the bank was struck by plummeting property prices in 1984–85. As he put it, "We lent a lot of money all over the place."[67]

While Basir cited Malaysia's Banking Secrecy Act in declining to identify delinquent borrowers, records from a court case revealed how politically-connected clients had treated the publicly-owned bank as their own private account. According to the records, the major offender was UMNO, which borrowed RM200 million from Bank Bumiputra in September 1983 to build a convention centre and office tower in Kuala Lumpur to house the party's headquarters. For the huge project, UMNO also borrowed RM50 million from state-controlled Malayan Banking Bhd., and RM13 million apiece from United Malayan Banking Corporation and Perwira Habib Bank Malaysia Bhd.[68] UMNO for years failed to repay any of the loans or the interest on the loans, which by July 1988 amounted to nearly RM300 million owed to Bank Bumiputra alone. The details were contained in records released in a legal suit after Malaysia's High Court ruled in early 1989 that Bank Bumiputra could foreclose on UMNO's Putra World Trade Centre, as the headquarters complex was known. Bank Bumiputra filed the suit, uncharacteristically, only after UMNO was declared illegal in 1988 and its assets surrendered to an Official Assignee, a government official.[69] Consistent with Bank Bumiputra's plundered history, UMNO avoided foreclosure after "negotiations", during which the party agreed to repay the loans but resisted the payment of interest,[70] which was estimated at RM126 million in late 1989.[71]

Petronas and Bank Bumiputra split towards the end of 1990. Typically, the sale of the bank to the government was not announced at the time, but Petronas confirmed it when queried by foreign reporters. The energy company said it wanted to "concentrate on its core business and other businesses with strategic fit to its core business". The price, also unannounced, was estimated RM1.15 billion.[72] Since Petronas did not have to disclose its financial details, it was hard to calculate how much it lost in total when acting as Bank Bumiputra's holding company and financial saviour.

Although Petronas was out of the picture, Bank Bumiputra failed to mend its wayward ways. It went bust twice more in the next eight years, each time being kept afloat by a government ever willing to reload the vaults by the back entrance as fast as the funds were handed out through the front door. The bank announced growing profits in the early 1990s boom times and often proclaimed that it was committed to purely commercial objectives, as the government prepared to list it on the stock exchange. Abdul Khalid Sahan, the latest executive chairman, declared in late 1996 that the "dark days" were over, with strong recent profits due largely to "more sound management and improving the quality of loans".[73] But with Bank Bumiputra answerable to only a single shareholder, the Minister of Finance Inc., and still not in the hands of independent professional managers, it continued to be afflicted by a civil-service mentality and addicted to bad habits.

The onset of the Asian economic crisis in 1997 revealed familiar weaknesses that belied the hype. Bank Negara said in March 1998 it had stress-tested Bank Bumiputra's loan portfolio, and that in a worst-case scenario the bank would need RM750 million to meet capital adequacy requirements.[74] Six months later, after the bank posted a loss of RM1.4 billion for the year ended 31 March 1998, the government pumped in RM1.1 billion – RM350 million beyond the imagined limit.[75]

Just six months after that, in what amounted to the fourth bail-out of Bank Bumiputra in 15 years, it was merged with Commerce Asset-Holding Bhd., Malaysia's sixth-largest banking group. They formed Bumiputra Commerce Bank, a new entity with RM65 billion in assets that was listed and would be punished by the market for poor future performance. At RM1.58 billion, Commerce Asset got a bargain: Bank Bumiputra's commercial-banking operations with a clean balance sheet. In a fit of generosity that matched previous decisions on the bank, the government agreed to take over all non-performing loans, estimated at RM7 billion, at face value. The government agency set up to buy bad loans and clean up a banking system damaged by the regional crisis paid as little as 60 per cent in the case of other banks. Also, the government pledged that the agency would accept at face value any Bank Bumiputra credits that turned sour during an 18-month period after the merger was finalized.[76] The only consolation for most Malaysians was the disappearance of Bank Bumiputra, a pet monster that gorged itself on RM10 billion or more of their money in a decade and a half.

The forex fiasco

On 16 September 1992, ever after known as Black Wednesday, George Soros made himself famous and US$1.1 billion richer when Britain devalued the pound. He bet London would be forced to withdraw from the European Exchange Rate Mechanism, which was designed to reduce exchange-rate volatility and achieve monetary stability in preparation for the introduction of a single European currency. His wager took the form of selling short more than US$10 billion in pounds. He won when Britain was reluctant to either raise its interest rates to the levels of other participating countries, or to float its currency. For his victory, he was dubbed "the man who broke the Bank of England".

Unbeknown to Soros, he also broke Bank Negara Malaysia, which had wagered a substantial proportion of its assets on Britain being able to hold the line on sterling. Faced with huge losses, Malaysia's central bank kept trading in the hope that the market would give back what it had snatched away. In two years the bank gambled away between RM16 billion and RM31 billion in the biggest Malaysian scandal of all.

Bank Negara's debacle introduced Dr. Mahathir, at a distance, to American Soros and the mysterious and largely invisible world of currency trading that was to grow exponentially with globalization. A Hungarian Jewish immigrant who made a fortune from financial investing and speculation, Soros became a high-profile philanthropist with his support of democratic causes worldwide. While Dr. Mahathir did not actually meet Soros then, he was familiar with his exploits from media accounts. Later in the decade, when Malaysia got pummeled in the Asian financial crisis, Dr. Mahathir blamed predatory currency traders and financial speculators for the regional devastation. Calling for the regulation of hedge funds and currency traders, he denounced a system in which greed rules and where the value of money ranks higher than the value of human lives and human welfare. Currency trading, he said, was "unnecessary, unproductive and immoral".[77] It had "severely impoverished countries and regions, causing millions to lose their jobs, riots and strikes, political and social instability".[78] He singled out Soros as the main villain in the piece.

Those sentiments, expressed so frequently and forcefully, represented a 180 degree turnaround for Dr. Mahathir, who was once happy enough to join the rush to make a buck from nervy currencies. His Bank Negara engaged in so much speculative activity in the second half of 1989 that the U.S. central bank, the Federal Reserve Board, privately asked the Malaysians to cool it.[79] The Bank of England offered similar unsolicited advice.[80] Bank Negara complied to a certain extent, but only temporarily. While denying it had been speculating, the bank explained that at a time of volatile exchange rates it was "actively" managing its external reserves to maintain their value. The main objective was "to be able to hedge, not to speculate", the bank said.[81]

In treasury departments of banks across Asia, however, Bank Negara's trading was the source of astonishment. On some days, it would trade anywhere from US$1 billion to US$5 billion. While that was a drop in the US$400 billion global bucket, it was an enormous amount for a single central bank, and a huge chunk of Malaysia's approximately US$6.5 billion in foreign reserves. The Bank of Japan, by contrast, would rarely reach US$1 billion when it intervened in the foreign-exchange market in an attempt to drive the yen up or down. The United States set a record for itself earlier in the year when it sold US$11.9 billion in dollars, but that was over a three-month period, and only at the peak of those operations did it sell US$1 billion a day.[82]

A central bank normally traded in the foreign-exchange market to influence the exchange rates of its country's currency, to buy other currencies in order to pay overseas obligations, or to occasionally adjust and balance its foreign-exchange reserves. Denials notwithstanding, Bank Negara was out to turn a profit. It actually needed cash on the way to buying heavily into the transportation industry. In September 1989, Bank Negara acquired 21 per cent of Malaysian Airlines System from the Minister of Finance Inc. for about RM772 million, raising its stake in the national flag carrier to 42 per cent. And in June the bank paid an estimated RM680 million to increase its stake to about 30 per cent in Malaysian International Shipping Corporation, the country's largest shipping company operating overseas.[83] The transactions were made by Finance Minister Daim Zainuddin to enable the government to pre-pay foreign debt.[84]

It was precisely in this period, between June and September, that other traders reported Bank Negara entering the market at the same time almost daily: at the start of morning activity, before the market had established a clear trend. Its heavy trading volume was enough to influence the direction of the market during Asian trading hours. Carrying out much of its trading in the highly liquid Singapore market, Bank Negara was able to cause the dollar to move up or down by between 0.75 yen and 1 yen.[85]

The bank cleaned up nicely at first, even if it irked the Fed on principle and upset the central banks of other major industrialized countries, which were trying to weaken the value of the dollar while Bank Negara's trades often attempted to strengthen it. Boasting one of the most sophisticated trading rooms in the world, Bank Negara turned itself into a profit centre for the government by using the country's rapidly mounting gold and foreign currency reserves to play the markets in Asia, Europe and the United States.

In retirement, Dr. Mahathir confirmed he had given Bank Negara the green light to continue currency trading after he was told about it. "They had a trading room and they informed us, and I went to see the trading room. I was quite impressed...I thought it was great and I did not disapprove of it," he said. Dr. Mahathir said the young people doing the trading were "very quick in making decisions" and he described their activities thus: "Not so much manipulation, which I was much against, but they were seeing the movement of currencies and they thought that if they are judicious in the management they can make money."[86]

As always, Dr. Mahathir was keen to take on the developed countries at their own games. He and other Malaysian leaders deplored what they saw as the arrogance of currency initiatives taken by the key industrial nations without consulting the rest of the world. Rather than submitting to such dictates, Bank Negara was encouraged to go on the offensive, joining the pack of private currency traders trying to outwit the major central banks.[87]

Dr. Mahathir was particularly unhappy about the 1985 Plaza Accord, by which the then G-5 – the United States, France, West Germany, Japan and Britain – agreed to devalue the dollar in relation to the yen and deutsche mark. The aim was to reduce the U.S. current account deficit and help the American economy emerge from recession. The dollar declined by 51 per cent against the yen over the next two years. Malaysia and some other Southeast Asian countries reaped huge benefits as Japanese manufacturers moved offshore in search of cheaper land and labour to remain competitive. But there was a downside, too, as the plethora of yen loans that Malaysia sought under the government's Look East policy became much more expensive to repay.

Dr. Mahathir focused on the negative side. In one of many criticisms of the Plaza Accord, he branded it "a political decision made largely because Japan's trade rivals wanted to reduce the competitiveness of Japan". The yen appreciated to the detriment of the Japanese economy and made life more difficult for people in many poor countries, for whom cheap Japanese goods meant higher living standards, he said.[88]

Bank Negara revelled in its anomalous reputation as a "maverick, yet conservative institution".[89] Under Governor Jaffar Hussein, it won respect for nursing Malaysia's shaky financial system back to health after a recession in 1985–86.[90] Central bank inspectors became adept at detecting bad loans, mismanagement and fraud, swooping on errant banks, finance and insurance companies, and savings and credit societies. Where necessary, Bank Negara did not hesitate to take them over temporarily. But by engaging in unbridled currency trading, Bank Negara was not only assuming irrational risk but also indulging in monumental hypocrisy. Part of its mandate was to curb speculation, and it periodically reprimanded or punished foreign banks for what it called currency manipulation and rigging.[91]

Finding itself on the losing end of George Soros's bet against sterling on that fateful day in September 1992, Bank Negara was helplessly exposed. Rather than admit that it behaved irresponsibly and grossly misread the market, the bank tried to conceal the disaster. Bank Negara buried a brief reference to a charge of RM9.3 billion against special reserve funds deep in its balance sheet at the end of its 1992 calendar year annual report, which ran to nearly 300 pages. The depth of the hole simply was not immediately apparent among discrepancies and accounting changes noted in the balance sheet. Only in response to written questions from the foreign press did the bank issue a three-page statement, attempting to explain the 93 per cent plunge in special reserve and contingency funds to RM752.6 million at the end of 1992 from more than RM10 billion a year earlier.[92]

Bank Negara attributed the charge almost solely to the appreciation of the Malaysian ringgit against the bank's foreign-exchange holdings. It did not mention going for broke on the British pound and other currencies that fluctuated wildly and fell before and after the crisis in the European Exchange Rate Mechanism. To meet its low-inflation target, the bank said it soaked up the heavy flow of foreign funds into the booming Malaysian economy. It diversified the inflow, mostly denominated in U.S. dollars, into other currencies in an attempt to protect the value of its external reserves, it said.[93]

The trouble with this explanation was that the dollar depreciated far less than some of the currencies of Malaysia's other trading partners. In fact, the ringgit appreciated against the currencies of all Malaysia's major trading partners, but only marginally against those of the United States, Japan and Singapore, the largest of its partners. This indicated that Bank Negara's foreign-exchange portfolio was heavily weighted in favour of currencies less relevant to Malaysia. Chief suspect: the pound, against which the ringgit appreciated 29.1 per cent during the year and as much as 33.6 per cent at its peak.[94]

Bank Negara advanced another reason for the charge against reserves. It said a portion of the amount could be attributed to a change in its customary accounting policy to value its gold and foreign reserves at prevailing market levels. In the past, the bank had valued its reserves at the lower of historical cost or market rates. The adjustment took the book value of Malaysia's reserves to a whopping RM46 billion at the end of 1992 from RM29.2 billion a year earlier.

The RM9.3 billion charge nearly wiped out all of the special reserves set up by Bank Negara. They comprised the Exchange Rate Fluctuation Reserve, the Investment Fluctuation Reserve, the Insurance Reserve and the Contingency Reserve. The bank said in its statement that "such reserve accounts were created precisely for this purpose, i.e., to act as cushion for undue and unpredictable changes, emanating in most part from international developments completely beyond the control of the bank, and to enable the bank to meet its objectives of policy without unleashing destabilizing effects on its normal operations".[95]

Although fighting inflation was bound to have cost Malaysia, few economists or money market professionals accepted that it could account for the entire loss, while the revaluation of the reserves seemed like no more than an attempt to dress up the balance sheet. The sensitivity of the matter was reflected in the caution of the local media, which did not report the bad news for two weeks after the 30 March release of Bank Negara's report. Even then it took the form of a comment by the new Minister of Finance, Anwar Ibrahim, that he had asked Bank Negara for additional information about its losses. Anwar said later he had issued "strong advice" to the central bank in March to cease speculating.[96] It emerged that the bank might lose considerably more on foreign-currency trades anyway. A figure of RM2.7 billion in contingent liabilities mentioned in the bank's report represented foreign-exchange contracts carried forward into the following year. Whether that sum translated into profit or loss would depend on exchange-rate fluctuations in 1993.

In Parliament, Lim Kit Siang called for a royal commission to inquire into the losses, which he attributed to Bank Negara pouring "tens of billions of ringgit" into the pound and hoping "to make a killing" by buying long, expecting the pound to recover with the support of the British government.[97] Although criticism was growing in the absence of a plausible explanation, Dr. Mahathir indicated that Bank Negara would not be blamed. He told reporters, "There were times in the past when we made profits. At that time, we kept quiet but now when there is a fall, we want to take action. That is not the way."[98]

In the closing days of 1993, Bank Negara took advantage of its ongoing battle with speculators to depress the value of the Malaysian currency, which improved the bank's year-end financial position by raising the value of its foreign currency and gold reserves in ringgit terms. For months, the bank used a variety of tactics, some of them unusual, to try and dissuade speculators from thinking that they could make quick profits on a rising ringgit. By dumping large amounts of ringgit into the market to buy dollars towards the end of December, the bank pushed the local currency down to a two-year low of around RM2.73 to the dollar from RM2.55 for most of the year.[99]

The government also rushed through the sale of Bank Negara's 42 per cent of Malaysian Airlines, effectively privatizing the carrier. A 32 per cent stake realized RM1.79 billion, at the time an inexplicable windfall for the central bank, as businessman Tajudin Ramli, a protégé of Daim Zainuddin, the former finance minister, agreed to pay RM8 a share when the market price was only RM3.50. Bank Negara sold its remaining shares to another government-controlled agency.[100] Driven by Dr. Mahathir, the deals were arranged hurriedly in the last two weeks of December 1993 to bolster the bank's bottom line.[101] In 2000, the government repurchased Tajudin's stake at RM8 a share, when it was trading at around RM3.60, provoking an outcry that Dr. Mahathir's administration was bailing out a crony. In 2006, Tajudin alleged in a lawsuit that he was forced to buy Malaysian Airlines in the first place as a "national service". He said he was directed to do so by Dr. Mahathir and Daim, who told him the acquisition was to save the central bank.[102]

Neither the accounting slight of hand nor the abrupt disposal of the airline could hide the ugly truth, however: more huge losses from foreign-currency transactions. The 1993 losses, artificially depressed to RM5.7 billion, nevertheless wiped out Bank Negara's remaining reserves and paid-up capital of nearly RM3.8 billion, and would have crippled the bank except for government help.[103] According to a note in the annual accounts, the RM5.7 billion represented the bank's "net deficiency", and the government had undertaken "to make good this deficiency as and when required to do so by the bank".[104]

Lim Kit Siang renewed his calls in Parliament for an investigation, but was ignored by a government with an unassailable majority. He accused Bank Negara of "dishonest and unethical accounting" to cover up losses amounting to billions of dollars in "a conspiracy of disinformation and misinformation". Rather than the almost RM16 billion in losses reported for 1992 and 1993, he said the actual figure could be as high as RM30 billion.[105] Former finance minister Tengku Razaleigh Hamzah, who had formed the opposition Semangat '46, put the two-year losses at RM31 billion.[106] Bank Negara took ten years to fully amortize the loss, finally closing the books on it in 2003.[107]

Jaffar Hussein, the Bank Negara governor, took the rap and quit, along with Nor Mohamed Yakcop, the third in command at the bank and the official in charge of foreign-exchange operations. "I take full responsibility," Jaffar told the press. "In the absence of perfect hindsight, mistakes will be made; indeed, mistakes were made." He listed "errors of judgment" in anticipating global currency gyrations and in not installing trading safeguards to limit the central bank's losses.[108]

Nagging questions remained, however. With his commitment to "profit optimization and market expertise" in managing the country's reserves,[109] Jaffar undoubtedly allowed the bank to speculate. But it was out of character for him, an accountant by training, to have permitted the undisciplined trading to persist on such a scale for so long. In nine years while he was governor, Bank Negara proved itself a strong and vigilant regulator of other financial institutions, while failing to keep its own currency traders in check.

Both Daim Zainuddin, who was finance minister from 1984 to 1991, and Anwar Ibrahim, who replaced him until 1998, said they did not know Bank Negara, which the finance ministry supervised, was speculating. This is especially puzzling in the case of Daim, a confidant of Dr. Mahathir, who not only knew about the speculation but tacitly approved it. Daim said that when he learned what was going on in 1989, he called Jaffar Hussein and cautioned him, but "he said 'not to worry; we've got everything under control'. I said OK".[110]

Years after he had been dismissed and jailed by the prime minister, Anwar said Dr. Mahathir and Daim were responsible for the currency speculation with Nor Mohamed, behind the late Jaffar Hussein's back.[111] Anwar said it was only after he took over as finance minister and travelled abroad that a Swiss friend had told him Bank Negara was one of the top three speculators and considered a rogue bank. He said he was incredulous and sought clarification from Jaffar, who was similarly in the dark. Attempts to sort it out with Dr. Mahathir had gotten nowhere, Anwar said: The prime minister played down the problem and accused the Western media of trying to undermine Malaysia.

The mystery only deepened with time. In 1998, Dr. Mahathir appointed Nor Mohamed Yakcop, who had undertaken the gambling spree and departed for the private sector four years earlier in disgrace, to the post of economic adviser to the government. When Abdullah Badawi took over as prime minister in 2003, he promoted Nor Mohamed to second finance minister.

The Perwaja perils

In one of those moments that return to haunt politicians, Dr. Mahathir visited steelmaker Perwaja Trengganu Sdn. Bhd. in 1991 and declared, "Perwaja is one of the most successful government-owned companies in the country, and it has made all of us proud."[112] He was not merely premature, but ignominiously incorrect. Perwaja was Malaysia's biggest industrial basket case then, and it went downhill afterwards.

As a showcase element in Dr. Mahathir's state-led industrialization drive in the 1980s, Perwaja looked like no more than a shining example of a politically conceived, commercially questionable and poorly executed enterprise that predictably failed. Despite lavish funding, a robust economy much of the time and protection from competing imports in the form of both tariffs and quotas, the company was never able to produce steel profitably. It suffered from chronic operating problems and a crushing debt load, including stiff foreign-exchange losses on heavy borrowing abroad. Even after the government decided to swallow RM9.9 billion in accumulated losses and privatize Perwaja in 1996, it continued to flounder.

Yet there was a more sinister side to Perwaja that guaranteed it an exalted place in the pantheon of Malaysian financial scandals. An unknown portion of the RM15 billion or more that the company consumed was ripped off in various rackets and ruses. Although both internal and external reports confirmed that the company was bled white, almost nothing was done to bring the culprits to justice and recover the funds. Eric Chia, a former chief executive officer, was arrested only after Dr. Mahathir left the prime minister's office, and he was eventually found not guilty of criminal breach of trust involving the relatively paltry sum of RM76.4 million.

The integrated steel complex in Trengganu state was meant to supply domestic needs using energy from offshore gas fields to fire the rapid development of a heavy industrial base. Built first was a RM1 billion plant to smelt imported iron ore into hot briquetted iron, also known as sponge-iron, which then would be converted into billets, the material used for manufacturing a variety of steel products. The project was undertaken in 1982 by a joint venture between state-owned Heavy Industries Corporation of Malaysia, which took 70 per cent of the equity, and a big-name Japanese group led by Nippon Steel Corporation, which held the rest. Significantly, the Japanese government and consortium members financed most of the cost with concessional yen credits.

As the yen appreciated dramatically after the Plaza Accord was signed in 1985 and interest payments mounted, Perwaja encountered production problems and racked up large debts. In 1987, the direct-reduction plant that was supposed to produce sponge-iron but never functioned properly, was closed. Frustrated by the setbacks, Dr. Mahathir stripped the Heavy Industries Corporation of its stake in Perwaja and handed it to the Ministry of Finance. Nippon Steel and its partners eventually relinquished their shareholding, leaving the company in the hands of Malaysian federal and Trengganu state government agencies. Dr. Mahathir said later that the people who were put in charge initially "had no idea of managing a steel mill at all....So I had to change" them.[113]

Dr. Mahathir turned to his friend, Eric Chia.[114] The burly, tough-talking Chia, who once headed UMW Holdings Bhd., an auto and heavy-equipment assembler, took over Perwaja in 1988 as the prime minister's personal troubleshooter with the authority to do what was necessary to turn it around. Just how much latitude he had became clear when a finance ministry representative on Perwaja's board tried to tighten internal financial procedures. Chia told him to get lost: He was reporting to Dr. Mahathir and had approval to do as he pleased.

With characteristic gusto, Chia plunged into the task of revamping Perwaja and building an integrated steel industry around it. The company poured in a further RM2 billion, building a new direct-reduction facility in Trengganu, and a rolling mill and a beam-and-section plant in Kedah. The funding included a fresh government equity injection of RM650 million. Perwaja also borrowed heavily from local and overseas banks, among them Bank Bumiputra, whose loans to the steelmaker totaled RM860 million. The Employees Provident Fund, the national pension plan that was used as a conduit for bumiputra share allocations in the tin caper, extended a loan of RM130 million, guaranteed by a group of Malaysian banks.

Chia's hustle and confidence seemed to work. He announced Perwaja's first profit in the early 1990s, winning praise from Dr. Mahathir, who visited the Trengganu site and basked in the glow of apparent success. Chia's boast that the government would recoup its investment quickly by privatizing the main operating unit, Perwaja Steel Sdn. Bhd., and listing it on the stock exchange, appeared close to reality.[115]

Then everything fell apart. Actually, it was an illusion all along, discovered after Chia resigned abruptly in August 1995 with scarcely a word of explanation for his seven years as managing director. Anwar Ibrahim, the finance minister, told the Malaysian Parliament that Perwaja lost RM376.5 million in the year ended 31 March 1995.[116] It swelled total losses since Perwaja was formed to RM2.49 billion, two and a half times the company's paid-up capital and reserves, and up from RM1 billion in accumulated losses when Chia took control. Long-term debt was threatening to obliterate the company.[117] Anwar, whose finance ministry's holding unit owned 81 per cent of Perwaja, announced that the government would honour all Perwaja's commitments and repayments. The pledge was considered vital, as a default on one loan could trigger cross-default clauses in loan agreements with other creditors, exposing Malaysia to a potential banking crisis.[118] Anwar ordered a comprehensive external audit of the company's finances and management by accounting firm Price Waterhouse & Company.

A confidential report prepared by Perwaja's new management team, under Managing Director Wan Abdul Ghani Wan Ahmad, was even more stunning. It sent shockwaves through Malaysia's political and business establishment after it was submitted to Anwar at the end of 1995 and leaked to the press. Perwaja's situation was perilous, requiring at least RM400 million in cash immediately to keep going. Unable to pay some creditors, it was seeking a moratorium on repayment of interest and principal on part of its RM5.7 billion in bank borrowings. "In the current global steel scenario, where competition is overwhelming and margins are thin, Perwaja's strategy of over-gearing is suicidal," the report said. It added, "Perwaja is over-borrowed, over-geared and insolvent."[119]

It was the report's findings of alleged mismanagement under Eric Chia, however, that were the most explosive. Among other things, it alleged that the company's finances were damaged by inaccurate accounting records and by hundreds of millions of ringgit in apparently unauthorized and one-sided contracts with Malaysian and foreign companies. It also listed instances of successful and attempted alleged misappropriation of Perwaja funds, including the overseas payment of 2.89 billion yen, over which Chia was eventually charged – and cleared. The report strongly suggested that the irregularities contributed to Perwaja's financial and operational problems. In one case, Perwaja Rolling Mill & Development Sdn. Bhd., the other main operating unit, allegedly misused the proceeds of a US$196 million loan from three Japanese companies. The loan was meant for spare parts and services for the beam-and-section mill. Instead, it was "fully utilized for other purposes", such as unrelated capital expenditures and repayment of unrelated debt. As a result, the new mill needed RM70 million to buy spare parts and had still to be commissioned.[120]

According to the report, between 1992 and 1995 Perwaja signed 25 maintenance contracts valued at RM292 million with local companies whose lack of experience undermined Perwaja's operations. The contracts were allegedly exorbitantly priced and permitted some contractors to purchase parts independently and bill Perwaja for them. One contractor bought RM103 million of spare parts of "questionable" quality for Perwaja Rolling Mill, "far beyond" what the company needed, but still Perwaja paid up. Another company was getting almost RM200,000 a month for gardening, cleaning and vehicle maintenance, showing "the degree of absurdity of such contracts that Perwaja had entered into".[121]

Some business arrangements with foreign contractors were equally dubious. One Japanese company was being paid commission of US$3 a tonne for iron-ore pellets and scrap purchased on world markets, when the international rate was about US$0.75. A Singapore commodity-trading outfit had been engaged to market Perwaja's direct-reduced products at a shipment price of US$112 a tonne, when the quoted market price was US$150.

The preliminary findings of the Price Waterhouse audit, which Anwar disclosed in Parliament in mid-1996, essentially confirmed the internal assessment. In what was the government's first detailed account of what went wrong, Anwar said, "The practices and the way business was carried out by the Perwaja group is [sic] very disappointing, and it is no surprise that Perwaja is facing a financial crisis." Price Waterhouse, he said, criticized Perwaja's lack of financial controls, its tendering procedures for supply and capital-investment contracts, and the absence of performance-evaluation controls for contractors. The company's board, consisting mostly of retired diplomats, civil servants and politicians, knew little of Perwaja's activities and was often left out of major financial, contracts and policy decisions. Spending and business plans apparently were never presented to the board.

Large contracts were awarded without any call for tenders or any competitive bidding.[122]

Among the cases mentioned by Anwar was the award of contracts valued at RM957 million to the Man Shoon Group and companies affiliated with businessmen Kok Mew Shoon and Ng Kim Lin. Price Waterhouse could not find documentation for RM103 million of the contracts. Unstated was that Kok, who controlled Man Shoon, was a long-time associate of Eric Chia. Legwork by reporters at the Registrar of Companies office unearthed the fact that the Man Shoon companies had done little business before they began to land the Perwaja contracts. For example, revenue at Man Shoon Enterprise Sdn. Bhd. jumped to RM234 million in 1994 from less than RM2 million in 1991. Another affiliate, Sinar Sdn. Bhd., did not do any business at all in 1991 and had paid-up capital of RM3. But by 1995, the company had annual revenue of more than RM80 million.[123]

With the government destined to be the big loser if Perwaja defaulted, Anwar said the immediate goal was to rescue the company. After considering offers from four companies, the government opted for a joint venture with a private investor, surprisingly selecting a small steel and property group, Maju Holdings Sdn. Bhd., ahead of much stronger candidates to lead the salvage effort. Maju's own steel business had been unprofitable, and it was hard to see how the privately held group would be able to raise the finance necessary to resuscitate Perwaja.[124] Maju, controlled by businessman Abu Sahid Mohamed, known best for driving a shocking pink Volvo stretch limousine, was given 51 per cent of the venture, Equal Concept Sdn. Bhd., and the government retained the rest. Perwaja's steel assets were transferred to Equal Concept free of debt, which was assumed by the government. In echoes of Eric Chia's boosterism, Abu Sahid told reporters the company would show "significant changes" within three years and be profitable within six years.[125]

Four years later, however, Equal Concept-managed Perwaja was mired deeper than ever in a financial swamp. The company had amassed another RM800 million in accumulated losses and was continuing to bleed red ink. Perwaja's net liabilities climbed to more than RM9.1 billion at the end of 1998 from RM6.94 billion three years earlier, while state-guaranteed borrowings rose to RM5.1 billion from RM3.19 billion. The Asian economic crisis had knocked 34 per cent off the value of the ringgit, making imported iron ore and scrap iron much more expensive and depressing demand for steel. Maju, as expected, lacked the financial means to spearhead any turnaround in Perwaja's fortunes.[126] A reporter who visited the site along the coast of northeastern Trengganu in 1999 found the sprawling complex almost deserted, its rusting chimneys smokeless in the blazing sun. To save money, the plant was working only one daily shift, overnight, but was still losing about RM35 million a month on its operations alone.[127]

Reviewing Perwaja, Dr. Mahathir described it as a "good project", but said he "couldn't help it if the management did not know how to run it".[128] He was relaxed about the losses, which he said totaled "maybe RM1 billion or RM2 billion", not "RM15 billion or anything like that....It's not something we couldn't overcome".[129]

In fact, based on incomplete public information, RM15 billion was a conservative estimate of Perwaja's losses. Similarly, Bank Bumiputra dropped at least RM10 billion. Bank Negara's foreign exchange forays drained perhaps RM23 billion from Malaysia's reserves. The cost of trying to push up the price of tin seemed paltry by comparison, maybe RM1 billion. The total, RM50 billion or so, could have easily doubled if a professional accounting had been made, factoring in all the invisibles, from unrecorded write-offs to blatant embezzlement and opportunity costs.

Notes

1   V. Kanapathy, "The Mahathir Era: A Brief Overview", in *The Mahathir Era: Contributions to National Economic Development* (Petaling Jaya: International Investment Consultants, undated), p. 21.

2   R.S. Milne and Diane K. Mauzy, *Malaysian Politics Under Mahathir* (London: Routledge, 1999), p. 162.

3   Ibid., p. 68.

4   Raphael Pura, "Malaysia Plan to Control Tin Led to Disaster", *Asian Wall Street Journal* (hereafter *AWSJ*), 22 September 1986. Extensive details of Malaysia's secret plan are drawn from this article.

5   Dr. Mahathir made his attitude to tin producers crystal clear: "On the one hand, they operate stockpiles, which is a monopolistic activity. On the other, they recently resented the rise in the price of tin, accusing Malaysia of manipulating the market. If placing tin on to the market is not manipulating prices, I don't know what is. I can't understand this double standard in which one can take action to depress the price but nobody can do anything to raise the price. This is something that I just cannot understand." "Interview/Mahathir Mohamad: Problems and Power", *Far Eastern Economic Review* (hereafter *FEER*), 30 October–5 November 1981, p. 31 <http://www.feer.com/articles/archive/1981/8111_05/P037.html> (accessed 25 January 2006).

6   Interview with Mahathir Mohamad, 31 March 2008.

7   Raphael Pura, "Tin Council Approves Price Increase, But Rise Still Short of Producer Goal", *AWSJ*, 19 October 1981.

8   Raphael Pura, "Malaysia Protests U.S. Move on Tin Sales", *AWSJ*, 24 December 1981.

9   Raphael Pura, "Malaysia Plan to Control Tin Led to Disaster".

10 Raphael Pura, "Malaysia Tin Mines Facing Hard Times as Glut Persists", *AWSJ*, 5 August 1982.

11 Neil Behrman and John Berthelsen, "Sudden Halt to Tin Trading Poses a Threat", *AWSJ*, 25 October 1985.

12 John Berthelsen, "Ipoh Hit Hard by Malaysia's Tin Slump", *AWSJ*, 3 February 1986.

13 Interview with Mahathir Mohamad, 31 March 2008.

14   Raphael Pura, "Mystery State Firm Puzzles Malaysians", *AWSJ*, 10 July 1986.
15   Raphael Pura, "Malaysia Plan to Control Tin Led to Disaster".
16   Ibid.
17   Nick Seaward, "Malaysia Tin Ramp Cost M\$660.5 million", *FEER*, 20 November 1986, p. 12 <http://www.feer.com/articles/archive/1986/8611_20/P014.html> (accessed 26 June 2006).
18   Vaudine England, "The Credibility Gap: Malaysia Faces Distrust as It Tries to Rally the ATPC", *FEER*, 13 November 1986, p. 115 <http://www.feer.com/articles/archive/1986/8611_13/P074.html> (accessed 25 January 2006).
19   Raphael Pura, "Tin Producers Hit Exports by Singapore", *AWSJ*, 16 January 1984.
20   Raphael Pura and Matt Miller, "Bank Bumiputra's Ills Begin to Shake Malaysia", *AWSJ*, 17 March 1983.
21   Interview with Mahathir Mohamad, 31 March 2008.
22   Raphael Pura, "Bank Bumiputra Change was Expected", *AWSJ*, 22 March 1982.
23   Raphael Pura, "Bank Bumiputra Faces Bad Debts from Heavy Lending in Hong Kong", *AWSJ*, 10 November 1982.
24   Raphael Pura and Matt Miller, "Bank Bumiputra's Ills Begin to Shake Malaysia".
25   Matt Miller and Raphael Pura, "Check Raises Questions on Bank Bumiputra Ties to Eda", *AWSJ*, 18 March 1983.
26   Raphael Pura, "Razaleigh Says Probe Continues into Bad Loans", *AWSJ*, 17 March 1983.
27   Raphael Pura, "Bank Bumiputra's Lending in Colony Chided by Aide", *AWSJ*, 4 April 1983.
28   Raphael Pura and Matt Miller, "For Bank Bumiputra, Some Troubling Questions Remain", *AWSJ*, 1 July 1983.
29   Raphael Pura, "Bank Bumiputra Unit's Hong Kong Loans Soar", *AWSJ*, 28 June 1983.
30   Raphael Pura and Matt Miller, "For Bank Bumiputra, Some Troubling Questions Remain".
31   Ibid.
32   Raphael Pura, "Mahathir Says Loans to Colony a 'Mistake'", *AWSJ*, 10 July 1983.
33   Raphael Pura, "Malaysia Due to Debate Loan Scandal Today", *AWSJ*, 11 March 1986. Dr. Mahathir's comments were contained in a letter appended to a white paper released by the government with the 1,075-page final report by a three-man committee of inquiry into BMF's Hong Kong lending.
34   Ibid.
35   Stephen Duthie, "Bank Bumiputra Suit May Rely on '86 Probe", *AWSJ*, 27 February 1992.
36   Stephen Duthie, "Bank Bumiputra is Target of Suit Filed in the U.S.", *AWSJ*, 26 February 1992. The suit was originally filed by Hong Kong-based Sinclair Nominees Ltd., which was later replaced by Capri Trading Corporation. Stephen Duthie, "Bank Bumiputra Faces Questions in Suit Involving Carrian Group", *AWSJ*, 29 April 1992.
37   Stephen Duthie, "Bank Bumiputra Suit May Rely on '86 Probe".
38   Stephen Duthie, "U.S. Federal Court Dismisses Suit Against Bank Bumiputra Malaysia", *AWSJ*, 24 February 1993.
39   Stephen Duthie, "Bank Bumiputra is Target of Suit Filed in the U.S.".
40   Stephen Duthie, "Bank Bumiputra Suit May Rely on '86 Probe".
41   Raphael Pura, "Malaysia Continues Investigation into Carrian Loans", *AWSJ*, 14 December 1984.

42 Raphael Pura, "Malaysian Banker's Murder Escalates Scrutiny on Loans", *AWSJ*, 25 July 1983.

43 Raphael Pura, "Prime Minister's Press Conference Sheds Light on Bumiputra Finance", *AWSJ*, 12 January 1984.

44 Later renamed the InterContinental Hong Kong.

45 Raphael Pura and Matt Miller, "Prosecutor Links Malaysian's Death to Carrian", *AWSJ*, 17 April 1984.

46 Matt Miller, Robert Magnuson and Raphael Pura, "Undisclosed Loans to Carrian Discovered", *AWSJ*, 16 September 1983.

47 K. Das, "A Gathering Storm: Kuala Lumpur is Embroiled in Mounting Debate Following the Revelation of Bank Bumiputra's Loans Debacle in Hong Kong", *FEER*, 3 November 1983, p. 90 <http://www.feer.com/articles/archive/1983/8311_03/P054.html> (accessed 25 January 2006).

48 Raphael Pura, "Bumiputra Finance Officials Resign Over Loans", *AWSJ*, 3 November 1983.

49 Raphael Pura, "Bank's Writs Reawaken Carrian Questions", *AWSJ*, 4 January 1984.

50 Raphael Pura, "Malaysia Begins Official Inquiry of Carrian Loans", *AWSJ*, 12 January 1984.

51 Raphael Pura, "Malaysia Steps Up Carrian-Loan Probe", *AWSJ*, 14 December 1984.

52 Ibid.

53 Raphael Pura and Matt Miller, "Mahathir Tilts to Theories Faulting Motives of Colony", *AWSJ*, 30 May 1984.

54 Raphael Pura, "Bumiputra Bank Panel Finishes Report", *AWSJ*, 9 December 1985.

55 John Berthelsen, "Malaysian Prime Minister Hits Bank Bumiputra Panel", *AWSJ*, 20 January 1986.

56 Raphael Pura, "Bank Bumiputra's Inquirer Wins Praise", *AWSJ*, 13 March 1985.

57 Raphael Pura, "Bank Bumiputra Reports Large Loss for Last Year", *AWSJ*, 21 September 1984.

58 Ibid.

59 Raphael Pura, "Malaysian Bank Rescue Will Be Costly", *AWSJ*, 17 September 1984.

60 Ibid.

61 John Berthelsen, "Malaysian Vote Sanctions Bank Rescue", *AWSJ*, 15 April 1985.

62 John Berthelsen, "Mahathir Draws Fire on Bumiputra Plan", *AWSJ*, 22 September 1986.

63 Raphael Pura, "Malaysia Steps Up Carrian-Loan Probe".

64 John Berthelsen, "Malaysia's Biggest Bank Explains Losses", *AWSJ*, 24 June 1985.

65 Stephen Duthie, "Bank Bumiputra Seeks New Rescue Plan", *AWSJ*, 9 October 1989.

66 Stephen Duthie, "Petronas to Help Bank Bumiputra Again", *AWSJ*, 16 October 1989.

67 Stephen Duthie, "Bank Bumiputra's Troubles Blamed on Property Loans", *AWSJ*, 18 October 1989.

68 A confidential review commissioned by UMNO showed that the party actually borrowed RM199.5 million from Bank Bumiputra and RM64.9 million from Malayan Banking for the project. "Khidmat Bersatu Sdn. Bhd.: Accountants'

Report for the Period from 1st June 1981 to 31st March 1986", Hanafiah Raslan & Mohamad, Kuala Lumpur.

69   Stephen Duthie, "Bank Bumiputra Seeks New Rescue Plan".

70   Interview with Daim Zainuddin, 18 October 2007. Daim said UMNO "subsequently" repaid the loan, but "There was a haircut on interest."

71   Stephen Duthie, "Bank Bumiputra Seeks New Rescue Plan".

72   Stephen Duthie, "Bank Bumiputra is Sold to Government", *AWSJ*, 17 January 1991.

73   Leslie Lopez, "Fattened Up by Big Profits, Malaysian Bank Fields Offers", *AWSJ*, 8 November 1996.

74   Leslie Lopez, "Bank Bumiputra May Need Bailout as Problems Mount", *AWSJ*, 2 July 1998.

75   Leslie Lopez, "Government to Take Over Bank Bumiputra Bad Loans", *AWSJ*, 9 February 1999.

76   Ibid.

77   Alan Friedman, "Soros Calls Mahathir a 'Menace' to Malaysia", *International Herald Tribune*, 22 September 1997 <http://www.iht.com/articles/1997/09/22/soros.t.php?page=1> (accessed 24 March 2009).

78   Mahathir Mohamad, *Reflections on Asia* (Subang Jaya: Pelanduk Publications (M) Sdn. Bhd., 2002), p. 87.

79   Cynthia Owens, Stephen Duthie and David Wessel, "Malaysia is Said to Slow Activity in Currencies", *AWSJ*, 5 December 1989.

80   Interview with Daim Zainuddin, 18 October 2007.

81   Cynthia Owens, Stephen Duthie and David Wessel, "Malaysia is Said to Slow Activity in Currencies".

82   Ibid.

83   Ibid.

84   Nick Seaward, "Malaysia's Controversial Finance Minister Proves an Able Economic Manager: The Daim Stewardship", *FEER*, 1 September 1988, p. 52 <http://www.feer.com/articles/archive/1988/8809_01/PO62.html> (accessed 25 January 2006).

85   Cynthia Owens, Stephen Duthie and David Wessel, "Malaysia is Said to Slow Activity in Currencies".

86   Interview with Mahathir Mohamad, 31 March 2008. Elsewhere, Dr. Mahathir said Bank Negara's currency trading room that he visited was in London: Pauline Ng, "Mahathir Denies Involvement in MAS Deal", *Business Times* (Singapore), 26 July 2006.

87   Stephen Duthie, "Bank Negara Chief Finds Gratitude Doesn't Last", *AWSJ*, 4 April 1994.

88   Mahathir Mohamad, *Reflections on Asia*, p. 140.

89   Doug Tsuruoka, "Malaysia: Testing Times", *FEER*, 17 October 1991, p. 78 <http://www.feer.com/articles/archive/1991/9110_17/P056.html> (accessed 23 January 2006).

90   Stephen Duthie, "Bank Negara Chief Finds Gratitude Doesn't Last".

91   John Berthelsen, "Malaysia Hits Hongkong Bank for Speculation", *AWSJ*, 21 August 1986.

92   Stephen Duthie, "Huge Charge at Bank Negara Startles Analysts", *AWSJ*, 2 April 1993.

93   Ibid.

94   Ibid.

95   Ibid.

96   Stephen Duthie, "Bank Negara Aims New Rules at Speculators", *AWSJ*, 24 January 1994.
97   Stephen Duthie, "Bank Negara is Criticized in Parliament", *AWSJ*, 28 April 1993.
98   Ibid.
99   Stephen Duthie, "Can Bank Negara Keep a Good Currency Down?", *AWSJ*, 18 January 1994.
100   Edmund Terence Gomez and Jomo K.S., *Malaysia's Political Economy: Politics, Patronage and Profits* (Cambridge: Cambridge University Press, 1999 edition), pp. 94–95.
101   Doug Tsuruoka, "Change in the Air: Bank Negara Moves to Sell Malaysian Airlines Stake", *FEER*, 23 December 1993, p. 52 <http://www.feer.com/articles/archive/1993/9312_23/P053.html> (accessed 23 January 2006).
102   In response to Tajudin's suit, Dr. Mahathir told reporters he agreed to the privatization after Daim approached him and said Tajudin wanted to buy the airline. Dr. Mahathir said he did not know who set the price for the shares. "I only decide on principles," he said. Pauline Ng, "Mahathir Denies Involvement in MAS Deal".
103   Stephen Duthie, "Bank Negara Posts Another Huge Loss", *AWSJ*, 1 April 1984.
104   Ibid.
105   Stephen Duthie, "Malaysia's Lim Seeks Central-Bank Probe", *AWSJ*, 13 April 1994.
106   "Tengku Razaleigh Responds to Dr Mahathir's Allegations Against Him", *Aliran Monthly*, 1994: 11, p. 36.
107   Email correspondence with Bank Negara, 22 August 2008.
108   Stephen Duthie, "Bank Negara Posts Another Huge Loss".
109   Stephen Duthie, "Bank Negara Chief Finds Gratitude Doesn't Last".
110   Interview with Daim Zainuddin, 18 October 2007.
111   Arfa'eza A. Aziz, "Forex Losses: Anwar Names Those Responsible", 19 July 2006 <http://www.malaysiakini.com/news/54097> (accessed 30 August 2008). Jaffar Hussein passed away in 1998.
112   Raphael Pura, "Malaysian Steelmaker Spouts Red Ink and Recriminations", *AWSJ*, 9 February 1996.
113   Interview with Mahathir Mohamad, 31 March 2008.
114   Eric Chia passed away in 2008.
115   Raphael Pura, "Malaysian Steelmaker Spouts Red Ink and Recriminations".
116   Raphael Pura, "Malaysia Discloses Hefty Loss at Perwaja", *AWSJ*, 19 October 1995.
117   Raphael Pura, "Malaysian Steelmaker Spouts Red Ink and Recriminations".
118   Leslie Lopez, "Malaysia Says It Will Bail Out Ailing Perwaja", *AWSJ*, 13 March 1996.
119   Leslie Lopez and Raphael Pura, "Steel Fiasco May Rattle Malaysian Government", *AWSJ*, 16 February 1996.
120   Ibid.
121   Ibid.
122   Leslie Lopez and Raphael Pura, "Malaysia Says Perwaja Faces Financial Crisis", *AWSJ*, 22 May 1996.
123   Leslie Lopez and Raphael Pura, "Steel Fiasco May Rattle Malaysian Government".
124   Leslie Lopez and Raphael Pura, "Malaysia Picks Firms for Rescue of Steelmaker", *AWSJ*, 19 June 1996.

125 Raphael Pura and Leslie Lopez, "Maju is Confident That It Can Turn Perwaja Around", *AWSJ*, 26 June 1996.
126 Leslie Lopez, "Malaysia's Perwaja Sees Losses Mount", *AWSJ*, 12 June 2000.
127 Ibid.
128 Steven Gan, "Interviewing Dr M", 23 May 2006 <http://www.malaysiakini.com/editorials/514647> (accessed 30 August 2008).
129 Interview with Mahathir Mohamad, 31 March 2008.

7
Big, Bigger, Bust

Of all the slogans associated with Dr. Mahathir's rule, the most resonant was not created by, or for, him. As far as anyone knows, *Malaysia boleh* was the tagline used in a marketing campaign for a health beverage in the 1980s. It translates as "Malaysia can", or more grammatically, "Malaysia can do it", and with Dr. Mahathir at the helm it became the battle cry of the nation. It echoed from the stadium as Malaysian sportsmen upheld national honour on the field, and it rang out in response to any news that could be construed as a Malaysian triumph.

The sentiment embodied in *Malaysia boleh* fit Dr. Mahathir's can-do personality perfectly. He wanted his fellow Malaysians, especially the Malays, to be proud, capable and confident. While Dr. Mahathir pursued initiatives meant to eliminate vestiges of colonial thinking at home and show that Malaysia was taken seriously abroad, he built for the ages on a scale that impressed Malaysians and foreigners alike. The north-south highway stretched from the tip of southern Thailand to the outskirts of northern Singapore. Connecting Penang island to the mainland was the longest bridge in Asia. An international airport for the capital matched the region's biggest and best. A proposed dam in Sarawak state would flood an area roughly the size of Singapore. Kuala Lumpur, once a nondescript urban tangle, took shape as a modern metropolis distinguished by eye-catching architecture that included iconic twin towers, the world's tallest. *Malaysia boleh!*

Driven by a nationalistic vision and paying due regard to aesthetics, Dr. Mahathir's building frenzy created a buzz among Malaysians. The doctor-politician diagnosed that they were suffering from a dire case of inferiority complex, and they responded with puffed chests to the treatment he prescribed and administered. As Dr. Mahathir explained, his monumental projects were "good for the ego" of a developing country. "To be noticed when you are small, sometimes you have to stand on a box," he said.[1] Ignoring critics, Dr. Mahathir kept on building in ever more spectacular style: a Formula One racing circuit, a government-guided version of California's

Silicon Valley and a brand new administrative capital for the future Malaysia.

After the Malaysian government made it into *Guinness World Records* with the world's highest flagpole, individual Malaysians went scrambling up Mount Everest, crossed the Antarctic and sailed the oceans in search of more records. If they did not qualify for the real thing, they found recognition in the *Malaysia Book of Records*, a home-grown version that let them create their own categories of accomplishments.

Dr. Mahathir championed the record making and breaking, sometimes appearing at events to participate, or commend the performers, reinforcing the belief that they were doing their bit to turn Malaysia into a mighty country. He embraced corporate executives who delivered, such as Ting Pek Khiing, a brash entrepreneur from Sarawak who made his fortune in construction and timber. Ting left an enduring impression on Dr. Mahathir by hurriedly building resort facilities on the island of Langkawi in time for Malaysia's first international air show in 1991.[2] Dr. Mahathir later boasted that "we" designed, built and equipped a 170-room, five-star hotel on Langkawi in four months, while deciding half way through to make up for a projected shortfall in accommodation by adding a 300-room, three-star hotel; it was finished in 53 days. Both were records and deserved a place in *Guinness*, he declared.[3]

At its best, the *Malaysia boleh* fervour engendered patriotism and encouraged Malays, Chinese, Indians and other minorities to forget their ethnic differences and take pride in being Malaysian. While it remained a noble cause for some, however, it degenerated into farce for others. As political opponents attacked Dr. Mahathir's "mega-projects" for their extravagance, his Malaysia set the unofficial world record for setting records, many of them banal, bizarre or plain wacky. They included the largest gathering of old people at a circus, the most number of heads shampooed in one day at a shopping mall and the highest backward climb up a staircase.

In conjunction with a World Youth Games in Moscow organized by the International Olympic Committee in 1998, Malaysia dispatched a 16-member team to participate in a mass jump on the North Pole.[4] The think-big wrinkle: With the help of the Russian military, the Malaysians floated a Proton Wira down to the icy waste, prompting some of their countrymen to "mock the inanity" of seeking to have their national car become the first Asian auto to arrive in the Arctic by parachute.[5]

Five Malaysian skydivers took aim at the South Pole in a trumpeted "Millennium Jump" at the turn of the century, only to miss their target by a thousand kilometres or so. They landed at Patriot Hills in the Chilean-claimed western Antarctic, disappointing Malaysia's youth and sports ministry, which had advanced the organizers RM780,000 to help make the polar bid. Stoically, Ong Tee Kiat, a deputy minister, pointed out that a jump had occurred and the team "should be praised for accomplishing the feat under difficult circumstances".[6]

Detractors derided "Bolehland" and a local satirical troupe, Instant Café Theatre, staged a spoof "Bolehwood" awards ceremony.[7] In another production, Instant Café offered a politician vying for the post of "deputy minister of misinformation" declaiming, "Yes, we know that we do not have a very good human rights record. That is why we are trying to have all the other records...".[8]

Even when he stuck to basic infrastructure, Dr. Mahathir courted controversy with the sheer dimensions and sweep of his plans. "I think very far ahead, not ten years, twenty years, [but] one hundred years", he said.[9] The 966-kilometre north-south highway system, which took 13 years to complete, cut travel time from one end of peninsular Malaysia to the other by two-thirds. Begun by the government, the project became contentious when a company controlled by Dr. Mahathir's UMNO was given a RM3.42 billion contract to complete the network, which was then privatized under a consortium led by the same company, with the right to operate it and collect tolls.

If anyone had any doubts, the replacement Kuala Lumpur International Airport provided an insight into the extent of Dr. Mahathir's ambitions. While some argued that the existing Subang airport could be expanded, he chose a remote site 70 kilometres from the capital, on which Kisho Kurokawa, the noted Japanese architect, designed an airport to handle eventually up to 100 million passengers a year. An entire section of rain forest was transplanted from the jungle, roots and all, to decorate the satellite building at which aircraft docked. At 130 metres, the control tower was then the world's tallest. The RM9 billion airport signalled that Malaysia aspired to compete with Singapore, Bangkok and Hong Kong as a regional transportation and logistics hub.

When it came to the Penang bridge, Dr. Mahathir solidified his reputation by making it a reality. Others had talked about it, studied the feasibility and promised to do something for a decade or more, especially at election time. Less than a week after becoming premier, Dr. Mahathir disclosed that a "non-Caucasian" company – South Korean, it transpired – had been chosen to do the bulk of the work.[10] Costing RM740 million, the toll bridge was the final link in an east-west highway network, and at 13.5 kilometres – 8.4 kilometres of it over water – it was the third-longest bridge in the world.[11] Driving a Proton Saga, the new national car, over the Penang bridge to celebrate its completion in 1985, Dr. Mahathir "brought together two potent symbols of modernity, Malaysian-style".[12]

With an audacious initiative to include Malaysia in Formula One, the world's most expensive sport, Dr. Mahathir successfully grabbed international attention. His government sponsored the construction of a RM270 million racetrack, which was sited at Sepang near the new airport.

Dr. Mahathir envisioned a glamorous grand prix, with a worldwide television audience of tens of millions and a loyal following among travelling spectators, as a magnetic tourist attraction. In addition, he saw it as a platform for the promotion of Malaysia's event-management industry and a showcase for the Proton.[13]

A car-racing fan, Dr. Mahathir flew to Europe to lobby Bernie Ecclestone's Formula One Administration personally to ensure that the prestigious race was held in Malaysia by 1999. Ecclestone said Dr. Mahathir's enthusiasm "more than convinced" the organizers.[14] The Petronas Malaysian Grand Prix took its place in the Formula One series, along with traditional venues in Britain, France, Germany, Italy, the United States and Monaco.

Just how far Dr. Mahathir was ahead of the game became clear much later. Only Australia and Japan in the Asian region were on the limited-race circuit when he seized the opportunity. China subsequently signed up Shanghai, Singapore secured the first night race in 2008 and India reached agreement to join in 2010, leaving Russia and others clamouring to get in. With aspirations to be a global city in the twenty-first century, Singapore regretted that it did not seek admission to the exclusive Formula One club much earlier. The republic's founding father, Lee Kuan Yew, publicly chastised himself for having rejected the idea in the 1990s, which he called a "stupid decision".[15]

The massive Bakun dam that Dr. Mahathir approved in Sarawak in 1993, after 14 years of studies and delays, incorporated nearly everything about his leadership that supporters admired and detractors despised. To generate 2,400 megawatts of electricity, it was planned to block the upper reaches of the Rejang River deep in Sarawak's interior to create a giant island-studded lake. About 80,000 hectares of tropical forest were to be cleared and 10,000 rural dwellers relocated. At least two 670-kilometre submarine transmission lines, the world's longest, would carry power across the South China Sea to the national grid in peninsular Malaysia.

To tame the Borneo jungle, Dr. Mahathir turned to Ting Pek Khiing, the tycoon who enjoyed close and cordial relations with the premier after establishing his credentials on Langkawi. Ting's flagship company, Ekran Bhd., assumed the lead role in the RM15 billion privatized venture, which was the biggest Malaysia had attempted, the costliest infrastructure undertaking in Southeast Asia and one of the world's largest engineering works. Dr. Mahathir gave the nod to Ekran in early 1994 after Ting and Sarawak's powerful chief minister, Abdul Taib Mahmud, privately negotiated a deal in just a few weeks.[16] There was no competitive bidding. Ekran, which lacked relevant experience, apparently did not even submit a proper proposal to the state government before it got the contract, and Ting produced his environmental impact study almost six months after the award.[17] "It's a project whose time has come," declared Dr. Mahathir.[18]

Alas, not only the timing was off. While Ting bragged about enhancing his reputation for fast work – "maybe we can do this in six or seven years", instead of the ten-year timetable suggested in studies – he encountered obstacles at every stage.[19] Ekran was dogged by green groups, opposition political parties, the financial community and Sarawak residents due to be displaced. They argued that the rock-filled dam, the world's highest, would be environmentally risky and commercially questionable. Ting multiplied the stakes by talking of plans to build a 14,000-hectare industrial park, Asia's largest, in Sarawak at an estimated cost of RM20 billion, to house makers of equipment for the hydroelectric project.

Although the Ekran-led main operating company projected income of RM38.6 billion from its 30-year concession, including a profit of RM1.47 billion in the first full year of power production, the market remained skeptical.[20] After announcing he had secured a crucial agreement to sell 70 per cent of the output to Tenaga Nasional Bhd., the national power company, Ting had to endure the embarrassment of further negotiations that reduced the price.[21] Ekran and its partners clashed. Swiss-Swedish engineering powerhouse Asea Brown Boveri Ltd., chosen by the Malaysian government to head the consortium to build the dam, objected to RM9 billion of contracts being given without tender to four companies controlled by Ting.[22] He sacked ABB. Two influential Malaysian minority shareholders in the operating company resisted Ekran's demand for management fees of more than RM1 billion as the main promoter of the project.[23] After almost three years of bickering, Ting suffered a stroke which, though mild, was extremely bad news for a man who ran his empire almost single-handedly.

As the Asian economic crisis struck Malaysia, the government in September 1997 decided to suspend work on several big-ticket items, Bakun among them. Because Ting wanted to proceed, the government cancelled Ekran's contract, agreed to pay compensation for preliminary work and took control of what was declared to be a "national" project. State funds were used to finish some of the work, including tunnels to divert the river.

One gigantic project that escaped the freeze was the RM20.1 billion administrative capital known as Putrajaya, along with its associated Multimedia Super Corridor. Located 30 kilometers south of Kuala Lumpur, about half way to the showpiece airport, Putrajaya was designed to be the nation's centre of government. Almost all the federal ministries, courts and agencies would migrate there – though not the Parliament – along with about 76,000 state employees and an anticipated population of 250,000. Reflecting his enthusiasm for Putrajaya, set on 4,581 hectares that once supported rubber and oil palm plantations, Dr. Mahathir made it a federal territory and home to the prime minister's office and official residence. He vowed to be the first to relocate.

Named after Malaysia's first prime minister, Tunku Abdul Rahman Putra, Putrajaya appeared to have been put on the slow track when the government announced general spending cuts with the onset of the crisis. Only the initial stage, begun two years earlier, would be implemented, while the others would be staggered over a "very long period", the government said.[24] But out of public view, an army of construction workers toiled at a frenetic pace on that RM5 billion first phase. Although extensive, the work avoided scrutiny because it was financed largely by the internal resources of state-owned oil and gas company Petronas, the city's main developer, and because details were deliberately withheld from the media.[25]

The opposition Parti Islam Se-Malaysia created a sensation in late 1998 by publishing a rare photo of the prime minister's partially completed residence, Seri Perdana, on the front page of its newspaper. It labelled the sprawling complex "Mahathir's *mahligai*", an otherworldly, or celestial, palace. Hours before he was arrested in 1998, sacked deputy prime minister Anwar Ibrahim fanned gossip about lavish spending on the palatial abode. He told an international television audience that Dr. Mahathir wanted "to live in a world of fantasy", and that the house would cost taxpayers RM200 million, not RM17 million as Parliament had been informed.[26] From his cell in Sungai Buloh jail, Anwar later wrote that he knew how the official figure had been manipulated. "The building will be the biggest and most sophisticated palace in the country," he said. "It is designed personally by Dr. Mahathir. Everything about it is French."[27]

Putrajaya's promoters opened the city to reporters for the first time in 1999, just before Dr. Mahathir and his staff were due to move in. Government officials leading the tour were happy to show off general activity – roaring dump trucks and bulldozers, cranes hoisting steel girders, a team of engineers putting the finishing touches on a dusky-pink mosque with a 116-metre minaret. But they seemed embarrassed to discuss the prime minister's new home, on a bluff across a huge man-made lake from his green-domed office complex. One official was asked if the press could visit the residence. "You mean that building?" he replied, gesturing across the water. "That's just a mirage."[28]

Actually, it was the cost of Seri Perdana, not the bricks and mortar, that proved illusory. As speculation and criticism mounted in 1998, a deputy minister in the Prime Minister's Department told Parliament that the residence was divided into "public amenities" and "private quarters", and the private areas would cost "only" RM17 million. In response to Anwar's revelations, the deputy minister adjusted the cost of the private quarters to RM17.5 million and disclosed that the other facilities, such as a banquet hall and state rooms for visiting dignitaries, would amount to RM57.5 million.[29] In 1999, the deputy minister added an extra RM45 million to the bill – for "software", he told Parliament.[30] That would raise the overall cost to about RM120 million, but in 2003 an opposition legislator received a written reply from the

Prime Minister's Department with a fresh tally. The final cost: RM201 million, exceeding Anwar's shocking figure.[31]

Incredibly, Dr. Mahathir argued that he designed Seri Perdana so big specifically to accommodate Anwar, who has a large family. Had he resigned in 1998 and Anwar taken over as planned, Dr. Mahathir would not have moved to Putrajaya at all, he said. "And the house for the prime minister, because the incoming prime minister, I thought, was going to have six children, so I built six [bed]rooms, not for me. This is for the future. We would like to have, for the residents there, like a White House....Not, whenever you change prime minister, you change residence because it's not big enough".[32]

In fact, it was Dr. Mahathir who made a habit of changing official homes, Seri Perdana being the second prime ministerial residence he built for himself. His immediate predecessors, Razak Hussein and Hussein Onn, occupied what was supposed to be the permanent quarters for Malaysian premiers, Sri Taman in Kuala Lumpur's Lake Gardens. Dr. Mahathir turned Sri Taman into a memorial for Razak and spent RM11 million, not counting the cost of land, to build the first Sri Perdana in Kuala Lumpur, completed in 1983.[33] It became Galeria Sri Perdana, a memorial for Dr. Mahathir, when he relocated to Putrajaya in 1999.[34]

As an Asian Silicon Valley, the RM8 billion Multimedia Super Corridor was envisaged by Dr. Mahathir as an information nucleus not only for Malaysia but for the entire region. Launched in 1996, it consisted of a zone 50 kilometres by 15 kilometres linking Kuala Lumpur with Putrajaya and the airport. Wired with advanced telecommunications, it served as an industrial park to attract high-tech industries to Malaysia. Dr. Mahathir recruited a high-profile panel, consisting of a who's who among global information technology players, led by Microsoft's Bill Gates, to advise him on the strategic direction of the venture. But it did not take off fully, partly because the government failed to gear Malaysia's universities to produce specialist graduates required by a knowledge economy.[35] It also lacked the equivalent of a Stanford University, a dynamic research centre where imaginative ideas found urgent commercial solutions to technical problems.[36] The Multimedia Super Corridor generated just US$2 billion in economic activity in a decade, missing the tech outsourcing boom that went mainly to India.[37]

Even as Dr. Mahathir prepared to move out of Kuala Lumpur, he sought to upgrade it into a more cosmopolitan commercial capital befitting the Malaysia of his dreams. Founded as a bedraggled tin-mining town in 1857, Kuala Lumpur was still largely an urban hodgepodge more than a century later. Officially made the capital of Selangor state in 1880, replacing the port of Klang, it became the capital of Malaya/Malaysia, but was granted city status only in 1972 and declared a federal territory two years later. By separating Kuala Lumpur from surrounding Selangor, the government ensured that the capital could not be controlled by an opposition party, at the same time weakening Chinese influence in the state. The first time Dr. Mahathir caught sight of Kuala Lumpur, he thought it very bleak. "I said, 'why don't you plant trees?' I kept on saying this but it never happened...until you have the authority to say, 'Plant!'"[38]

Armed with prime ministerial authority, Dr. Mahathir did a great deal to create a greener capital immediately after he came to power in 1981. In 1997, he ordered Malaysians to start planting seriously, with the target of adding three million trees throughout the country by 2000 – Kuala Lumpur's quota was 220,000 – and 20 million by 2020. An interim goal was to create a garden nation by 2005. The campaign got a boost on 15 October 2000, World Habitat Day, when Dr. Mahathir joined many other Malaysians in planting 110,461 trees in just one minute. Sure enough, it was sufficient to claim a world record, dwarfing the previous best effort, 24,199 trees planted in a week, set in Sao Paolo, Brazil, in 1976.

Acting as the de facto lord mayor, Dr. Mahathir took a personal interest in Kuala Lumpur's transformation, nothing being too small to overlook. According to Chandran Jeshurun, an academic who researched a book on the capital,[39] Dr. Mahathir paid close attention to heritage conservation and directly contributed to the preservation of some treasures. One was an old railway station with Moorish-style minarets and domes. It was renovated and extended, "with a very sensitive touch for historical and architectural detail".[40]

In 1984, Dr. Mahathir offended the local construction industry by insisting that the contract for the Dayabumi complex, a showcase commercial building and then the city's tallest, go to two Japanese companies that were outbid by a Malaysian one. He was less interested in cutting costs than ensuring the realization of the Japanese design, which was visually stunning. "It was a remarkable combination of Islamic motifs and steel structure, and it marked a turning point in Kuala Lumpur's modern heritage," wrote Chandran Jeshurun.[41]

There followed a succession of noteworthy high-rises, including the Putra World Trade Centre, which housed UMNO's headquarters, the "curvaceous" head office of the Pilgrims Fund Board, and next to it the "uniquely Malaysian design" of the National Equity Corporation headquarters.[42] The Kuala Lumpur Tower, used for communications and containing a revolving restaurant, featured an antenna that soared 421 metres into the tropical sky. On the strength of visits to "nearly every country in the world", Dr. Mahathir expressed the view that it was the most beautiful tower ever built.[43]

They were heady days for Malaysia's leading architects, a rare chance to let their imaginations soar. One, Ken Yeang, observed that few places had ever seen building of such magnitude and scale. "In the last ten years we have built more, in terms of square footage, than in the last one hundred years...," he said.[44]

The crowning glory was the 88-storey Petronas Twin Towers, designed by the late Cesar Pelli, the celebrated Argentinian-born American who created New York's World Financial Centre and Canary Wharf in London. With a steel and glass façade evoking traditional Islamic art and architecture – the floor pattern was based on an eight-point star, reduced from 12 points at Dr. Mahathir's suggestion – the building was engineered to the most demanding international standards.[45] The elegantly proportioned, identical slender towers rose in the heart of the capital, linked by a double-decker skybridge at the forty-first and forty-second floors. They were anchored in a six-level, crescent-shaped shopping mall, part of a fully-integrated town called the Kuala Lumpur City Centre, with hotels, condominiums and a public park.

Pelli did not set out to collect the "world's tallest" tag with the twin towers, until Dr. Mahathir casually raised it with him over tea one afternoon in 1994.[46] It would take an additional 16 metres to match the 443-metre Sears Tower in Chicago. With construction well underway, Pelli frantically re-did the mathematical calculations and deemed it doable, not by increasing the number of floors, but by raising the height of the "pinnacles".[47] From tip to toe, the completed building was almost 452 metres, and it gave Malaysia the excuse to claim another world record – for the continuous pouring of concrete.[48]

Although the twin towers ran into a definitional dispute over being the tallest building, they were undoubtedly the highest twin towers, and they became identified with Kuala Lumpur as much as the Opera House is with Sydney or the Eiffel Tower with Paris. Sean Connery and Catherine Zeta-Jones swung beneath the skybridge in the Hollywood movie *Entrapment*. Certainly no regional city could boast such a landmark, most definitely not serious and successful Singapore, which preferred safe and sensible structures. "We lack a daring, pioneering spirit," lamented a Singaporean architect as his government turned down a phantasmagorical wave-like design for an integrated resort and casino proposed by acclaimed Canadian-American architect Frank Gehry.[49] Dr. Mahathir backed the twin towers precisely to convey that spirit. "Indeed, they stand out prominently against the skyline of Kuala Lumpur to symbolize courage, ingenuity, initiative and determination, energy, confidence, optimism, advancement and zest of a nation that will bring worldwide recognition and respect to all Malaysians," he said at the opening. It was 31 August 1999, the last national day of the century, the last of the millennium.

As if to pre-empt the inevitable comments about an edifice complex, Dr. Mahathir conspicuously forbid his name to be attached to any physical feature, man-made or natural. The only trace while he held office was his old MAHA Clinic in Alor Star, which retained the name long after he had abandoned medical practice permanently. "It would be an act of arrogance if I were to allow buildings and so on to be named after me," he said on more than one occasion.[50] Asked bluntly by the foreign press if "all the dams, tall buildings and new cities" appearing in Malaysia were "merely monuments to Mahathir," he replied, "I really don't need any monuments. These are necessities, and they are necessities we can afford."[51]

Dr. Mahathir would have been more persuasive if he had not encouraged, or at least permitted, the growth of a personality cult.[52] In 2001, his political secretary urged institutions of higher learning to offer a course on the thoughts of the prime minister, a comment considered so noteworthy it was disseminated by Bernama, the national news agency.[53] Other supporters made at least two attempts to obtain a Nobel Prize for him. At the instigation of Minister of Science, Technology and Environment Law Hing Dieng, a fairly high-powered committee in 1999 prepared a formal nomination document that was submitted to the Nobel Foundation in Oslo. And in 2006, Dr. Mahathir's son Mukhriz called a meeting of prominent Malaysians with the idea of building a case for his father to be awarded the Nobel Peace Prize.[54] While nothing came of these efforts, other initiatives also sought to accord Dr. Mahathir exceptional, personal status. In 1999, a CD entitled "CEO Malaysia Inc.", was made of his major speeches, he featured in a 14-part television dramatization of his life, had an UMNO seminar devoted to "The Thoughts of Dr. Mahathir", and had an album of ten patriotic songs released in his honour. He also accepted a Rotary award as Man of the Millennium.[55]

While Dr. Mahathir could justify much of the infrastructure to accelerate economic development, he was less than convincing when claiming as essential the colossal investment in skyscrapers and some of the other creations. As his other comments testified, the buildings were supposed to be more than utilitarian. They were meant to impress, to take the breath away and engender awe. Opponents who carped that the money should have been spent instead on education, health, welfare, poverty reduction, public housing, security or even the environment had a point, but they ignored Dr. Mahathir's point, which was something else entirely. As for the cost, Malaysia could afford his grandiose schemes as long as the economy steamed along, and while the country kept pumping oil and gas.

At its peak, the surge of new-found confidence was so pervasive that Chandran Jeshurun, the academic researcher, concluded that *Malaysia boleh* should be translated as "anything you can do I can do better".[56] Amid signs of hubris, Dr. Mahathir increased the tempo of *Negaraku*, the national anthem, to give it a more martial beat – in keeping with lofty economic goals, as an official put it. He also had the nation's coat of arms touched up to make its two tigers look more rampant.

Until the economic crisis forced a halt, developers seemed bent on outdoing each other with the expense and expanse of their projects. When the government temporarily suspended the privatization programme in

September 1997, proposals totalling about RM90 billion were awaiting approval.[57] It was not just the staggering cost, but the type of venture being contemplated that thrilled or appalled Malaysians, depending on their political and social outlook. Dr. Mahathir had already endorsed Linear City, the world's longest building, a ten-storey, two-kilometre, tunnel-like structure to be built for RM10 billion along and above a river flowing through central Kuala Lumpur. Another plan, costing RM30 billion, involved building a string of artificial islands along the coast of Kedah, on which would be developed a RM2.5 billion airport for Penang and a seaport, as well as industrial, commercial and residential properties. Also proposed was a "mountain highway" to open the rugged interior of peninsular Malaysia to tourism by linking a series of jungled, upland resort areas stretching from Genting Highlands, near Kuala Lumpur, north to Cameron Highlands.

As economic conditions eased, Dr. Mahathir quietly revived some of his mega-projects, a term he detested, which nevertheless had become part of Malaysia's political lexicon due almost entirely to his efforts. In 2000, the government said it was going ahead with a scaled-down version of Bakun dam: The generating capacity was maintained, but the plan to transmit power by underwater cable was scrapped. Syed Mokhtar Albukhary, who had emerged in two years as one of the country's most influential businessmen, took a controlling stake in the again-privatized venture. Construction of a monorail through downtown Kuala Lumpur, part of the original Linear City proposal, also proceeded.

But in traumatized, post-crisis Malaysia, where the landscape was strewn with corporate wreckage and deep resentment over government bail-outs, big was no longer so beautiful. For example, public protests thwarted government plans to build a RM1.5 billion incinerator – yes, the biggest of its kind in the world, capable of burning 1,200 tonnes of rubbish a day – at two locations on the outskirts of the capital. When the popular demand was for good governance, transparency and an end to cronyism, yet more record-setting invoked wry humour if not outright cynicism. Typically, one local analyst noted that the Malaysian Parliament, with 93 of its 219 members appointed as ministers, deputy ministers and parliamentary secretaries, had perhaps the world's largest executive, while Malaysia's 33 ministers gave the country a bigger cabinet than Britain, India or Australia. "Maybe this is what we call *Malaysia boleh*," he wrote.[58]

From prison, Anwar Ibrahim helped spread the feeling that jingoistic sloganeering had run its course, and that Dr. Mahathir was more concerned with establishing a legacy than tending the national interest. Although it was self-serving for Anwar to discredit Dr. Mahathir, he had a large and loyal following among Malaysians, especially the young, and they resented his dismissal. His eviction from the centre of Dr. Mahathir's inner circle permitted him a certain credibility to describe his long-time mentor's alleged descent into delusional glory:

> Driven by a self-induced frenzy to pursue his megalomaniacal fantasies, he became increasingly divorced from the real world. He could not differentiate the wants and needs of the people from his own egotistical desires. In the last few years, he has become increasingly isolated as he got impatient to get things done so that they would serve as monuments to his majestic rule. Surrounded by sycophantic courtiers, he failed to realize that his ideas were getting obsolete and irrelevant. He has delusions of grandeur and cannot but associate his rule with mega-projects and superlatives – the longest bridge, the tallest building, the grandest airport, the most awesome dam....[59]

Abdullah Badawi was aware of the changing mood on the ground well before he moved into Seri Perdana. It was in line with his personal philosophy, which was always restrained. "I'm not into big projects," he told a meeting of senior government officials early in 2003.[60] Abdullah cancelled, postponed or downgraded several of Dr. Mahathir's huge commitments, incurring his unyielding enmity. Although Abdullah accepted an invitation in 2006 to launch the tenth edition of the *Malaysia Book of Records*, the private-sector bible of the think-big movement, he sounded a different tune. While "it is admirable to achieve the biggest, the tallest and the largest of everything, it may not always be meaningful or beneficial" to Malaysia's becoming a fully developed country, Abdullah said. "Malaysians should focus on quality, world-class achievements which will add value to our society, enrich our culture, strengthen our moral fibre and provide strong role models for young Malaysians." He called for a nation of *cemerlang, gemilang dan terbilang* – excellence, glory and determination.[61] Officially, *Malaysia boleh* was history.

Notes

1   S. Jayasankaran, "The New Way: Think Small", *Far Eastern Economic Review* (hereafter *FEER*), 6 November, 2003, p. 15.

2   Raphael Pura, "Ekran is Tapped to Construct Malaysian Dam", *Asian Wall Street Journal* (hereafter *AWSJ*), 31 January 1994.

3   Mahathir Mohamad, "Views and Thoughts of Dr. Mahathir Mohamad, the Prime Minister of Malaysia", in Ahmad Sarji Abdul Hamid, ed., *Malaysia's Vision 2020: Understanding the Concept, Implications & Challenges*, (Petaling Jaya: Pelanduk Publications (M) Sdn. Bhd., 1997), p. 3.

4   "International Parachute Expedition to the North Pole 1998" <http://www.skypole.ru/north98/north98_e.htm> (accessed 6 April 2009).

5   Thor Kah Hoong, "For One Brief Moment...", *Malay Mail*, 19 August 2008 <http://www.mmail.com.my/For_one_brief_moment_-d–d–d–.aspx> (accessed 5 April 2009).

6   S. Jayasankaran and Simon Elegant, "Down to Earth", *FEER*, 23 March 2000 <http://www.feer.com/articles/2000/0003_23/p19.html> (accessed 23 January 2006).

7   Jonathan Kent, "Malaysia's Record-Breaking Obsession", in *BBC News*, 24 February 2003 <http://news.bbc.co.uk/go/pr/fr/-/1/hi/world/asia-pacific/2793415.stm> (accessed 22 January 2007).

8   Anil Netto, "Laughing Out of Control", in *Aliran Monthly*, 2003: 6, p. 22.

9   Hannah Beech, "Not the Retiring Type", *Time*, 29 October 2006 <http://www.time.com/time/magazine/article/0,9171,1552090,00.html> (accessed 4 September 2008).

.0   K. Das, "The Great Divide", *FEER*, 27 November 1981, p. 53.

.1   "Penang: The Golden Umbilicus 8.4 Miles Over the Sea", *FEER*, 28 August 1981, p. 64.

.2   Halinah Todd, "The Proton Saga Saga", *New Internationalist*, No. 195 (May 1989), pp. 14–15.

.3   Leslie Lopez, "Malaysian Grand Prix Stalls Out as Fans Pass Up Race Tickets", *AWSJ*, 14 March 2001.

.4   V.G. Kulkarni, S. Jayasankaran and Murray Hiebert, "Dr. Feelgood", *FEER*, 24 October 1996, p. 18.

.5   Peh Shing Huei, "Why Hosting F1 is a Winning Formula for Singapore", *Straits Times*, 2 February 2007.

.6   Raphael Pura, "Ekran is Tapped to Construct Malaysian Dam".

.7   Edmund Terence Gomez and Jomo K.S., *Malaysia's Political Economy: Politics, Patronage and Profits* (Cambridge: Cambridge University Press, 1999 edition), pp. 110–111.

.8   Raphael Pura, "Ekran is Tapped to Construct Malaysian Dam".

.9   Ibid.

.0   Chen May Yee and Raphael Pura, "BHC Projects Flow of Earnings from Dam Deal", *AWSJ*, 14 May 1997.

.1   Leslie Lopez, "Malaysian Dam Project Clears Bid-Award, Power-Price Barriers", *AWSJ*, 14 June 1996.

.2   Leslie Lopez, "Clash May Trim Ekran's Profits on Bakun Dam", *AWSJ*, 18 April 1997.

.3   Leslie Lopez, "Shareholder Row Delays Malaysian Dam", *AWSJ*, 30 September 1996.

.4   Leslie Lopez and Raphael Pura, "Anwar to Defer Large Projects, Cut Spending", *AWSJ*, 11 September 1997.

.5   Leslie Lopez, "Building the Future: New City isn't a Capital Idea, Malaysian Critics Complain", *AWSJ*, 10 June 1999.

.6   Liew Chin Tong, "Seri Perdana's Cost: 'Now, What Shall We Tell 'em?'", 22 November, 2005 <http://www.malaysiakini.com/opinions/43423> (accessed 28 August 2008).

.7   Anwar Ibrahim, "From the Halls of Power to the Labyrinth of Incarceration", letter from Sungai Buloh Prison, 3 November 1998, p. 5.

.8   Leslie Lopez, "Building the Future: New City isn't a Capital Idea, Malaysian Critics Complain".

.9   Ibid.

.0   Liew Chin Tong, "Seri Perdana's Cost: 'Now, What Shall We Tell 'em?'".

.1   Ibid.

.2   "Full Version", Malaysiakini interview <http://www.asiafinest.com/forum/lofiversion/index.php/t76432.html> (accessed 6 April 2009).

.3   Both Sri Taman and Sri Perdana in Kuala Lumpur used the old spelling for "sri", while Seri Perdana in Putrajaya was spelled the new way.

.4   Liew Chin Tong, "Putrajaya", 28 May 2006 <http://liewchintong.blogspot.com/2006/05/putrajaya.html> (accessed 6 April 2009). Liew won the Bukit Bendera parliamentary constituency for the Democratic Action Party in the 2008 general election.

35 Marika Vicziany and Marlia Puteh, "Vision 2020, the Multimedia Supercorrido and Malaysian Universities", proceedings of 15th Biennial Conference of the Asian Studies Association of Australia, Canberra, 29 June–2 July 2004.

36 Ibid.

37 Eric Ellis, "Protonomics", *Fortune*, 10 July 2006, p. 20.

38 R.S. Milne and Diane K. Mauzy, *Malaysian Politics Under Mahathir* (London Routledge, 1999), p. 174.

39 Chandran Jeshurun, *Kuala Lumpur: Corporate Capital, Cultural Cornucopia* (Kuala Lumpur: Arus Intelek Sdn. Bhd., 2004).

40 Chandran Jeshurun, "Kuala Lumpur: The City that Mahathir Built", in Bridge Welsh, ed., *Reflections: The Mahathir Years* (Washington: Southeast Asia Studie Program, The Paul H. Nitze School of Advanced International Studies, John Hopkins University, 2004), p. 392.

41 Ibid., p. 392.

42 Ibid., p. 392.

43 R.S. Milne and Diane K. Mauzy, *Malaysian Politics Under Mahathir*, p. 67.

44 Chandran Jeshurun, "Kuala Lumpur: The City that Mahathir Built", p. 396.

45 Ibid., p. 393.

46 "Dare to Dream", excerpted from www.thestar.com.my <http://www.kiat.net towers/dream.html> (accessed 2 February 2007).

47 Ibid.

48 R.S. Milne and Diane K. Mauzy, *Malaysian Politics Under Mahathir*, p. 67.

49 Ong Soh Chin, "Dare We Build a True Icon?", *Straits Times*, 31 October 2006.

50 Zainuddin Maidin, *The Other Side of Mahathir* (Kuala Lumpur: Utusan Publication & Distributors Sdn. Bhd., 1994), p. 279.

51 Donald Morrison, Sandra Burton and John Colmey, "Mahathir on Race, the West and His Successor", *Time Asia*, 9 December 1996, p. 31.

52 In retirement, Dr. Mahathir boasted, "Today there is nothing named after me except an orchid flower", adding, "I never liked personality cults." Dr. Mahathir Mohamad, "Fitnah", 15 February 2009 <http://chedet.co.cc/chedetblog/2009/02 fitnah.html> (accessed 20 March 2009).

53 Patricia Martinez, "Mahathir, Islam, and the New Malay Dilemma", in Ho Kha Leong and James Chin, eds, *Mahathir's Administration: Performance and Crisis i Governance* (Singapore: Times Media Pte. Ltd., 2001), p. 216.

54 Email correspondence with a Malaysian familiar with both Nobel Prize initiatives 9–10 December 2008.

55 John Funston, "Malaysia's Tenth Elections: Status Quo, *Reformasi* or Islamization?" *Contemporary Southeast Asia* 22, no. 1 (April 2000): 54.

56 Chandran Jeshurun, "Kuala Lumpur: The City that Mahathir Built", p. 393.

57 Leslie Lopez and Raphael Pura, "Anwar to Defer Large Projects, Cut Spending".

58 Liew Chin Tong, "Malaysia's XXL-size cabinet", 27 August 2004 <http://www malaysiakini.com/opinions/43423> (accessed 28 August 2008).

59 Anwar Ibrahim, "From the Halls of Power to the Labyrinth of Incarceration", p. 5.

60 S. Jayasankaran, "The New Way: Think Small".

61 Abdullah Ahmad Badawi, speech, "Malaysia Book of Records Awards Night" 6 June 2006 <http://www.pmo.gov.my > (accessed 22 January 2007).

8
An Uncrowned King

Before Dr. Mahathir became prime minister and consolidated his power, Malaysia's royal families could get away with murder. Constitutionally, the sultans, or rulers of the nine Malay states, were above the law and could not be subjected to any legal proceedings. Ignoring convention, they sometimes played politics, leveraged their positions for financial gain and indulged in fairytale-like extravagance at public expense. Although not meant to engage in commerce, they were actually so deeply involved that they were resented in the business community. If they transgressed too blatantly, the ruling UMNO leadership took up the matter with them in private. The two sides would reach an accommodation, usually on royalty's terms, as it suited the politicians to protect a system that was seen as essential to perpetuate Malay political dominance.

Dr. Mahathir, who was critical of feudalism, did not object to the existence of a purely ceremonial monarchy.[1] As a commoner and politician, though, he was less tolerant of interference and excess by members of royal families than his blue-blooded predecessors. After a confrontation with the royals early in his prime ministership, he came to view the monarchy as a rival centre of power that had to be permanently restrained. His success in taming the monarchy in a bruising, episodic battle that extended over more than a decade gave him the chance to display his formidable political skills and grit.

The failure of some of the sultans to stay within unwritten limits invited Dr. Mahathir to cut them down to size, which he did by reducing their standing in the eyes of the Malaysian public. Historically, the sultans were seen as the protectors of Malay interests, in return for which their subjects gave them unquestioned loyalty, though the rulers lost some of their prestige when they failed to back nationalist campaigns against the British colonial authorities. Dr. Mahathir had to overcome fear in the Malay community that his constitutional changes would undercut the privileged position of the Malays in a multiracial society in danger of being destabilized by the effects of modernization. His audacity in facing down the monarchs, diehard royalists and political opponents testified to how strongly he felt about his development agenda, and how ready he was to crush anyone or anything that got in his way.

Dr. Mahathir's personal triumph, however, came at a cost to both constitutional development and missed opportunity to genuinely reform the feudalistic monarchy. Malaysia's separation of powers doctrine, with power divided among different organs of government – legislative, judicial and executive – provides for a system of checks and balances. The Conference of Rulers – comprising the Malay hereditary rulers of the nine states, who routinely choose one among themselves to serve a five-year term as king, and the appointed governors of four states – is part of the system. Dr. Mahathir's two major clashes with the monarchy upset the balance of powers by strengthening the executive at the expense of the rulers, the balance further skewed by his simultaneous subordination of the judiciary.

Malaysia is one of four nation-states in Southeast Asia where once prevalent kingdoms, empires and principalities survived the depredations of Western colonialism or the nationalist revolutions it spawned. The nine royal houses were the remnants of as many as 30 small sultanates that prospered a thousand years ago along the Malay Peninsula. The grandest was Malacca, a great cosmopolitan trading port that flourished in the fifteenth century, before falling to European invaders. Surviving Malay monarchies benefited from indirect rule, in which colonial Britain found it expedient in the nineteenth century to impose control through traditional political structures. Outside Malacca and Penang, which were colonies where non-Malays formed a majority of the population, Britain kept the façade of royal legitimacy to simulate Malay political sovereignty. In reality, the sultans were obliged to accept the advice of a British official stationed in each state in all matters except Malay custom and the Muslim religion.

British intervention strengthened the royal houses by centralizing power within each state and regularizing succession in a single line. Chiefs, who headed major regions and lower divisions down to village level, lost out. Provided with funds to carry out their royal duties as well as substantial personal allowances, the sultans saw their prestige rise along with their lifestyle. British recognition of the sovereignty of the sultans, amidst massive Chinese and Indian immigration, turned them into living symbols of the status of all Malays as the true sons of the soil.[2]

After World War II and the Japanese occupation, the returning British introduced a radical plan that stripped the sultans of their sovereignty and combined the nine states with Malacca and Penang to form a single colony called the Malayan Union. Although Malay nationalists were able to mobilize and form UMNO to block the Malayan Union, the rulers stood accused of selling out. They had signed treaties transferring sovereignty to the British crown, and though they claimed they acted under duress, the demystification of the monarchy had begun.[3] Malay-language newspapers charged the rulers with betraying the Malays and committing treason. UMNO's first leader, Onn Jaafar, coined the cry *"Hidup Melayu"*, long live the Malays, adapted from the familiar *"Hidup Raja-raja Melayu"*, long live the *rajas*, kings. The rulers heeded an UMNO warning not to attend the inauguration of the Malayan Union in 1946, marking the point at which the will of the people prevailed over traditional power.[4]

The Federation of Malaya, negotiated with the British by a joint committee of UMNO and the rulers and formed in 1948 to replace the Malayan Union, recovered the thrones for the sultans. They became constitutional monarchs, remaining the head of religion in their own states, to safeguard Malay rights and privileges and be symbols of Malay identity and paramountcy. Under the Federation of Malaya Agreement, the sultans had special veto powers on immigration, which could be employed to prevent a further influx from China and India. Each state got its own constitution, and the sultans governed in accordance with British advice as before. Non-hereditary governors were appointed in Malacca and Penang. Although each sultan exercised the authority of the state, it was a pure formality as he was required to give assent to bills passed by the state legislature.

At independence in 1957, the federal Constitution stipulated that a king would replace the British High Commissioner as head of state. The unique concept of the rulers regularly electing one among themselves to be *Yang di-Pertuan Agong*, king, was adopted at the suggestion of Tunku Abdul Rahman, the first prime minister and head of UMNO. Malay supremacy was thus symbolically extended to the whole of Malaya, including Malacca and Penang, and to Sabah and Sarawak as well on the formation of Malaysia in 1963. The king was to give effect to provisions safeguarding "the special position of the Malays", such as fixing quotas in the civil service, schools and universities, and allocating scholarships and commercial licences, a duty he exercised in practice on the advice of the prime minister. The Conference of Rulers, which for some specific purposes consists of only the nine sultans, was given a veto over any laws directly affecting their "privileges, position, honours or dignities".

Having stayed above the turbulent political fray in the 1960s, the rulers had their collective role strengthened when the Malaysian Parliament was restored in 1971, following its suspension at the time of the racial riots in 1969. Controversially, the Constitution was amended to require Conference of Rulers' consent in the passing of a number of important kinds of legislation, including some constitutional amendments. Principally, the laws entrenched in this way relate to matters popularly known as the "sensitive issues": citizenship, the special position of the Malays and natives of Sabah and Sarawak, and the legitimate interests of others, the national language and the rulers themselves.[5] Moreover, both the Constitution and the Sedition Act were amended to make it illegal to question these matters, even in Parliament. These severe restrictions were imposed on freedom of speech and expression to limit public discussion of topics that might again upset racial harmony. Reinforcing the rulers' position by adding "reassurance to assurance", as one analyst termed it, was part of a multi-pronged effort to make Malays feel more secure about their place in multi-ethnic Malaysia.[6]

While the arrangements worked fairly well in the early years, there were signs that some of the rulers had not fully subscribed to the concept of constitutional monarchy. Based on the Westminster model, Malaysia's Constitution is one in which convention rather than law is a major source of rules.[7] The sultans had a different notion of their prerogatives from that which is scrupulously observed by their British counterparts.[8] For example, they found it hard to grasp that while they held "discretionary powers" to appoint the state political leader – the chief minister, known as *mentri besar* in the sultanates – it was no longer their prerogative to do so. According to the principles of constitutional monarchy, they were expected to accept the nomination of the ruling party, which usually meant the prime minister's choice. Similarly, giving royal assent to laws passed by elected state legislatures was supposed to be a formality. But some rulers still interfered in the appointment of chief ministers and members of executive councils, which functioned as state cabinets. They also lobbied hard and embarrassingly for increased personal allowances and handouts, while spending conspicuously and often frivolously.

In 1963, Prime Minister Tunku Abdul Rahman reminded the sultans of Perak and Selangor, who were at odds with their state governments, that they were symbols and must steer clear of politics. The same year he also had to settle a fuss made by the Selangor sultan, who called a press conference to complain about conditions that the state government imposed on ten acres of land it granted him in Kuala Lumpur. Declaring himself personally insulted, he said, "As a ruler, I have power over land matters in the state of Selangor."[9] True enough, under the federal Constitution land was a state responsibility – and a source of wealth as the Malaysian economy took off and the New Economic Policy kicked in – but control of land was devolved to elected politicians. Yet this sultan and others were able to exert considerable influence because the momentum of their traditional role carried over into what was ostensibly a fully representative and democratic system.[10] The Constitution notwithstanding, it was simply hard to say "no" to a ruler. In Kelantan in the 1970s, the sultan demanded and received a new palace "for his indulgence towards certain questionable dealings in timber and other concessions", by which Chief Minister Mohamed Asri Muda attempted to raise funds simultaneously for the state budget, his Parti Islam Se-Malaysia and private pockets.[11] As the New Economic Policy opened business opportunities for bumiputras, a similar "economic nexus in ruler-executive relations" spread to nearly every Malay state.[12]

As the Father of Independence and a prince himself, Tunku Abdul Rahman was uniquely placed to offer gentle advice to erring sultans and their ever more numerous – and sometimes arrogant, wayward and avaricious – relatives. For the most part, though, the subject remained taboo, with potential critics deterred by the constitutional prohibition on questioning the sovereignty of the rulers, the widened Sedition Act, and a general belief that they were courting trouble if they spoke up. Chandra Muzaffar, a prominent intellectual, made a cautious case in 1979 for critically examining the behaviour of rulers. He said some aspects of the institution could – and should – be discussed in public: "The alleged utilization of public funds for private purposes, the apparent extravagance in lifestyles, involvement in businesses, interference in strictly political matters, the inability to uphold high ethical standards and most of all, the absence of an image of excellence which can inspire emulation...".[13] Although his study was a persuasive argument for a responsible public debate, it was not forthcoming.

Dr. Mahathir's tenure as deputy prime minister coincided with a bout of "political activism" by the royalty, which began in the mid-to-late 1970s.[14] The Sultan of Kelantan persuaded the regent, who happened to be his son and crown prince, to postpone dissolution of the state legislature, recommended by Chief Minister Mohamad Nasir after he lost a no-confidence vote. The sultan was manoeuvring to keep Parti Islam Se-Malaysia in power without having an election, but the UMNO-led federal government stepped in amidst the turmoil and imposed central control on the state. In Perak, the sultan got rid of Chief Minister Mohamed Ghazali Jawi after a long campaign, expressing his delight by shaving off his protest beard and turning the occasion into a fireworks and drum-beating celebration for family members, civil servants and community leaders. A similar situation occurred in Johore, where the sultan prevailed on the federal government to remove Chief Minister Othman Saat.

In the case of Pahang, Prime Minister Hussein Onn, who was committed to reducing corruption, imposed his choice of Abdul Rahim Bakar as chief minister on the protesting sultan. While the sultan sought to invoke the principle of consultation, with the implication of a possible veto, he was actually seeking a "malleable" chief minister who was "essential for the rapid or rule-bending processing of land alienation at preferential rates".[15] Already feeling slighted, the sultan was doubly annoyed to find the able and honest Rahim made life difficult for those who had in the past been able to acquire timber concessions through high-level local patronage.[16] After the sultan became king in 1979, his son, who was acting as regent in his absence, refused to sign money bills. With dozens of bills awaiting royal assent and important development projects threatened, Rahim finally quit in November 1981, by which time Dr. Mahathir had taken over as premier.

Having been involved in the tussle with the Pahang throne for more than three years, Dr. Mahathir felt the sting of the government's retreat. In case anyone missed the significance of Rahim's departure, the regent reminded them by signing the delayed Pahang bills almost immediately.

Other instances of royal recalcitrance also embarrassed and disturbed Dr. Mahathir. His government had to bail out one ruler who lost heavily at gaming tables abroad.[17] The sultans of Perak and Johore, asserting themselves as head of religion in their states, clashed with the federal government over the date for the end of Ramadan. By determining the timing locally and using a different method, they ended up with a fasting month one day longer or shorter than the rest of the country, causing confusion among Malays and disrupting holiday arrangements.

That Dr. Mahathir would respond forcefully to royal abuses was a matter of how and when, not if. He had never had much sympathy for the rulers. While writing as C.H.E. Det in his student days, Dr. Mahathir had warned them that too often they were on the wrong side of history. In 1949, he criticized the Conference of Rulers for rejecting UMNO's recommendation that a Malay commoner he appointed deputy high commissioner of the Federation of Malaya. The rulers' objection on the grounds that it would lower their dignity, he said, pitted them against "the people". The hitherto unquestioned devotion of Malays to their rulers was at stake: Unless the rulers changed their minds, "there is no doubt that they will lose, perhaps forever, the confidence and loyalty of their subjects".[18] Elsewhere, Dr. Mahathir also wrote of the "new force" of Malayan democracy that was likely to eclipse feudalism.[19]

In *The Malay Dilemma* in 1970, Dr. Mahathir insinuated that the rulers in earlier centuries were more concerned about feathering their own nests than helping the Malays obtain a fair deal from visiting Indian, Arab and Chinese traders. He said the rulers appropriated "a certain portion of goods belonging to their subjects" and exchanged them for imported items, enabling them to amass "vast amounts of clothing and jewellery". He also said the Chinese merchants' "habit of giving expensive gifts to the ruling class ingratiated them with all levels of authority", facilitating a greater influx of Chinese merchant-adventurers and allowing a system of Chinese retail shops to penetrate "every nook and corner" and "become an established feature of life in the old Malay sultanates".[20]

In other historical references, Dr. Mahathir held the rulers partly responsible for the Malays being dispossessed and colonized for "400 years". He said, "There was always a monarch who was prepared to help a foreign power for personal gain", noting that Singapore "came into being because one monarch" handed over "that part of the Johore empire".[21] And he never forgave the rulers for agreeing to British plans for the objectionable Malayan Union. Self-interested political groups were trying to disrupt Malay unity, he wrote in the 1970s, "Just as at one time monarchs without thrones were prepared to betray their people in their greed for power...".[22]

In 1983, Dr. Mahathir – and every other politician in Malaysia – could see more trouble coming in the form of the new king to be chosen in early 1984. Under the rotating system, it would be either Perak's or Johore's turn as all the other states had occupied the throne once. Both had sultans who were usually referred to as strong-willed, a euphemism for being prepared to ignore political advice when it suited them. Sultan Idris Shah of Perak had seniority, having assumed the throne earlier than his southern counterpart, but indicated he might decline the post as he had done twice before. He was insisting on constitutional changes that would allow him to remain Sultan of Perak while he was king, which the federal government said was out of the question.[23]

The alternative, having Sultan Mahmood Iskandar of Johore installed as Malaysia's eighth king, filled the political establishment with greater foreboding. It was not just that he was from a family with a history of defying the central government, his grandfather having ridiculed the idea of independence for the Malays in 1955. He also had a long record of criminal behaviour, exuded an aura of violence and inspired fear.[24] When a lawyer overtook the sultan's car on the road in 1972, he had the man stopped and beaten.[25] On separate occasions, he physically assaulted members of the Pahang and Trengganu royal families, apparently in the belief they were impersonating members of his family.[26] He once ordered a policeman who had offended him confined to a dog kennel.[27] In the most controversial case, the sultan was convicted in 1977 of culpable homicide for the shooting of a man he said he thought was a smuggler. He was sentenced to six months imprisonment, but pardoned by his father and never spent a day in jail.[28] Although he was the eldest son, he was removed as successor by his father in 1961. In mysterious circumstances, his father restored him to the line of succession on his deathbed at the age of 86.

As if the prospect of a wilful and politicized king were not enough, the government received reports that Sultan Mahmood Iskandar had boasted that he would, in effect, stage a coup d'etat after he was enthroned. He told a gathering that once elected king, he would declare a state of emergency unilaterally, take over with the help of the army and throw out all the politicians.[29]

According to an associate, Dr. Mahathir "had long nursed an ambition to settle this problem once and for all", after watching each of his predecessors "put up with the antics" of the rulers. Having to placate the Sultan of Pahang himself and pay off a ruler's gambling debts "strengthened his resolve to act quickly to put an end to it all".[30] The prospect that a rebellious king might frustrate Dr. Mahathir's legislative programme elevated a priority to "almost an obsession".[31]

Dr. Mahathir's pre-emptive strike, which was designed to do more than close constitutional loopholes before the installation of the next king, was titled the Constitution (Amendment) Act 1983. Introduced on 1 August, it contained three sensitive measures. The crucial one declared that if the king did not give royal assent to a bill passed by Parliament within 15 days, it would become law anyway. Similarly, state constitutions would be altered so that legislation passed by a state would become law after 15 days even if a ruler did not give his assent. Another amendment would transfer the right to declare a state of emergency from the king – acting on government advice, which implied consultation with the Cabinet – to the prime minister personally. The House of Representatives, by a 136–9 vote, adopted the package with minimal debate and delay. As he had obtained King Ahmad Shah's approval in advance, Dr. Mahathir hoped to wrap up the whole exercise before any serious opposition developed around the country.[32]

But the king had second thoughts when he saw the content of the bill, and consulted his fellow sultans. They were offended by being bypassed and objected to the substance as well. They persuaded him not to grant assent. The king made their collective displeasure known by withholding assent from a couple of other bills passed by Parliament as well. The very situation that the amendments were designed in part to prevent had become a reality, and the government faced a crisis.

Dr. Mahathir's secretive strategy, which led directly to the confrontation, contrasted sharply with his rhetoric about the importance of transparency during his first two years on the job. "I believe in open discussion and solving problems openly", he declared on one occasion. "Hiding things...does not take us very far."[33] Setting out to define strictly the powers of the rulers, however, Dr. Mahathir opted for a stealth seldom previously seen in national life.

The three contentious changes were buried among 22 constitutional amendments contained in the bill that was presented to Parliament. Contrary to an undertaking Dr. Mahathir had given to consult lawyers on all proposed laws, the bill was not made available beforehand to the Malaysian Bar Council.[34] The editors of local news organizations were summoned and instructed not to report the changes affecting the rulers. Government legislators played their part by also ignoring those amendments during two days of debate in the House, with the result that the public had almost no idea what was at stake. Lim Kit Siang, the leader of the opposition Democratic Action Party, called it a *wayang kulit*, a traditional shadow puppet play: "We see the shadows but not the substance...".[35]

Dr. Mahathir had several reasons for trying to sneak the changes through Parliament without publicity, and unknown to the sultans. The first reason was Article 38(4) of the Constitution, which stated flatly that "no law directly affecting the privileges, position, honours or dignities of the rulers shall be passed without the consent of the Conference of Rulers." Without their prior approval, the amendments more than likely were unconstitutional.

As leader of the exclusively-Malay UMNO, Dr. Mahathir also wanted to avoid alarming his core constituents. He could not afford to appear anti-monarchist, which might incense and alienate the rulers and be interpreted as less than totally pro-Malay. Even knowing his remarks would not be reported in the local papers, Dr. Mahathir was unwilling to admit that the powers of the rulers were being curbed. He argued implausibly that it was the executive which was surrendering some of its authority. In a constitutional monarchy, he said, formalities required everything to be done in the name of the king, who acted on the advice of the prime minister and Cabinet. With a 15-day limit for the king to sign bills, "the right of the Cabinet to advise the king is also gone after 15 days. It will mean it's the Cabinet that loses, not the king."[36]

For Lim Kit Siang, a trained lawyer representing a multiracial but predominantly Chinese party, the amendments were the most important since independence, with grave and far-reaching consequences. Eliminating the need for royal assent might be construed as a step towards a republican philosophy, he said. As for transferring the right to order a state of emergency to the prime minister, any such proclamation would be above the law, regardless of whether the premier acted in bad faith or wrongfully. Lim raised the dire possibility that those participating in the parliamentary debate might be guilty of sedition. "In excluding the need for the royal assent in certain circumstances, aren't we taking an action which would be tantamount to a derogation of the sovereignty of the rulers? Aren't we in fact challenging and questioning the sovereignty of the rulers...?"[37]

While Dr. Mahathir could hustle the bill through both houses of Parliament in three days, he could not persuade King Ahmad Shah to put his signature to it, so it was not published in the government gazette and did not become law. The king was in an invidious position: If he were tempted to accede to the advice of the government of the day, he could be removed from office by a majority vote of the Conference of Rulers. A dismissal resolution supported by five fellow rulers would demote him from king to sultan, and send him packing back to Pahang.

The government also felt the pressure as the 22 amendments that remained blocked included day-to-day matters, such as ending civil appeals to Britain's Privy Council, expanding the scope of deputy ministers and parliamentary secretaries, and increasing the number of parliamentary seats. Until the bill went through, the electoral authorities could not redraw the boundaries, and they might not be ready for the next general election. Among the other bills the king was ignoring to make his point was one containing the 1984 budget appropriations, which needed to be approved soon or the government would shut down.

The public, which had no knowledge of the stalemate for a couple of months, learned of it through an open letter by Senu Abdul Rahman, an UMNO veteran and former cabinet minister, who wrote to Dr. Mahathir opposing the amendments. Malay and English versions of his letter were widely distributed, sparking the sort of grass-roots ferment that Dr. Mahathir had sought to avoid. Tunku Abdul Rahman joined in the criticism in his weekly newspaper column. He declared that the bill contravened "one of the most important articles of our Constitution" – the one requiring Conference of Rulers consent for any law affecting the sultans.[38] Having rejected a personal appeal by Dr. Mahathir, the defiant rulers convened on 20 November at the court of the Sultan of Selangor, named Heavenly Hill Palace, in an ostentatious show of tradition and modernity to consider a compromise proposal delivered by an UMNO delegation:

> It was a uniquely Malaysian gathering of the clans. The sultan of Perak packed a pistol on his hip and wore green combat fatigues and a red beret. The man who could be Malaysia's next king gave a jaunty clenched-first salute as he popped out of his Mercedes. The sultan of Johore, another ruler fond of firearms and the Perak sultan's main rival for the kingship, preferred more formal officer's dress. For security he traveled in a jet-black army sedan with blacked-out windows and brought along a special escort with a sub-machine gun. The sultan of Trengganu rolled up in an elongated golden Cadillac equipped with a television antenna in the shape of water buffalo horns. The raja of Perlis, a portly man in a rumpled beige suit, arrived in a more traditional chariot, a powder-blue Rolls Royce....[39]

Even before the rulers voted down the revisions, Dr. Mahathir reversed course and appealed directly to the public. His hastily assembled Plan B involved persuading the royalty that the vast majority of the Malays backed the legislation, and the rulers risked their prestige by resisting the tide. Dr. Mahathir and other leaders addressed rallies organized by UMNO that sought to evoke the spirit of the anti-Malayan Union campaign, with its overtones of the people coming to the rescue after royal perfidy. Party cheerleaders with bullhorns adapted the old battle cry *"Hidup Melayu"* for the new imperative *"Hidup* Mahathir".[40]

Where the press had obediently remained silent earlier, the papers now carried articles explaining the necessity of the constitutional amendments and reporting a groundswell of government support across the country. In fact, the Malay community was almost evenly split, with rural and elderly people – and women particularly – sympathetic to the monarchy. Royalists sponsored their own rallies, which were much better attended than the controlled press reported. The differences showed up within UMNO's senior ranks, with a party vice president and at least two cabinet ministers siding silently with the sultans.[41] Although he revelled in the rallies, Dr. Mahathir had uncomfortable moments. Criticized by sections of UMNO for being autocratic and ignoring traditions of consultation and consensus building, he was forced to deny that he would resign. Dr. Siti Hasmah noticed the tell-tale signs of stress in her husband, a reddening in the eye, and feared for his safety as large and enthusiastic crowds surged around him at meetings throughout the country. For the first and only time in his political career, she said, "both eyes were red".[42]

A settlement reached in early December was a compromise that pleased nobody beyond the relief it brought that the five-month confrontation had ended. In an embarrassing retreat, the government allowed the king to retain the formal right to declare an emergency, while the sultans' obligations to assent to state legislation were left unchanged, though they undertook orally not to block bills without reasonable cause. In his attempt to remove royal assent to legislation passed by Parliament, Dr. Mahathir actually gave the king an explicit legislative role for the first time.[43] Under the compromise, the king could no longer block legislation by refusing to sign it into law, though he would be able to delay it for at least two months. Once legislation was passed by Parliament, the king would have 30 days to sign it. If he objected to the bill within that period, he could return it to Parliament with a statement of his reasons for further consideration. If Parliament then reaffirmed support for the measure, it would be resubmitted to the king and automatically would become law after another 30 days. Money bills, an exception, would become law automatically after the initial 30-day period.

Government leaders could call the agreement a "triumph of rationality" and political maturity that did not favour either side, but it fell far short in Dr. Mahathir's terms.[44] While he gained a crucial legal point – depriving the king of the power to thwart the elected leadership by refusing to sign legislation – his victory was incomplete. Certainly it had not solved the problem of constitutional impropriety at state level, where it was acute. Politically, the episode dented Dr. Mahathir's standing, though if adversaries expected him to retreat, they still had much to learn about their leader. For someone of Dr. Mahathir's temperament and convictions, it was a case of unfinished business.

Although the government feared the worst when Sultan Mahmood Iskandar was made king in 1984, after Sultan Idris Shah died on the eve of the electoral conclave, he and Dr. Mahathir learned to coexist amicably after a few early bumps. The new king made a positive start by donating his and the queen's federal salaries to charity. He confirmed his eccentricity by refusing to live at the national palace in Kuala Lumpur, preferring the official residence provided by the state of Johore. He had to be talked out of wearing a military uniform and into traditional dress for his coronation. He shocked many Malays by demanding, after prayers at the National Mosque during Ramadan, that Deputy Prime Minister Musa Hitam, a Johore subject, apologize publicly for insulting him during the previous year's constitutional crisis. When Musa stood as directed, kissed the monarch's hand and apologized, the congregation broke out in applause. For the most part, though, the king performed dutifully, and he and Dr. Mahathir found it served their individual interests to cooperate. Indeed, Dr. Mahathir did nothing to expose a serious crime in 1987 – the king killed his golf caddy – which, if known, would have ruined and probably ended the king's reign.

For his part, the king visibly acquiesced the following year in Dr. Mahathir's siege of the judiciary that left its independence in tatters.

In the states, however, some of the familiar frictions were at work. Kedah Chief Minister Syed Nahar Shahabuddin resigned, apparently a victim of the fallout from the constitutional crisis that left him uncomfortably opposed to his uncle, Tunku Abdul Rahman, and the rulers.[45] The Sultan of Selangor had a public row with the state's chief minister, Muhammad Muhammad Taib, over land development, complicated by the terms of Muhammad's divorce settlement with the sultan's daughter.[46] In Kelantan, the situation was much more serious, with the sultan accusing the UMNO chief minister of being corrupt. The sultan was targeted by UMNO after his uncle, Tengku Razaleigh Hamzah, broke with UMNO and formed his own party, which contested the 1990 general election in alliances with Parti Islam Se-Malaysia and with another opposition party. Dr. Mahathir and his supporters blamed the sultan's "political interference" for the loss of all of Kelantan's 13 parliamentary seats and 39 Legislative Assembly seats, a body blow to UMNO's pride.

A more general and widespread complaint came from the growing ranks of Malay businessmen, newly enfranchised by affirmative action policies, who found themselves shut out of some of the most lucrative investment fields by the web of interests associated with the royal houses. Young, self-confident and usually members of UMNO, these Malays saw little need to rely on the sultanates for symbolic protection. On the contrary, they resented the business competition, being particularly incensed by the alliances that some sultans had formed with established Chinese companies. According to Finance Minister Daim Zainuddin, the rulers had no compunction about writing directly to him seeking government contracts.[47]

Malay concerns about the rulers' ventures into both politics and business spilled into the open at UMNO's General Assembly in 1990, resulting in a unanimous resolution urging the royal families to uphold the federal and state constitutions. Emboldened, the delegates at the party's gathering a year later advocated a royal code of conduct. Negotiated by UMNO representatives and the rulers, the seven-page Proclamation of Constitutional Principles issued by the king on 4 July 1992 was of limited value. It was murky on many points and signed by only six sultans – the Johore, Kedah and Kelantan rulers declined – and while they said they would stay out of politics, accept federal government appointments to their respective states and refrain from active involvement in business, the code lacked constitutional force.[48]

Realizing that the consensual approach had failed, the government laid the groundwork to use its two-thirds parliamentary majority to change the Constitution and compel the sultans to behave, even though it would require the consent of the Conference of Rulers.[49] With Dr. Mahathir's tacit approval, the Malaysian press abandoned the free ride it had long given the sultans and their offspring, pouncing instead on any royal indiscretion. In one case, the out-of-favour Sultan Ismail Petra of Kelantan attracted a torrent of publicity when he walked into the customs cargo centre at Kuala Lumpur's airport and drove off in a Lamborghini Diablo, without paying the RM2.1 million import duty on the sports car. The sultan had exceeded his duty-free quota of seven cars, the government tax authorities ruled, and he must pay up. Several local businessmen ended the incident by taking up a collection and settling the bill for him.[50]

It was Sultan Iskandar's reversion to violent form, however, that "enabled shadow boxing to give way to a serious, and historic, confrontation" between the elected leadership and the monarchy.[51] Back in Johore after completing his term as king without public scandal, Sultan Iskandar was furious when his youngest son, 22, was suspended from field-hockey competition for five years for assaulting a Perak goalkeeper after a match. The sultan decided that if his son could not play, nobody else in Johore would either. On his orders, Johore hockey teams were withdrawn from competition, often at the last minute. When a leading Johore secondary school team was pulled out of a national tournament hours before it was due to start, coach Douglas Gomez criticized the decision. The sultan summoned Gomez to the palace on 30 November 1992 and thrashed him.

Seizing the moment, Dr. Mahathir's government moved swiftly to stoke popular revulsion over the assault and build a national consensus for a fresh effort to curb the monarchy. In fact, the Cabinet had laid the groundwork earlier by issuing a statement that royalty could not expect criminal behaviour to be covered up, a strong signal of support for the hockey authorities to impose the ban on the young prince. After encouraging Gomez to file a police report, Dr. Mahathir declared, "The royalty is not above the law. They cannot kill people. They cannot beat people."[52]

Less than two weeks after Sultan Iskandar's attack, the Malaysian Parliament took the unprecedented step of censuring him, with the 96 members of the 180-seat House of Representatives present at the session finding common cause. The motion said "all necessary action must be taken to ensure that a similar incident" did not happen again. It was the first time that the opposition had joined with parties from the ruling coalition to support a motion presented by the government.[53] It was also the first time a motion of formal reproof directed at a royal personage was accepted by the House. In the past, the government had rejected such motions, insisting they were prohibited by the Constitution and the Sedition Act.

Deputy Prime Minister Ghafar Baba, who introduced the motion, indicated that condemning Sultan Iskandar was a step towards reforming the monarchy to safeguard its long-term survival. If the government did not put an end to transgressions by the Malay rulers, he said, "the people" might lose patience and overthrow the monarchy, as they had done in other countries. He quoted a Malay proverb with an implicit warning to the monarchy: A just king is adulated, but an unjust one is to be shunned.[54]

The government's target was the monarchy's constitutional shield: Article 181(2) said "no proceedings whatsoever shall be brought in any court against the ruler of a state in his personal capacity". On government instructions, Abdul Majid Idris, second in line to succeed his father as Sultan of Johore, was charged with assault. Although he was subsequently acquitted when the victim accepted RM1,000 in compensation, an arrangement permitted under Malaysia's criminal code, his prosecution was highly significant. Royal personages below the level of sultan rarely had been charged previously, even though they were not protected from prosecution. Indeed, the prince was only the second leading member of Malaysia's royalty to face a criminal offence, the first being his father back in the 1970s.

The Constitution (Amendment) Act 1993, introduced on 18 January, removed judicial immunity from rulers in their private capacity, though they still would be protected in the exercise of their official functions. As the bill was not made retroactive, it ruled out prosecution for past offences. In the future, though, the long arm of the law would reach inside royal palaces, breaching their customary legal sanctity. A late compromise measure stipulated that sultans accused of breaking the law would be brought before a "special court" rather than the courts for commoners. Sultans and appointed state governors would be unable to pardon themselves, their wives or their children. The post-1969 gag on legislators debating royal misdeeds would be lifted: No member of Parliament or a state Legislative Assembly "shall be liable to any proceedings in any court" for anything they say about the king or the sultans, though they would still not be permitted to advocate "the abolition of the constitutional position" of the king or sultans.[55]

In pushing the amendments through Parliament, Dr. Mahathir ignored their formal rejection by the sultans, moving Malaysia close to the brink of another constitutional crisis. He said the sultans "must heed the advice of the government", and if they failed to endorse the amendments, the courts would settle the matter.[56] Opposition members who earlier condemned Sultan Iskandar's beating of Douglas Gomez did not support the legislation, even though they agreed that no ruler should be above the law. Their reservations were part of a backlash that questioned Dr. Mahathir's motives in wanting to subdue the monarchy so forcefully. The suspicion was that Dr. Mahathir, having greatly expanded the prime minister's executive power over the years, was using royal misdeeds as a pretext to eliminate yet another check and balance in his domineering stewardship of the government.[57] "One question that is forefront in the minds of Malaysians is whether the removal of the rulers' immunity will only result in the greater immunity of the political leadership in government," said Lim Kit Siang, the opposition leader.[58] Declared an editorial in the Bar Council's journal, "Far from protecting the institution, the amendments will, in fact, arm the executive with the power to subjugate the rulers through threats of prosecution for any offences, however minor. The rulers will be at the mercy of the executive."[59]

Dr. Mahathir had calculated shrewdly and waited for the right time to strike, having discarded from the Cabinet and UMNO's Supreme Council those politicians who sympathized or sided with the monarchy during the first crisis. He figured that with the growth of the Malay middle class, fewer Malays would look to the monarchy for symbolic protection. They owed their improved status to specific policies, and they would have faith in the political system that delivered those policies to secure their future. In case the rulers were slow to pick up on these trends, Dr. Mahathir held their feet to the fire.

Unleashed anew, the press paraded a catalogue of royal horrors that had been known only to a few insiders for years and deemed unfit to print. Effectively, the Sedition Act was suspended, since it required the attorney general to authorize a prosecution and he was not about to do that. As the dark and expensive side of the monarchy was exposed, nothing was off limits except direct attacks on the institution itself.

State-owned Radio Television Malaysia aired old movies that portrayed the rulers in ancient times as base or brainless. An opposition member revealed in Parliament that Sultan Iskandar had not been a model king during his 1984–89 reign after all. He had killed his caddy with a golf club. An UMNO member of parliament said the sultan and his eldest son were implicated in 23 incidents of criminal activity over the past two decades, including rape, assault and murder.[60] A former group editor and a senior reporter of a Malay-language newspaper published their first-hand account of being harassed by the king in 1985. They had been summoned to his Johore palace and threatened, after the national daily criticized his gift of a rare Sumatran rhinoceros to a zoo in Thailand.[61] The sultan had used his private army, the 337-man Johore Military Force, established with British help in 1886, to "aid and abet" some of his "wrongdoings".[62]

With scant regard for their historical role in protecting the Malays or their current obligation to uphold Islam, the rulers had accumulated enormous wealth at the expense of fellow Malaysians. They were among the main beneficiaries of government policies aimed at eradicating poverty, being guaranteed millions of dollars in profits from secret allotments of shares in publicly listed companies. They borrowed millions from banks and often did not repay. Illegally importing luxury cars and selling them to friends and family was a common cash-raising exercise. Some of the sultans gambled and celebrated Christian holidays, despite Islamic prohibitions.[63]

On top of the privy purse – salaries, allowances and expenses to maintain the sultans' primary dwellings – which totaled about RM200 million annually, "they've always asked for more, like land and timber concessions", said Dr. Mahathir.[64] The rulers were each entitled to reside in more than seven palaces, and had been granted more land and logging concessions than could be traversed in weeks of hiking. Pahang's Sultan Ahmad Shah, one of the country's richest rulers, had at least a dozen palaces, his own Boeing 727 and 200 polo ponies kept in air-conditioned stables. According to state officials, the prime timber concessions allocated to him in the previous five years were estimated to be worth RM270 million.[65]

As if the disclosure of the scandalous waste of public funds was not enough, Dr. Mahathir announced that the royal households would be squeezed financially. Henceforth, they would receive only what was specified in the federal and state constitutions. As the extras were withdrawn, to curb what Dr. Mahathir called their "lavish lifestyle",[66] the sultans would find themselves without government-paid air transport, outriders and special hospital wards. Free postage facilities were being restricted or withdrawn altogether. Most members of royal families would be denied the diplomatic passports they were accustomed to, and Malaysian missions abroad would be forbidden to entertain rulers' families during private visits and help with such tasks as booking airport VIP rooms.

If the sultans were tempted to go to court, they would probably regret it. UMNO officials indicated that, if challenged, the government was prepared to produce evidence to substantiate the need for the amendments. It might involve calling the victims of rape or torture to testify in open court, or providing details of cheating, smuggling and over-spending by royal family members, with the prospect of even more horrific revelations.

With this sort of heavy artillery arrayed against them, the rulers capitulated. Their surrender was presented as a face-saving agreement after negotiations, but the minor modifications to be made to the bill could not hide the truth. The alterations dealt primarily with the procedures to be followed by the special court, though one also specified that no sultan could be charged without the personal consent of Malaysia's attorney general.[67]

Not content with this success, Dr. Mahathir used the introduction of the modifications in Parliament to torment the only one of the rulers still prepared to stand and argue. Already unpopular with UMNO for politicking for the party's opponents in Kelantan, Sultan Ismail Petra continued to denounce the amendments as unconstitutional. Dr. Mahathir said the sultan's remarks cleared the way for commoners to question the validity of his appointment and installation as head of the state's royal household. The press dutifully followed up Dr. Mahathir's attack with stories suggesting that Sultan Ismail, born of a commoner mother, was not the rightful successor and that his cousin, a businessman, should have become ruler.

Hardly had that controversy faded than Dr. Mahathir moved with supreme confidence to demonstrate the total subjugation of the monarchy. The Constitution (Amendment) Act 1994, introduced without warning in May, sealed the rulers' fate in a welter of provisions that affected the judiciary as much as the monarchy. One removed the king's right to delay a bill with a statement of reasons, which was the compromise ten years earlier. The king must now give assent within 30 days, or the bill would become law automatically. A similar provision applied to the sultans and state legislation, the very reason they had dug in their heels previously. In contrast with the titanic struggles of 1983–84 and 1992–93, the rulers uttered not a squeak of protest this time. Mindful that their mandated allowances could be cut and their access to business squeezed, they had lost the will to fight another round with Dr. Mahathir.

Tunku Abdul Rahman was convinced that Dr. Mahathir was trying to abolish the monarchy and install himself as the president of a Malaysian republic. In conversations with his official biographer in 1988, the Tunku condemned Dr. Mahathir as "irresponsible" and added, "He cares nothing for class, for law, for order, for the Constitution. What suits him, he just does it."[68]

There was considerable truth and a hint of revenge in the Tunku's trenchant observations. From the political wilderness in 1970, Dr. Mahathir had condemned the Tunku's administration, not least for its willingness to rewrite the independence Constitution: "The manner, the frequency and the trivial reasons for altering the Constitution reduced this supreme law of the nation to a useless scrap of paper."[69] Yet under Dr. Mahathir the pace of constitutional change did not slacken, his government pushing 25 amendments through Parliament in 22 years.[70] The record showed he did not accept the opinion of constitutional experts, much less his own declaration,[71] that Malaysia's Constitution should indeed be supreme, above all the institutions of government.

But while Dr. Mahathir had little time for the royalty where it represented a feudal order, he never seriously contemplated reforming the monarchy or eliminating it altogether. His basic requirement was that the monarchy should not obstruct him and his nation-building goals. A powerful prime minister with a reformist bent might have taken steps to persuade the sultans to behave as real and admired constitutional monarchs. He could have issued instructions through the chief ministers of the Malay states to ensure the sultans stayed out of business and the appointment of local officials, eschewed gambling and other social vices and generally comported themselves in an exemplary manner. Dr. Mahathir's failure to project a model institution worthy of emulation, as Chandra Muzaffar termed it,[72] meant the problem would inevitably recur. And, indeed, some royal households began flexing their political muscles again, intervening to get their nominees appointed as chief ministers of Trengganu and Perlis in 2008, as Malaysia sank into despair under Prime Minister Abdullah Badawi's weak and indecisive leadership.[73]

By exposing the sultans' all too human frailties and treating them with such disdain, Dr. Mahathir reduced them to figurehead status, if only for as long as he governed. "The heirs to the 'glory of Malacca' look distinctly overawed", commented academic specialist Roger Kershaw.[74] The erosion of the rulers' stature and influence "diminished their constraining role in tempering the exercise of executive powers",[75] which Dr. Mahathir proceeded to wield with unprecedented latitude. In a remade constitutional landscape, he had no need to contemplate a republic. He was the uncrowned king.

Notes

1   Email correspondence with Mahathir Mohamad, 17 June 2008.
2   Roger Kershaw, *Monarchy in South-East Asia: The Faces of Tradition in Transition* (London: Routledge, 2001), p. 28.
3   Cheah Boon Kheng, *Malaysia: The Making of a Nation* (Singapore: Institute of Southeast Asian Studies, 2002), p. 16.
4   Ibid., p. 17.
5   Andrew Harding, *Law, Government and the Constitution in Malaysia* (London: Kluwer Law International, 1996), p. 74.
6   Roger Kershaw, *Monarchy in South-East Asia*, p. 101.
7   Andrew Harding, *Law, Government and the Constitution in Malaysia*, p. 105.
8   Ibid., p. 75.
9   Zainuddin Maidin, *The Other Side of Mahathir* (Kuala Lumpur: Utusan Publications & Distributors Sdn. Bhd., 1994), p. 77.
10 David Jenkins, "A Focus for Identity, Traditional Rulers Adjust to Change: Sultans as Symbols", *Far Eastern Economic Review* (hereafter *FEER*), 30 June 1983 <http://www.feer.com/articles/archive/1983/8306_30/P032.html> (accessed 25 January 2006).
11 Roger Kershaw, *Monarchy in South-East Asia*, p. 62.
12 Ibid., p. 102.
13 Chandra Muzaffar, *Protector?: An Analysis of the Concept and Practice of Loyalty in Leader-led Relationships within Malay Society* (Penang: Aliran, 1979), p. 74.
14 Roger Kershaw, *Monarchy in South-East Asia*, p. 101.
15 Ibid., p. 102.
16 David Jenkins, "A Focus for Identity, Traditional Rulers Adjust to Change: Sultans as Symbols".
17 Zainuddin Maidin, *The Other Side of Mahathir*, p. 79.
18 Dr. Mahathir Mohamad, "The Rulers are Losing Loyalty", in *The Early Years: 1947–1972* (Kuala Lumpur: Berita Publishing Sdn. Bhd., 1995), pp. 47–48.
19 Dr. Mahathir Mohamad, "Rulers and Rakyat – Climax is Near", in *The Early Years*, p. 58.
20 Mahathir bin Mohamad, *The Malay Dilemma* (Singapore: Times Books International, 1999 edition), pp. 33–35.
21 Mahathir Mohamad, *The Challenge* (Petaling Jaya: Pelanduk Publications (M) Sdn. Bhd., 1986), p. 155.
22 Ibid., p. 158.
23 K. Das, "We are Not Amused: Hereditary Rulers Opposed to Federal Government Attempts to Limit Their Powers May Force a Constitutional Crisis", *FEER*, 15 September 1983 <http://feer.com/articles/archive/1983/8309_15/P030.html> (accessed 25 January 2006).
24 John Berthelsen, "Malaysian King Sails through First Months on the Job", *Asian Wall Street Journal* (hereafter *AWSJ*), 19 April 1985.

25 Ibid.
26 Ibid.
27 Ibid.
28 Ibid.
29 R.S. Milne and Diane K. Mauzy, *Malaysian Politics Under Mahathir* (London: Routledge, 1999), p. 32.
30 Zainuddin Maidin, *The Other Side of Mahathir*, p. 79.
31 Raphael Pura, "Malaysia Deadlocked by Royalty Crisis", *AWSJ*, 17 November 1983.
32 Ibid.
33 J. Victor Morais, *Mahathir: A Profile in Courage* (Petaling Jaya: Eastern Universities Press (M) Sdn. Bhd., 1982), p. 46.
34 K. Das, "Less Ado About Anything: Mahathir Moves Quietly to Reduce the Constitutional Role the Sultans Play in the Nation's Legislative Process", *FEER*, 25 August 1983 <http://www.feer.com/articles/archive/1983/8308_25/P033.html> (accessed 25 January 2006).
35 Ibid.
36 Barry Wain, "Trying to Limit the Role of Malay Hereditary Rulers", *AWSJ*, 5 September 1983.
37 K. Das, "Less Ado About Anything: Mahathir Moves Quietly to Reduce the Constitutional Role the Sultans Play in the Nation's Legislative Process".
38 Raphael Pura, "Malaysia Deadlocked by Royalty Crisis".
39 Raphael Pura, "Gun-Toting Sultans Arrive in Style at Royal Palace in Selangor State", *AWSJ*, 21 November 1983.
40 Raphael Pura, "Mahathir Whips Up Support at Rallies", *AWSJ*, 12 December 1983.
41 Raphael Pura, "Mahathir Won't Retreat from His Battle Royal", *AWSJ*, 5 December 1983.
42 Interview with Siti Hasmah Mohamad Ali, 17 January 2008.
43 Andrew Harding, *Law, Government and the Constitution in Malaysia*, p. 71.
44 Raphael Pura, "Malaysian Rulers Compromise on Veto", *AWSJ*, 16 December 1983.
45 R.S. Milne and Diane K. Mauzy, *Malaysian Politics Under Mahathir*, p. 37.
46 Michael Vatikiotis, "A Code for the Royals: UMNO Seeks a Deal on Role of Hereditary Rulers", *FEER*, 12 March 1992 <http://www.feer.com/articles/archive/1992/9203_12/P013.html> (accessed 23 January 2006).
47 Cheong Mei Sui and Adibah Amin, *Daim: The Man Behind the Enigma* (Petaling Jaya: Pelanduk Publications (M) Sdn. Bhd., 1995), p. 127.
48 Roger Kershaw, *Monarchy in South-East Asia*, p. 109.
49 Andrew Harding, *Law, Government and the Constitution in Malaysia*, p. 77.
50 Stephen Duthie, "Alleged Beating Puts Sultans of Malaysia in Firing Line", *AWSJ*, 10 December 1992.
51 Roger Kershaw, *Monarchy in South-East Asia*, p. 110.
52 Stephen Duthie, "Alleged Beating Puts Sultans of Malaysia in Firing Line".
53 Stephen Duthie, "Malaysia Sultan is Censured by Parliament", *AWSJ*, 11 December 1992.
54 "A Just King is Adulated, but an Unjust King is to be Shunned", speech by Deputy Prime Minister Ghafar Baba in the House of Representatives, 10 December 1992, *The Other Side of Mahathir*, Appendix 2, p. 294.
55 Stephen Duthie, "Malaysian Royalty Faces Limit to Powers", *AWSJ*, 13 January 1993.

56   Stephen Duthie, "Malaysia Nears Crisis as Sultans Reject Curbs", *AWSJ*, 19 January 1993.
57   Ibid.
58   Stephen Duthie, "Malaysian Government is Unlikely to Put End to Clash with Royalty", *AWSJ*, 10 March 1993.
59   Stephen Duthie, "Malaysian Royalty Faces Limit to Powers".
60   Stephen Duthie, "Malaysia Sultan is Censured by Parliament".
61   Stephen Duthie, "Mahathir is Likely Victor in 2nd Round with Royalty", *AWSJ*, 14 December 1992.
62   Ibid.
63   Stephen Duthie, "Royalty's Pampered History Returns to Haunt Malaysia", *AWSJ*, 5 February 1993.
64   Stephen Duthie, "Malaysia to Cut Outlays for Royalty's Expenses", *AWSJ*, 27 January 1993.
65   Stephen Duthie, "Royalty's Pampered History Returns to Haunt Malaysia".
66   Stephen Duthie, "Malaysia to Cut Outlays for Royalty's Expenses".
67   Stephen Duthie, "Royal Rights Compromise Backed by Malaysia's King", *AWSJ*, 19 February 1993.
68   Kua Kia Soong, ed., *K. Das & the Tunku Tapes* (Petaling Jaya: Strategic Info Research Development, 2002), pp. 128, 131, 132.
69   Mahathir bin Mohamad, *The Malay Dilemma*, p. 11.
70   Email correspondence with Param Cumaraswamy, 14 May 2008.
71   Mahathir Mohamad, speech at the Asean Law Association General Assembly, University of Malaya, Kuala Lumpur, 26 October 1982.
72   Interview with Chandra Muzaffar, 16 August 2007.
73   Chow Kum Hor, "Rulers Get Their Way in Choice of MBs", *Straits Times*, 28 March 2008. Malaysia's king, Sultan Mizan Zainal Abidin of Trengganu, not only refused to appoint Abdullah's candidate as chief minister of the state, but also led a campaign by the Conference of Rulers to refuse to accept the government's nominees for two top judicial appointments. Leslie Lopez, "Malaysian Royals Start to Flex Their Muscles", *Straits Times*, 28 July 2008.
74   Roger Kershaw, *Monarchy in South-East Asia*, p. 117.
75   H.P. Lee, *Constitutional Conflicts in Contemporary Malaysia* (Kuala Lumpur: Oxford University Press, 1995), p. 119.

9

The Perils of a Pragmatic Islam

For Dr. Mahathir, Islam was more than a personal creed. It was a tool to help uplift the Malays and pursue his dreams of a fully developed Malaysia.[1] The problem, as he saw it, was that Islam-dominated Malay culture was an obstacle to their advancement. It was not so much the religion itself, he believed, but the local interpretation of Islamic doctrines that caused the trouble. So he defined for Malaysian Muslims an interpretation of Islam that was meant not only to take care of their spiritual well-being, but to secure material benefits for them as well.

Quick to recognize the significance of a global Islamic resurgence, Dr. Mahathir harnessed it to legitimize his administration and make Islam an integral element of his commitment to an increased Malay stake in the economy. Establishing Islamic institutions, such as a university, a bank and various business bodies, he promoted economic development and prosperity as compatible with the ethics, theology and philosophy of Islam.[2] He went further, asserting that it was incumbent upon Muslims to embrace modernity and economic progress to overcome their backwardness and recover Islam's past glory. Dr. Mahathir's pragmatic strategy won him a glowing reputation throughout the Islamic world, but he stumbled badly as he succumbed to political expediency in the final years of his leadership of Malaysia.

By equating Islam with ethnicity in pursuit of his grand design, Dr. Mahathir ensured that religion became an even more vital part of Malay identity, which led to significant numbers of Malay Muslims questioning many aspects of Malaysian society. Holding their leaders to Islam's strict ethical standards, these Malays were alienated by the rampant corruption and cronyism spawned by Dr. Mahathir's economic vision, centred on the government's affirmative action programme. Dr. Mahathir's abrupt dismissal and vilification of his deputy, Anwar Ibrahim, in 1998 stripped the administration of much of its remaining moral authority in the eyes of Malays, leaving the prime minister exposed and vulnerable to electoral punishment and heavily dependent on non-Malays to remain in office.

The major beneficiary of Dr. Mahathir's perceived ethical collapse was the opposition Parti Islam Se-Malaysia (PAS), the direct ethnic rival of his UMNO. Ironically, it was PAS, which always wanted Malaysia turned into an Islamic state, that Dr. Mahathir had tried to undercut by adopting moderate Islamization policies back in the early 1980s. With disillusioned, disenchanted and disgusted Malays deserting UMNO in droves in the 1999 general election, however, PAS vaulted from its provincial base to become the formal leader of the opposition in the national Parliament. The measure of PAS's success was the extent of Dr. Mahathir's failure.

Recast overnight by his critics as an "anti-Muslim villain" and contemptuously labelled *Mahazalim, Mahakejam* and *Mahafiraun*[3] – the Great Oppressor, the Cruel One and the Great Pharaoh: in summary, the cruelest of them all – Dr. Mahathir chose not to address the many sources of Malay discontent. Instead, he tried to recover Malay affection by further outbidding PAS on religion, offering some of the items on the fundamentalist agenda he had always opposed.[4] Encouraged and emboldened, religious bureaucrats flexed their muscles and tried to impose a grim form of Islamic orthodoxy. The whole sorry saga culminated in a declaration by Dr. Mahathir in late 2001 that Malaysia was, in fact, already an Islamic state – a day that in local terms is likely to live in infamy.

It was possible for Dr. Mahathir to make such a controversial claim because the Federation of Malaysia's Constitution is ambiguous on this crucial point. An Islamic state is commonly understood to mean a country where Islamic law, known as sharia, is the supreme law of the land. The alternative is secularism, where the state professes no religion and does not side with any religion. The Malaysian Constitution states that Islam is "the" religion of the nation, though freedom of worship is guaranteed for all. Despite that constitutional guarantee, in practice freedom of religion is qualified. Muslims – all ethnic Malays are automatically registered as Muslims – are answerable to sharia courts, which usually deny them the right to leave Islam or convert to another faith. Indeed, apostasy or conversion is a punishable offence in most states, either with a fine or a jail sentence, or both.

In a memorandum to the Reid Constitutional Commission, which drafted the Constitution before independence in 1957, the governing Alliance said the country should be secular, with Islam made the official religion.[5] An Islamic state was not one of the commission's terms of reference. A White Paper dealing with the constitutional proposals specified that Islam's status would "in no way affect the present position of the Federation as a secular state".[6] But the language ultimately adopted was thought sufficient to convey that notion without actually mentioning the word "secular".[7] At the same time by designating, in effect, an official religion, Malaysia's Constitution allowed the government to fund certain Islamic activities – building mosques, holding Qur'an-reading competitions and organizing the hajj, the annual pilgrimage to Mecca in Saudi Arabia that every Muslim is expected to make at least once.

Back in those more relaxed days it was expected that Islam would play a declining role in national affairs. The departing British handed over to an UMNO-led democratic government with a Western-educated leadership that was focused on economic development. Malaysia's Sunni Muslims were easy-going, coexisting peacefully enough with the Chinese and Indian minorities – predominantly Buddhists, Christians and Hindus – who made up half the population.[8] Few Malay women wore head-coverings, the men were clean-shaven and Muslims generally felt comfortable eating their pork-free meals in non-Muslim restaurants and homes.

Contrary to expectations, however, Islam gradually became more important in the country's politics and the daily lives of Muslims, especially after PAS proved a serious contender for Malay political allegiance. Formed in 1951 by the defection of UMNO's religious department, PAS attracted members with varied interests, including Malay nationalists demanding independence and conservatives from the ranks of the religious elite.[9] PAS captured two states, Kelantan and Trengganu, in the first post-independence general election, held in 1959, surprising UMNO and permanently splitting the Malay community on political lines. Although its fortunes in terms of legislative representation fluctuated over the years, PAS always won between 30 per cent and 50 per cent of the Malay vote.[10]

With religion falling under the jurisdiction of the states and their sultans, the federal government initially had only a limited involvement in Islamic affairs. In 1968, however, the Council of Rulers, consisting of the sultans of the nine Malay states, formed the Malaysian National Council for Islamic Affairs, chaired by the prime minister with a secretariat in his department. Expanding quickly in the early 1970s, the council became one of the major institutions for formulating policy on Islamic matters. Operating alongside the civil court system, the sharia courts – which deal with marriage, divorce and death and hear cases against Muslims accused of religious offences – were taken over from the states and reorganized on a federal basis in 1998.[11] Still, the individual states retained the exclusive right to enact laws on Islam, giving rise to different versions throughout the country.

After the 1969 election, which threatened Malay political supremacy and precipitated racial riots, UMNO sought to recoup political losses by polishing its Islamic credentials. In addition to reinforcing affirmative action for the Malays in the form of the New Economic Policy (NEP), UMNO announced a new cultural policy centered on Islam and beefed up the religious bureaucracy in the Prime Minister's Department. When the three-party Alliance was expanded in 1974 into the much larger National Front coalition, it included four former opposition parties, among them PAS.

As the worldwide tide of Islamic revivalism lapped Malaysian shores in the early 1970s, the government offered other gestures to show its commitment to the religion – introducing the *azan*, the call to prayer, over state-run radio and TV, publishing Islamic literature and establishing an Islamic Research Centre and an Islamic Missionary Foundation. With its quest to re-establish Islamic values, practices and laws, the resurgence took the form of numerous *dakwah*, missionary, groups. They found fertile ground especially among Malaysia's young, educated, urban middle class. Malay women took to covering their heads with various versions of the veil, some adding an ankle-length, long-sleeved robe that left only the face and hands visible. Many men grew beards and some also wore robes, to emulate the Prophet Muhammad and his companions. They sprinkled their conversation with Arabic terms, regarded as authentically Islamic. Muslims not only avoided pork, specifically prohibited in the Qur'an, but became sensitive to the presence of gelatin in chocolates, cakes and tomato sauce.[12] The more devout were no longer willing to dine with non-Malay friends, or with lax fellow Malays for that matter. They insisted that their food be strictly *halal*, prepared in accordance with Islamic prescriptions.

The *dakwah* groups concentrated not on converting non-Muslims but on creating conditions that allowed Islam a larger role in the personal lives of adherents and in the conduct of public affairs. Rural-born Malays who migrated to the cities under rapid industrialization were prospective members of organizations that could give them a sense of belonging, and where they would renew their commitment to an Islamic way of life. The groups – tolerant and liberal at first, though some became more militant later – looked to Islam for what its teachings could offer as solutions for Malay problems, such as poverty, lack of education and corruption.

The "intellectual powerhouse" of the resurgence was the Malaysian Islamic Youth Movement, known by its Malay acronym as ABIM, co-founded by Anwar Ibrahim in 1971 after he graduated with honours in Malay studies from the University of Malaya.[13] A former student leader and fiery political orator, Anwar led non-partisan ABIM through a period of spectacular growth, finishing the decade with a membership of 35,000 in 86 branches. ABIM published its own monthly journal, produced and marketed Islamic books, maintained a library, ran an economic cooperative and organized leadership training courses and Islamic study groups. Ever-ready to back its demands with direct action, ABIM argued that the Malaysian economy benefited only a small group of local and foreign capitalists and was in need of reform. ABIM also spearheaded complaints against Harun Idris, the chief minister of Selangor,[14] which eventually led to his conviction on several corruption charges.

As a fresh graduate, Anwar declined an invitation to join UMNO as well as offers of plum jobs in order to continue addressing questions of Malay backwardness. He opened a school under ABIM's auspices for Malay-medium dropouts from the government education system, collecting a monthly subsistence salary of RM350, as principal and board chairman, for the next ten years. Arrested in December 1974 after backing mass student demonstrations in support of Malay peasants who were suffering acute economic hardship in Kedah, Anwar spent almost two years in prison. Accused of anti-government

ctivities going back five years, he was never charged with a crime and continued to guide ABIM from detention. On his release, he picked up from
where he had left off, sometimes working with the government, more often
thorn in its side.[15]

A number of other ABIM leaders left in the late 1970s to join PAS, which
after four years had broken with UMNO and departed from the National
Front, and many expected Anwar to follow. A visit to Iran soon after Aya-
tollah Khomeini's Islamic revolution in 1979 sharpened Anwar's radical
image. In 1981, he linked up with non-Malay groups to head a broad public
campaign against government amendments to the Societies Act, which were
designed to limit the political activities of non-governmental organizations.
Then, in March 1982, in the middle of this campaign, Anwar stunned the
country by accepting Dr. Mahathir's invitation to join UMNO and contest a
parliamentary seat in a general election two weeks later.[16]

Dr. Mahathir had long held strong views on Islam, the practice of which
he believed should be drastically reformed in Malaysia, and he saw in the
charismatic and popular Anwar an agent of change. Islam of the Shafi'i
school, introduced to Malaysia by Arab and Indian traders and scholars
around the beginning of the fourteenth century, might be moderate and
enlightened, but Dr. Mahathir identified it as a cause of Malay failure and a
barrier to national development. He touched on the subject in *The Malay
Dilemma*[17] in 1970 and elaborated on it in *Menghadapi Cabaran*,[18] published
in 1976, which appeared later in English as *The Challenge*.[19] Dr. Mahathir
wrote that the Malays' value system and code of ethics, on which Islam was
the single greatest influence, were "impediments to their progress".[20] He
blamed "Malay-style" Islam for fatalistic tendencies, a disinclination to
compete and a preference for spiritual over material pursuits.[21] But he said
there was no reason why the Islamic faith, "properly interpreted", could
not achieve spiritual well-being as well as material success for the Malays.[22]

Although Dr. Mahathir had no claim to religious expertise – he was not
educated in the Islamic school system or in Arabic[23] – with the help of
expert assistants and advisers he described in some detail the way Islam
should be redefined.[24] Drawing on Islamic texts, with verses quoted in Arabic,
he took issue with Muslims who saw their religion as either opposed to
modernity, or as the equivalent of socialism. He said, "Islam accepts the
reality that in any society there will be rich and poor, king and commoner,
leader and follower."[25] Despite the way the Qur'an reverberates with the ethos
of social justice, as one analyst noted, Dr. Mahathir declared the teachings
and spiritual values of Islam to be entirely compatible with the pursuit of
materialism.[26] He said the ownership of property did not mean loss of spirit-
uality, and Muslims "need not reject wealth or endeavours which lead to
wealth...".[27] Indeed, Muslims must be equipped with knowledge and other
"tools and skills of the modern world" to uphold spiritual values, for "without
wealth and efficiency, the Muslims will be oppressed and finally spiritual

values too will be lost".[28] Bottom line: Malays had almost a religious obligation to change their character and participate wholeheartedly in Malaysia's
development.

With acute political instincts, Dr. Mahathir spotted the domestic effects
of the international Islamic awakening before most others, and planned to
engage and reshape it with Anwar's help. Nevertheless, he significantly
underestimated the extent to which Malaysian Islam would be "Arabized"
and come under Salafi influences from the Middle East.[29] As a member of
UMNO's Supreme Council in the early 1970s, Dr. Mahathir had tabled a paper
warning of a growing Islamization among Malays, but party seniors dismissed
his concern because he was not a religious expert.[30] UMNO and the government were content to keep responding piecemeal to the proliferating and
diverse *dakwah* groups, whose aspirations varied from communal living
and producing their own products, to forming a religious party and establishing an Islamic state. State governments set up educational foundations in
rural areas to compete with ABIM, while the federal authorities launched a
"*dakwah* month" in 1978 and opened Pusat Islam, in effect the government's
own *dakwah* group, in 1980.[31] These official efforts were widely derided by
UMNO's opponents as little more than token concessions meant to control
and manipulate the growing Islamic consciousness.[32]

Dr. Mahathir's co-option of Anwar soon after becoming prime minister was
a masterstroke, because it not only took much of the steam out of ABIM but
also deprived PAS of a valuable ally, regardless of whether he would have
joined the opposition party. Most of all, it gave the government the services
of arguably the most influential thinker on religion and politics outside
the political parties.[33] It also strengthened Dr. Mahathir's "Islamic" image
and enabled him to make a coordinated and comprehensive response to
the *dakwah* phenomenon. He entered directly into Islamic competition with
PAS, choosing consciously to fight Islam with more Islam, which had the
predictable effect of intensifying Islamization in Malaysia.[34]

At the 1982 UMNO General Assembly, Dr. Mahathir declared that "the
biggest struggle...[is] to change the attitude of the Malays in line with the
requirements of Islam in this modern age....UMNO's task now is to
enhance the Islamic practices and ensure that the Malay community truly
adheres to Islamic teachings".[35] The government banned the import of
non-*halal* beef, prohibited Muslims from entering the country's only casino
at Genting Highlands and introduced compulsory courses on Islamic civilization at universities. Under a slogan of "Inculcation of Islamic Values",
the government also promoted in the civil service such virtues as justice,
honesty, dedication, diligence and self-discipline, which had the added
attraction of being universal human values.

Systematically, the government set up a series of Islamic institutions. An
Islamic bank, which treated earnings as profits and not interest to conform
to Islamic principles, opened in 1983. Catering mostly to rural Malays, it

was offered as an addition to Malaysia's commercial banking system. An International Islamic University, co-sponsored by the multinational Organization of the Islamic Conference, aspired to be the Malaysian counterpart of Egypt's renowned Al Azhar University. It began teaching in 1983 with an international faculty and student body. There followed an Islamic insurance agency, a sharia advisory council for the Securities Commission and Islamic unit trusts for Muslim investors. The overtly political Institute for Islamic Understanding, known by its Malay acronym as IKIM, opened in 1992, with one of its main tasks to channel the ongoing Islamic revival along state-defined lines.[36]

Dr. Mahathir had no patience with *ikhtilaf,* the tradition of scholarly disagreements and varieties of opinion in interpreting Islam.[37] He complained that while Muslims endlessly debated "the minutiae of our religion", Islamic countries were unable to cope with change and were dominated by others.[38] Anyway, he argued, all those options confused Malays without specialized knowledge of religion, leading them to make unwise choices that were "dangerous to the individual and to society".[39] Consistent with his idea of strong leadership, he proceeded to make the interpretation himself.[40]

Bold and driven as ever, Dr. Mahathir deployed an abiding pragmatism to accompany his deep conviction of what was necessary to develop Malaysia. As political scientist Khoo Boo Teik put it, Dr. Mahathir was not concerned with offering startling premises on Islam, or in seeking a systematic engagement with the principal debates sweeping Islamic communities worldwide. He was a Muslim politician "who, in surveying the world of Islam, thought he had important insights into the contemporary Muslim condition, its failings, and what is more, its much-needed correctives".[41]

The Mahathir administration's "correct" Islam was a close reflection of the prime minister's personal and political philosophy outlined years earlier. Essentially an interpretation of an Islamic value system, it specified what the religion did or did not encourage, what it prohibited and what it allowed. Islam was intimately linked to the government's development goals, specifically the NEP and Dr. Mahathir's declared objective of making Malaysia a fully developed nation by 2020. It was a modern Islam, progressive and open to foreign investment and technology, and prepared to learn from the West.[42]

The core message, that there is no conflict between Islamic values and Malaysian-style capitalism, development and prosperity, was conveyed in speeches by cabinet ministers and leading government officials.[43] IKIM, the institute responsible for promoting an understanding of Islam as defined by the Mahathir administration, churned out books and articles making the point. One such article, directed at pious Muslims concerned about usury or interest, said that the basic aim in business "is to make profits, and making profits is nothing negative religiously".[44] In another publication, a writer claimed Islamic endorsement for the government's mega-projects, such as the Petronas Twin Towers, the new Putrajaya administrative capital and the Kuala Lumpur International Airport.[45]

Waging war against narrow-minded Islam, Dr. Mahathir lectured Malays with logic and commonsense. He said a Muslim who blamed fate when it was within his capacity to change his lot lacked faith in the justice of Allah. "Those with mouths but do not eat or drink will die," he said. "Death, when it comes, will be fate, but if the person had food and drink and had the energy to live, then that too would have been fated."[46]

In a celebrated case, Dr. Mahathir chastised a Muslim women doctor who, loath to touch a male patient during diagnosis, prodded him with a pencil. In a letter to a local newspaper, Dr. Mahathir wrote, "The purpose of treatment is to restore the patient's health, not to protect the doctor from sin. This failure to give him sincere and proper examination is an act of cruelty, and cruelty is not part of the teachings of Islam...". If a doctor's faith were shaken by the conduct of his or her duty, Dr. Mahathir said, it would be better for the person not to be a doctor at all. But then there would be no Muslim doctors, a situation he suggested that might be "in dereliction of the Muslims' general obligation".[47]

Dr. Mahathir was withering about Muslims who opted for empty rituals and cosmetic appearances, valuing form over substance. He poured scorn on Malays who adopted an uncritical attachment to lifestyles from the early days of Islam in seventh-century Arabia, rebuking those who claimed women with covered heads were more virtuous and Islamic than others. At the National University of Malaysia, he intervened to prevent the cancellation of a concert by a popular male singer after Muslim undergraduates opposed it, keen to avoid the appearance of "a victory for the external groups that were orchestrating the opposition".[48]

Quite apart from the fact that Dr. Mahathir appropriated Islam for political purposes and to confer legitimacy on his administration,[49] his validation of a singular approach to the religion was bound to be controversial. For a start, as Patricia Martinez, a non-Muslim Malaysian expert in Islam, pointed out, Dr. Mahathir did not follow traditional Islamic scholarly practice of invoking sources from *tafsir*, the formal discipline of Qur'anic interpretation.[50] He and his administration, "even the regular columns by government institutions", defined Islam largely through literal interpretations, the approach usually adopted by fundamentalists.

But just as he had little use for theological interpretations of Islam,[51] Dr. Mahathir conceded not an inch to the theologians and other intellectuals trained in Islam who objected to his pronouncements. Indeed, he willingly confronted the *ulama,* specialists highly educated about Islam, upon whom usually rested the task of interpreting the Qur'an and the Hadith, the account of the words and deeds of the Prophet.[52] Criticized by some *ulama* for venturing into their territory without the necessary academic credentials,

Dr. Mahathir called them arrogant and ignorant, even if they had yards of paper qualifications. "Religion should bring success to its people, but what is being constantly hammered home to Muslims is happiness in the hereafter," he said. "And these interpreters of religion are the cause of backwardness and ignorance in Muslim society."[53]

Dr. Mahathir linked his disdain for *ulama* critics to one of his favourite refrains, that what ailed Islam across the ages was bad leadership that abused the power to define the religion for followers.[54] An example he cited was a small group in Egypt, claiming to be following the only true teachings of Islam, who incited rebellion against the government when it was facing threats from Israel, knowing that if they were successful it would result in victory for the Israelis. "Thus something manifestly bad can be interpreted as being good by Muslims when they have a leader who deviates from the norm," he said.[55]

In assuming the power to define, to impose *his* norm, Dr. Mahathir drew a line that was as much political as religious. With UMNO positioning itself as moderate and responsible, the ruling party freely assigned the label of extremism to its political opponents, including PAS and any religious movements expressing a dissenting Islamic interpretation.[56] The government banned dozens of books and leaflets judged contrary to Islam, and refused to allow Shi'a Muslims to practise openly, regarding their teachings as deviant.[57] It also allocated RM40 million to build two Islamic faith rehabilitation centres, which were "urgently needed" by the mid-1990s.[58]

While Dr. Mahathir preferred to persuade, cajole and implore to enforce the official interpretation of Islam, he did not hesitate to threaten or use coercion when deemed necessary. Some leading UMNO politicians were even more heavy-handed.[59] A deputy minister said the Internal Security Act, which provides for indefinite detention without trial, would be used against persons promoting religious fanaticism among Muslims. He identified several PAS chiefs allegedly guilty of it, among them Kelantan Chief Minister Nik Abdul Aziz Nik Mat, who served as the party's spiritual adviser.[60]

For its part, PAS proved more than a willing participant in what turned out to be one of the nastiest features of Dr. Mahathir's tenure, a conflict with UMNO over Islam that tore apart the Malay heartland. Known as *kafir-mengkafir*, accusations of apostasy, it describes the fury of mutual condemnation. After an internal upheaval in which the so-called *ulama* faction took over in 1982 and established a supreme council of 12 religious scholars, PAS presented itself as the only true Islamic political party in the country. Leaders resorted to *takfir*, "the ultimate polemic in Muslim politics", by calling UMNO politicians not only infidels but apostates, persons who have abandoned their faith.[61] A journalist who visited rural communities in Trengganu, Kelantan and Kedah found PAS propagating "an extremist ideology of hate", which led to separate prayer services and burial grounds, boycotts of feasts and even family break-ups.[62] As government attempts to curb "extremism" increasingly involved questions of religious authority and the toleration of divergent views, the two sides engaged in recurrent cycles of abuse, slander and hate-mongering, all in the name of godliness.

The government outlawed several Islamic groups after branding them deviant, though the circumstances served as a reminder that politics informed the definition of deviancy. In 1985, 18 people died, including four members of a police raiding party, as they attempted to arrest a PAS Islamic preacher named Ibrahim Libya, who had established a following in the remote village of Memali, Kedah. Tough action was also taken against the Al-Ma'unah cult, 15 of whose members attacked two army camps in Perak in 2000, seizing weapons and taking hostages, two of whom were later murdered. Government officials linked PAS to both groups, though many Malays believed otherwise, convinced that security forces mishandled the incidents or were implicated in them.[63]

Even more suspect was the crushing of the passive Darul Arqam in 1994, a full 26 years after it was founded by a charismatic religious teacher, Ashaari Muhammed. The movement followed a traditionalist approach to Islam, with members eating Arab-style, the men wearing green robes and turbans and the women in purdah most of the time. Followers established self-contained communes with houses, mosques, schools, clinics and vegetable plots, their factories producing items for sale in their own shops. Nation-wide, Darul Arqam ran 250 kindergartens and grade schools, and operated enterprises spanning food processing and property to textiles and health services, with assets of about RM300 million.[64] In the years before it was banned, the government quietly cleared the way for the group to expand to counter PAS.[65] When the National Fatwa Council, a government body, declared Darul Arqam a deviant Islamic sect, its leaders were detained under the Internal Security Act for allegedly endangering national security. They were not charged with sharia violations. In the absence of any evidence to support a host of fuzzy accusations, including one that the organization was training a military wing in Thailand to wage war on the Malaysian government, analysts concluded that the reasons for the ban lay elsewhere. With a membership of tens of thousands and attracting upwardly mobile and professional Malays, not to mention founding a dynamic business conglomerate without NEP patronage, Darul Arqam presented essentially a political challenge to the government. Ashaari's claim, that he was more popular than Dr. Mahathir and would one day lead the country, could not be ignored.[66]

The export version of what sometimes was called the Malaysian model of Islam sold well in other Islamic countries.[67] What Dr. Mahathir devised for Malaysian Muslims, welding Islam with modernity, he essentially prescribed for the worldwide *umma,* the community of believers. At the same time, however, steps were taken to ensure that the many progressive Islamic books and articles being produced in Indonesia since the 1970s were not circulated widely in Malaysia. Leading Indonesian Islamic intellectuals, such as Nurcholish Majid, might have enjoyed good personal relations with figures as senior as Anwar Ibrahim, but their innovative ideas were regarded as too controversial for Malaysia.[68] In regular visits and speeches abroad, Dr. Mahathir said that if historically Islam had rescued the world from the Dark Ages and set it on course for modern civilization, Muslim society currently faced an aimless future. And while it was possible to see the hand of Islam's foes at work, the fault lay primarily with Muslims themselves. It was the same old problem of Muslims interpreting Islamic teachings "so that the bounties of Allah fall beyond our reach". Identifying with the major Islamic issues of the time, Dr. Mahathir used them as case studies to drive home his points. The plight of the Palestinians and Soviet-occupied Afghanistan showed "how frequently Muslim countries fall into the hands of non-Muslim enemies because of the weakness or incompetence of Muslims". As for the Iran-Iraq war, it was tragic proof that in the Middle East more Muslims were killed by Muslims than by their infidel enemies. Dr. Mahathir said violence had achieved nothing for Muslims, and their governments should be funding education rather than buying arms.[69] He urged them to embrace science and technology and build dynamic societies equal to the best in the West. The way for Muslims to regain respect was to seek knowledge, work hard, be thrifty, acquire wealth and achieve economic progress.

From the periphery of Islam in Southeast Asia, Dr. Mahathir expressed an unpalatable critique that nevertheless resonated in the Middle East, the traditional heartland of Islamic teaching and political thought. Representing a successful and independent-minded Muslim country that sparkled in contrast with most economically and intellectually stagnant Arab states, he was heard with respect, garnering immense prestige for Malaysia. On the ground, he had name recognition. Abdul Rahman Aziz, an academic in Mecca for the hajj in 2005, was stopped at the Great Mosque's King Fahd Gate by a fellow pilgrim, a provincial court judge from Pakistan, who wanted to know if he was a Malaysian. When Abdul Rahman confirmed it, the judge gushed, "Please send my regards to Dr. Mahathir. Tell him he is a great Muslim leader and will go straight to *jannah*," heaven.[70] No other Muslim with pretensions to leadership had the courage and credibility to "tell it like it is". As Patricia Martinez remarked, "In his pragmatic understanding of – and agenda for – Islam and its *umma*, Mahathir was the best contemporary leader in the Muslim world."[71]

At the same time, Dr. Mahathir's international acclaim had an important domestic dimension. By focusing on Islamic trouble spots, he was able to contrast their problems with the success of his own government's Islamic policies. The implied warning, which he sometimes made explicit, was that if local Muslims did not unite and instead fell prey to different doctrines, they might end up like Muslims in Palestine, Afghanistan or Azerbaijan, subjugated by their enemies. Translated, that meant support the government and reject PAS. Above all, "Mahathir's acquired status of an Islamic statesman" contributed significantly to "the propagation of his version of 'modern' Islam at home".[72]

Still, the risks involved in Dr. Mahathir's Islamization programme in Malaysia were considerable. While he hoped to blunt PAS's appeal for the establishment of an Islamic state, which to all non-Muslims and a reasonable number of Muslims collided with the notion of a modern democracy, the conflict with PAS pushed Malaysia in a more conservative direction. In trying to match PAS, Dr. Mahathir made one concession after another, not just inflating and prolonging the Islamic resurgence but allowing it to move in dangerously illiberal directions, in ways that ultimately were completely at odds with the process of modernization and intellectual growth that Dr. Mahathir was seeking to promote.[73] In 1988, he amended the Constitution to raise the sharia courts to "co-equal" status with the civil law courts, which was to prove his "most fateful, yet ill-advised, innovation".[74] Henceforth, sharia court decisions, in their own area of jurisdiction, could not be appealed – and thus reversed – by any action in a civil court. The incessant UMNO-PAS contest raised expectations among some Muslims that the government would soon eradicate "all those values which were regarded as un-Islamic", leading to a more religious and puritanical order. Conservatives demanded the closure of nightclubs and discos, and attacked state-owned Radio Television Malaysia and UMNO-owned TV3 over their Western-oriented programmes and commercials.[75] The danger was that Dr. Mahathir would take one step too far and be unable to stop.

Dr. Mahathir's high-wire act was never more obvious than in 1992, when the PAS-dominated Kelantan government proposed the adoption of *hudud*, the Islamic criminal code that prescribes such punishments as amputation of the hand for theft, flogging for drinking alcohol and fornication, and stoning to death for adultery. UMNO voted for the *hudud* laws. Dr. Mahathir did not object to the concept of Islamic law, but attempted to brand the Kelantan legislation as a deviation from true Islam.[76] While subtly indicating that his government had no intention of introducing similar legislation, he said, "This does not mean that we reject the *hudud*. We only reject the interpretation and laws of Kelantan PAS, which are not compatible with the sharia."[77] Although legislated in the state in 1993, *hudud* could not be implemented without Parliament amending the Constitution.

So anxious was Dr. Mahathir to avoid handing PAS a political advantage that he chose not to round up a group of Indonesian Islamic extremists, who were on the run from the Suharto regime and proselytizing in Malaysia. Among them was Abu Bakar Ba'asyir, a preacher from Central Java, who emerged as the head of a regional terrorist organization, Jemaah Islamyiah, with links to Osama bin Laden's al-Qaeda. Committed to establishing an Islamic caliphate in Southeast Asia, Jemaah Islamyiah later carried out a series of bombings in Indonesia and the Philippines in which hundreds of people died. Abu Bakar Ba'asyir, who fled to Malaysia in 1985, remained in the country until after Suharto fell in 1998. According to Leslie Lopez, a Malaysian journalist whose reports did much to expose the shadowy network, Malaysian authorities monitored the group for years, but had no idea it was plotting violence. Dr. Mahathir vetoed police plans to detain the radicals because he had little time for Suharto and did not want to play into PAS's hands, Lopez said.[78]

As UMNO and PAS engaged in yet another round of what was dubbed holier-than-thou polemics, the distinction between them blurred: What were once considered extreme demands by PAS became government policy.[79] The battle also opened the way for a vast expansion and empowerment of the religious bureaucracies at state and federal level, all filled with graduates of conservative Middle Eastern institutions whose understanding of Islam was a good deal more reactionary and narrow than that of the prime minister.[80] State Islamic departments reached beyond supervising mosques and Islamic schools, collecting *zakat,* the wealth tax, and certifying those authorized to preach. They enforced Islamic law much more strictly with their own moral police, whose job it was to ensure Muslims observed regulations relating to fasting, decent attire and *khalwat,* close proximity between unrelated members of the opposite sex. The mufti, an official appointed by each state administration who usually sat as an ex officio member of the state Executive Council, emerged as a particularly powerful individual. As a jurist, he had the authority to issue a *fatwa,* a legal opinion with the force of law.[81]

For several reasons, including historical tension between the center and states, the jostling for authority and control did not always follow party lines. Many of the *ulama* had studied in the Middle East together and shared the same deeply conservative opinions, whether employed by UMNO or PAS.[82] As Dr. Mahathir clashed with *ulama* in National Front-controlled states as well as PAS strongholds, the ranks of religious officialdom swelled inexorably, with functionaries devising new laws and restrictions that invaded the most private spaces of Muslim lives. Rather than contributing to the opening of the Muslim mind in Malaysia, the Islamization race actually restricted it even further.[83]

Objecting to "the steady encroachment of a particularly rigid" form of Islam, Farish Noor, a Malay intellectual, complained that Muslims were forced to negotiate "a gamut of bureaucratic hurdles" to do the most basic things – like getting married. Farish, a political scientist specializing in Islamist politics, described as "pathetic" his own three-day marriage class. All he learned was "the benefit of strawberry-flavoured condoms", while the religious teacher compared making love to playing football "in such a ridiculous way that I now understand how the Malaysian football team could lose to Laos nil-6".[84]

Farish and a number of like-minded liberal Muslims paid dearly for having the temerity to challenge Islamic clerics and scholars. Accused by the Malaysian Ulama Association of "insulting Islam", they were verbally abused and threatened with rape and death. Their "living hell" ended when they eventually were able to explain themselves at public forums and in talks with state religious authorities.[85]

Chinese and Indian Malaysians, the vast majority of whom are not Muslims, had their own complaints. In 1982, an Islamic consultative body proposed new regulations that would allow sharia courts to punish non-Muslims, as well as believers, in *khalwat* cases. The proposal was clearly in breach of the Constitution, which allows state governments to legislate on Islam only for Muslims. After non-Malays strongly protested, the mooted regulations were never implemented. In 1989, the Selangor government revised a law to permit, among other things, non-Muslim children to convert to Islam on reaching puberty. After behind-the-scenes lobbying by the Malaysian Chinese Association, UMNO's coalition ally, the offending provision was quietly withdrawn.[86]

It was with his core Malay constituency, however, that Dr. Mahathir came unstuck. Their consciousness raised by years of immersion in narrow readings of Islam at odds with traditional Malay tolerance and creativity,[87] the Malays elevated Islam to the main marker of their identity, superseding language and custom, as defined in the Constitution. With economic progress an integral part of their Islamic lives, as hammered home in countless Dr. Mahathir harangues, many Malay-Muslims came to view critically the NEP and its successor policies. They were better educated and better off than their parents, with a nominally deeper commitment to the practice of Islam. While the country had experienced remarkable development, they could also see that the gains were not being distributed in a fair and reasonable manner. Indeed, Dr. Mahathir's objective of creating Malay millionaires by definition endorsed favouritism, if not cronyism, while financial scandals and massive corruption were endemic and seemingly tolerated. While the power and privilege of those in the upper echelons of a prosperous urban-industrial economy were reinforced, the poor and deprived struggled. In brief, the most basic principle of governance in Islam, social justice, was missing. As the Islam expert Patricia Martinez put it, "It is Islam that defines Malay identity and Islam that proscribes perceptions of wrong doing…".[88] Islam deployed as "catalyst and legitimacy" for the objectives of the Mahathir administration came home to roost as the "idiom and metaphor" for Malay disgruntlement.[89]

A contributing factor was the alternative example provided by PAS, which expanded its membership and branch network with a limited budget and sheer hard work. Attracting little publicity or praise in the mainstream press, the party built a grassroots organization with individual donations and mass support on the back of volunteers willing to contribute without monetary reward.[90] In stark contrast with UMNO luminaries, PAS's *ulama* leaders for the most part led exemplary lives, free of ostentation and the hint of corruption.[91]

Nik Abdul Aziz, the Kelantan PAS boss accused by the government of spreading religious fanaticism, set the tone. After being elected chief minister in 1990, he eschewed the grand official residence and continued to live in the humble wooden house in which he was born, ten kilometres outside the state capital, Kota Bharu.[92]

For large numbers of Malay-Muslims, the dramatic sacking of Anwar Ibrahim in 1998, after a year of financial and economic turmoil, confirmed their judgment that the Mahathir administration was degenerate. Anwar, the second-most powerful politician in the nation and the one providing UMNO with its Islamic ballast, was denounced as both a womanizer and a gay. Dismissed as deputy prime minister and finance minister and stripped of his UMNO deputy presidency and party membership on successive days, he was in the dock a few weeks later being prosecuted as a common criminal. It was all too sudden and shocking. Moreover, it was unbelievable.

Even less acceptable in Malay culture was the way Anwar was shamed and humiliated. Arrested at his home by balaclava-clad, M-16 wielding police special forces who broke down an open door, he was held under the Internal Security Act for allegedly endangering public security. Bashed in custody by Malaysia's police chief, he was left untreated for days and without access to a lawyer or his family. When he appeared in court with a black eye nearly closed, his face bruised and puffy, Dr. Mahathir suggested Anwar may have inflicted the wounds himself to gain sympathy. The government's defensive response to Anwar's later physical deterioration in jail, together with reports showing a high level of arsenic in his blood, indicated little apparent concern for his physical safety. Anwar's chances of getting a fair trial – he was initially charged with five counts of corruption and five of sodomy – receded as Dr. Mahathir repeatedly declared, in disregard of court warnings, that Anwar was a homosexual and an adulterer.[93]

As the Malay community split into two mutually antagonistic and irreconcilable camps, members left UMNO in droves for the only logical alternative, PAS, among them many young, middle-class professionals. PAS offices worked around the clock, signing up 15,000 new members a month at the height of the stampede. Smaller numbers joined the National Justice Party, a multi-ethnic grouping formed much later by Anwar's wife. As if Anwar's incarceration was not enough, the arrest of many of his supporters, sometimes in mosques, left the government's Islamic image in tatters. To his many detractors, Dr. Mahathir was identified with everything un-Islamic in Malaysia. Farish Noor, the academic-commentator, wrote that "whatever the man says – even if he claims that two plus two equals four – is now dismissed as the words of the great *Mahazalim*, who is cruel, tyrannical and unjust...the charm of the old spell has been broken".[94] The minimum standards of respect, which had remained intact through the most bitter political clashes in the past, collapsed. Dr. Mahathir was pelted with used paper drinking cups by Anwar supporters as he left the UMNO

Supreme Council meeting that expelled Anwar, and Malaysia's foremost novelist, Shahnon Ahmad, directed a political satire at the prime minister. It was simply titled *Shit*, and it became a best seller.

Anwar's treatment dominated the dirtiest election campaign in Malaysian history, held in late 1999 after another year of high drama and confrontational politics. Dr. Mahathir prepared for the poll on 29 November by relinquishing the finance and home affairs portfolios, appointing Abdullah Badawi deputy prime minister and reshuffling his Cabinet. The ruling National Front faced a coalition of major opposition parties that for the first time was pledged to a common reform platform. Four parties – PAS, the Democratic Action Party, the National Justice Party and the small socialist People's Party of Malaysia – formed the Alternative Front. They named Anwar, who at that time had been sentenced to six years imprisonment for corruption and faced further charges in a legally disputed trial, as their leader.

Apart from the government's alleged cruelty, symbolized by ubiquitous posters of Anwar and his black eye, issues that figured prominently were those highlighted by the *Reformasi* movement that emerged with the Asian economic crisis in 1997 – corruption, economic mismanagement, injustice and lack of transparency and accountability. Islam was also a factor, the prime minister having defined his deputy's dismissal with the statement, "I am a better Muslim than Anwar is."[95] As if to underline the point, Dr. Mahathir and several close associates went on the hajj to Mecca early in the year. PAS's goal of an Islamic state was not included in the manifesto of the Alternative Front, which campaigned generally for vastly improved democratic governance.

Although the government retained a two-thirds majority in the House of Representatives, regarded as a necessary minimum, UMNO suffered the worst electoral setback since the first post-independence election in 1959. Its parliamentary representation collapsed from 94 seats to 72, with four ministers and five deputy ministers being defeated. In his constituency, Dr. Mahathir's majority fell from 17,226 to 10,138. Overall, more than half the Malay vote went to the opposition. PAS retained power in Kelantan and took control of Trengganu for the first time since 1959. Holding 27 of the 45 non-government seats in Parliament, PAS assumed the leadership of the opposition from the Democratic Action Party.[96]

It seemed obvious that UMNO needed to change its policies and address demands for reform in order to rescue the party's claim to majority Malay support. Anecdotal evidence, supported by subsequent interviews, confirmed that UMNO was identified with gross abuse of power. For example, the majority of Muslims interviewed in Trengganu who voted for PAS said they cast their ballots in anger and frustration: Like their non-Muslim counterparts, they regarded the National Front state government as thoroughly corrupt. They did not vote for PAS because they wanted to live in an Islamic state.[97] Dr. Mahathir claimed otherwise. He insisted UMNO's reversal was due to

Anwar and allies spreading lies, Malay ingratitude and PAS's bribery in promising a passage to heaven for its followers.[98] Rather than admit to a deficient performance that might warrant a *mea culpa* over Anwar and a wide policy front, Dr. Mahathir embarked on what he portrayed as a renewed mission to thoroughly Islamize the party, the government and the nation.[99]

Although popular sentiment clearly favoured good governance, PAS sometimes acted as if it had received an endorsement of its Islamic state agenda. After party leaders continued to restate their intention to create a juridical Islamic state if they obtained power at the federal level, the Democratic Action Party withdrew from the opposition coalition, effectively dismantling the Alternative Front. At the state level, PAS demonstrated its commitment by trying to impose the *kharaj*, land tax, on non-Muslims in Trengganu, the scene of its latest electoral triumph.[100] Following Kelantan's earlier example, Trengganu's PAS government forced through unconstitutional legislation adopting *hudud*, but went further by providing for the execution of apostates.[101] Those laws were "inspired by the most conservative, narrow and chauvinistic interpretation of the Qur'an".[102] Prodded by the Dr. Mahathir-directed federal government, UMNO-ruled states began passing Islamic laws that were almost as harsh.[103] Thus was "moderate" Malaysia subjected to an ever-escalating "Islamic policy auction", with mounting implications.[104]

From April 2000, various National Front-controlled state legislatures began considering their own laws to stop Muslims from straying religiously. Perlis adopted legislation, prepared in the Prime Minister's Department, which allowed the state's religious authorities to take criminal proceedings against Muslims accused of heresy, deviation or other "crimes" related to their beliefs. The bill provided for an accused to be confined to a "faith rehabilitation centre" for up to a year, to allow him or her to be "brought back" to the proper fold of Islam. Those judged unredeemable would be declared apostates and lose their rights as Muslims.[105] A more extreme version of the law, which would have allowed for the prosecution of a Muslim accused of misleading fellow Muslims to vote for an opposition party, was considered during the debate.[106] Johore provided for caning and jail sentences for lesbians, prostitutes and pimps, and for those found guilty of sodomy, pre-marital sex and incest.[107] At a special meeting, UMNO agreed to introduce full Islamic law, including *hudud*, in the state at an appropriate time.[108] In Pahang, all Muslim businesses were required to close during evening prayers, and in Malacca the state government issued an edict directing all female employees, non-Muslims included, not to reveal their elbows and knees.[109]

The federal government began monitoring mosques to ensure that the standard sermon was delivered, and to keep tabs on other activities. In 2001, 15 Muslims were charged in the sharia court for contravening an order by the Federal Territory Islamic Council regarding Friday prayers. It was a criminal offence, punishable by up to two years in jail or a hefty fine, to pray separately from the main congregation or question the authority of the imam leading

the prayers – a PAS tactic. Although there was no basis in Islam for criminal-
izing such disobedience, a version of the law was enacted in many states.[110]

An attempt to force PAS to drop its Islamic banner failed when the Council
of Rulers, consisting of the nine sultans who have authority over religion in
their states, denied a federal government request to ban Islam from the names
of political parties. The government kept the heat on PAS in threatening to
criminalize the party's "religious extremism" by using the Penal Code, which
prohibits uttering words to deliberately wound religious feelings or cause
disharmony. In another move to check "extremism" – and PAS – Dr. Mahathir
in late 2002 halted state funding for private Islamic schools, hoping to stran-
gle them financially and encourage their student body of up to 100,000 to
attend "national" schools instead.[111]

Having abandoned its historically moderate position in the course of
the struggle with PAS for Islamic legitimacy, UMNO teetered on the brink of
radicalism. On 29 September 2001, two weeks after Islamic terrorists mounted
devastating suicide attacks on New York and Washington, Dr. Mahathir
stepped off the cliff by declaring Malaysia an "Islamic state". Although he had
often said the same thing before, and he no doubt sought to outflank PAS
tactically after declaring all-out support for the United States in the "war
on terror" that followed "September 11", Dr. Mahathir was serious this
time. He made the announcement at a meeting of Parti Gerakan Rakyat
Malaysia, an UMNO coalition partner, and called a gathering of all National
Front members to endorse the move. He later told Parliament that Malaysia
was a "fundamentalist Islamic state".

Although Dr. Mahathir claimed that the leaders of the coalition component parties were "comfortable" with his concept, his declaration caused
an uproar throughout the country, which the mainstream press consciously
ignored. Much of the concern was expressed in closed-door meetings or
anonymously on the Internet. Senior government officials insisted it was a
matter of semantics, that nothing had changed in terms of policy or law, and
nor would there be any change.[112] In reality, Dr. Mahathir's announcement
increased UMNO-PAS friction and made life more problematic for Buddhists,
Hindus, Christians, Sikhs and other religious minorities, comprising 40 per
cent of the population. The Information Department distributed a booklet,
"Malaysia is an Islamic State", giving four supporting definitions by *ulama*,
which the government mistakenly assumed would end the debate.[113] Instead,
the publication inflamed the situation by clearly relegating non-Muslims to a
secondary position, and eventually was withdrawn.[114] Government officials
sought to reassure non-Muslims that they were protected by the constitutional guarantee of freedom of worship, but that was cold comfort in
view of Dr. Mahathir's frequent amendment of the Constitution for political
reasons.

Under pressure to produce an operational blueprint for its own proposed
Islamic state, PAS released a document at the end of 2003 that reinforced

the party's hardline image. Until then, PAS had been able to tiptoe around the subject by pointing to its constitution, which identified the party's objective as a vague and more benign "Islamic society". Any chance of persuading the public that PAS's Islamic state would be moderate was lost when Fadzil Mohamad Noor, the party's accommodative president, died in 2002 and was replaced by the conservative Abdul Hadi Awang, chief minister of Trengganu. While the PAS plan did not specifically mention a theocratic state, the press portrayed it otherwise,[115] and Hadi's advocacy of *hudud* and death for apostasy in Trengganu gave the party an uncompromising face. Although PAS condemned the "September 11" attacks, a party initiative to declare non-violent jihad against the United States after its invasion of Afghanistan, together with its support for al-Qaeda's Osama bin Laden and the Mullah Omar-led Taliban regime, further battered the party's reputation as a responsible, democratic movement dedicated to gradualist change.[116]

Confusing matters, Dr. Mahathir started referring to himself as a "Muslim fundamentalist", somehow identifying with the Islamists against whom he had long waged ideological war. Of course, Dr. Mahathir had not changed his outlook. His facile explanation, "I follow the fundamentals of the Muslim religion", betrayed a tactical objective. By describing himself as a fundamentalist, Dr. Mahathir was taking a jab at the West over its preference for "moderate" as opposed to "fundamentalist" Muslims in the "war on terror", and displaying his unhappiness with the West's negative portrayal of Islam generally. It helped get his tough message across in the Muslim world and afforded him some political protection in Malaysia against the stridently anti-American PAS.

Most non-Muslim Malaysians ignored such rhetoric and rallied behind Dr. Mahathir as the extent of the global terrorists threat became apparent and the government's policy of detaining Islamic extremists appeared vindicated. But the Malays remained as divided as ever over Dr. Mahathir. As soon as he retired in October 2003, his successor did what was required to win an imminent election: Abdullah Badawi waged rhetorical war on corruption, cancelled huge infrastructure projects and acted as if *Reformasi* was his natural platform. His greatest assets were his agreeable personality, his Islamic scholarly background and the fact that he was not the demonized Dr. Mahathir. In lieu of further concessions to PAS, Abdullah produced a new formulation called Islam Hadhari, or Civilizational Islam, his own vehicle for showcasing Malaysia as a moderate Muslim country promoting economic development, progress and harmony. Abdullah's crushing victory, capturing 199 of 219 parliamentary seats, was achieved mainly at the expense of PAS, whose representation dropped from 27 seats to 6, while the party also lost control of Trengganu and held Kelantan by a thread. Although PAS actually recorded a slight increase in the popular vote from 1999, the election was a significant setback for the party.

Yet neither Abdullah's huge majority nor Islam Hadhari's stress on universal values would arrest the advance of a strict Islamist ideology, which had built up momentum over a couple of decades and taken on a life of its own. Righteous officials in bloated federal and state religious bureaucracies raided homes in the name of moral policing, splitting families where spouses were of different faiths and separating children from their parents.[117] Non-Muslims who sought legal redress were stymied by Dr. Mahathir's 1988 constitutional amendment giving sharia and civil courts mutually exclusive jurisdiction. Civil courts generally refused to hear cases involving family and Islamic matters, even where non-Muslims were trying to free their wives from rehabilitation centers or recover their children. In what amounted to a rebuke to the Mahathir administration, Judge Abdul Hamid Mohamad said in a ruling in the Federal Court, Malaysia's highest court, that Parliament should act to define jurisdictions clearly, rather than expect the courts to resolve the issue.[118]

In a closely-followed case, a Malay convert to Christianity was denied the right to switch religions. After converting at 26 and being baptized in 1998, Azlina Jailani applied to have her conversion legally recognized. Although her name change to Lina Joy was accepted in 1999 and noted on her identity card, her change of religion was not. Hoping to live openly as a Christian, she filed suit in the Federal Court, but in 2007 it rejected her appeal to have the word "Islam" deleted from the document. Two judges said in their majority decision that "a person cannot, at one's whims and fancies, renounce or embrace a religion".[119] Unable to remove the legal barrier to marrying her Christian fiancé – he would have had to convert to Islam – Lina Joy is believed to have gone abroad to start a new life.

Despite Abdullah's enthusiasm for Islam Hadhari, one of whose ten principles is "protection of the rights of minority groups", he showed little interest in defending religious freedom. Unlike Dr. Mahathir, who at least slapped down those extremists he considered a threat to his interests, Abdullah governed passively and let religious zealots mock his claim to be heading a moderate Muslim administration. He seemed unable to resist pressures to increase the pace and range of Islamization. All policewomen, regardless of race and religion, were required to wear the traditional *tudung* head-covering for official functions. Mainstream books were banned, among them three by British religious writer Karen Armstrong described by Chandra Muzaffar, a public intellectual, as "intellectually illuminating and fair in their treatment of Islam".[120] When Islamic militants demonstrated against attempts to hold an inter-faith dialogue organized by "Article 11", a coalition of 13 religious and human rights groups named after the constitutional article that guarantees religious freedom, Abdullah backed the extremists. He shut down "Article 11" in 2006 in the interests of peace on the streets.

The extent of the morass bequeathed by Dr. Mahathir and aggravated by Abdullah, with Islam defining and dividing Malaysian politics, was clear by the firestorm ignited by Deputy Prime Minister Najib Razak's comment on 17 July 2007. He said Malaysia was an Islamic state and had never been secular.[121] It contradicted the historical record and split the Cabinet and the community.[122] Abdullah expressed his opinion, that Malaysia was neither a theocratic nor a secular state but a parliamentary democracy, implicitly repudiating both his predecessor and successor.[123] After 50 years of independence that included 22 years of Dr. Mahathir trying to reinvent Islam and out-pray PAS, Malaysia's record of religious and racial tolerance was under serious threat.

Notes

1   Patricia Martinez, "Perhaps He Deserved Better: The Disjuncture between Vision and Reality in Mahathir's Islam", in Bridget Welsh, ed., *Reflections: The Mahathir Years* (Washington: Southeast Asia Studies Program, Paul H. Nitze School of Advanced International Studies, Johns Hopkins University, 2004), p. 28.
2   Ibid., p. 30.
3   Farish A. Noor, "How Mahathir Became 'Mahazalim'", in *The Other Malaysia: Writings on Malaysia's Subaltern History* (Kuala Lumpur: Silverfishbooks, 2002), pp. 142–144.
4   Patricia Martinez, "Perhaps He Deserved Better", p. 36.
5   John Funston, "Malaysia", in Greg Fealy and Virginia Hooker, eds, *Voices of Islam in Southeast Asia: A Contemporary Sourcebook* (Singapore: Institute of Southeast Asian Studies, 2006), p. 54.
6   M. Sufian Hashim, "The Relationship between Islam and the State in Malaya", *Intisari*, vol. 1, no. 1, 1962, pp. 7–22.
7   John Funston, "Malaysia", in *Voices of Islam in Southeast Asia*, p. 54.
8   Ibid., p. 51.
9   Ibid., p. 54.
10 Ibid., p. 58.
11 Ibid., pp. 55–56.
12 Chandra Muzaffar, *Islamic Resurgence in Malaysia* (Petaling Jaya: Penerbit Fajar Bakti Sdn. Bhd., 1987), p. 3.
13 R.S. Milne and Diane K. Mauzy, *Malaysian Politics Under Mahathir* (London: Routledge, 1999), p. 83.
14 John Funston, "Political Careers of Mahathir Mohamad and Anwar Ibrahim: Parallel, Intersecting and Conflicting Lives", IKMAS Working Papers (Institute of Malaysian and International Studies, Universiti Kebangsaan Malaysia), no. 15 (July 1998): i–iv, 1–32.
15 Ibid.
16 Ibid.
17 Mahathir bin Mohamad, *The Malay Dilemma* (Singapore: Times Books International, 1999 edition).
18 Mahathir Mohamad, *Menghadapi Cabaran* (Kuala Lumpur: Pustaka Anatara, 1976).
19 Mahathir Mohamad, *The Challenge* (Petaling Jaya: Pelanduk Publications (M) Sdn Bhd., 1986).
20 Mahathir bin Mohamad, *The Malay Dilemma*, p. 173.
21 Ibid., pp. 157–173.

22   Ibid., p. 173.
23   Patricia Martinez, "Mahathir, Islam, and the New Malay Dilemma", in Ho Khai Leong and James Chin, eds, *Mahathir's Administration: Performance and Crisis in Governance* (Singapore: Times Media Pte. Ltd., 2001), p. 221.
24   Email correspondence with Greg Barton, Herb Feith Research Professor for the Study of Indonesia, Monash University, 4 June 2008.
25   Mahathir Mohamad, *The Challenge*, p. 64.
26   Patricia Martinez, "Mahathir, Islam, and the New Malay Dilemma", p. 223.
27   Mahathir Mohamad, *The Challenge*, p. 74.
28   Ibid., p. 82.
29   Email correspondence with Greg Barton, 4 June 2008.
30   Musa Hitam, "We Were Followers", *Far Eastern Economic Review* (hereafter *FEER*), 9 October 2003 <http://www.feer.com/articles/2003/0310_09/p024region.html> (accessed 19 January 2006).
31   R.S. Milne and Diane K. Mauzy, *Malaysian Politics Under Mahathir*, p. 85.
32   Khoo Boo Teik, *Paradoxes of Mahathirism: An Intellectual Biography of Mahathir Mohamad* (Kuala Lumpur: Oxford University Press, 1995), p. 161.
33   R.S. Milne and Diane K. Mauzy, *Malaysian Politics Under Mahathir*, p. 85.
34   Patricia Martinez, "Mahathir, Islam, and the New Malay Dilemma", p. 218.
35   Mahathir Mohamad, speech at UMNO General Assembly, 10 September 1982.
36   R.S. Milne and Diane K. Mauzy, *Malaysian Politics Under Mahathir*, p. 86.
37   Patricia Martinez, "Mahathir, Islam, and the New Malay Dilemma", p. 219.
38   Mahathir Mohamad, speech in London 2000, cited in Patricia Martinez, "Mahathir, Islam, and the New Malay Dilemma", p. 219.
39   Mahathir Mohamad, *The Challenge*, pp. 105–106.
40   Patricia Martinez, "Mahathir, Islam, and the New Malay Dilemma", p. 219.
41   Khoo Boo Teik, *Paradoxes of Mahathirism*, p. 162.
42   Shanti Nair, *Islam in Malaysian Foreign Policy* (London: Routledge, 1997), p. 91.
43   Patricia Martinez, "Mahathir, Islam, and the New Malay Dilemma", p. 232.
44   Ibid., p. 233.
45   Ibid., p. 235.
46   Mahathir Mohamad, speech at UMNO General Assembly, 8 November 1991.
47   Zainuddin Maidin, *The Other Side of Mahathir* (Kuala Lumpur: Utusan Publications & Distributors Sdn. Bhd., 1994), pp. 119–120.
48   Ibid., pp. 117–118.
49   Patricia Martinez, "Mahathir, Islam, and the New Malay Dilemma", p. 224.
50   Ibid., p. 222.
51   Ibid., p. 219.
52   Patricia Martinez, "Perhaps He Deserved Better", p. 34.
53   Mahathir Mohamad, speech at UMNO General Assembly, 8 November 1991, cited in *The Other Side of Mahathir*, p. 114.
54   Patricia Martinez, "Mahathir, Islam, and the New Malay Dilemma", p. 222.
55   Mahathir Mohamad, *The Challenge*, p. 105.
56   Patricia Martinez, "Mahathir, Islam, and the New Malay Dilemma", p. 242.
57   Ibid., pp. 238–239.
58   Ibid., p. 240. The role of such rehabilitation centres was publicized in 2007, when the opposition Democratic Action Party supported the case of an Indian, Revathi Masoosai, 29, the daughter of Muslim converts who was raised as a Hindu by her grandmother. When Revathi applied to a sharia court in Malacca to leave Islam officially, she was charged with apostasy and confined to an Islamic rehabilitation centre in Selangor for six months. Her baby, 15 months, was

taken from Revathi's Hindu husband and given to her Muslim parents. Revathi said that during her detention in jail-like conditions, she was denied visitors and religious officials tried to force her to pray, wear a headscarf and eat beef, forbidden for Hindus. Claudia Theophilus, "Malaysian Family Split by Faith", *AlJazeera.net*, 7 May 2007 <http://english.aljazeera.net/news/asia-pacific/2007/05/200852513390760277.html> (accessed 9 April 2009). "Malaysia Woman Freed after 180 Days in Detention for Apostasy", *Kyodo News*, 6 July 2007 <http://asia.news.yahoo.com/070706/kyodo/d8q70sq00.html> (accessed 8 April 2009).

59 Patricia Martinez, "Perhaps He Deserved Better", p. 37.
60 Patricia Martinez, "Mahathir, Islam, and the New Malay Dilemma", p. 239.
61 Patricia Martinez, "Perhaps He Deserved Better", p. 37.
62 Zainah Anwar, "Don't Let Moderate Islam Get Hijacked", *Straits Times*, 8 November 2006.
63 John Funston, "Malaysia", in *Voices of Islam in Southeast Asia*, p. 58.
64 Stephen Duthie, "Al-Arqam Sect Faces Wrath of Malaysia, Other Nations", *Asian Wall Street Journal* (hereafter *AWSJ*), 4 August 1994.
65 Ibid.
66 John Funston, "Malaysia", *Voices of Islam in Southeast Asia*, p. 58, fn 7.
67 Patricia Martinez, "Mahathir, Islam, and the New Malay Dilemma", p. 232.
68 Email correspondence with Greg Barton, 4 June 2008.
69 Dr. Mahathir did, however, believe in the use of violence in certain circumstances. For example, he secretly provided the Muslim Bosnians with heavy weapons when war broke out in the former Yugoslavia in the early 1990s.
70 Interview with Dr. Abdul Rahman Aziz, deputy director of the Institute of Tun Dr. Mahathir Mohamad's Thoughts, 26 February 2007.
71 Patricia Martinez, "Perhaps He Deserved Better", p. 38.
72 Karminder Singh Dhillon, *Malaysian Foreign Policy in the Mahathir Era (1981–2003): Dilemmas of Development* (Singapore: NUS Press, 2009), p. 255.
73 Email correspondence with Greg Barton, 4 June 2008.
74 Clive S. Kessler, "Faith on Trial in Malaysia" <http://www.atimes.com/atimes/printN.html> (accessed 24 November 2005).
75 Zainuddin Maidin, *The Other Side of Mahathir*, p. 118.
76 Harold Crouch, *Government & Society in Malaysia* (Sydney: Allen & Unwin, 1996), p. 172.
77 Ibid., p. 172, fn 62.
78 Email correspondence with Leslie Lopez, 3 May 2008.
79 Shanti Nair, *Islam in Malaysian Foreign Policy*, p. 43.
80 Email correspondence with Greg Barton, 4 June 2008.
81 John Funston, "Malaysia", *Voices of Islam in Southeast Asia*, p. 55.
82 Patricia A. Martinez, "The Islamic State or the State of Islam in Malaysia", *Contemporary Southeast Asia* 23, no. 3 (December 2001): 478.
83 Farish A. Noor, "PAS Post-Fadzil Noor: Future Directions and Prospects", in *Trends in Southeast Asia*, no. 8 (August 2002), Institute of Southeast Asian Studies, p. 15.
84 Farish A. Noor, "Pharisees at My Door", in *The Other Malaysia*, pp. 250–251.
85 Farish A. Noor, "There Was Once a Religion Called Science: A Fable for Our Troubled Times", in *The Other Malaysia*, p. 319.
86 Harold Crouch, *Government & Society in Malaysia*, pp. 169–170.
87 Email correspondence with Greg Barton, 4 June 2008.
88 Patricia Martinez, "Mahathir, Islam, and the New Malay Dilemma", p. 247.
89 Patricia Martinez, "Perhaps He Deserved Better", p. 32.

90 Farish A. Noor, "'Malaysia Boleh?' – PAS and the Malaysian Success Story", in *The Other Malaysia*, pp. 127–128.

91 Patricia A. Martinez, "The Islamic State or the State of Islam in Malaysia", p. 480.

92 Stephen Duthie, "Kelantan Chief Eschews Showy Trappings", *AWSJ*, 18 February 1991.

93 John Funston, "Malaysia's Tenth Elections: Status Quo, *Reformasi* or Islamization?", *Contemporary Southeast Asia* 22, no. 1 (April 2000): 26, 38.

94 Farish A. Noor, "How Mahathir Became 'Mahazalim'", in *The Other Malaysia*, pp. 144–145.

95 *Utusan Malaysia*, 23 September 1998, cited in John Funston, "Malaysia's Tenth Elections", p. 37.

96 John Funston, "Malaysia's Tenth Elections", p. 51.

97 Patricia A. Martinez, "The Islamic State or the State of Islam in Malaysia", p. 480.

98 John Funston, "Malaysia's Tenth Elections", pp. 56–57.

99 Patricia Martinez, "Mahathir, Islam, and the New Malay Dilemma", p. 245.

100 Ahmad Fauzi Abdul Hamid, "The Islamic Opposition in Malaysia: New Trajectories and Directions?", p. 4, paper presented at a seminar on "Islam in Malaysia" at S. Rajaratnam School of International Studies, Nanyang Technological University, Singapore, 11 September 2007.

101 Farish A. Noor, "PAS Post-Fadzil Noor: Future Directions and Prospects", p. 13.

102 Shad Saleem Faruqi, "Removing the Confusion Between Radical and Tolerant Islam", in "Perspectives on Doctrinal and Strategic Implications of Global Islam", *Trends in Southeast Asia*, no. 11 (2003), Institute of Southeast Asian Studies, p. 19.

103 Yukiko Ohashi, "Malaysia: The Elusive Islamic State" <http://www.atimes.com/atimes/printN.html> (accessed 31 March 2006).

104 Clive S. Kessler, "Faith on Trial in Malaysia".

105 Farish A. Noor, "PAS Post-Fadzil Noor: Future Directions and Prospects", p. 15.

106 Patricia A. Martinez, "The Islamic State or the State of Islam in Malaysia", p. 482.

107 Ibid., p. 481.

108 John Funston, "Malaysia", *Voices of Islam in Southeast Asia,* p. 60.

109 Patricia A. Martinez, "The Islamic State or the State of Islam in Malaysia", p. 482.

110 Ibid., p. 483.

111 S. Jayasankaran, "A Plan to End Extremism", *FEER*, 26 December 2002–2 January 2003, p. 12.

112 Patricia A. Martinez, "The Islamic State or the State of Islam in Malaysia", p. 494.

113 Ibid., p. 492.

114 John Funston, "Malaysia", *Voices of Islam in Southeast Asia,* p. 60.

115 Ahmad Fauzi Abdul Hamid, "The Islamic Opposition in Malaysia".

116 Farish A. Noor, "PAS Post-Fadzil Noor: Future Directions and Prospects", p. 13.

117 Clive S. Kessler, "Faith on Trial in Malaysia".

118 Reme Ahmad, "KL Judge: Syariah Court Not for Cases Involving Non-Muslims", *Straits Times,* 27 July 2007.

119 "Lina Joy: Facts, Discussion Forum, and Encyclopedia Article", *Absolute Astronomy. com* <http://www.absoluteastronomy.com/topics/Lina_Joy> (accessed 9 April 2009). "Chief Justice Tun Ahmad Fairuz Sheikh Abdul Halim's Judgment on Lina Joy's

Case", The Malaysian Bar <http://www.malaysianbar.org.my/index.php?option=
com_docman&task=cat_view&gid=380&Itemid=120> (accessed 9 April 2009).

120   Interview with Chandra Muzaffar, 22 September 2007. The three books: *The Battle
for God: Fundamentalism in Judaism, Christianity and Islam; A History of God: The
4,000-Year Quest of Judaism, Christianity and Islam;* and *Muhammad: A Biography of
the Prophet.*

121   Hazlin Hassan, "Malaysia an Islamic State, and Never has been Secular: Najib",
Straits Times, 18 July 2007.

122   Carolyn Hong, "Leaders Must Speak Up on Religious Issues: Minister", *Straits
Times*, 18 August 2007.

123   "Malaysia Neither Secular nor Theocratic State, says Abdullah", *Sunday Times,*
5 August 2007.

10
A Strident Voice for the Third World

One indication that Malaysia's place in the world would change drastically under Dr. Mahathir came early, as the U.S. ambassador in Kuala Lumpur made a courtesy call on the newly installed prime minister. The ambassador cheerfully informed him that, though it was not easy, he was making arrangements for Dr. Mahathir to meet with President Ronald Reagan in Washington. Although an audience with the leader of the Free World was the imprimatur sought by the head of almost every non-communist government, "I didn't want to have anything to do with America," Dr. Mahathir said later. He told his Foreign Ministry to tell the ambassador he would not visit the United States anytime soon.[1]

It was not so much that Dr. Mahathir was anti-American, though a central strand in his international outlook – "I was deliberately against people who wield a big stick"[2] – ensured he would clash often with the United States. It was more a case of Dr. Mahathir being sceptical of the West in general, and more than a little miffed by the ambassador's assumption that Malaysia would do what was expected of it. The failure to acknowledge Malaysia's independent status was a cardinal sin in Dr. Mahathir's book, an affront to him, the Malays and the entire nation. "The big countries take you for granted, sometimes look upon you with disdain", while small countries "appreciate the friendship" more, he said.[3]

With an instinct of sympathy for the underdog, while seeking respect and retaliating against anyone perceived to have given offence, Dr. Mahathir repositioned Malaysia, forging a more independent and activist foreign policy. A small country in a distant corner of the world, Malaysia punched above its weight, acquiring many of the attributes of a middle power.[4] It was driven hard and almost solo by Dr. Mahathir, who refused to modify his abrasive and outspoken style for the sake of diplomatic etiquette. More than any other non-Western political leader of his time, wrote political scientist Johan Saravanamuttu, Dr. Mahathir proved to be "the quintessential iconoclast of world politics".[5]

In essence, Dr. Mahathir was continuing a nationalistic line in Malaysian foreign policy, which he aggressively improvised and pugnaciously delivered, that could be traced to the 1969 racial riots, when pro-British Prime Minister Tunku Abdul Rahman effectively lost power. The Tunku's rivals who took over set about carving out a distinctive role for the country in international affairs.[6] Confident that Malaysia's political maturity and standing justified a more independent expression in the international arena, the post-1970 leadership sought recognition and acceptance as an equal.[7] Dr. Mahathir, never one to do anything by halves, came close to demanding it. The countries that found it hardest to adjust to the change were those inclined to look back nostalgically to the Tunku years, especially Britain and Australia.[8]

Often correcting course melodramatically, Dr. Mahathir used foreign policy to drive the development of Malaysia, always his central objective – encouraging exports, opening new markets, securing foreign investment, acquiring technology and finding opportunities for Malaysian entrepreneurs to invest in developing countries. Nevertheless, he imposed sanctions on Britain to remind the former colonial master, as well as the traditionally Anglophile Malaysian elite, that the master-servant days were long gone. Extolling "Asian values", he clashed with the Australians, declaring them too deficient in manners and pale of skin to join Asian institutions. He condemned the United States for attempting to impose its system of liberal democracy and neo-liberal economics on ill-prepared developing countries. In looking eastward to Japan, Dr. Mahathir found an alternative development model that did not seek to export unwanted values along with its goods and capital.

Blunt and seemingly fearless, Dr. Mahathir targeted the international economic system, which he believed was rigged in favour of the industrialized West that devised it, to the crippling disadvantage of poor countries. Taking up the cause of all victimized economies, he voiced the criticisms that others dared not utter and became a spokesman for the Third World. Along the way he added the plight of the Palestinians and other high-profile Islamic causes to his portfolio, making himself a hero to Muslims from Pakistan to Gaza and Bosnia. With his credibility anchored in a strong economic performance while maintaining harmony in a multi-ethnic, Muslim-majority society, the peripatetic Dr. Mahathir rebuked the West and preached global restructuring. Conferring with overseas leaders as naturally as he once made house-calls on sick farmers in Kedah, he put Malaysia on the map and gave most Malaysians a reason to take pride in the country.

With Dr. Mahathir, though, it was essential to distinguish between rhetoric and reality. His anti-West diatribes, even when espousing principled positions, were grounded in domestic politics, aimed at enhancing his own nationalist standing and attempting to strengthen what political scientist Joseph Liow called "the Malaysian psyche and national identity".[9] That involved,

Dr. Mahathir seemed to suggest, getting rid of a massive inferiority complex, a colonial legacy he appeared to share with the rest of the country, reflected in his references to the peoples of the West as "whites". While indulging in such "protest diplomacy", though, Dr. Mahathir rarely jeopardized Malaysia's core interests. He artfully operated on a double track, maintaining sound, functional relations with Western governments while sometimes feuding with their leaders, media and non-governmental organizations. Malaysia needed the West's money and know-how, and overwhelmingly pragmatic Dr. Mahathir – "for all his ranting", as Joseph Liow noted – never forgot it.[10]

While skewering First World hypocrisy, double standards and unprincipled inconsistency, Dr. Mahathir walked a fine line between being reasonable and ridiculous. His inflammatory language and extreme positions at times threatened to undermine his genuine grievances and useful suggestions. He was branded anti-Semitic for periodic, disparaging remarks about Jews. He made enemies of some governments that would have been useful allies, and too often he chose personal whim over strategic value. The overriding characteristic that defined foreign policy under Dr. Mahathir was aptly described as "diplomatic adventurism".[11]

Although Dr. Mahathir had a hand in almost every aspect of government policy, the extent of his contribution was not always apparent. With foreign policy, however, there was no doubt. It was all his. As one foreign ambassador in Kuala Lumpur put it, Dr. Mahathir kept Malaysia's relations with the world "in his own hands, defining, monitoring, controlling, directing and redirecting them". In another office in another building, the foreign minister of the day waited to hear "an idea or instruction from 'the boss', and only then" was he able to embark on a diplomatic venture.[12]

While Dr. Mahathir had the services of a specialist in Ghazali Shafie, his first foreign minister, the prime minister did not fully trust any of his Foreign Ministry professionals. Dr. Mahathir personally instructed his ambassadors to be more assertive, and even belligerent and rude, in pushing Malaysia's foreign policy goals.[13] Ghazali, who served as permanent secretary of the Foreign Ministry before entering politics and had extensive regional contacts and friends in Washington and London, complained privately about what amounted to a change in diplomatic culture.[14] Dr. Mahathir bypassed not only the Foreign Ministry but also his Cabinet in launching some of his most spectacular foreign initiatives.

Before Dr. Mahathir took over, little was known of his views on foreign affairs and defence. As a backbencher, he had shown an aversion for militarism – indeed, pacifist tendencies.[15] He was among the nationalists who criticized Tunku Abdul Rahman for maintaining close economic and security ties with Britain after 1957. Dr. Mahathir accused the Tunku of having an "apron-string complex" that betrayed a lack of confidence in independent Malaysia.[16] He was on record describing the consultative Five

Power Defence Arrangements – linking Britain, Australia and New Zealand to protect Singapore and Malaysia – as written on a "worthless scrap of paper", because they offered no protection against "the very real threat" of communist insurgency.[17] But on assuming the Malaysian leadership in strategically uncertain times – the Cold War and Sino-Soviet rivalry still gripped East Asia – Dr. Mahathir made himself defence minister and took a cautious line. He made no move to abandon the five-power pact – in fact, he later strengthened it – or to remove Australian and New Zealand forces from Malaysian soil. Dr. Mahathir also ordered the occupation of the first of several atolls and islets to stake Malaysia's claim to part of the hotly disputed Spratly Islands in the South China Sea.

Six years after the American defeat in Vietnam, the Association of Southeast Asian Nations (ASEAN) was cooperating with China and the United States in trying to force Vietnamese troops to withdraw from Cambodia. Dr. Mahathir, however, looked askance at China, which had attacked Vietnam in retaliation, merely to teach Hanoi "a lesson". Beijing was known to be helping Malaysian Chinese visit China clandestinely in breach of Malaysian law. Beijing was also giving moral support to the sputtering, predominantly-Chinese communist rebellion in Malaysia, despite Kuala Lumpur's formal recognition years earlier of the People's Republic as the sole government of China. Dr. Mahathir declared the Chinese not only a threat to Southeast Asia, but a greater danger than Vietnam.[18]

His was not only a minority view, but was also expressed without the customary consultation with ASEAN. With Foreign Minister Ghazali scrambling to explain to his startled regional counterparts the new prime minister's comments, the episode was a sharp reminder that as leader Dr. Mahathir would sometimes play the diplomatic game by his own rules. Two years earlier, at the height of the "boat people" exodus from Vietnam, he had shocked the international community by declaring that Malaysia would arm itself with the power to "shoot on sight" refugees attempting to land on its shores. Although Dr. Mahathir claimed privately that he had been "misunderstood", he declined to retract or clarify his outburst, saying it had served a purpose by drawing attention to the severity of the refugee problem.[19]

Malaysia announced a fresh set of foreign-policy priorities that were supposed to reflect, in order of importance, Dr. Mahathir's global view: ASEAN, then a five-member group that was struggling to represent a Southeast Asian region split ideologically after recent communist revolutions in Vietnam, Cambodia and Laos; the Organization of the Islamic Conference (OIC), an intergovernmental outfit seeking, fairly unsuccessfully, to promote and protect Muslim interests; the Non-Aligned Movement, a collection of developing countries trying to survive in a bipolar universe; and the downgraded Commonwealth of Nations, usually known as the Commonwealth, a club of mostly former British colonies. But this reordering was a rough guide only, serving to obfuscate as much as illuminate the foreign policy drama that unfolded.

A scant three months after taking office, Dr. Mahathir snapped Malaysia out of its pro-West default position by instituting a Buy British Last policy. Any government purchase from Britain had to be referred to his office for clearance, together with an alternative, non-British tender. Four months later, Dr. Mahathir dropped the other shoe by unveiling the Look East policy, nominating Japan as the country from which Malaysia could learn and benefit most as it industrialized. So while Malaysia looked East with fresh eyes, it also symbolically turned its back on the West as represented by the former colonial power, temporarily at least.

As Malaysia's major trading partner and biggest investor at the time, Britain was a risky target for punitive action. Malaysia had been a member of the Commonwealth since independence, and Britain was the country of choice for most Malaysians studying abroad. The British had defended Malaysia during Confrontation with Indonesia and throughout the communist insurgency, and Kuala Lumpur still had joint defence arrangements with London.[20] Dr. Mahathir, however, regarded Britain as a nation in precipitate decline, a long way from its glory days.[21]

While Japan in many ways was a logical development model, it did not figure at all in the priority list. From the ashes of World War II, Japan had risen to become the world's second-largest economy, turning out products from cars to computers and cassettes that were conquering all markets. Singapore, ever ready to seize a competitive edge, launched a "Learn From Japan" campaign in 1978, and even some Americans were suggesting they should imitate selected Japanese production and managerial methods. For Dr. Mahathir, Japan also had some less obvious attractions that he had noted on trips to the country as trade and industry minister. The capitalist system that Japan practiced was strongly directed by the state, while still allowing the private sector to flourish, in contrast with the laissez-faire approach inherited from Britain and generally favoured by the West.

Critically, Dr. Mahathir believed not just Britain but the West itself was no longer worthy of automatic emulation. He theorized that the post-World War II loss of colonies and the wealth that went with them deeply affected the Western psyche. Moreover, the U.S. debacle in Vietnam undermined self-confidence and further "enfeebled" Western spirits. Over time, Dr. Mahathir observed, despondent Western powers had abandoned the values, systems and qualities that made them great – for one thing, opting for unlimited freedom over discipline. Their decline was reflected in a new generation "sporting shirts and jeans that are unseemly, torn, patched, dirty and old", and young men with long hair and in worn slippers or barefoot. What disturbed Dr. Mahathir was that Asians, Malays included, were mindlessly aping these "bad" habits.[22] "The East is now going through a phase in which independence in the physical sense has been achieved but the influence of Western imperialism is still pervasive," he wrote in the 1970s.[23]

Loosening the straightjacket of colonial thinking was an unstated aim of Look East and Buy British last. As an endorsing editorial in the *New Straits Times* commented, "Only Anglophiles are likely to be flabbergasted...Their bias has been inherited from another era under Pax Britannica".[24] The twin moves had the desired effect, shocking the Malaysian establishment to the core.[25]

Dr. Mahathir let it be known that Buy British Last was the result of negative British attitudes towards Malaysia built up over a long period. One sore point was the start of a London-Singapore supersonic Concorde service on a temporary route through Malaysian air space in 1977: The British "never asked us, never even informed us", he said.[26] The prime minister was also irked by the imposition of higher tuition fees for foreign, non-European Economic Community students in Britain, among them thousands of government-sponsored Malaysians. He was unhappy, too, about the treatment of Malaysian officials visiting the UK, and the way two prominent British companies had restructured under the New Economic Policy (NEP) without giving preference to bumiputras. Britain's refusal to grant Malaysia additional landing rights at Heathrow airport was also resented. The last straw was the London Stock Exchange's revision of its takeover code shortly after a Malaysian state-owned corporation acquired venerable British plantation company Guthrie Corporation in a four-hour share-buying blitz in 1981, dubbed a "dawn raid" by critics. To Dr. Mahathir, the introduction of a seven-day waiting period suggested the Malaysians had acted improperly, and that the British wanted to block similar actions in future. It was especially galling to Dr. Mahathir that Guthrie management, the British government and some newspapers called the purchase back-door, or subtle, nationalization. He considered nationalization unethical, and any hint of it likely to deter investors.

Regardless of those irritations, Dr. Mahathir was bound to adjust what was often called a special relationship, which he regarded as unequal. He had no compunction about severing the sentimental attachments to Britain held by Tunku Abdul Rahman and his two successors, all of whom were British-educated and from the traditional Malay ruling class. Far from sharing their unquestioning attitude to British intentions towards Malaysia, Dr. Mahathir, the outsider, always suspected the worst, until it was proven otherwise.

Not that his fiercely anti-colonial outlook was the result of personal experience. By his own telling, he enjoyed a happy childhood under the British and "yearned" for their return after Japan's defeat in World War II.[27] Dr. Mahathir's explanation for the depth of his resentment – he realized British weakness during the swift Japanese conquest of Malaya, and "I became very agitated" after the war when they tried to impose the Malayan Union[28] – was true enough but insufficient to explain his conversion. After all, when the Malayan Union proposal died within two years, most of his contemporaries moved on.

What really bothered Dr. Mahathir was his perception that colonization had left Malaysia with a "psychological burden" that weighed heavily long after the colonialists had retreated: "the belief that only Europeans could govern our country effectively". What was needed, he said, was "decolonization of the mind". Dr. Mahathir said, "Most Asians felt inferior to the European colonisers…Asia was a region without pride and self-confidence…".[29] Changing that mindset – the nearest Dr. Mahathir came to explaining what he saw as a national inferiority complex – and restoring pride and confidence, infused much of his policy making.

This explained Dr. Mahathir's willingness, even eagerness, to forgive the Japanese for the suffering they inflicted on Malaya from 1941 to 1945. While they awakened national consciousness and expedited the struggle for independence, Japanese troops committed a number of massacres and atrocities during their occupation.[30] In addition to transferring the four northern Malay states to Thailand, leaving the Malays in a minority in both countries,[31] the Japanese exacerbated inter-ethnic tensions and conflicts.[32] Their use of Malay policemen against the guerrillas in the Chinese-dominated Malayan People's Anti-Japanese Army set the stage for reprisals once the war was over. Indeed, some historians trace the starting point of racial cleavages in Malaysia to the Japanese period.[33] While acknowledging Japan's responsibility for immense hardship across Asia, however, Dr. Mahathir encouraged the official Malaysian view that emphasized remembering the positive rather than the negative aspects of the war.[34] To him, the Japanese invasion "convinced us that there is nothing inherently superior in the Europeans. They could be defeated, they could be reduced to grovelling before an Asian race…if we wanted to, we could be like the Japanese…and compete with the Europeans on an equal footing".[35] In 1994, Dr. Mahathir told visiting Prime Minister Tomiichi Muruyama there was no need for Japan to keep apologizing for its wartime conduct.[36]

Ever ready to make amends for Malaysians who had felt "the bitterness and pain of life as a colonized people",[37] Dr. Mahathir targeted a symbol that had long offended his nationalistic sensibilities: "Carcosa", a magnificent colonial house on a hill above Kuala Lumpur's Lake Gardens. Built in 1904, it was traditionally home to Britain's most senior representative. Tunku Abdul Rahman had presented the deeds to the mansion and surrounding acres to the British government in 1956, a goodwill gesture that was anathema to those who felt Malaysia was extending to Britain "the ultimate in privilege and status" that was denied to other governments.[38] They also believed that the gift of the highest point in the capital "had a negative psychological effect on the Malaysian people".[39]

As soon as he got the chance a quarter of a century later, Dr. Mahathir orchestrated a campaign from behind the scenes to evict Britain's high commissioner from "the house on the hill", as it was known. It sounded innocent enough when the matter was raised at the UMNO General Assembly in 1982 by a woman delegate. "It serves no purpose for the government to give too much to people who have colonized this country for so long while the people and the nation derive no benefits from them," she said. They were actually Dr. Mahathir's words, planted by him to get the ball rolling.[40] And Britain was expecting it: Dr. Mahathir had sent a private emissary, his businessman-politician friend and informal adviser Daim Zainuddin, to London to let the government know they would have to relinquish "Carcosa".[41] The British initially took the view that it would not be appropriate to return the property while the Tunku was still alive, but they acquiesced in 1984, years before his death. Although not paid compensation, they were granted land for a new residence in the fashionable Ampang area.

Downgrading the Commonwealth to the bottom of Malaysia's foreign policy agenda was another way of putting Britain in its place. Dr. Mahathir declined to attend the biennial Heads of Government Meeting in Melbourne in 1981 and again in New Delhi in 1983. His view was that he could achieve more by staying home than going abroad to just "talk with no tangible results". Staying home on special occasions became a Mahathir trait.

It was the tough-minded British Prime Minister Margaret Thatcher, herself a mold-breaking politician and outsider, who worked out how to repair relations with Malaysia. After her foreign secretary and defense minister returned empty handed from a trip to Kuala Lumpur early in 1982, Thatcher took it upon herself to end the estrangement. In hosting Dr. Mahathir in London in early 1983, she showed the deference that made the difference. Thatcher entertained Dr. Mahathir at a so-called "peace-meal" at No. 10 Downing Street, the grand occasion attended by an array of dignitaries whose presence underlined Dr. Mahathir's VIP treatment.[42] The British government subsequently agreed to allow Malaysia's national airline to carry more passengers on the Kuala Lumpur-London route. On his return to Malaysia, Dr. Mahathir announced the end of Buy British Last. He attended the 1985 Commonwealth Heads of Government meeting, and at the next gathering two years later offered to host the 1989 meeting and the Commonwealth Games in 1998. It was quite a turnaround for the man who had described the Commonwealth as a "creature of the past".

The limited boycott was to have lasted until Dr. Mahathir judged not only the British government but also business, the press and other institutions to be showing Malaysia more respect. By the time he lifted the restrictions, after 18 months, British companies were hurting and complaining about the loss of contracts estimated at between 20 million and 50 million pounds. Dr. Mahathir told the Malaysian Parliament that the British had shown "a comprehensive change in attitude and thinking towards Malaysia as a sovereign and independent country". One basic adjustment in London was the acceptance that Britain in future would have to compete with the field for commercial contracts, and perhaps sweeten major deals with government inducements.[43]

While Dr. Mahathir had made his point, his underlying pragmatism was undiminished, as indicated by the speed by which bilateral relations recovered and British investment in the Malaysian economy simultaneously spiked. Although the West might be rotting morally, it remained an essential market and source of capital for Malaysia's ambitious development. Thatcher's hand-crafted settlement was critical. It confirmed that the supersensitive Dr. Mahathir sought consideration, appreciation and homage from the West, particularly from the country that had lorded over Malaysia for more than a century. It also reinforced Dr. Mahathir's belief that it did not necessarily pay to be nice to everyone. As it was, Thatcher found in Dr. Mahathir a kindred spirit, "almost a man to envy".[44] Her feelings were fully reciprocated, with Thatcher being awarded an honorary degree from a university in Dr. Mahathir's constituency.

While the bilateral relationship remained warm until Thatcher was deposed by her party in 1990, Dr. Mahathir was prepared to slap down the British again if they overstepped some invisible mark, or Malay confidence faltered before what one analyst called "the British aura of superiority".[45] London's *Sunday Times* obliged in 1994, when John Major was prime minister, by reporting "high-level corruption" around a tendering process in Malaysia. It came as the British Parliament and press probed possible illegal links between a 1.3 billion pounds arms sale to Malaysia, signed by Dr. Mahathir and Thatcher in 1988, and aid for the Pergau hydroelectric dam in Kelantan. Angered by the British government's failure to defend both the deal and his integrity, Dr. Mahathir launched another boycott of British commerce, including the cancellation of some major projects on the eve of closure. The decision was announced by Deputy Prime Minister Anwar Ibrahim, who echoed Mahathir's "obsession with white racism" by trying to portray the *Sunday Times* report as a slight on all Malaysians.[46] In a lengthy letter to the *Financial Times*, Dr. Mahathir said, "Of course the natives are corrupt. They must be because they are not British and not white."[47]

While Dr. Mahathir's reaction seemed to expose his insecurities, Major's condescending comment, immediately after the prohibition was imposed, betrayed traces of the colonial mentality Dr. Mahathir detested. Major suggested that the reason Malaysia was prosperous was due to British trade and investment.[48] He had learned nothing from his predecessor where Dr. Mahathir was concerned. Just the same, Dr. Mahathir moved quickly to limit the scope and shorten the duration of the boycott this time – seven months – mindful that London might retaliate with the backing of its European partners.

Although Dr. Mahathir initially deflected American overtures and spent the next couple of years criticizing the West, especially the United States, for failing to understand or support the economic aspirations of developing countries, he soon made amends. The United States was one of Malaysia's most important economic partners, and American capital and appetite for Malaysian goods were an essential part of Dr. Mahathir's plans to develop the country. On his first official visit to Washington in 1984, Dr. Mahathir travelled with some of Malaysia's most influential businessmen and bankers, their way smoothed by Daim Zainuddin, dispatched by Dr. Mahathir nine months earlier, again as a personal envoy. Daim had persuaded the Americans to limit sales of stockpiled tin in view of weak world demand for a key Malaysian export, and the success of his representations prompted Kuala Lumpur to intensify its lobbying efforts in Washington.[49] Dr. Mahathir got to meet what diplomats called the "first team": President Reagan, Vice President George Bush, Treasury Secretary Donald Regan and Defense Secretary Caspar Weinberger.

The most far-reaching outcome of the visit, however, was a security – not an economic – agreement, what one analyst called, when details began to leak almost two decades later, "a secret defense treaty".[50] Without informing his countrymen and women, Dr. Mahathir threw in his lot with the Americans, agreeing to naval ship visits, ship and aircraft repairs, joint military exercises in Malaysia and close cooperation between the two militaries. Thereafter, Dr. Mahathir could launch regular rhetorical broadsides at the United States, winning a name in Malaysia and the rest of the developing world for his courage in standing up to Washington, knowing his relations with the Americans rested on a secure bedrock. When the United States lost the use of major military bases in the Philippines in 1991–92, the Malaysians criticized Singapore for offering to accept a small number of military personnel and provide facilities to enable the U.S. Seventh Fleet to retain a forward presence in Southeast Asia. Yet Malaysia covertly was providing similar facilities, which allowed the Americans to implement a "places not bases" strategy. Dr. Mahathir publicly disputed the need for the U.S. Navy to patrol the region, but privately helped make it possible. And while he noisily disagreed, from the early 1990s, with Western officials who worried that a powerful China might become a neighbourhood bully, in practice he indulged in classic hedging: He contributed to a balance of power arrangement and effectively paid insurance premiums to the United States in case anything went wrong.

The innocuous sounding Bilateral Training and Consultation (BITAC) agreement entered into by Malaysia and the United States in 1984 established a series of working groups for exercises, intelligence sharing, logistics support and general security issues.[51] Officially, it was not an agreement at all, according to a former American air attaché in Kuala Lumpur, William E. Berry, Jr., "because that was too structured for that crafty old fox, Mahathir". The prime minister was being careful because of his public opposition to foreign military bases in the region, Berry explained.[52] The Americans played along, doing nothing to draw attention to the commitment and allowing Dr. Mahathir to flaunt his independence and claim, "We are aligned with no one."[53]

Nevertheless, BITAC was the basis for vastly expanded military cooperation between the two countries. The U.S. Air Force and navy made use of its provisions to establish air-to-air and air-to-ground training, while the U.S. army got access to the excellent jungle warfare training school at Pulada in Johore. With Malaysian assistance, the U.S. Navy developed a small-ship repair facility at Lumut on the West Coast, and the U.S. Air Force later established a facility in Kuala Lumpur to repair C-130 Hercules transport aircraft. As the Philippine bases closed, particularly Crow Valley, the main bombing range of U.S. forces in the western Pacific, the Malaysian training grounds became even more important. For the Malaysian air force and navy, the major benefit was the opportunity to train with American forces. For example, Cope Taufan, an annual air force exercise, in 1996 provided the first chance for the Malaysian Air Force to use its Russian MiG-29s with American F-15s. Internally, both sides expressed "great satisfaction" with the war games.[54]

In 1994, Malaysia and the United States signed an Acquisition and Cross-Servicing Agreement, which allowed American naval vessels and aircraft to transit Malaysia for re-supply and maintenance. This agreement, too, remained secret until 2005, when it was publicly renewed for another ten years. Even after some Malaysians heard about periodic American ship visits and exercises in Malaysia, the government was reluctant to identify BITAC and disclose details to Parliament.[55] Finally, in 2002, 18 years after Dr. Mahathir and the Reagan administration had sealed the original deal, Defence Minister Najib Razak partially lifted the curtain on what he called a "well-kept secret": More than 75 U.S. military ships had docked at Malaysian ports in the past two and-a-half years.[56] In addition, the two countries were holding joint exercises annually on land and sea, Malaysians were training in the United States and an extensive two-way student exchange programme was in place.

In retirement, Dr. Mahathir acknowledged and defended BITAC, which he said was suggested by Caspar Weinberger, Reagan's defence secretary, and involved no more than "normal arrangements that the United States has with many, many countries". Malaysia's military brass favoured the agreement for the benefits it brought, and "I think it is good for them. They should get to know new tactics, new strategies and things like that. That's why I agreed".[57] The U.S. perspective, however, was quite different, seeing BITAC as an original template for wider application. By 1996, it had become "the model for the establishment of military ties with other countries with which the United States is associated".[58] Dr. Mahathir acknowledged the secrecy surrounding the 1984 and 1994 agreements. "Maybe they were not broadcast widely, but I didn't see anything wrong with that," he said. And he continued to insist, contrary to the end result, that "I didn't like the idea of the Seventh Fleet hovering around here."[59]

Australia was another developed country with which Malaysia had long and friendly ties, including security links, which were periodically troubled after Dr. Mahathir appeared on the scene. Australia's closest regional ally in the 1950s and 1960s, Malaysia became the neighbour that Canberra found the most challenging in the following decades. Given its past as an aid donor, Australia was slow to jettison its paternal attitude and recognize the importance that the post-1970 Malaysian leadership attached to issues of national pride. For their part, Malaysian leaders sometimes used extravagant rhetoric in criticisms of Australia, and too often assumed that views expressed by the media represented those of the government.[60] The crucial element, however, was Dr. Mahathir's prickly personality. Where his predecessors might have overlooked an Australian barb or gaffe, Dr. Mahathir allowed nothing to pass that he found offensive. He had difficulties with Australian prime ministers on most of his watch, regardless of political affiliation: Bob Hawke (Labor), in 1986, for describing the execution of two Australian drug traffickers as "barbaric"; Paul Keating (Labor), in 1993, over calling Dr. Mahathir "recalcitrant" for not attending the first summit of the Asia-Pacific Economic Cooperation forum; and John Howard (Liberal), in 1998–99, for expressing concern about former deputy premier Anwar Ibrahim's arrest and trials.

In the late 1970s, relations were buffeted by a series of bilateral trade disputes, but the issues that rocked the relationship in the Mahathir era were overwhelmingly about national self-esteem.[61] For a year from late 1990, Malaysia downgraded relations with Australia in protest over the showing of a drama series on Australian TV, *Embassy*, set in a fictitious Ragaan, which the Malaysians assumed was a caricature of Malaysia. In one scene a Ragaan leader prepared to "shoot" Vietnamese boat people, later to claim he had merely meant to "shoo" them, a dramatization of the incident in the early 1980s, when Home Minister Ghazali Shafie sought to defuse the furore over Dr. Mahathir's threat against refugees. Malaysia-Australia projects and visits were frozen, and officers at the Australian mission in Kuala Lumpur were excluded from routine diplomatic contacts. Things returned to normal after Hawke agreed to disassociate Australia from media reports that Malaysia found objectionable. After Keating called Dr. Mahathir recalcitrant in late 1993, the Malaysian Cabinet authorized individual ministries to take such measures against Australia as they saw fit. Australian-made television shows and commercials were banned from Malaysian TV, and the minister for posts and telecommunications said his department would review its dealings with Australian companies. After three weeks, during which the Australians let it be known they were contemplating serious retaliatory action, Malaysia accepted Keating's expression of regret for any unintended offence. Characteristically, Dr. Mahathir took Hawke's 1986 description of the act of hanging the two drug dealers – "barbaric" – as an insult that applied to the entire Malaysian population. Hawke "called Malaysians barbarians", Dr. Mahathir said.

Dr. Mahathir had acquired a jaundiced view of Australia early in his political career as a result of an Australian diplomatic faux pas. In the late 1960s, Canberra invited him, as a first-term parliamentarian and rising star, to visit the country on an all-expenses paid programme as a guest of the foreign ministry. After he lost his seat in the 1969 election and a few days before he was due to depart, the Australians asked him to postpone the trip, with officials reporting variously that the visitor programme was overloaded or short of funds. Suspecting he was dropped because of his political setback, which included expulsion from UMNO, Dr. Mahathir admitted to being "hurt".[62] Two years later he accepted an Australian government offer to visit Canberra after attending a seminar at his own expense at Monash University, only to find the official hospitality in the capital as bleak as the winter weather. An embarrassed junior official tried to save the occasion, on his own initiative, by hosting a dinner for Dr. Mahathir.[63] Nearly 40 years later, Dr. Mahathir had not forgotten how he was treated by the Australians when "out of the government". He said, "They invited me to visit, and then they cancelled it." Was it a calculated snub? "I don't know whether it was deliberate, but anyway they cancelled it."[64]

In government, Dr. Mahathir did not try to hide his dislike of Australia. Hosting a state dinner in Kuala Lumpur for Prime Minister Malcolm Fraser in 1982, Dr. Mahathir delivered caustic comments that were "unnecessarily provocative and in extremely poor taste", according to a Malaysian account.[65] On his only official visit to Australia in 1984 he was immensely sympathetic to Prime Minister Hawke, who broke down and wept during their meeting, having just learned of his daughter's potentially fatal drug addiction. Responding both as a fellow parent and doctor, Dr. Mahathir went to considerable personal lengths to get information that he thought might help the Hawke family.[66] But politics was something else. Dr. Mahathir's failure to make another official visit to Australia in 18 years was an expression of disapproval by one of Asia's most travelled leaders.

His general gripe was that Australians, in or out of government, were too fond of criticizing – "that we are not up to their mark and we don't know how to run our country; we don't practice human rights; our democracy is defective…".[67] An exchange in 1988 showed just how deeply Dr. Mahathir resented such unsolicited advice. Responding to a protest by more than 100 Australian members of parliament over the detention without trial of Malaysian politicians, activists and intellectuals in Operation Lalang, Dr. Mahathir wrote, "When Australia was at the stage of Malaysia's present development, you solved your aborigines problem by simply shooting them". After explaining the need for "harsh" laws to ensure tensions were contained in a multi-racial country, he told the parliamentarians to "please concentrate on fair treatment for the aborigines and the Asians in your midst and leave us alone".[68] While Dr. Mahathir was prime minister, bilateral relations would remain in what Malaysian academic Shamsul Amri Baharuddin called a state of "stable tension" – trouble could flare at any time.[69]

Dr. Mahathir's regular skirmishes with Western governments, together with his use of crude language and references to race and religion, invited the judgment that he was blindly anti-Caucasian – and anti-Semitic, since the religion he targeted was usually Judaism. Yet he formed close personal friendships not only with Margaret Thatcher, but other prominent Western officials such as Henry Kissinger, the Jewish former U.S. secretary of state. He also courted leading international corporate figures, persuading the likes of Microsoft founder Bill Gates to act as an adviser to Malaysia's Multimedia Super Corridor.[70] In fact, most of Dr. Mahathir's anti-West rhetoric was designed to provide him with political cover on the domestic front, or give Malaysians a reason to close ethnic ranks and rally behind the government. It was a potent tool when Dr. Mahathir's leadership of the party or country was under threat.[71]

As for his outrageous and sometimes odd remarks about Jews, Dr. Mahathir chose to live recklessly. His statements no doubt were anti-Semitic at times, and to the New York-based Anti-Defamation League, formed specifically to fight anti-Semitism, Dr. Mahathir was an "unrepentant anti-Semite".[72] But he denied it, and almost no one who knew him well or observed him at close quarters for any length of time believed he was anti-Semitic. Dr. Mahathir had the habit of denigrating anyone or anything he did not like, and he was not about to restrain himself over Jews. One problem was that he failed to distinguish between "Jews" and "Israel" or "Israelis", using the terms interchangeably. As one of Israel's fiercest mainstream critics – Malaysia did not recognize Tel Aviv – Dr. Mahathir was irked that Muslims could so easily be labelled terrorists, while any condemnation of Israel – a "terrorist state", as he called it – brought an outcry alleging anti-Semitism. Another problem was that Dr. Mahathir had long presented his views of race in terms of stereotypes, distinguished not only by ethnic origin but also other characteristics. As an illustration, he said in *The Malay Dilemma* that Jews "are not merely hook-nosed, but understand money instinctively".[73] He also wrote: "Jewish stinginess and financial wizardry gained them the commercial control of Europe and provoked an anti-Semitism...".[74] Dr. Mahathir dealt similarly, and at length, with Malaysia's Chinese and Malays – complete with theories of inbreeding – reserving his harshest judgment for his own community. He described the Malays as chronically backward and subservient. So while his analytical approach was hardly scientific and his conclusions questionable, he clearly did not discriminate on the basis of religion or ethnicity.

The record showed that the New York Philharmonic cancelled a proposed visit to Malaysia in 1984 after the government demanded that a work by Swiss Jewish composer Ernest Bloch be removed from the programme, and Steven Spielberg withdrew "Schindler's List" from distribution in Malaysia after the Cabinet ruled in 1994 that several scenes be cut from the movie. Dr. Mahathir voiced no public objection when some UMNO members handed out copies of American industrialist Henry Ford's anti-Semitic book, *The International Jew*, at the UMNO General Assembly in

2003.[75] Dr. Mahathir countered that he personally invited 14 Israeli high school students to visit Malaysia in 1997, followed soon after by an Israeli cricket team. "I have friends who are Jews," he said, without a trace of irony or embarrassment.[76]

Dr. Mahathir, the politician and Islamic statesman, used extreme language against the perceived enemies of Islam as a device to get his message across in the Muslim world. The message was as pragmatic as it was uncompromising, that if 1.3 billion Muslims were oppressed and humiliated it was largely their own fault, and only they could rescue themselves. Dr. Mahathir couched his problematic statements in the "dichotomies of the world-versus-Islam", familiar to his Muslim audience, to open their minds for the unpalatable advice that inevitably followed.[77] The speech he gave to the opening of the OIC summit in Kuala Lumpur two weeks before he retired in 2003 was typical, if more acerbic than usual. His comment, that "the Jews rule this world by proxy" and "get others to fight and die for them", made headlines around the world and was widely condemned.[78] The 56 other Islamic leaders in Dr. Mahathir's audience also heard him urge Muslims to summon the political will to build stable and well administered countries, "economically and financially strong, industrially competent and technologically advanced".[79] His speech was nuanced enough for him to note that "not all non-Muslims are against us" and even many Jews "do not approve of what the Israelis are doing.... We must win their hearts and minds".[80]

Throughout the 1980s, Dr. Mahathir caught international attention by denouncing the West for policies that furthered its prosperity at the expense of developing countries. Based on Malaysia's experience producing tin and rubber, he complained that commodity prices were manipulated by rich countries to make money for middlemen, while the prices of imported manufactured goods were set by the Western countries to ensure a hefty profit. He said speculators, including banks, could alter exchange rates as they wished, turning the trade in commodities into a trade in currencies. Taking up the cause of all small and developing countries, Dr. Mahathir said they were "victims of an unjust and inequitable economic system that seeks to deny us the legitimate rewards of our labour and natural resources".[81] He attacked the "free traders of convenience" in the West, who resorted to protectionism in the form of quotas, tariffs, high interest rates and exorbitant freight charges, once developing countries became competitive.[82] Observing that the big powers formed exclusive "economic clubs" to guard their own interests, such as the Group of Seven industrialized nations, he charged them with bullying, hypocrisy and deceit. The uncaring North, as he collectively called them, enforced a "cycle of low income, lack of capital and know-how and continuing low income" that entrapped most developing nations, the South.[83]

It was a withering critique, one Dr. Mahathir could deliver because Malaysia was less dependent on foreign aid and assistance than other potential critics and less susceptible to retribution by the major powers.[84] True, he sometimes went overboard and claimed to fear "a new form of colonialism".[85] He also indulged in his own deceit, not only ignoring Japan's protectionist policies but pretending Japan was not part of the industrialized world. He once told a business audience – disingenuously, as an analyst noted[86] – that "Japan may be classified as developed but it is still developing vigorously".[87]

Pronouncing the North-South dialogue dead, Dr. Mahathir unveiled a series of initiatives aimed at encouraging cooperation among poorer countries and making them less dependent on the industrialized world. Working through the Non-Aligned Movement and the once-shunned Commonwealth Heads of Government Meetings, he was instrumental in forming the South-South Commission, whose first secretary-general was a Malaysian. Dr. Mahathir also set up the Group of 15, a core of developing countries that first met in Kuala Lumpur in 1989 to explore closer economic ties. His other contributions included a bilateral payments arrangement enabling any two participants to settle their trade without using foreign currency, and a data exchange centre to provide advice to small and medium-sized industries in the South.

The end of the Cold War and its promise of a new world order opened the way for more assertive types of leaders from developing countries, such as Dr. Mahathir, to make their mark internationally. Having vanquished his political foes and seen the underground Communist Party abandon its 40-year insurgency, Dr. Mahathir carefully reoriented external relations towards developing countries without damaging ties to the developed world. With the Malaysian economy starting to catch fire again, delegations from developing countries dropped in to learn his secrets, and Dr. Mahathir was in demand as a speaker at global forums. Named chairman of a group to plot the long-term future of the Commonwealth, he also headed another outfit to find a solution to apartheid South Africa's political quagmire.[88] Reflecting his activism, Malaysia was elected to a non-permanent seat on the United Nations Security Council in 1998–99, the second term during Dr. Mahathir's premiership, and to the presidency of the U.N. General Assembly. "By the 1990s", wrote Joseph Liow, the political scientist, "Mahathir Mohamad had firmly established himself as a charismatic leader with a reputation for outspokenness and daring to challenge prevailing norms in international relations".[89]

Malaysia identified diplomatic niches where its limited resources might be stretched to play a leading role. For example, based on a peacekeeping tradition that began in 1962, Malaysia became one of the top ten troop contributors to U.N. operations in the early 1990s, when it simultaneously dispatched forces to Somalia and Bosnia-Herzegovina.[90] During the decade, Malaysia also sent peacekeepers to the Iran-Iraq border, Namibia, Cambodia, Kuwait and East Timor. It opened a peacekeeping training centre in Malaysia, to which more than a dozen countries, among them the United States, Canada and France, sent trainees.[91]

Mindful of the worldwide Islamic resurgence and its impact on Muslim-majority Malaysia, where the opposition Islamic party was pushing for an Islamic state, Dr. Mahathir crafted a foreign policy to serve that specific need. By winning international recognition as a champion of Islamic causes, he made it almost impossible for the opposition to claim he was neglecting Islam. It is doubtful, though, that Dr. Mahathir's commitment went beyond posturing, as when the crunch came – for instance, over Iraq's 1990 invasion of Kuwait – Malaysia ignored public opinion and voted with the United States in the U.N. to use force to evict the Iraqis.

Inheriting a concern for the liberation of Palestine, Dr. Mahathir pursued the issue with added fervour, excoriating Israel and its Western supporters, exposing what he called Zionist influence in international news organizations and straining relations with Singapore by objecting to Israeli President Chaim Herzog's visit to the city-state in 1986. Through the OIC, Dr. Mahathir also got involved in trying to settle the eight-year Iran-Iraq war, and actively supported the *mujahidin* in their resistance to the Soviet Union's occupation of Afghanistan. But it was the defence of Muslims in Bosnia-Herzegovina, as war broke out in the former Yugoslavia, which proved to be Dr. Mahathir's Islamic preoccupation. He secretly provided the Bosnians with heavy weapons.[92] It was an ideal tragedy on which to unleash his polemical skills and flay the West for practising double standards over its reluctance to stop Serbian ethnic cleansing. Dr. Mahathir's efforts to reactivate the Non-Aligned Movement in the post-Cold War era and galvanize it to adopt a resolution calling for the expulsion of the rump state of Yugoslavia from the U.N. caught the movement's imagination at a conference in Jakarta in 1992. Dr. Mahathir emerged as the "New Voice for the Third World", as a cover of the weekly *Far Eastern Economic Review* proclaimed.[93]

Under fire by Western environmentalists over its forestry practices, Malaysia also rallied developing countries to ensure their views were heard at a landmark U.N. sponsored Earth Summit in Rio de Janeiro in 1992. Dr. Mahathir told ministerial representatives of more than 50 developing economies, who gathered in Kuala Lumpur beforehand, that the industrialized world's fear of environmental degradation provided them with leverage that had not previously existed. He asserted that developed nations, if they wanted to save the forests in poorer countries, had a responsibility to provide the funds and technology to enable them to shift to other sources of income. As the *Economist* noted, the Malaysians "emerged as the leaders of the developing world on the road to Rio".[94] Moreover, at the summit, Dr. Mahathir and his officials maintained the pressure so that the general development interests of the South were persistently linked to the overall discussion of environmental issues.[95]

As Third World champion, Dr. Mahathir took a prominent part in a debate on "Asian values" that raged the length of East Asia and across the Pacific in

the early 1990s. Triumphant after the demise of Communism, President
Bill Clinton's first administration aggressively sought to spread its victor-
ious version of democracy and human rights among the unconvinced and
unconverted. Dr. Mahathir joined government-employed Singaporean
intellectuals in counter-attacking by contending that Asian values, in
contrast with Western values, put greater stress on community than
individuals, and emphasized economic and social, rather than civil and
political, rights.

Dr. Mahathir had longed railed against the British for ruling Malaya in
authoritarian fashion, only to insist that the inexperienced country practice democracy the instant it became independent. In the name of Asian
values, which conveniently deflected attention from his own blemished
record, Dr. Mahathir listed societal defects – crime, violence, drug addiction, homosexuality, chronic vandalism, illegitimate births – to suggest the
American political system did not suit Asia. Is there only one form of
democracy or only one high priest to interpret it, he asked rhetorically.
Attempts by the West to impose democracy and human rights were disguised efforts to weaken Asian countries and undermine their competitiveness, he said, and a U.S. move, backed by labour unions, to increase wages
in Asia had the same objective. He was particularly outraged by the West's
efforts to link human rights with aid or trade. Malaysia and Singapore were
the active participants at a preparatory meeting in Bangkok that staked out
a loose common Asian stand for a U.N. Conference on Human Rights in
Vienna in 1993. The debate showed Dr. Mahathir's gift of invective at its
best, while his "exposure of some Western illogicalities was devastating".[96]

Combining his Third World spokesmanship with vigorous commercial
diplomacy, Dr. Mahathir was able to open the way for Malaysian companies in some of the poorest developing and former communist countries.
On his frequent trips abroad, he packed his aircraft with local business
people and helped them find markets for Malaysian manufactured goods
and investment opportunities in impoverished corners of Europe, Africa,
the Americas and wide swaths of Asia. Malaysian companies signed contracts
for everything from housing in Albania, to flower farming in Uzbekistan, gold
exploration in Kazakhstan, road building in India and bridge construction in
Uruguay.[97]

Dr. Mahathir's anti-West stance translated into commercial benefits in
several countries that were hostile to the United States, among them Iran,
Somalia and Liberia. Petronas, Malaysia's national oil and gas company,
took a 30 per cent stake in an Iranian oil venture, despite an American law
that penalized foreign companies doing business with the Islamic republic.
"We will not submit to what the United States dictates to us," Dr. Mahathir
declared.[98] Dr. Mahathir's staunch opposition to apartheid and friendship
with Nelson Mandela paid off in the form of large housing, township and
harbour development contracts after his African National Congress came to

power in 1994. They were awarded to Malaysian companies, despite substantially lower bids by international developers.[99] In some of the remote markets, the Malaysians were treated like royalty.[100] "When I go to Argentina, all doors are open," commented businessman Salehuddin Hashim. "That's the impact of what Dr. Mahathir has done with his pushing of South-South cooperation."[101]

But much of the activity was hasty and ill-conceived and did not pay dividends to Malaysia Inc. Many projects, announced with much fanfare and little research, were primarily political and did not get beyond the memorandum of understanding stage. "It's well known in Malaysia that one of our biggest exports is MOUs," quipped Ananda Krishnan, one of the country's most successful entrepreneurs.[102]

Some investments proved embarrassing, as when evidence surfaced of unofficial associated payments. The "tea money" for a large, private Malaysian port-city redevelopment in Cambodia included the gift of an aircraft for one of the country's two premiers.[103] In post-apartheid South Africa, where Malaysia surprisingly emerged as the second biggest source of foreign investment, the "Malaysian state or state-linked corporate sector" donated about six million rand to the African National Congress just before the 1994 elections.[104] Malaysia's reputation was also tarnished by environmental studies criticizing Malaysian logging practices in Guyana, Cambodia, Papua New Guinea and other South Pacific countries.

One notorious deal placed Dr. Mahathir in an intimate embrace with Zimbabwe's dictatorial and increasingly erratic president, Robert Mugabe. After a Malaysian company bought a controlling stake in Zimbabwe's biggest thermal power plant, beating out six Western companies, the United States criticized the transaction, while the local trade union movement condemned it as "asset stripping", and the entire board of the electricity authority joined the chorus of protest. The Zimbabwean government sacked the board and went ahead anyway.[105]

The main aim of so-called reverse investment was to repatriate profits to Malaysia to offset a worrying deficit in the country's services account, itself caused by foreign investors taking out their profits.[106] It was always going to be a long-term gamble, with Malaysian companies prepared to ignore red tape, corruption and political volatility to be first into new markets, counting on Dr. Mahathir to sort out any difficulties they encountered. With the conspicuous exception of Petronas, few of these overseas operations survived the 1997–98 Asian economic crisis. The saving grace for Malaysia was that Dr. Mahathir, for all his Third World and Islamic bombast, did everything necessary to ensure that economic relations with the West prospered while he postured.[107]

Malaysia's search for prospective markets closer to home prompted Dr. Mahathir to seize the enormous opportunities offered by China's opening, once he was persuaded that the danger of subversion had passed with the formal end of the communist insurrection in 1989. On four trips to China in the 1990s with senior executives in tow as usual, he pushed an economic agenda that was open to all Malaysians, including ethnic Chinese. Malaysian companies invested US$3.1 billion in China between 1996 and 2003, while two-way trade ballooned to US$14.11 billion from US$3.76 billion in the same period.

In pursuit of commercial returns, as well as regional solidarity, Dr. Mahathir also became an eager advocate of further expanding ASEAN. It had been enlarged to six countries with Brunei's membership in 1984, and Dr. Mahathir wanted to include the rest of the then ten Southeast Asian nations. Recognizing the economic potential of authoritarian states Vietnam, Cambodia, Laos and Myanmar as they switched from central planning to market economies, he correctly calculated they would appreciate his efforts to get them into ASEAN, by offering trade and investment opportunities. Malaysia duly became the biggest foreign investor in Cambodia and secured significant contracts in Vietnam and Myanmar.

The withdrawal of Vietnamese forces from Cambodia in 1989 opened the door for Cambodia, Vietnam and Laos to join ASEAN. Vietnam was admitted in 1995. But Myanmar's proposed membership was internationally contentious, since the ruling military junta had ignored the decisive victory of democracy leader Aung San Suu Kyi's party in a 1990 election and also had an abysmal record on human rights, forced labour and the use of child soldiers. Dr. Mahathir's was the loudest Southeast Asian voice telling American and European critics, and even some within ASEAN, to mind their own business. ASEAN decided to admit the three remaining countries simultaneously. With Malaysia occupying the rotating chairmanship of ASEAN on its 30th anniversary in 1997, Kuala Lumpur played host and prepared to celebrate as the three became members and fulfilled the ASEAN founding fathers' dream of One Southeast Asia. Amid the preparations, Malaysia unveiled a new ASEAN logo of ten rice sheafs.[108] Unexpectedly, however, Cambodia rained on Dr. Mahathir's parade. After bloody, armed clashes between the ruling coalition partners, Phnom Penh was forced to wait until 1999 to join ASEAN.

Despite his success in resisting Western pressure over Myanmar, Dr. Mahathir often stumbled in his Asian diplomacy as he sought to play on the world stage and neglected events in his own backyard. And despite his invocation of Asian values, his own failure to observe some of Southeast Asia's rituals and courtesies sometimes put him at loggerheads with neighbours. "He would make sensible suggestions at the ASEAN leaders meetings, but there was, in many cases, no follow-up," said Rodolfo C. Severino, a former secretary-general of ASEAN. Contradicting the Malaysian foreign policy priority list, Dr. Mahathir was more active in the OIC, the Non-Aligned Movement and other Third World forums than in ASEAN, Severino said.[109]

Dr. Mahathir miscalculated as he followed up Myanmar's admission to ASEAN with an attempt to help bring about reconciliation between Aung San Suu Kyi and the country's xenophobic leadership. A close Malaysian associate, Razali Ismail, a retired diplomat who was appointed the U.N. secretary-general's special envoy for Myanmar, managed to get the two sides into secret, confidence-building talks in 2000.[110] Frustrated over their failure to move on to substantive issues, Dr. Mahathir wrote more than once to Than Shwe, the five-star general who was head of state, and visited Myanmar in 2002.[111] "Very interested in finding a solution to support Myanmar," as a senior Malaysian official put it, and presumed to be carrying a bagful of goodwill, Dr. Mahathir encountered a clique of hidebound generals impervious to a sales pitch, whether from the East or West. Denied a meeting with Aung San Suu Kyi,[112] he abandoned his mission and began vilifying the junta for being an "embarrassment to ASEAN". Engaging in the sort of sniping he once rejected as interference, Dr. Mahathir even raised the possibility that the group might expel Myanmar.

While Dr. Mahathir was one of the strongest proponents of an ASEAN Free Trade Area (AFTA) that was formed on Thailand's initiative in 1992, he did AFTA no favours when it came to self-interest. With his national car project endangered by the Asian economic crisis, Malaysia sought exemption from the requirement to reduce tariffs on imported foreign vehicles and those assembled locally from imported kits. After heated debate and with great reluctance, AFTA changed its rules to accommodate Malaysia,[113] allowing it a further six years of protection. While the move had little practical effect, it encouraged the Philippines to follow suit with some petrochemical products and reinforced the widespread impression that ASEAN was not serious about economic integration.

Malaysia took a deep interest in new institutions that were fashioned for Asia after the Cold War, getting involved in the shape and composition of the ASEAN Regional Forum (ARF) on security that was formed in 1994. While government rhetoric conveyed the message that Malaysia was quite at ease with Beijing's rising military profile, Kuala Lumpur sought to use ARF to both engage China and encourage it to play by international rules. With a membership that included China's rivals – the United States, Japan, Russia and India – ARF would, in Malaysia's calculations, balance China if it tried to be more assertive.[114]

When it came to forming a counterpart economic organization, however, Dr. Mahathir got into a diplomatic dogfight that contributed to his legend. Australia in 1989 proposed the Asia-Pacific Economic Cooperation (APEC) forum, with a core membership of Australia and New Zealand, the United States, Japan, South Korea and the six ASEAN states. The following year Dr. Mahathir launched his rival East Asia Economic Caucus (EAEC), whose proposed membership was limited to ASEAN and the rapidly integrating economies of Northeast Asia: Japan, China and South Korea. Both had their

origin in the worrying state of the global economic system, spreading protectionism and a declining U.S. commitment to the values of multilateral,
non-discriminatory trade. But they represented vastly different visions:
Australia was driven by fear of being shut out if the world fractured into
three competing economic blocs, while Malaysia was inspired by a pan-
Asian nationalism to create an East Asian identity.

Ironically, Australia outmanoeuvred Malaysia with the sort of culturally
sensitive, deft diplomacy that Dr. Mahathir insisted was alien to the Australians and which made them unsuitable participants in Asian affairs. Knowing
that ASEAN held the key, the Australians addressed the group's primary
concern, that APEC should not undermine ASEAN's strength and cohesion.
They agreed that the annual APEC ministerial meeting would be held in an
ASEAN country every second year, and that the secretariat would be located in
Southeast Asia – Singapore, as it happened. Crucially, Canberra dispatched
one of its most seasoned diplomats, Richard Woolcott, as the prime minister's
emissary to sell the concept in each ASEAN country. Having served in the
key ASEAN capitals, Woolcott headed first for Jakarta, where he respectfully
sought "advice and guidance" from President Suharto, acknowledged as
ASEAN's unofficial leader. The reward for this "proper show of respect" was an
expression of Suharto's willingness to think about the idea, which was enough
for Woolcott to parlay into ASEAN endorsement by the end of his shuttle.[115]

By contrast, Dr. Mahathir had not consulted any of his fellow ASEAN
members when he floated the idea of an East Asia Economic Group, as it was
first called. He also made the mistake of suggesting that it should become
"an economic bloc" to "countervail the other economic blocs", which he
identified as the North American Free Trade Agreement and the European
Economic Community. Later, he backtracked and said that "it should not be a
trade bloc". Still, the damage was done. Livid over Dr. Mahathir's rudeness,
Suharto vetoed the Malaysian plan, making known his displeasure. Other
ASEAN member-states were also concerned about the lack of consultation,
and some had misgivings about Dr. Mahathir's anti-Western tone.[116] Australia
sided with the United States in opposing an Asians-only grouping, fearing it
would draw a line down the Pacific, and Washington pressured Tokyo not
to join. The proposal was watered down to the EAEC – a caucus rather than
a group, which detractors derided as a "caucus without Caucasians" – and
effectively buried within APEC.

Even after the first APEC ministerial meeting had been held in Canberra,
the Malaysians made a serious effort to kill the fledgling process. They arrived
at an ASEAN gathering in the East Malaysian city of Kuching in early 1990,
arguing that ASEAN should withdraw support for APEC. Indonesia decisively
blocked the Malaysian challenge.[117] Protesting over what he called broken
promises not to institutionalize APEC, Dr. Mahathir boycotted the first meeting of the group's leaders, hosted by President Clinton in Seattle in 1993.
While Dr. Mahathir won an apology from Australia's Paul Keating for calling

him "recalcitrant" over his no-show, Dr. Mahathir misjudged where APEC was heading. When Suharto, encouraged by Australia, offered to host a second summit the following year, turning it into an annual event, Dr. Mahathir had little choice but to attend. In what amounted to a Javanese command, Suharto said, "I will invite him and I expect that he will come".[118]

Long of memory and reluctant to retreat, Dr. Mahathir found a way over the next decade to both revive his EAEC and take revenge on Australia for his loss of face. He directed Malaysian diplomacy to the goal of excluding Australia as much as possible from regional political life. By denying Canberra a seat at the first biennial Asia-Europe summit in 1996, Dr. Mahathir was also able to restrict the Asian side to the potential members of his EAEC: ASEAN plus China, Japan and South Korea. While hosting the annual ASEAN summit in 1997, Malaysia invited the leaders of China, Japan and South Korea to meet with those of ASEAN together and individually. They continued to meet annually in a forum known as ASEAN + 3, which differs only in name from EAEC. ASEAN + 3 activities proliferated, forming the basis of an East Asian community along the lines Dr. Mahathir envisaged.

So keen was Dr. Mahathir to pursue his vendetta against Australia that he actually harmed ASEAN. In 2000, again using the ASEAN consensus rule that allowed just one country to exercise the right of veto, Malaysia blocked a plan to link Southeast Asia with Australia-New Zealand in a free-trade area. Malaysia did this against the recommendation of an ASEAN task force, which said such a union was "not only feasible but also advisable".[119] As one independent study noted, Australia, in particular, "was made to feel an outsider and a supplicant", despite being a longtime supporter of ASEAN and a contributor of emergency financial assistance to Indonesia and Thailand during the 1997–98 regional economic crisis.[120]

As Southeast Asia, stripped of much of its economic lustre by the crisis, tried to regain its vitality, it went without some of the US$25.6 billion in gains that the task force estimated would have accrued to the ASEAN side from a free-trade area over ten years. Australian and New Zealand traders, investors and business executives had alternatives, especially the huge markets of Northeast Asia and South Asia, and "They prospered as ASEAN struggled to recover."[121]

Unfazed by such self-inflicted damage, Dr. Mahathir maintained his ban on Australia's further participation in ASEAN-led regionalism until he retired, justifying it on racial and cultural grounds, a position adopted by no other Asian government. He described Australia, whose 20 million population included six million migrants from about 200 countries, as "some sort of transplant from another region". It was "basically European", he asserted, and could be part of Asia only after 70 per cent of its population was Asian. On another occasion he said, "Australia and New Zealand are not East Asian countries. Geographically maybe they are, but in terms of culture they are not...".[122] "Some of the Asian culture", he said, "should be accepted if not adopted" by the Australians.[123]

President Suharto felt the same way about Dr. Mahathir, that he should acknowledge the culture of the "Malay world" and be more respectful to a neighbour, namely Indonesia. Historically, Indonesia and Malaysia have a special relationship rooted in *serumpun,* similar stock, and the idea of blood brotherhood. After Confrontation, in which Indonesia tried to crush the new-born Malaysia militarily, reconciliation was effected gradually in the 1970s through Jakarta's pragmatic policies and Kuala Lumpur's willingness to concede primacy to the Indonesians and their new leader, Suharto, who had replaced the bellicose Sukarno.[124] Malaysia was prepared to play *adik,* little brother, to *abang,* big brother, Indonesia.

Dr. Mahathir, the nationalist, put a swift end to that. His initiatives on South-South cooperation, Islamic policies, peacekeeping, resuscitating the Non-Aligned Movement and active politicking at the U.N. clashed with Indonesia's own ambitions to return to international affairs after a period of dormant diplomacy.[125] Fluent in English, articulate and familiar with global institutions, Dr. Mahathir pressed his advantage at Indonesia's expense. His performance at the Non-Aligned Summit in Jakarta in 1992 in upstaging Suharto, the taciturn host, incensed the Indonesians. They began calling Dr. Mahathir a "little Sukarno", and not just for the fun of it. His Malaysia posed a challenge to Indonesia's regional leadership "on the back of the same anti-Western crusade that is identifiable with Sukarnoism".[126]

The depth of the antipathy between the two men imposed serious strains on ASEAN, since the two countries were often acknowledged as the corner-stone of the organization. "We could contain it below the leaders' level," said a senior Southeast Asian official, who was deeply involved in ASEAN affairs. "A casual observer would hardly notice it."[127] Looking back on his relationship with Suharto, Dr. Mahathir was unrepentant. "I wasn't rude to him or anything, but I went my own way," he said. "I am not going to be treated like...a little brother."[128]

Singapore's elder statesman Lee Kuan Yew levelled precisely the same accusation at Dr. Mahathir's Malaysia: seeking an *abang-adik* relationship with the city-state that was once part of the federation. In truth, their rela-tionship was characterized by interdependence, since they remained con-nected by historical, familial, cultural, political, economic and strategic ties, not to mention the pipeline that carried vital supplies of Malaysian water to the republic.[129] "When non-vital interests were at stake, we were prepared to humour *abang,* but not when *adik* had legitimate interests to defend...," Lee wrote in his memoirs.[130]

Having clashed directly with Dr. Mahathir in Parliament in the old days, Prime Minister Lee initiated a dialogue with him when Dr. Mahathir became deputy prime minister "to clear away the debris of the past". It seemed to work. As prime minister, Dr. Mahathir exchanged visits with Lee and they quickly resolved a number of issues. Although spats occurred fairly often, Lee noted that on his retirement in 1990 he had made more progress solving bilateral problems in nine years with Dr. Mahathir than in 12 years with his two predecessors.[131]

Yet relations were souring even as Lee stepped down. An agreement he signed the day before leaving office, covering the joint development with Malaysia of portions of the Malayan Railway land that stretched some 20 kilometres into downtown Singapore, would unravel. Lee had negotiated with Malaysian Finance Minister Daim Zainuddin, who had been designated by Dr. Mahathir to settle the terms. While the Singaporeans regarded it as a legally binding agreement, Dr. Mahathir repudiated it later on the grounds that it was unfair.

After Goh Chok Tong succeeded Lee, discussions about several important matters went nowhere – the long-term supply of water, the relocation of a Malaysian railway immigration checkpoint in Singapore, the timing of pension payments to peninsular Malaysians who had completed employment contracts in Singapore, and Malaysia's request for a new bridge to replace the causeway linking the two countries. Citing environmental concerns, Malaysia in 1997 banned the sale of sand to Singapore, which needed vast quantities over the coming decades to meet its reclamation plans. The following year Kuala Lumpur, without explanation, banished Singapore air force planes from Malaysian airspace, an inconvenience for training and search and rescue operations. Friction increased against the background of a massive Malaysian armed forces modernization and buildup that went some way to reducing Singapore's overwhelming military superiority.

After two particular incidents, Dr. Mahathir had basically given up on Singapore. He was upset when his security services uncovered a Singaporean spy ring in 1989, arresting five Malaysian military officers and their two Singaporean handlers.[132] Dr. Mahathir's first official meeting with Goh in Singapore in 1990, soon after he assumed the Singapore leadership, also went badly, though it was not apparent at the time. Dr. Mahathir subsequently complained that the new prime minister kept him waiting. The Singaporeans denied it, and said Dr. Mahathir's real beef was that Goh did not go downstairs to greet him but waited in his office, which was his normal practice. Regardless, it was enough to help put Malaysia-Singapore relations in the cooler for the rest of the decade. Dr. Mahathir delegated Foreign Minister Syed Hamid Albar to receive and farewell Goh on subsequent official visits.[133] As Senior Minister in Goh's cabinet, Lee Kuan Yew travelled twice to Kuala Lumpur in just over a year in an attempt to break the stalemate. But while he was able to sign a "skeletal" agreement in 2001, none of the main issues was resolved.[134] Singapore concluded that progress was unlikely while Dr. Mahathir was in power.[135] His announcement in 2002 that Malaysia would unilaterally build half a bridge to connect at the mid-point of the causeway captured the essence of the troubled bilateral relationship.[136]

Some of the Southeast Asian resentment against Dr. Mahathir surfaced after he sacked and jailed his deputy, Anwar Ibrahim, in 1998. Joining predictable Western outrage, the leaders of Indonesia and the Philippines criticized Dr. Mahathir, and Thailand expressed concern. Cory Aquino, a former Philippine president who carried considerable moral authority, also rebuked him, while regional newspapers, non-governmental organizations and commentators denounced his conduct in unprecedented fashion.

In the United States, where Dr. Mahathir was already notorious for blaming "rogue speculators" led by George Soros for the Asian economic crisis, President Bill Clinton's administration treated him as a virtual pariah. Deputising for Clinton at an APEC summit in Kuala Lumpur in November 1998, Vice President Al Gore infuriated his hosts by publicly backing Anwar's *Reformasi* movement. Dr. Mahathir continued to attract adverse publicity over currency controls, Anwar's trials and a crackdown on political opponents. "September 11" rescued him. After terrorists crashed hijacked aircraft into the World Trade Centre in New York and the Pentagon in Washington on 11 September 2001, President George W. Bush, who had been reluctant to meet Dr. Mahathir, embraced Malaysia as a partner in his "war on terror".

What Bush did not know was that Dr. Mahathir, at the height of his unpopularity over Anwar, had decided it was time to mend fences with Washington. Mahathir associates secretly paid US$1.2 million to American lobbyists to arrange the rapprochement, the money being channeled through the well-connected Jack Abramoff, who was subsequently jailed for improperly influencing members of Congress and their aides.[137] Only when scandal engulfed Abramoff years later did it become known that he was being paid by the Malaysian embassy in Washington, and that some of the funds went to analysts in the United States writing favourable commentaries about Malaysia. Kuala Lumpur also won points by cooperating with U.S. authorities in passing on intelligence about some of the "September 11" hijackers who had passed through Malaysia and others with al-Qaeda connections. The outcome was a meeting in Washington in 2002 between Dr. Mahathir and Bush, which both sides sought, as Dr. Mahathir made his first visit to the United States in eight years.

In their three-hour session, Bush did not mention Anwar's mistreatment, and he later praised Dr. Mahathir for his strong support in combating terrorism. The president hailed Malaysia as "a modern, moderate and prosperous Muslim state", and "an important example to the region and the rest of the world".[138] Bush obviously hoped Dr. Mahathir, who was to chair both the Non-Aligned Movement and the OIC, beginning in 2003, would help swing moderate Muslims behind Washington's anti-terrorist campaign.

It did not work out like that. As the United States-led forces attacked Iraq in early 2003, Dr. Mahathir slipped back into his anti-American rhetoric, describing the superpower as a "cowardly and imperialist" bully[139] that was using "September 11" as an excuse to attack Muslim nations.[140] He deeply angered the Americans by referring to victims of the September 11 attacks and the Bali bombing in October 2002 as collateral damage.[141] The vitriolic denunciations persisted, becoming ever more shrill and "going beyond normal expressions of opposition", as a senior American official put it, until Dr. Mahathir retired later in the year.[142]

With Dr. Mahathir's departure and the installation of Abdullah Badawi in 2003, the tone of Malaysia's relations with the United States, Australia and Singapore changed overnight. Abdullah made arrangements to visit the three countries, signalling an end to the open hostility and giving Dr. Mahathir another reason to feel betrayed by his successor. Dr. Mahathir complained to a friend that Abdullah had "completely" reversed his policy towards Washington, Canberra and Singapore.[143] A significant by-product of Kuala Lumpur's about-face was the inclusion of Australia and New Zealand in regional councils. Their prime ministers were invited to the annual ASEAN Summit in 2004, and ASEAN asked them to resume talks on the long-delayed free-trade area.[144] Moreover, Australia and New Zealand, along with India, were included in the line-up for the inaugural East Asia Summit in 2005. Dr. Mahathir was still protesting their inclusion when it opened in Kuala Lumpur.

Notes

1   Interview with Mahathir Mohamad, 14 August 2007.
2   Ibid.
3   Ibid.
4   Kim Richard Nossal and Richard Stubbs, "Mahathir's Malaysia: An Emerging Middle Power?", in Andrew Cooper, ed., *Niche Diplomacy: Middle Powers after the Cold War* (Houndmills: Macmillan Press, 1997), pp. 147–163.
5   Johan Saravanamuttu, "Iconoclasm and Foreign Policy – The Mahathir Years", in Bridget Welsh, ed., *Reflections: The Mahathir Years* (Washington: Southeast Asia Studies Program, The Paul H. Nitze School of Advanced International Studies, Johns Hopkins University, 2004), p. 307.
6   John Funston, "Australia-Malaysia Relations: A Maturing Partnership", in Zaniah Marshallsay, ed., *Australia-Malaysia Relations: New Roads Ahead* (Clayton: Monash Asia Institute, 1996), p. 91.
7   Shamsul A.B., "Australia in Contemporary Malaysia's Worldview", in *Australia-Malaysia Relations*, p. 70.
8   John Funston, "Australia-Malaysia Relations: A Maturing Partnership", p. 91.
9   Joseph Liow, "Personality, Exigencies and Contingencies: Determinants of Malaysia's Foreign Policy in the Mahathir Administration", in Ho Khai Leong and James Chin, eds, *Mahathir's Administration: Performance and Crisis in Governance* (Singapore: Times Books International, 2001), p. 157.
10 Ibid., p. 154.
11 Joseph Chinyong Liow, *The Politics of Indonesia-Malaysia Relations: One Kin, Two Nations* (London and New York: RoutledgeCurzon, 2005), p. 134.
12 Hajrudin Somun, *The Secret of the Malaysian Success* (Subang Jaya: Pelanduk Publications (M) Sdn. Bhd., 2003), p. 176.

13 Email correspondence, 25 July 2008, with Marvin C. Ott, professor, National Security Strategy, National War College, Washington, D.C., who is researching a book on Malaysian foreign policy.

14 Ibid.

15 Chandran Jeshurun, "Malaysian Defence Policy Under Mahathir: What has Changed?", in *Reflections*, p. 335.

16 Mahathir Mohamad, "Trends in Foreign Policy and Regionalism", in "Proceedings and Background Paper of Seminar on Trends in Malaysia", edited by Patrick Low, *Trends in Southeast Asia*, no. 2 (1971), Institute of Southeast Asian Studies, p. 33.

17 Ibid., p. 36.

18 Joseph Liow, "Personality, Exigencies and Contingencies", p. 129.

19 Barry Wain, *The Refused: The Agony of the Indochina Refugees* (New York: Simon and Schuster, 1981), pp. 96–97, 274–275, fn 1.

20 Karminder Singh Dhillon, *Malaysian Foreign Policy in the Mahathir Era (1981–2003): Dilemmas of Development* (Singapore: NUS Press, 2009), p. 161.

21 Ibid., pp. 163–164.

22 Mahathir Mohamad, "West and East", in *The Challenge* (Petaling Jaya: Pelanduk Publications (M) Sdn. Bhd., 1986), pp. 46–47.

23 Ibid., p. 54.

24 *New Straits Times*, 16 July 1982.

25 K. Das, "Malaysia's 'Restoration'", *Far Eastern Economic Review* (hereafter *FEER*), 11 June 1982, p. 38.

26 Interview with Mahathir Mohamad, 14 August 2007.

27 Mahathir Mohamad, *A New Deal for Asia* (Subang Jaya: Pelanduk Publications (M) Sdn. Bhd., 1999), p. 16.

28 Interview with Mahathir Mohamad, 14 August 2007.

29 Mahathir Mohamad, *A New Deal for Asia*, pp. 14–15.

30 Cheah Boon Kheng, "The 'Black-out' Syndrome and the Ghosts of World War II: The War as a 'Divisive Issue' in Malaysia", in David Koh Wee Hock, ed., *Legacies of World War II in South and East Asia* (Singapore: Institute of Southeast Asian Studies, 2007), pp. 47, 48.

31 Paul A. Kratoska, *The Japanese Occupation of Malaya: A Social and Economic History* (London: Hurst & Co., 1998), p. 86.

32 Cheah Boon Kheng, "The 'Black-out' Syndrome and the Ghosts of World War II", p. 48.

33 Ibid., p. 51.

34 Ibid., p. 47.

35 Mahathir Mohamad, *A New Deal for Asia*, pp. 16–17.

36 "Forget the Past, PM tells Muruyama", *Star*, 28 August 1994, cited in Cheah Boon Kheng, "The 'Black-out' Syndrome and the Ghosts of World War II", p. 49.

37 Mahathir Mohamad, "Quo Vadis Malaysia?", in *The Challenge*, p. 163.

38 Zainuddin Maidin, *The Other Side of Mahathir* (Kuala Lumpur: Utusan Publications and Distributors Sdn. Bhd., 1994), p. 97.

39 Ibid., p. 97.

40 Ibid., p. 97.

41 Interview with Daim Zainuddin, 18 October 2007.

42 Roger Kershaw, "Brown Humanity Strikes Back: Confronting Britain in a Good Cause?", in *Reflections*, p. 347.

43 Ibid., pp. 347–348.

44 Ibid., p. 347.

45 Ibid., p. 344.
46 Ibid., p. 349.
47 Mahathir Mohamad, Appendix 5, in *The Other Side of Mahathir*, pp. 303–306.
48 Karminder Singh Dhillon, *Malaysian Foreign Policy in the Mahathir Era (1981–2003)*, p. 170.
49 Raphael Pura, "Mahathir's U.S. Trip Showcases Better Ties", *Asian Wall Street Journal* (hereafter *AWSJ*), 10 January 1984.
50 Jomo K.S., *M Way: Mahathir's Economic Legacy* (Kuala Lumpur: Forum, 2003), p. 40.
51 William E. Berry, Jr., "Threat Perceptions in the Philippines, Malaysia and Singapore", INSS Occasional Paper 16, September 1997, USAF Institute for National Security Studies.
52 Email correspondence, 28 November 2007, with William E. Berry, Jr., U.S. air attache in Kuala Lumpur 1990–93.
53 Mahathir Mohamad, speech in conjunction with the celebration of the 41st anniversary of the United Nations, 25 October 1986, cited in Khoo Boo Teik, *Paradoxes of Mahathirism: An Intellectual Biography of Mahathir Mohamad* (Kuala Lumpur: Oxford University Press, 1995), p. 96, fn 131.
54 William E. Berry, Jr., "Threat Perceptions in the Philippines, Malaysia and Singapore".
55 Anil Netto, "Fear, Fanaticism and an Asian Tightrope Act", *AsiaTimes Online* <http://www.atimes.com/atimes/printN.html> (accessed 18 July 2007).
56 Najib Abdul Razak, "U.S.-Malaysia Defence Cooperation: A Solid Success Story", address to the Heritage Foundation and Centre for Strategic and International Studies, Washington, 3 May 2002. Heritage Lecture no. 742.
57 Interview with Mahathir Mohamad, 14 August 2007.
58 William E. Berry, Jr., "Threat Perceptions in the Philippines, Malaysia and Singapore".
59 Interview with Mahathir Mohamad, 14 August 2007.
60 John Funston, "Australia-Malaysia Relations: A Maturing Partnership", p. 91.
61 David Camroux, "'Looking East'...and Inwards: Internal Factors in Malaysian Foreign Relations During the Mahathir Era, 1981–1994", Australia-Asia Papers no. 72, October 1994, Griffith University, p. 44.
62 Barry Wain, "Malaysia's New Priorities in Foreign Policy", *AWSJ*, 16 November 1981.
63 John Funston, "The Legacy of Dr. Mahathir", *Australian Financial Review*, 30 July 2004.
64 Interview with Mahathir Mohamad, 14 August 2007.
65 Chandran Jeshurun, *Malaysia: Fifty Years of Diplomacy 1957–2007* (Kuala Lumpur: The Other Press Sdn. Bhd., 2007), p. 170.
66 Greg Sheridan, *Tigers: Leaders of the New Asia-Pacific* (Sydney: Allen & Unwin, 1997), p. 169.
67 Interview with Mahathir Mohamad, 14 August 2007.
68 "The Full Text of Datuk Seri Dr. Mahathir's reply dated April 25", *New Straits Times*, 30 May 1988.
69 Shamsul A.B., "Australia in Contemporary Malaysia's Worldview", pp. 71–72.
70 John Funston, "The Legacy of Dr. Mahathir".
71 Joseph Liow, "Personality, Exigencies and Contingencies", p. 157.
72 Statement by Abraham H. Foxman, National Director, Anti-Defamation League, "ADL Calls on Leaders of Civilized Nations to Condemn Call for Holy War Against Jews", 16 October 2003.

73   Mahathir bin Mohamad, *The Malay Dilemma* (Singapore: Times Books International, 1999 edition), p. 84.
74   Ibid., p. 84.
75   Leslie Lopez, "Malaysia Strains U.S. Tolerance", *AWSJ,* 27 June 2003.
76   "Malaysian Prime Minister Mahathir Mohamad: On the Jews", interview with *Bangkok Post*, 21 October 2003, cited on Anti-Defamation League website <http://www.adl.org/Anti_semitism/Malaysian_1.asp> (accessed 27 January 2006).
77   Patricia Martinez, "Perhaps He Deserved Better: The Disjuncture between Vision and Reality in Mahathir's Islam", in *Reflections*, p. 35.
78   "Mahathir Attack on Jews Condemned", *CNN.com*, 16 October 2003 <http://cnn.worldnews.printthis.clickability.com/pt/cpt?action=cpt&title=CNN.com+-+> (accessed 27 January 2006).
79   Mahathir Mohamad, speech at the Tenth Islamic Summit Conference, Putrajaya, Malaysia, 16 October 2003.
80   Ibid.
81   Mahathir Mohamad, speech at the Foreign Policy Association, 19 January 1984, cited in Khoo Boo Teik, *Paradoxes of Mahathirism,* p. 59.
82   Mahathir Mohamad, speech at the dinner hosted by Japanese Prime Minister Yasuhiro Nakasone, 24 January 1983, cited in Khoo Boo Teik, *Paradoxes of Mahathirism*, p. 59.
83   Mahathir Mohamad, keynote address at the ASEAN-EEC industrial sector conference, 28 February 1983, cited in Khoo Boo Teik, *Paradoxes of Mahathirism*, p. 62.
84   Ministry of Foreign Affairs, Malaysia <http://www.kln.gov.my/english/foreign-affairs/foreignpolicy/myforeign.htm> (accessed 31 March 2006).
85   Khoo Boo Teik, *Paradoxes of Mahathirism*, p. 64.
86   Ibid, p. 62.
87   Mahathir Mohamad, speech at 5th joint conference MAJECA/JAMECA, 8 February 1982, cited in Khoo Boo Teik, *Paradoxes of Mahathirism*, p. 62.
88   Joseph Liow, "Personality, Exigencies and Contingencies", p. 148.
89   Ibid., p. 148.
90   Captain Johari Ramzan Ahmad, "Malaysia's Peacekeeping Effort: A Personal Perspective", *The Liaison*, 3, no. 1 <http://www.coe-dmha.org/Liaison/Vol_3No_1/index.htm> (accessed 30 November 2007).
91   Ibid.
92   Chandran Jeshurun, *Malaysia: Fifty Years of Diplomacy 1957–2007*, pp. 252–253.
93   "Malaysia's Mahathir: New Voice for the Third World", *FEER*, 20 August 1992, cover.
94   Kim Richard Nossal and Richard Stubbs, "Mahathir's Malaysia: An Emerging Middle Power?", p. 155.
95   Ibid., pp. 155–156.
96   R.S. Milne and Diane K. Mauzy, *Malaysian Politics Under Mahathir* (London: Routledge, 1999), p. 139.
97   S. Jayasankaran and Nate Thayer, "From Logs to Lotus", *FEER*, 12 December 1996, pp. 64–69.
98   Ibid., p. 66.
99   Karminder Singh Dhillon, *Malaysian Foreign Policy in the Mahathir Era (1981–2003)*, p. 252.
100 Jomo K.S., "Introduction", in Jomo K.S., ed., *Ugly Malaysians?: South-South Investments Abused* (Durban: Institute for Black Research, 2002), p. 11.

101   S. Jayasankaran and Nate Thayer, "From Logs to Lotus", p. 66.
102   Ibid., p. 66.
103   Ibid., p. 69.
104   Vishu Padayachee and Imraan Valodia, "Developing South-South Links?: Malaysian Investment in Post-Apartheid South Africa", in *Ugly Malaysians?*, p. 36.
105   S. Jayasankaran and Nate Thayer, "From Logs to Lotus", p. 69.
106   Ibid., p. 65.
107   Kaminder Singh Dhillon, *Malaysian Foreign Policy in the Mahathir Era (1981–2003)*, p. 257.
108   Ian Stewart, *The Mahathir Legacy: A Nation Divided, a Region at Risk* (Sydney: Allen & Unwin, 2003), p. 3.
109   Interview with Rodolfo C. Severino, 29 March 2006.
110   Barry Wain, "U.N. Myanmar Envoy Hints at Resignation If Talks Don't Proceed", *AWSJ*, 19 November 2002.
111   Barry Wain, "Yangon Doesn't Want Reconciliation Help", *AWSJ*, 26 August 2002.
112   Barry Wain, "Mahathir Won't Meet Dissident", *AWSJ*, 19 August 2002.
113   Rodolfo C. Severino, *Southeast Asia in Search of an ASEAN Community: Insights from the Former ASEAN Secretary-General* (Singapore: Institute of Southeast Asian Studies, 2006), p. 227.
114   Kaminder Singh Dhillon, *Malaysian Foreign Policy in the Mahathir Era (1981–2003)*, pp. 217–218.
115   Graeme Dobell, *Australia Finds Home* (Sydney: ABC Books, 2000), p. 36.
116   Rodolfo C. Severino, *Southeast Asia in Search of an ASEAN Community*, p. 266.
117   Graeme Dobell, *Australia Finds Home*, pp. 37–38.
118   Ibid., p. 40.
119   *The Angkor Agenda: Report of the High-Level Task Force on the AFTA-CER Free Trade Area* <http://www.aseansec.org/angkor_agenda.pdf> (accessed 2 September 2008).
120   Chin Kin Wah and Michael Richardson, *Australia-New Zealand & Southeast Asia Relations: An Agenda for Closer Cooperation* (Singapore: Institute of Southeast Asian Studies, 2004), pp. 27–28.
121   Ibid., p. 28.
122   Jeremy Hurewitz, "Interview", *FEER*, March 2006, p. 54.
123   Greg Sheridan, *Tigers*, p. 200.
124   Joseph Chinyong Liow, *The Politics of Indonesia-Malaysia Relations*, p. 132.
125   Ibid., p. 136.
126   Ibid., p. 167.
127   Interview with senior Southeast Asian official, 3 November 2006.
128   Interview with Mahathir Mohamad, 14 August 2007.
129   K.S. Nathan, "Malaysia-Singapore Relations: Retrospect and Prospect", *Contemporary Southeast Asia* 24, no. 2 (August 2002): 404.
130   Lee Kuan Yew, *From Third World to First: The Singapore Story: 1965–2000* (Singapore: Times Media Pte. Ltd., 2000), p. 280.
131   Ibid., pp. 275, 279–281, 289.
132   Kaminder Singh Dhillon, *Malaysian Foreign Policy in the Mahathir Era (1981–2003)*, p. 136, fn 93, citing *Straits Times*, 18 February 1990. Suhaini Aznam, "Neighbourly Interest", *FEER*, 21 December 1989, p. 20.
133   Chandran Jeshurun, *Malaysia: Fifty Years of Diplomacy 1957–2007*, p. 297.
134   K.S. Nathan, "Malaysia-Singapore Relations: Retrospect and Prospect", pp. 398–399.
135   K. Kesavapany, "Promising Start to Malaysia-Singapore Relations", in Saw Swee-Hock and K. Kesavapany, eds, *Malaysia: Recent Trends and Challenges* (Singapore: Institute of Southeast Asian Studies, 2006), pp. 275–286.

136   Kaminder Singh Dhillon, *Malaysian Foreign Policy in the Mahathir Era (1981–2003)*, p. 132.

137   Tom Hamburger and Peter Wallsten, "Abramoff Bragged of Ties to Rove", *latimes.com*, 15 February 2006 <http://www.latimes.com/news/printedition/la-na-abramoff15feb,1,927022,full.story?coll=la-headlines-politics> (accessed 13 March 2006).

138   Jim Lobe, "Mahathir Gets White House's 'Rehabilitation'", *AsiaTimes Online*, 17 May 2002 <http://www.atimes.com/sea-asia/DE17Ae03.html> (accessed 27 January 2006).

139   Ahmed Rashid, "What Do You Think of America Now?", *FEER*, 3 April 2003, p. 12.

140   Leslie Lopez, "Malaysia Strains U.S. Tolerance".

141   Barry Wain, "Washington to Reward Its Friends", *AWSJ*, 28 April 2003.

142   "Mahathir's Criticism Causes Tension", *FEER*, 10 April 2003, p. 8.

143   Interview with Abdullah Ahmad, 23 March 2007.

144   ASEAN, Australia and New Zealand concluded their negotiations on a free-trade agreement in Singapore in 2008.

Global exposure: Mahathir with United Nations Secretary General Kofi Annan. Mahathir used regular appearances at the U.N. General Assembly to lash the West and promote his pet causes.

Source: Perdana Leadership Foundation

Anti-apartheid allies: Mahathir with South African President Nelson Mandela. Malaysian companies made a major investment in South Africa after Mahathir campaigned to end white rule and the two countries developed close ties.

Source: Perdana Leadership Foundation

276

Wary neighbours: Mahathir with Singapore Prime Minister Lee Kuan Yew. Political adversaries from the time Singapore was part of Malaysia in 1963–65, they settled some bilateral issues, but problems remained.

Source: Perdana Leadership Foundation

11
The Destruction of a Designated Heir

In the most sensational 48 hours in Malaysian politics, Dr. Mahathir in 1998 sacked Anwar Ibrahim as deputy prime minister and finance minister and had him expelled from UMNO. Not since the 1969 racial riots, which were confined largely to Kuala Lumpur, had the country been gripped by such drama. And that was only the beginning. As Dr. Mahathir sought to crush Anwar politically with the full weight of the state, he was pilloried by the police and press, arrested under emergency laws and bashed in jail. Married with six children and a reputation as a principled and thoughtful Muslim leader, Anwar was accused of being both a womanizer and a homosexual, financially corrupt and a threat to national security.

Like the 1987 UMNO factional fight, the Mahathir-Anwar rupture split the Malay community down to family level and reverberated beyond the political system itself. It brought a sharp reaction from many regional and world capitals, where Anwar was known and respected. As he was dismissed from the government the day after Malaysia imposed capital controls to deal with the Asian economic crisis, the international community took an even keener interest in his removal. Dr. Mahathir and Anwar had diverged in their responses to the crisis, and the deputy premier's departure was as unwelcome to foreign investors as the restrictions on the outflow of funds.

Protesting his innocence and claiming to be the victim of a "conspiracy at the highest level of government", Anwar refused to go quietly.[1] He slipped back into the adversarial role he once played as a student and Islamic leader, rallying Malaysians to demand widespread reform before being arrested. Considered a political prisoner by international human rights groups, Anwar was jailed for 15 years after two trials that failed to meet minimum standards of justice. With Dr. Mahathir's assistance, Anwar's enemies in UMNO had achieved their aim of denying him the top political prize, though his own miscalculations contributed to his downfall. Dr. Mahathir continued to insist that Anwar was dropped because he was morally unfit, but few believed it even after he had served a jail term. Rather, the evidence suggested that Dr. Mahathir had concluded that Anwar, the man he had brought into UMNO 16 years earlier and anointed as his successor, was planning to use the economic turmoil to dislodge him and take over the party and the country. Dr. Mahathir had struck pre-emptively to squash any possible challenge.

While Dr. Mahathir ensured that Anwar did not succeed him, it was something of a Pyrrhic victory. The episode exposed the deeply authoritarian nature of Dr. Mahathir's administration and the institutional rot that had set in during his long years at the helm. It also raised doubts about Dr. Mahathir's vaunted political judgment and renewed speculation about when, if ever, he intended to retire. Large numbers of Malaysians, especially Malays, remained alienated and looked upon Dr. Mahathir as an ogre. No matter how he tried, Dr. Mahathir could never bury the Anwar issue. Like a bad odour, it hung around as long as he stayed on, constantly testing his patience and permanently sullying his name.

Dr. Mahathir's dismissal of Anwar ended a relationship that was long, complicated and, in part, personal as well as professional. Although born more than two decades apart, the men shared similarities in their ideas and political careers. They were commoners in contrast with former UMNO leaders who had aristocratic backgrounds, though Anwar's middle-class upbringing was more comfortable than Dr. Mahathir's. The son of a hospital orderly who became an UMNO member of parliament, with a mother who also was an active party member, Anwar completed secondary school as a boarder at the elite Malay College in Kuala Kangsar, the country's most prestigious school. He excelled at debating, led Islamic study groups and eventually was appointed school captain.[2]

When they first met in the late 1960s, Anwar was a student leader at the University of Malaya and Dr. Mahathir was a first-term parliamentarian, both making a name for themselves as Malay nationalists. A skilful political strategist with clear views on what he wanted to achieve, Anwar – like Dr. Mahathir – had politics in his blood. In 1968, Anwar took over the two major Malay student organizations in the country, uniting the Malay nationalist and Islamic streams.[3] Under his direction, they addressed Malay backwardness in such areas as health, education and economics, while pressuring politicians to keep earlier promises to make Malay the sole national language. Anwar and other students would visit Dr. Mahathir at his residence in Kuala Lumpur, at his invitation, to discuss shared concerns.[4]

The venue was significant. It was the home of Dr. Mahathir's close friend and fellow UMNO member of parliament, Tunku Abdullah Tuanku Abdul Rahman, with whom Alor Star-based Dr. Mahathir often stayed when Parliament was in session. Tunku Abdullah was President of the Malaysian Youth Council, an umbrella organization for all youth groups, which would later include Anwar's Malaysian Islamic Youth Movement (ABIM). In 1972, Anwar would succeed Tunku Abdullah as head of the multiracial Malaysian

Youth Council, a post usually reserved for a senior UMNO member, providing Anwar with the opportunity to work beyond the Malay community.

Anwar and his followers admired the outspoken Dr. Mahathir, and they supported him when he lost his seat in the 1969 election and blamed Prime Minister Tunku Abdul Rahman's allegedly pro-Chinese policies for the "May 13" tragedy that followed. A few of the students helped circulate copies of Dr. Mahathir's notorious letter condemning the Tunku before it was banned. They also distributed copies of the first two chapters of *The Malay Dilemma,* which Dr. Mahathir passed to Anwar, before the complete book was published and proscribed. The students staged anti-Tunku demonstrations and continued to provide Dr. Mahathir with a platform after he was expelled from UMNO.

In the following decade, however, Dr. Mahathir and Anwar found themselves not only on opposite sides of the political fence, but in conflict. Readmitted to UMNO in 1972, re-elected to Parliament in 1974 and immediately appointed education minister, Dr. Mahathir took a hard line to quell academic and student protests. Dr. Mahathir strongly supported a government decision to arrest Anwar, then head of ABIM, without trial under the Internal Security Act, after he backed mass demonstrations to protest peasant suffering in Kedah in late 1974.[5]

Undeterred by 22 months in detention, Anwar was still head of ABIM and leading a broad coalition of non-governmental organizations against a proposed piece of legislation that would have tightened government control of voluntary associations, including religious and student organizations, trade unions and professional and consumer groups, when Dr. Mahathir recruited him as a candidate in 1982. Although Dr. Mahathir claimed later that he took Anwar in only to prevent a mischief-maker from joining the Islamic opposition, Anwar undoubtedly had star quality. He was an instant vote-winner and reinforced the impression that the relatively new Mahathir government was dynamic and serious about responding to the Islamic resurgence.

Toning down his radical rhetoric, Anwar became an obedient and "relatively quiet cog in the Mahathir administration machinery".[6] Mentor and protégé worked well together, with Anwar ready to do battle for some of Dr. Mahathir's favourite causes. As UMNO Youth leader, Anwar led the campaign to recover "Carcosa", the former home of British colonial rulers given to the British at independence, and articulately argued the case to reform the monarchy. Anwar was a member of the "AIDS" group – Anwar Ibrahim, Daim Zainuddin and Sanusi Junid – which provided crucial support for Dr. Mahathir against Tengku Razaleigh Hamzah in the battle for control of UMNO in 1987.[7]

In turn, Dr. Mahathir appointed Anwar to a succession of portfolios "tailor made to equip him to take over the top post".[8] After a year as a deputy minister attending mainly to Islamic affairs, Anwar was made minister for youth, culture and sports, going on to spend two years in the agriculture portfolio and five years in education before being named finance minister in 1991. His parallel rise through UMNO ranks was even more impressive. Narrowly capturing the UMNO Youth leadership only months after joining Dr. Mahathir in 1982, he was elected one of the party's three vice presidents six years later. In 1990, he secured the highest number of votes in the vice presidential contest, ranking him third in the party hierarchy, behind the president and deputy president.

A charismatic speaker and engaging conversationalist, Anwar sought to allay fears that he was an Islamic extremist in order to expand his appeal beyond his Malay-Muslim constituency – "learning how to eat with chopsticks", as one Chinese executive put it.[9] While supporting Dr. Mahathir's agenda, he remained quietly on the sidelines as political and business scandals periodically engulfed the government, telling old friends that he was working from the inside to influence policy instead of confronting opponents as in the past. An "unremarkable initiator of change" who produced few tangible achievements he could claim as his own,[10] Anwar nevertheless collected the credit as the Malaysian economy boomed in the 1990s. He travelled widely as finance minister and acquired a considerable international reputation.

Although Dr. Mahathir and Anwar both studied at local universities rather than overseas and experienced a period of political banishment, they were different in some obvious ways. Unlike Dr. Mahathir, who governed by the force of his will and professed no desire to be popular, Anwar's political style was "a canny mix of personal charm and cool pragmatism".[11] While Dr. Mahathir was practical, with little time for theory and fascinated by technological gadgets, Anwar had a more philosophical bent, equally at ease quoting the Qur'an to conservative villagers or citing Shakespeare to a more-Westernized audience.[12] Dr. Mahathir focused on economic growth, promoting his vision of a fully developed Malaysia by 2020 that bristled with skyscrapers, superhighways, bullet trains and other concrete symbols of modernity. Anwar talked more of poverty alleviation, low-cost housing and healthcare, and the hope that his generation would see greater liberty, less censorship and a flowering of civil society.

Although these differences were "matters of nuance, not of fundamentals",[13] strains showed as pundits repeatedly returned to their favourite guessing game: Who would succeed Dr. Mahathir, and when? A hint of dissension came at the 1993 UMNO General Assembly, when Anwar challenged Ghafar Baba for the deputy presidency against Dr. Mahathir's wishes. Anwar mounted his assault from behind a series of denials that sought to conceal his elaborate preparations. While Dr. Mahathir eventually did support Anwar's bid, prompting Ghafar to quit as deputy premier and withdraw from the party contest rather than be humiliated in a ballot, the prime minister would have preferred to keep them both in place and onside.

As political scientist John Funston commented, relations between Dr. Mahathir and Anwar could no longer be completely free of tension.

Dr. Mahathir had to keep on demonstrating that he remained in control, or party members would conclude he no longer was. Anwar, on the other hand, had to show that he was ready to take over whenever required, or someone else would emerge to challenge his newly acquired position as the heir apparent.[14] The key question: In the absence of a timetable, would Anwar patiently wait his turn, or be pressured by supporters into risking his post by challenging Dr. Mahathir?

Living in adjoining official residences in the fancy Damansara Heights section of Kuala Lumpur, Dr. Mahathir and Anwar and their families developed a comfortable personal friendship. Anwar had met his wife in 1980 when visiting Dr. Mahathir's sister-in-law in hospital, where she was being cared for by a recent Dublin medical school graduate named Wan Aziza Wan Ismail. Anwar and Wan Aziza married in 1981. As neighbours, Dr. Mahathir and Anwar went horse-riding together on Sundays, until Anwar broke his collarbone in a fall and gave it up. Their daughters were good friends and studied together in Assunta Secondary School in Petaling Jaya, sometimes riding in each other's car if one driver was late.[15] Anwar described Dr. Mahathir as his "mentor, leader and father in politics".[16]

After the government increased its majority in a general election in 1995, UMNO was riven by proxy battles between the leader and his deputy, which had the overall effect of weakening Dr. Mahathir's grip on the party.[17] As usual, the intense jockeying was conducted as political *wayang kulit,* shadow play, behind a veneer of normality and professions of loyalty and denials of rifts that fooled nobody. At the 1995 UMNO General Assembly, Dr. Mahathir said he would retire "soon" and reaffirmed that Anwar was his natural successor. Anwar declared that his loyalty to the president should not be questioned and said anyone proposing him as a candidate for the leadership would be wasting their time. Dr. Mahathir's supporters, though, took out a little insurance. They persuaded the assembly to adopt a resolution saying there should be no contest for the positions of president and deputy president in 1996, when the party's triennial elections were due.

Despite that apparent obstacle, some observers and participants thought Anwar's spreading influence might be sufficient for him to be tempted to try and nudge aside "the old man" at the UMNO General Assembly in October 1996. Dr. Mahathir, however, moved first. In the early part of 1996, he had the party's Supreme Council, which he chaired, pass three new rulings. Reinforcing the previous year's resolution, the Supreme Council directed that party divisions, which propose candidates for elections at the assembly, could nominate only Dr. Mahathir for president and Anwar for deputy. Further, all candidates for senior positions must register with UMNO headquarters five months in advance, a requirement that would not allow a challenger to hide his intentions as Anwar had in 1993 against Ghafar. Finally, the Supreme Council pushed through an unprecedented rule that banned all campaigning for the October party elections. While the restrictions were introduced in the name of noble causes – less politicking, more unity, a level playing field and reduced vote buying – they effectively entrenched Dr. Mahathir's presidency until 1999.

At the General Assembly, Anwar's faction showed its muscle early when Ahmad Zahid Hamidi defeated incumbent Rahim Tamby Chik for the leadership of UMNO Youth and Siti Zaharah Sulaiman took control of the women's wing from Rafidah Aziz. But while Dr. Mahathir endorsed candidates lost that round, they dominated the Supreme Council poll, and Anwar's allies failed to make inroads at vice presidential level. If Anwar's followers tried to create the impression that time was running out for Dr. Mahathir, he saw no reason to be rushed into retirement. A buoyant Dr. Mahathir subsequently declared he would not set a date for his departure. "The moment you give a timetable, you are a lame duck," he said. He added, "I can go anytime now or ten years later or whatever. Depends on what the situation is like." As for naming a successor, "Whoever is in place as my deputy will succeed me."[18]

With both men making light of speculation about their differences as they entered 1997, Anwar got a taste of the top job when Dr. Mahathir took two months leave in May. For the first time since the 1980s, Dr. Mahathir made his deputy acting prime minister, an indication of his confidence in Anwar and something of a trial run. As Dr. Mahathir joked when asked if it were to test whether Anwar was capable of succeeding him, "Yes, he has to sit for an examination. When I come back, I will make him sit down and answer questions. I will then mark the paper."[19] On his return in July, Dr. Mahathir declared himself satisfied with Anwar's management of the country.

But Acting Prime Minister Anwar's actions, specifically his declared war on corruption, alarmed sections of UMNO and the business community, and they joined Anwar's rivals in committing themselves to blocking his ascent.[20] The Anwar sponsored Anti-Corruption Bill 1997 increased penalties, enhanced the powers of the Anti-Corruption Agency and contained provisions allowing for the prosecution of a public official even after leaving office. Anwar won Cabinet acceptance of the proposed legislation over the objections of some ministerial colleagues. It was clear not only to Anwar's political adversaries, but also to some of Malaysia's well-connected corporate players, that he could not be relied upon to protect their interests if he became prime minister.[21]

In August 1997, a month before the annual UMNO General Assembly, Anwar's enemies struck, circulating *surat layang* aimed at his high moral character. While a common way to denigrate lofty aspirants in Malay politics, this onslaught of poison-pen letters came in more than half a dozen versions in what Anwar called the "most concerted, well organized and well orchestrated" effort to sabotage him politically. The letters alleged he had an affair with the wife of his private secretary and fathered her child, and also had a homosexual relationship with his former family chauffeur.

As some of the letters were sent to the prime minister and signed by their authors, they could be easily investigated by police, who were answerable to Dr. Mahathir as home affairs minister. After Anwar lodged a complaint with the police and they conducted inquiries, Dr. Mahathir told a press conference the allegations were "absurd" and just the usual slander to prevent Anwar's succession. "It is totally political. There is no truth in it," he said. Dr. Mahathir gave an example of the way the campaign to blacken Anwar was organized, with one person signing a letter dictated by another. "The letter was written in a language beyond the capacity of one of the writers," he said.[22]

With such a categorical dismissal of the "lies" by the person who mattered most in the prime ministerial stakes, the perpetrators might have been expected to retreat. But no action was taken against them, and the "flow of anti-Anwar literature was not stemmed".[23] Calumnious books appeared, one of them titled *Talkin Untuk Anwar Ibrahim* – Requiem for Anwar Ibrahim. The political conspiracy against Anwar was well-funded and real, confirmed by former deputy prime minister Musa Hitam, an UMNO elder who was neutral in the Mahathir-Anwar fallout. "Definitely", he said later. The people involved in the planning had told him, Musa said, "what will be done against Anwar to make sure he will be toppled".[24]

The Asian economic crisis, which originated in Thailand in July 1997, put additional strain on the relationship between leader and deputy as the effects spread to neighbouring countries. Dr. Mahathir's vilification of foreign equity and currency traders as "manipulators" and "criminals" accelerated the implosion of Malaysia's currency, stock and property markets. It fell to the more urbane Anwar, as finance minister, to calm growing domestic and foreign alarm over Dr. Mahathir's pronouncements and policies.[25] While playing good cop to Dr. Mahathir's bad cop boosted Anwar's reputation abroad as the voice of "reason and moderation",[26] it was deeply resented by Dr. Mahathir. And he was even more annoyed when some international media suggested that he should step down in favour of Anwar.[27]

As the recession bit deeper and government spending was reduced, tension between the two also increased over the continued financing of Dr. Mahathir's mega-projects and the rescue of favoured bumiputra corporations. Anwar had long grumbled about some of the big-ticket infrastructure items, and he took the first opportunity to shelve a few. Despite Anwar's public opposition to bailouts, the government threw lifelines to some major companies aligned with factions or prominent figures in UMNO. Anwar and Dr. Mahathir argued privately over payment to Ting Pek Khiing, the entrepreneur behind the postponed Bakun Dam, and to Mirzan Mahathir, the prime minister's eldest son, for the purchase of the entire shipping business and assets of his Konsortium Perkapalan Bhd. by Petronas.[28] Now, Dr. Mahathir had reason to share the doubts about Anwar's willingness to protect certain interests after Dr. Mahathir's premiership.[29] As Musa Hitam, the former deputy premier, said, "To put it simply, this is all about the search for the next leader who could ensure that the past leader and his cronies will not be in trouble."[30]

Although Anwar said later he thought Dr. Mahathir had made up his mind to remove him by December 1997, there was little sign of it at the time, though differences between them were beginning to show. The day after a pivotal cabinet meeting chaired by Dr. Mahathir on 3 December, before Anwar could announce a second austerity package to cope with the spreading economic malaise, Dr. Mahathir made a statement that suggested it was business as usual. He declared that a RM10 billion "land bridge", comprising a road, railway and a gas pipeline, between Malaysia and Thailand would go ahead. Anwar's measures, announced on 5 December, included more curbs on government spending and mega-projects, specifically reversing Dr. Mahathir's stand on the land bridge.[31]

Soon after, Dr. Mahathir took steps to dilute Anwar's voice in economic policy formulation. He created a National Economic Action Council to oversee the country's recovery and brought back Daim Zainuddin, the former finance minister and his most trusted lieutenant, to head it with the title of executive director. Dr. Mahathir became chairman and Anwar deputy chairman. The prime minister made it clear that Daim would exercise full power to carry out the council's directives.

Facing rare criticism in the local media over his controversial response to the worsening economic conditions, Dr. Mahathir sought to consolidate his leadership with a strong resort to nationalism. In addition to suggesting a Jewish conspiracy linked to American investor George Soros to block the progress of Muslims, he repeatedly warned that Malaysia's independence was threatened and appealed for unity. If Malaysia were forced to follow Thailand and Indonesia and go to the International Monetary Fund (IMF) for help, he said, the government would be compelled to increase taxes on an already impoverished people, charge higher lending rates and close most of the banks and finance companies. And foreign capitalists would be free to enter the Malaysian market and scoop up bargains, amounting to re-colonization of the country, he said.

After their breach, Dr. Mahathir blamed Anwar, aided by Bank Negara, the central bank, for having made "a bad situation worse" by slavishly following standard IMF prescriptions and adopting tight monetary and fiscal policies. Dr. Mahathir said they implemented a "virtual IMF without the IMF loans", pushing already suffering banks and businesses into "dire distress".[32] But as prime minister, and a particularly powerful one, Dr. Mahathir always had the final say in policy making and no course could have been pursued without his acquiescence at least. In reality, Malaysia's economic policies were worked out in consultation with the IMF until about the middle of 1998.[33] Internal discussions and disagreements, reflecting a wider international debate, resulted in austerity being gradually abandoned. Even the IMF adopted a more flexible stance. Along with others, Anwar modified his views, describing interest rates at the end of June as "prohibitively high".[34] A 200-page recovery plan, prepared by the National Economic Action Council and released in July, reflected the move towards looser monetary and fiscal policies, "but within a framework that economic commentators acknowledged as prudent".[35]

If there was one area in which Anwar sought to distinguish himself from Dr. Mahathir, it was over the meaning of the Asian economic crisis and what it portended for regional societies. Where Dr. Mahathir saw it purely as tragedy, it represented opportunity as well for Anwar, a chance to promote the idea that the old order should give way to a new and better one – code for fresh leadership. In an address to the Council on Foreign Relations in New York, Anwar described the contagion sweeping through East Asia as "creative destruction".[36] He said, "The pressure has been building up in recent months in the region itself and we are aware that unless we reform the system from within, changes will be imposed from without." While Dr. Mahathir initially accepted the logic of domestic reforms and an end to crony capitalism, his attitude changed after Indonesian President Suharto was driven from office on 21 May 1998 amid economic and political chaos. With Anwar and his supporters adopting the slogan of the Indonesian *Reformasi* movement, opposing *korupsi, kronyisma* and *nepotisma* – corruption, cronyism and nepotism – Dr. Mahathir had no doubt they were out to topple him.

As the June 1998 UMNO General Assembly loomed, Dr. Mahathir again took steps to restrict the possibility of being challenged, though party leadership elections were not due until 1999. He blocked moves for change by getting UMNO to limit contests for heads of divisions, each of which sent delegates to the assembly. Contests were prohibited where a Supreme Council member was a divisional head, while Supreme Council members who were not divisional heads were prevented from seeking the post. As a result, there were only 24 new faces among the 165 divisional chiefs, who were key operatives in the assembly.[37] The status quo was a positive outcome for Dr. Mahathir, a number of whose supporters otherwise would have had to defend their positions against Anwar's highly-organized machinery.

Additional measures were proposed by Dr. Mahathir's followers to protect his leadership in the form of resolutions to be considered at the assembly on 19–21 June, one a re-run of the "no contest" for president and deputy of three years earlier. If it were carried again this time, Dr. Mahathir would be insulated until 2002. But as the balance of power in the party shifted to Anwar, with public support for a change after 17 years, pressure built on Dr. Mahathir to allow competition. After Zahid Hamidi, the UMNO Youth chief and a prominent Anwar ally, decried the "no contest" idea as inimical to democracy, Anwar welcomed Zahid's willingness to face challenges in the 1999 elections to preserve "the spirit of the constitution as well as the democracy and the healthy culture in the party".[38] Their coordinated comments fuelled renewed speculation that Anwar would challenge Dr. Mahathir the following year.

Dr. Mahathir, however, was convinced that Anwar was intent on unseating him immediately. Less than two weeks before the 1998 assembly, Anwar told an UMNO meeting in Johore that without reform Malaysia faced the same fate as Indonesia. Zahid and other followers joined in, picking up the Indonesian battle cry against corruption, cronyism and nepotism. Anwar's campaign was intended as a "message" for Dr. Mahathir, to get him to "understand the undercurrents in the country....we should either make adjustments now or let a smooth transition take place eventually".[39] True, Dr. Mahathir had said in 1995 that he would not stay on if UMNO members sent him a message that they were not happy with him. But in these highly charged and difficult times, the message Dr. Mahathir received was a naked threat, a conspiratorial effort to discard him like Suharto.

According to Anwar, Dr. Mahathir had sleepless nights as the assembly approached, fearing the appearance of organized discontent, such as a no-confidence vote being taken against him, a banner calling for his resignation, or just jeering.[40] Going on the offensive, Dr. Mahathir issued a series of warnings, clearly aimed at Anwar's backers, not to make "unsubstantiated" claims about nepotism and cronyism. In a closed-door briefing the day before the youth and women's wings of UMNO were due to meet ahead of the assembly, Dr. Mahathir said delegates who raised issues that might destabilize the party must be accountable for their actions. He told a press conference, "If you want to bring up such matters, you must have the facts."[41] Daim, the prime minister's long-time confidant, called Zahid and advised him to back off from his tough talk about nepotism and cronyism for the sake of his political future.[42] It came just eight hours before Zahid was to address the UMNO Youth gathering. Zahid went ahead anyway, his attack on the existence of corruption, cronyism and nepotism approved by Anwar.[43]

Although Anwar's own speech to the combined UMNO youth and women's delegates contained no such criticism and he urged an end to factionalism and a united stand in support of Dr. Mahathir in facing the economic crisis, it was too late. Dr. Mahathir, in his opening speech to the assembly, hit back so hard at the cronyism critics that any incipient revolt was quelled. His view, that external forces were responsible for Malaysia's problems, was endorsed in a resolution that was carried unanimously. Dr. Mahathir also turned the tables on Anwar by releasing, without notice, lists of all the Malays who had benefited from privatization and government contracts. His son Mokhzani was listed, but so too were Zahid and members of Anwar's family. While it might have been a "cheap trick", as Anwar later claimed, because it did not differentiate "between projects worth a few million ringgit and those worth billions",[44] the ploy worked. With Dr. Mahathir declaring all Malays cronies because all had benefited from the government's affirmative action policies, *kronyisma* was wiped from the agenda.

A parallel development, played out in the shadows while the delegates debated, confirmed how seriously and quickly the tide had turned against Anwar. Among the items being peddled by the hawkers set up outside the assembly venue, the Putra World Trade Centre, was a book titled *50 Dalil Mengapa Anwar Tidak Boleh Jadi PM* – 50 Reasons Why Anwar Cannot be Prime Minister. The poison-pen letters of a year earlier had been embellished and packaged in a more permanent format, authored by Khalid Jafri, a former newspaper sports editor. Repeating the earlier sexual charges, the book accused Anwar of complicity in a murder, and called him the most corrupt man in the country and an agent of foreign powers who wanted to overthrow Malaysia's leadership. As soon as he learned of the book, Anwar obtained an injunction through a law firm to halt its publication and distribution before the assembly opened. He described the book as "a conspiracy to smear my image and topple me" and called on the authorities to take harsh action against the author and publisher and their agents.[45] Ominously for Anwar, however, in defiance of the court order the book was packed into delegates' souvenir bags by the UMNO secretariat.

Not only did Zahid's salvo fail to ignite a debate on domestic weaknesses and the need for reform, it also eroded any remaining trust Dr. Mahathir had in his deputy. Anwar disappointed some of his own troops by failing to back Zahid and leaving him exposed, or for not leading the charge himself against corruption, cronyism and nepotism. There was no doubt about public disquiet over the matter. In a by-election a week later, the opposition captured the parliamentary constituency of Arau in Perlis for the first time, the first parliamentary seat ever won by Parti Islam Se-Malaysia in the state. The critical factor, though denied by Dr. Mahathir: The UMNO candidate was the brother of the state's chief minister, a blatant example of nepotism that shaded into money politics and related abuses.

Over the next couple of months, Dr. Mahathir orchestrated a series of moves, using both the government and party, to weaken Anwar's position.[46] A few days after the convention, Daim was re-appointed to the Cabinet with the title of Special Functions Minister. Having acquired full ministerial rank in addition to his role as government economic adviser and head of the National Economic Action Council, he was assigned responsibility for coordinating economic recovery, further isolating Anwar as finance minister. The editors of the two major Malay dailies, Johan Jaafar of *Utusan Malaysia* and Nazri Abdullah of *Berita Harian,* were forced to resign, as was the director general of TV3. All strong Anwar allies, they were replaced by pro-Mahathir figures.

As police resumed investigations into *50 Dalil,* as it became known, they focused as much on Anwar as those responsible for the book. While charges were laid against Khalid Jafri, the editor, also arrested was Nallakaruppan Solaimalai, a businessman and occasional tennis partner of Anwar, who was alleged in the book to have arranged sexual liaisons for him. After police searched Nallakaruppan's house, he was charged under the Internal Security

Act with unlawful possession of live ammunition, an offence carrying a mandatory death sentence. The same offence under the Arms Act, more appropriate in the circumstances, carried a maximum penalty of seven years imprisonment and a RM10,000 fine. Attorney General Mokhtar Abdullah told reporters there might be more arrests. Anwar was outraged to find himself being pressed to take a DNA test to prove he had not fathered an illegitimate child, as the book claimed. DNA testing of his private secretary and secretary's wife, plus the child in question, confirmed it was theirs, relieving Anwar of the need to submit to analysis.

On 12 August, Daim approached Anwar and informed him that Attorney General Mokhtar had told him that Anwar was to be charged that morning with sexual misconduct, Official Secrets Act offences and possibly treason. Anwar stormed into Dr. Mahathir's office and demanded an explanation. After listening to him for a while, Dr. Mahathir called Mokhtar on the phone and told him to delay the charges. "Wait for my clearance," the prime minister said.[47] In public, however, Dr. Mahathir and Anwar maintained the pretence that nothing was amiss between them, though Anwar was forced to deny rumours that he would resign. Dr. Mahathir said in an interview, "Do I have to kiss him on the street before people will stop saying there is a rift?"[48] In one appearance together in Penang, Anwar professed his loyalty and love for Dr. Mahathir, whom he described as "a teacher" and himself as "a mere student".[49]

Dr. Mahathir toured the country, visiting all states, supposedly to explain the economic problems directly to the people, but in reality shoring up his own popularity and preparing the public for "drastic" and even "shocking" measures to follow. He was aided by souring relations with Singapore, a periodic occurrence, which enabled Dr. Mahathir to resort once again to "bristling nationalism", as a Singapore newspaper called it, and drape his leadership in the flag. An unexplained blip on 28 August was the resignation of the governor and deputy governor of Bank Negara, which was, in fact, their way of protesting the economic policies about to be adopted. On 1 September, with no public objections by Anwar, the government introduced capital controls.

If the unorthodox economic programme sent shockwaves through the region, what happened next was a political earthquake. At 12:15 p.m. the following day, 2 September, Dr. Mahathir told Anwar: "Resign or be sacked with grave consequences." Responded Anwar: "I'm innocent and I'll have to expose your conspiracy."[50] At 5:30 p.m. he was handed a letter dismissing him as deputy prime minister and finance minister, and his office was sealed. No reasons were given for his removal in the brief announcement that evening by Bernama, the national news agency.

But events the next day, 3 September, indicated the extent of the forces ranged against Anwar and how far they were prepared to go to put him out of action. In the morning, the prosecution in the case against Nallakaruppan produced four affidavits in court to support a decision to hold him at police headquarters instead of transferring him to a prison outside the city. For the most part, they were unrelated to the offence with which he was charged, possession of 125 bullets. Rather, one police affidavit outlined statements by seven unidentified witnesses, including a man who claimed he was sodomized 15 times by Anwar and a woman who alleged she was paid RM350 by Nallakaruppan after having sex with Anwar. There were also references to a driver who had been asked to fetch Chinese, Mexican, Eurasian and women of other races for illicit sexual activities, two women who rejected Anwar's advances and a third who reportedly said she discussed politics after having sex with him. According to the affidavit, police had received a complaint that Anwar had tried to seduce the wife of a businessman, when the couple were in Anwar's delegation on a trip to Washington. The affidavit said Nallakaruppan, who was believed to have access to national secrets through Anwar, frequently accompanied Anwar abroad and "his activities could be exploited by subversive elements in and out of the country which could jeopardize national security".[51] In another affidavit, Mokhtar, the attorney general, reaffirmed that the police investigations involved national security. If there was prima facie evidence, "Nallakaruppan and/or the national leader could be charged in court under the country's laws".[52]

While the judge, Abdul Wahab Patail, adjourned the hearing to consider a defence submission that the affidavits were irrelevant to the proceedings, he refused a defence request that the affidavits be embargoed pending his ruling. He said they had been filed and were therefore public documents, a legally defective decision that made a farce of his adjournment to consider the admissibility of the affidavits. Affidavits filed in court usually become public documents only after they have been read in court or when the trial is over. The *Malay Mail*, an afternoon paper, packed them into a special edition that day, while the major dailies splashed them across their front pages the next morning. Normally staid and squeamish, the Malaysian press repeated every lurid detail of the alleged sexual misdemeanors, corruption, intimidation of witnesses and possible sedition in what a "very concerned" Malaysian Bar Council called "a breach of the rules of natural justice and fair play".

Nallakaruppan's own statements – categorically denying the accusations, alleging police brutality in detention and attempts to get him to sign false confessions incriminating Anwar while being threatened with a charge carrying a mandatory death sentence – were swamped to the point of being almost invisible. Having served to stain Anwar's reputation, particularly among conservative Muslims, most of the scurrilous allegations were abandoned, never to be mentioned again. Anwar subsequently was prosecuted on charges of corruption and sodomy. While consensual sex between males had been decriminalized in many countries, it remained a serious offence in Malaysia, punishable by 20 years imprisonment and caning, though seldom enforced.

Homosexuality was not defined in the Malaysian Penal Code, instead being described by reference to "unnatural offences" deemed to be "against the order of nature".

On the evening of 3 September, a specially convened session of UMNO's Supreme Council voted to expel Anwar from the party. Before the meeting, members received faxed copies of the police affidavit against Nallakaruppan.[53] Not that any of them could have been unaware of the details, for the country was talking about little else. In Dr. Mahathir's version, the council's decision was unanimous, but Anwar said only five of the other 40-odd members clearly supported his dismissal while the majority wanted to suspend him until any legal processes had taken their course,[54] the party's customary practice. At that stage, he had not even been charged. It made no difference as Dr. Mahathir had opened the proceedings with a directive that Anwar be kicked out for sexual misconduct, and council members had no doubt that if they objected they would suffer the same fate.[55]

By eliminating almost any chance of Anwar making a comeback in UMNO, Dr. Mahathir was able to carry the senior ranks of the party with him. Within a few days of Anwar's expulsion, all UMNO members of parliament, chief ministers, cabinet ministers and deputies, parliamentary secretaries and UMNO divisional chiefs came out in support of Dr. Mahathir's stand.[56] Only a few UMNO officials defied him, an extraordinary situation considering Anwar was believed to command about half of the party's support a few months earlier. Some UMNO heavyweights felt Anwar was wrong to pressure the party leader when he was beset with problems and vulnerable, especially as Dr. Mahathir had sponsored Anwar's rise. A few were delighted that Anwar's downfall had thrown open the succession. Many others toed the Mahathir line, publicly and enthusiastically, because they feared he would not nominate them or their allies as candidates for the next general election, which had to be held before mid-2000.

Public opinion, however, was not so easily manipulated. Much to the surprise of the prime minister and his advisers, Anwar quickly developed a huge following, both on the street and online. Thousands flocked to his house nightly to lend moral support and listen to his inside tales of corruption and abuse of power. He tapped a deep vein of resentment, especially among Malays and young people, over the rampant use of money and connections by the UMNO political and corporate elite to enrich themselves. On a tour of the countryside, crowds estimated at between 20,000 and 50,000 – technically illegal since a gathering of more than four persons required a police permit – turned out to hear Anwar denounce Dr. Mahathir as a corrupt dictator who should resign. Anwar's *Reformasi* agenda was framed in the Permatang Pauh Declaration, named after his parliamentary constituency, which emphasized the rule of law, democracy, economic justice, eliminating corruption and a commitment to peaceful protest.

In Kuala Lumpur, members of the police Special Branch, a political-intelligence unit, were not encumbered by such lofty ideals as they compiled a case against Anwar. On 6 September, they arrested Sukma Darmawan Sasmitaat Madja, Anwar's adopted brother. Eight days later they detained Pakistan-born Munawar Ahmad Anees, a microbiologist with a doctorate from the United States and a major intellectual figure in the Islamic world, as author and social critic, who periodically wrote speeches for Anwar. They were held incommunicado under the Internal Security Act and brutalized into making false confessions implicating Anwar in homosexuality. In a statutory declaration, Munawar, married with two young children, later gave a chilling description of his ordeal, which read in part "like the memoirs of a Soviet-era East European political prisoner".[57] "Kidnapped" from his home by about a dozen men in plain clothes who produced no police identification or arrest warrant, he was confined to a windowless cell and forced to answer not to a name but to "Number 26". Drugged and deprived of sleep, he was relentlessly interrogated by men often screaming obscenities in his face and subjected to degrading treatment, including having his head shaved, being stripped and forced to simulate sex on the floor with an imaginary Anwar.[58]

On 19 September, Sukma, 37, and Munawar, 51, dazed and disoriented, appeared in separate courts, each pleading guilty with the encouragement of a police-provided lawyer, to a charge of committing an act of gross indecency by allowing Anwar to sodomize him. As veteran journalist Ian Stewart observed, two men pleading guilty to identical charges and receiving identical jail sentences in identical brief court proceedings on the same day was scarcely plausible.[59] Still, it did not stop the government controlled press going to town again the following day. "We were sodomized", screamed the *New Straits Times* over its page one report.[60] Shocking their readers, some papers printed all the details of the charge, which mentioned that each defendant had allowed Anwar "to introduce his penis into your anus".[61] It was unprecedented and undoubtedly done to destroy Anwar's aura of religious respectability, and it would not have been contemplated without official approval.

That day, 20 September, Anwar was arrested after addressing the biggest rally in the capital since 1969, his popularity continuing to soar despite the attempts to discredit him. Anywhere between 35,000 and 100,000 people clapped and cheered as Anwar, wife Wan Aziza by his side, addressed them on a sunny Sunday from a balcony of the National Mosque and later in Freedom Square in the city centre. They laughed at his jokes and roared in approval as he lashed the prime minister, the government, the establishment media and the police. With banners in the background reading "Power to the people", hawkers sold badges bearing photos of Anwar and the word "*Reformasi*", while people chanted "Long live Anwar" and "Mahathir resign". They simply did not believe the case against Anwar, and they sympathized with the perceived victim of a system they judged to be badly in need of repair.

If Dr. Mahathir's attempt to eliminate Anwar politically had begun poorly, it became a public relations disaster when he was taken into custody that evening. Dozens of police commandos, masked and brandishing automatic weapons, smashed their way into Anwar's double-storey house in an upmarket suburb of Kuala Lumpur while he was holding a news conference. Under the glare of television lights, as international and local reporters, photographers and cameramen watched in amazement and his supporters chanted "*reformasi*", he was whisked away into the night.

Within half an hour of being placed in a cell at police headquarters, Anwar was assaulted by the Inspector General of Police, Abdul Rahim Noor, after the nation's top law-enforcement official silently ordered subordinates to blindfold and handcuff the prisoner. Rahim beat Anwar so viciously about the head and neck that a government forensic specialist said later he was lucky to survive. Two senior police officers dragged Rahim away from Anwar. With blood oozing from his nose and lips, Anwar lost consciousness until the following morning. He was not permitted to see a doctor for five days.

Although Anwar was told he was to be charged in court under the Penal Code the day after his arrest, Rahim announced that the former deputy premier was being held under the Internal Security Act, which allows indefinite detention without trial. Dr. Mahathir said the police had to take Anwar in before they were ready to prefer charges because he was inciting violence, a reference to the clash the previous day between protesters and riot police firing tear gas and water canons. The advantage to the authorities in holding Anwar under the Internal Security Act, however, was that he was not permitted to make phone calls, consult a lawyer or have any contact at all with outsiders. Nobody except the police knew he had been beaten. Responding to expressions of concern over his disappearance, Rahim told the press after four days that Anwar was "safe and sound", when in reality he was injured and still being refused medical treatment.[62] The truth emerged on 29 September, nine days after his arrest, when Anwar appeared in court sporting the black eye that was to become infamous. Already shaky, the government's credibility all but evaporated.

Despite repeated denials, Dr. Mahathir was never able to shake the perception that he was complicit in the attack on Anwar, if, indeed, he had not actually ordered it. He did not help his cause by suggesting initially that Anwar's injuries might have been self-inflicted to gain sympathy. The announcement of an internal police inquiry, which Dr. Mahathir called "independent", was greeted cynically, justified when it took almost four months to confirm Anwar had been assaulted by police. Those responsible for the savagery remained unidentified, even after a former Anwar staffer in exile in Indonesia named Rahim as the culprit. While Rahim eventually confessed to a royal commission, belatedly established by the government

as public pressure mounted, his lenient sentence of two months jail reinforced the widespread view that he had not acted alone. In Malaysia's
feudal society – as John Funston, the political scientist, noted – no Malay
could believe that the police chief would act without at least the expectation that he was doing his boss's bidding.[63]

Dr. Mahathir, who had said earlier he fired Anwar for moral misconduct
and not because he feared a political challenge, explained to the press on
22 September why he believed in Anwar's guilt when he had not a year
earlier. He said he had personally interviewed six of Anwar's accusers, "the
people who were sodomized, the women whom he had sex with", with
no police officers present. They had provided "incontrovertible proof" that
the allegations were true, he said. Seeking to persuade a sceptical media,
Dr. Mahathir read from Munawar Anees's statement to police, graphically
describing – and miming buggery for television, as one disgusted critic
noted[64] – what Anwar was alleged to have done while engaged in a sexual
act with Munawar. Dr. Mahathir said he could not understand how a man
could "invent a story like that".[65] Munawar, of course, had not invented
the story. It was invented for him by Special Branch officers, who degraded
him to the point of being a "shivering shell of a man" willing to agree to
sign anything "to stop the destruction of my being".[66]

In standing trial, Anwar had to contend with more than a coerced confession by two of his alleged victims. By dismissing three senior judges in
1988, Dr. Mahathir had stamped his authority so firmly on the judiciary it
was doubtful that a court would act contrary to his administration's wishes
in a politically sensitive case.[67] Since Dr. Mahathir's intervention a decade
earlier, a number of junior and more pliant judges had been promoted
ahead of their independent-minded and experienced colleagues. Anwar recognized the problem. Although he was represented by outstanding
Malaysian lawyers who provided their services for a nominal fee, he treated
his trials essentially as theatre – more political than legal. Dr. Mahathir recognized the problem too. He said the government could not win, regardless
of the verdict. "If Anwar is found not guilty then we lose, and if he is convicted we will also lose because we will be accused of" rigging the outcome,
he said.[68]

Anwar was charged with five counts of corruption and five counts of
sodomy. The first trial, in which the prosecution proceeded with four of
the corruption charges, began in the High Court on 2 November 1998 and
lasted until 1 April 1999, making it the longest in Malaysian history.
Although "corrupt practice" was mentioned in the charges, which were
brought under an emergency ordinance introduced in 1970 in the wake of
the year-earlier riots, no money was involved. Rather, the term referred to
abuse of power. The accusation was that Anwar had told police to secure
retractions from two people who had made allegations against him in the
1997 poison-pen letters, Ummi Hafilda Ali, the estranged sister of his

private secretary, and Azizan Abu Bakar, a former driver for Anwar's wife and children. Anwar was alleged to have directed senior Special Branch officers to get a written admission from both Ummi and Azizan "to deny sexual misconduct and sodomy committed by you" for the purpose of protecting himself against any criminal action.

Mohamad Said Awang, Director of the Special Branch, testified that Anwar had asked him and other officers to frighten the pair. He said Anwar had used the Malay word *gempar*, which means to threaten or "put a little fear in them". Anwar agreed he had used the word, but said he intended to have his accusers scolded like children. Said, however, had given his subordinates just 24 hours to "turn over" Ummi and Azizan, meaning to have them recant. The Special Branch officers testified they obtained retractions by subjecting the two to night-long, non-stop interrogation and threats.

Presiding at the trial was Justice S. Augustine Paul, the most junior judge in the Criminal Division of the High Court, having only months earlier been promoted from the position of judicial commissioner in the state capital of Malacca. His appointment ahead of more senior colleagues to conduct such a politically sensitive trial was "almost bound to give rise to concern", reported an international legal mission that investigated the independence of the Malaysian judiciary. And what happened during the trial "only served to increase that concern", it said.[69] Paul denied Anwar bail. He announced, without explanation, a break in proceedings between 14 and 23 November, interpreted as an attempt to prevent the Anwar affair from overshadowing an Asia-Pacific Economic Cooperation summit in Kuala Lumpur, at which Dr. Mahathir hosted world leaders.

Early on, Paul warned that anyone commenting on Anwar's guilt or innocence outside the court would be committing contempt and punished. Dr. Mahathir, however, felt free to express his views frequently and forcefully, leaving no doubt he thought Anwar was guilty. Paul never rebuked the prime minister or carried out his threat and punished him.

After hearing summaries of the evidence to be given by a number of defence witnesses, the judge refused to let them testify. When a lawyer argued that the defence would be "impeded" and "hindered" if the proposed evidence were excluded, Paul called it an irresponsible statement and said the two words "bordered on contempt of court". Paul went even further when lawyer Zainur Zakaria filed an affidavit on Anwar's behalf seeking to have the chief prosecutor and his deputy removed from the case. The affidavit said the two prosecutors had offered a plea bargain arrangement to Nallakaruppan, Anwar's tennis partner, in return for false evidence against Anwar. Paul contended there was no basis for Zainur saying there had been a request for "fabricated evidence". When Zainur refused to tender an unconditional apology, Paul jailed him for three months for contempt, though another court suspended the sentence until his appeal was heard.

The composition of the prosecuting team, initially led by Abdul Gani Patail and his deputy, Azahar Mohamed, was highly controversial, though not just because Gani was the brother of Wahab Patail, the judge who had allowed Anwar to be besmirched in the Nallakaruppan case. In the course of the Anwar trial, Attorney General Mokhtar Abdullah joined in and took over as leader, despite being implicated, both personally and through his position in the government, by the defence allegations of a political and police conspiracy.[70] The defence wanted Gani and Azahar replaced because of what the prestigious Inter-Parliamentary Union later agreed were "attempts made by the prosecution to fabricate evidence" against Anwar.[71] The allegation, contained in a statutory declaration by Nallakaruppan's lawyer, was that Gani had offered to consider a lesser charge for Nallakaruppan if he implicated Anwar in sexual offences. Gani not only remained on the job, but by the time of Anwar's second trial had been appointed attorney general and again led the prosecution.

With the defence claiming the charges were "trumped up", Anwar testified that he had political foes who would stop at nothing to destroy him politically and that there were major differences between him and Dr. Mahathir. But Paul ruled that evidence of a "political conspiracy" against Anwar, the heart of his case, was irrelevant, though evidence of a police conspiracy was allowed subject to certain restrictions. Protested Anwar: "Your Lordship has said don't touch on political conspiracy. I do not know what to do with my defence because they are so inter-related. The police conspiracy cannot stand alone. I am helpless."[72]

As the prosecution sought to prove Anwar's unbridled bisexuality, the public was treated to another assault on the conventions of good taste and decency that had made publication of such details taboo in the past. Azizan Abu Bakar, the driver, claimed Anwar had sodomized him against his will several times in 1992. The daily *Star* reported his first day's testimony under a page-one banner that read, I WAS A SEX SLAVE.[73] Police hauled into court a king-size mattress, supposedly stained with semen and seized from an apartment where Anwar allegedly had sex with his private secretary's wife and allegedly had sodomized Azizan. Malay-language media had to coin new words to express the technical vocabulary of human sexuality, which "was once considered to be unspeakable in a Malay cultural context".[74] Appalled that local papers had taken to running headlines that would "curl the whiskers of a sewer rat", a prominent Malay writer asked on the Internet, "What next? Soiled underwear? Used condoms?"[75]

Difficulties arose for the prosecution when Azizan, under cross-examination, said he had not been sodomized. When pushed in re-examination, he changed his mind yet again and said he had been. He also changed the dates on which the alleged offences had occurred. The prosecution responded by applying, at the end of its case, to amend the four charges in a way that removed the need to prove the sexual acts took place in order to obtain a conviction on the corruption issue. Although the defence complained of an abuse of process that smeared Anwar and his secretary's wife, Paul saw no prejudice to the accused and allowed the amendment. He also expunged from the record all evidence relating to Anwar's alleged sexual misconduct and sodomy, which meant the defence was powerless to try and restore his reputation.

After the defence closed its case, Anwar's lawyers filed an application seeking to disqualify Augustine Paul from continuing to hear the case. Anwar contended he had not received a fair trail and had "grave apprehension" that the judge might not bring an impartial and unprejudiced mind in weighing the issues and reaching a verdict. On top of everything else, it was claimed, the judge kept "interfering" when defence lawyers were questioning witnesses "to the extent of himself taking on the mantle of the prosecution". On 23 March 1999, when the parties were invited to sum up, the defence refused to do so until the application had been dealt with by the judge. He insisted the case continue. When the entire nine-member defence team maintained its refusal, Paul held its members in contempt of court. But on 25 March, the defence lawyers were informed that Paul would hear the application for his removal on 27 March, a Saturday. After listening to arguments from both sides, he dismissed the application.[76]

The defence clashed again with the judge during the summing up. After Christopher Fernando, another defence lawyer, became embroiled in an exchange, Raja Aziz Addruse, Anwar's respected leading counsel, agreed that what Fernando had said was correct but expressed in the wrong way. He said he was sure Fernando did not mean to be impolite, adding, "That's his way of speaking." Replied Paul: "If the way of speaking is like an animal, we can't tolerate it. We should shoot him." Later, when Fernando sought to cite the judge for contempt of his own court, Paul said he had not intended to liken Fernando to an animal.[77]

On 14 April 1999, 11 days after the trial closed with the defence refusing to make a final submission, Paul found Anwar guilty of all four charges and jailed him for six years on each, the sentences to be served concurrently. Contrary to usual practice in Malaysia, he dated the sentences from the day before conviction and not from the time of arrest to take account of the almost seven months Anwar had spent behind bars. He also dismissed a defence application for a stay of execution and bail pending an appeal. The sentences were regarded as harsh, since the "corrupt practice" with which Anwar was charged was, as one Kuala Lumpur-based foreign journalist wrote, "a minor transgression compared with the widely accepted corruption rampant throughout all levels of the Malaysian government".[78]

Although Anwar's conviction was judged almost unanimously by international legal and human rights organizations as a miscarriage of justice, the Court of Appeal upheld the decision in April 2001. An appeal to the Federal Court was also rejected in July 2002. All levels of the Malaysian court system simply did not see, as expert observers did, violations of due process, mis-directions and unfair rulings by the judge and the admission of obviously inadmissible evidence.[79]

On 27 April, less than two weeks after his conviction, Anwar was back in court charged with "carnal intercourse against the order of nature". Prosecutors proceeded with one of the five sodomy charges, the one allegedly involving Azizan, attempting to prove what had eluded them in the first trial. They chose not to go ahead with the counts allegedly involving four other people, three of whom – including Sukma Darmawan, Anwar's adopted brother – had publicly claimed they were coerced by police into falsely accusing Anwar of sodomizing them. The government, however, charged Sukma with sodomizing Azizan and with abetting Anwar to sodomize Azizan. Anwar and Sukma were tried jointly in the High Court.

When Anwar's sodomy charge was first mentioned in a lower court, the date of the alleged offence was May 1994. At the preliminary hearing it had been changed to May 1992. As the trial got underway, the prosecution moved to have the charge amended to stipulate that the offence had been committed one night between January and March 1993. The reason for the latest switch was obvious: Anwar and Sukma had filed an advance notice of alibi, which showed that the apartment in which their offences were alleged to have been committed had not been completed for occupancy in May 1992. Anwar's lawyers accused the prosecution of acting in bad faith and sought to have the charges thrown out, but the judge, Ariffin Jaka, allowed the amendment.

Still, the prosecution had to rely heavily on the uncorroborated testimony of Azizan, who had given contradictory evidence earlier. Azizan had told the first trial he was sodomized by Anwar on more than one occasion in 1992, but that he had "no problems" with Anwar after that. At the second trial, Azizan said he meant he had not been sodomized in Anwar's house since 1992. After Azizan admitted under cross-examination that he had changed the dates at the request of police, the defence attempted to get his evidence struck out on the grounds that he had contradicted himself and lied to the court. Ariffin rejected the defence request again, even though he himself had remarked at one point that "this witness says one thing today and another thing tomorrow".

As in the first trial, one of Anwar's eight lawyers found himself in legal trouble over his conduct in court. Karpal Singh, a veteran advocate and opposition politician, suggested Anwar had been poisoned. He said a urine sample sent under a false name for analysis in Australia showed Anwar had a dangerous level of arsenic, 77 times above normal, and that someone might be trying to kill him. Calling for an inquiry, Karpal said he suspected some people in high places were "in all likelihood responsible for the situation". After Anwar was sent to hospital and tests showed his arsenic level was normal, without refuting earlier evidence that the level had been significantly elevated, the government slapped Karpal with a charge of sedition, which carried a maximum penalty of three years imprisonment.

Given more leeway this time to develop Anwar's argument of a political conspiracy, the defence was able to get support from an UMNO member, Raja Kamaruddin Wahid. He testified that Dr. Mahathir's political secretary, Abdul Aziz Shamsuddin, had told him on 26 June 1998 about plans to destroy Anwar's reputation so he could never become prime minister. He said Abdul Aziz had said he long wanted revenge against Anwar, and the best way to tarnish him was to make up sodomy and adultery charges. Abdul Aziz had said he was paying Azizan and Ummi Hafilda Ali to invent stories about Anwar, the witness said. Another witness, Nor Azman Abdullah, who said he once had an intimate relationship with Ummi, told the court she had admitted to pressuring Azizan to accuse Anwar of sodomizing him. Nor Azman said Ummi had told him she contributed to the book, *50 Dalil*, which was sponsored by prominent UMMO members. Ummi had said that after Anwar was brought down, she was to be given a RM10 million business contract. Nor Azman said Ummi had confirmed she wrote the original letter to Dr. Mahathir about Anwar, but said it had been altered by Abdul Aziz Shamsuddin, the prime ministerial aide.

But Justice Ariffin Jaka was unimpressed and said conspiracy was not an issue "in this case". On 8 August 2000, three weeks after the trial closed, he found Anwar guilty of sodomy and sent him to jail for nine years, fixing the sentence to begin when he had served the six years for his earlier conviction. Sukma, 39, was given six years imprisonment and two strokes of the cane on each of two charges, his jail terms to be served concurrently. Anwar, 53, escaped the cane because of his age.

After the Court of Appeal upheld the judge's decision in April 2003, attention focused on the part played by the judges who were involved in each stage of Anwar's legal ordeal. The three judges who heard the appeal were relatively junior in the Court of Appeal, and there was no explanation as to why more senior judges were bypassed.[80] When the extremely junior Justice P.S. Gill was selected to chair the panel, Malaysia's chief justice was warned privately it was being speculated in legal circles that Gill had been promised a promotion to the Federal Court in return for dismissing the appeal.[81] In any event, he was quickly promoted to the Federal Court. Similarly, Augustine Paul and Ariffin Jaka were elevated to the Federal Court, leap-frogging colleagues with longer and stronger records. Paul's bright career prospects seemed undimmed by a Federal Court decision that overturned lawyer Zainur Zakaria's conviction for contempt and prompted a judicial comment that Paul had acted more like a prosecutor than a judge in Anwar's first trial.[82]

In a statement after the Court of Appeal ruled against him on sodomy, Anwar attacked Ariffin Jaka, Augustine Paul and the three appeal court judges for having "wantonly sold their souls for worldly gains". He said the public believed these judges were "hand-picked, servile and compliant", and had been "promptly and generously rewarded with promotions, unfairly bypassing independent judges of integrity".[83]

International and independent local legal experts concurred that the two trials were deeply flawed and that the judges were culpable. Param Cumaraswamy, a Malaysian who at the time was United Nations Special Rapporteur on the Independence of Judges and Lawyers, said there was "no hope for judicial independence and impartiality" while some judges were prepared to compromise the values of their high office in politically sensitive cases.[84] In a report for the Australian Bar Association and the International Commission of Jurists, Queen's Counsel Mark Trowell said the Malaysian justice system "failed to act independently from the executive arm of government", which was largely identified with Dr. Mahathir's interests.[85] A joint report by a mission representing four international legal organizations agreed that executive influence severely compromised the judiciary during Anwar's trials.[86]

On 2 September 2004, precisely six years after Anwar was fired and almost a year after Dr. Mahathir had retired, the Federal Court overturned the former deputy prime minister's sodomy conviction. In a majority decision, the court found that Sukma's confession was inadmissible because it was "involuntary", and Azizan was an unreliable witness whose testimony had not been corroborated where he was obviously an accomplice. Two of the three judges concluded that the prosecution had not proved its case beyond a reasonable doubt, and both Anwar and Sukma should have been acquitted without having to enter a defence. Subsequently, after Sukma won a retrial for his original conviction, all charges against him were withdrawn. A similar appeal by Munawar Anees, who had become an American citizen and was living in France, was still pending in early 2009.

Most of the experts agreed that Anwar was exonerated only because Dr. Mahathir had left the scene and his successor, Prime Minister Abdullah Badawi, had made it clear he would not try to impose his will on the court. "Finally, justice has been done," said Param Cumaraswamy. "Since 1988, under the Mahathir regime, the judiciary did not have the courage to dispense justice independently."[87] Mark Trowell said the judiciary "simply failed to respond fairly and impartially to Anwar's complaints" until Dr. Mahathir's influence had been lifted by his departure from office. "Only then could the abuses and injustices of past legal proceedings be rectified," he said.[88] Anwar also credited Abdullah with keeping his hands off. "You've got to recognize the fact that his predecessor wouldn't have made this judgment possible," he said.[89]

But Anwar's vindication was qualified as well as belated. The two Federal Court judges who cleared him and Sukma of sodomy said there was evidence to confirm they had been involved in homosexual activities, though the judges failed to provide any explanation of how they had reached that conclusion. Their comment was derided as political by critics: "acquitted but guilty".[90] Anwar was freed immediately as he had already completed his sentence, reduced to four years for good behaviour, for the corruption offence. One final attempt to get the Federal Court to reverse its own decision allowing the corruption conviction, based on new evidence and a constitutional point, failed. The five outstanding charges against Anwar – one of corruption, four of sodomy – were dropped. He was barred from holding political office and sitting in Parliament until April 2008, five years after completing his sentence. The only way for an earlier return was to obtain a pardon from Malaysia's king, which required an admission of guilt, and that was out of the question for Anwar. He was adamant he was innocent.

Despite repeated efforts, Anwar was never able to confront Dr. Mahathir in a courtroom, where they would be sworn to tell the truth. Dr. Mahathir said he would have liked to have given evidence so he could explain "how be became convinced" by the allegations against Anwar, but he ducked every opportunity to do so. In the first trial, the defence said it intended to call the prime minister as a witness, but dropped the idea after complaining that Dr. Mahathir refused to make a written statement before his planned appearance. The judge in the second trial, supporting Dr. Mahathir's resistance to a subpoena, ruled that he would not be a material witness. Although Anwar's lawyers appealed to both the Court of Appeal and the Federal Court, they declined to reverse that ruling. After he was cleared of sodomy, Anwar attempted to sue Dr. Mahathir for defamation for continuing to call him a homosexual. Branding the action frivolous and an abuse of the legal process, Dr. Mahathir's lawyers persuaded the High Court in 2007 to reject the RM100 million suit. Anwar's appeal was still pending in early 2009.

If there was any consolation for Anwar in the ruins of a political career, it was that the conviction had little effect on his standing. After his release from prison and spinal surgery in Germany, he was treated as a wronged politician rather than a criminal who had served his time, in keeping with Amnesty International's adoption of him as a prisoner of conscience and a statement by a Human Rights Watch official that Anwar was the victim of a "political vendetta" by Dr. Mahathir. Anwar accepted attachments at three prestigious universities, Oxford in England and Georgetown and Johns Hopkins in the United States, and was in demand on the international lecture circuit, before returning to fulltime politics in Malaysia in 2006. He was touted as a possible head of the United Nations in 2007, and though he was never a serious candidate to replace Kofi Annan, the speculation reflected the esteem in which he was still held.

For Dr. Mahathir, Anwar's political evisceration carried a steep price. The entire episode exposed a pattern of political manipulation of Malaysia's key state institutions, among them the police, public prosecutor's office and the judiciary. Said Awang, the Special Branch director, testified that he might lie under oath if instructed to do so by the prime minister, and acknowledged a situation could arise where he might have to do something illegal if requested by Dr. Mahathir or the police chief.

Court testimony also reflected on Dr. Mahathir personally, suggesting he had blocked a corruption investigation only months before Anwar was arraigned for allegedly doing the same thing. Shafie Yahya, the former head of Malaysia's Anti-Corruption Agency, said Dr. Mahathir had told him in June 1998 to stop investigating Ali Abul Hassan Sulaiman, Director General of the Economic Planning Unit, the powerful agency that awarded privatization projects. Ali Abul Hassan was made governor of Bank Negara the day before Anwar was dismissed. The Anti-Corruption Agency, like the Economic Planning Unit, was part of the Prime Minister's Department. Shafie told the court that after he had responded to an official complaint and found large amounts of cash in a drawer in Ali Abul Hassan's office, he was called by Dr. Mahathir, who scolded him and told him to close the case. According to Shafie, Dr. Mahathir had said, "How dare you raid my senior officer's office", and accused Shafie of "trying to fix" Ali Abul Hassan. Shafie said he was disillusioned by Dr. Mahathir's intervention and wanted to resign, but his wife persuaded him to serve out the remaining months of his contract.[91]

If Shafie's account was untrue, as Dr. Mahathir claimed, Shafie should have been charged with perjury. But he was not. Nor did the police make any attempt to clear Dr. Mahathir's name or investigate him for a possible crime, though years later an official said the attorney general had decided not to pursue the matter because of inconsistencies in witnesses' statements and a lack of supporting evidence.[92] Lawyers who inquired informally in the attorney general's department were advised to be realistic – nobody would dare interrogate the prime minister.[93]

Notes

1 Raphael Pura, "Anwar Alleges 'Conspiracy' in His Dismissal", *Asian Wall Street Journal* (hereafter *AWSJ*), 4 September 1998.
2 John Funston, "Political Careers of Mahathir Mohamad and Anwar Ibrahim: Parallel, Intersecting and Conflicting Lives", IKMAS Working Papers (Institute of Malaysian and International Studies, Universiti Kebangsaan Malaysia) no. 15 (July 1998): i–iv, 1–32.
3 Ibid.
4 Interviews with Tunku Abdullah Tuanku Abdul Rahman, 22 March 2007; Mahathir Mohamad, 31 March 2008; and Anwar Ibrahim, 21 May 2008.
5 Interview with Mahathir Mohamad, 31 March 2008.
6 Stephen Duthie, "Malaysia Wonders if Anwar, Mahathir Can Make a Team", *AWSJ*, 1 October 1993.
7 Daim was finance minister, while Sanusi was agriculture minister and UMNO secretary general.
8 John Funston, "Political Careers of Mahathir Mohamad and Anwar Ibrahim: Parallel, Intersecting and Conflicting Lives".
9 Stephen Duthie, "Malaysia Wonders if Anwar, Mahathir Can Make a Team".
10 Ibid.
11 Raphael Pura, "Anwar Deftly Navigates Shoals of Malaysian Crisis", *AWSJ*, 18 September 1997.
12 Ibid.

13 John Funston, "Political Careers of Mahathir Mohamad and Anwar Ibrahim: Parallel, Intersecting and Conflicting Lives".
14 Ibid.
15 Interview with Siti Hasmah Mohamad Ali, 17 January 2008.
16 A. Kadir Jasin, "Anwar's Loyalty to Dr. M Not in Doubt", *New Sunday Times*, 15 October 1995.
17 In-Won Hwang, *Personalized Politics: The Malaysian State Under Mahathir* (Singapore: Institute of Southeast Asian Studies, 2003), p. 283.
18 V.G. Kulkarni, Murray Hiebert and S. Jayasankaran, "Tough Talk: Premier Mahathir Thrives on No-nonsense Policies", *Far Eastern Economic Review* (hereafter *FEER*), 24 October 1996, p. 23.
19 Ian Stewart, *The Mahathir Legacy: A Nation Divided, a Region at Risk* (Sydney: Allen & Unwin, 2003), p. 33.
20 John Funston, "A Fateful September", *Southeast Asian Affairs 1999*, p. 169.
21 In-Won Hwang, *Personalized Politics*, p. 289.
22 "Too Absurd to be Believed", *New Straits Times*, 25 August 1997, cited in Khoo Boo Teik, *Beyond Mahathir: Malaysian Politics and Its Discontents* (London: Zed Books Ltd., 2003), p. 78.
23 Khoo Boo Teik, *Beyond Mahathir*, p. 78.
24 Interview with Musa Hitam, 1 April 2008.
25 Raphael Pura, "Anwar Deftly Navigates Shoals of Malaysian Crisis".
26 Ibid.
27 John Funston, "A Fateful September", p. 168.
28 Anwar Ibrahim, "From the Halls of Power to the Labyrinth of Incarceration", a letter from Sungai Buloh Prison, 3 November 1998, p. 7.
29 In-Won Hwang, *Personalized Politics*, p. 293.
30 Interview with Musa Hitam, 1 April 2008.
31 In-Won Hwang, *Personalized Politics*, p. 296.
32 Ian Stewart, *The Mahathir Legacy*, p. 41.
33 John Funston, "A Fateful September", p. 166.
34 *Straits Times*, 30 June 1998, cited in "A Fateful September", p. 167.
35 John Funston, "A Fateful September", p. 166.
36 "Malaysia: The Feud", *Business Week*, 9 November 1998 <http://www.business-week.com/1998/45/b3603032.htm> (accessed 13 April 2009).
37 In-Won Hwang, *Personalized Politics*, p. 298.
38 "Anwar Backs Zahid's Call on Contests for Top Posts", *Star*, 11 May 1998, cited in *Personalized Politics*, p. 300, fn 80.
39 "'I Never Threatened the PM'", *Asiaweek*, 18 September 1998, p. 50.
40 Anwar Ibrahim, "From the Halls of Power to the Labyrinth of Incarceration", p. 8.
41 Ian Stewart, *The Mahathir Legacy*, p. 65.
42 In-Won Hwang, *Personalized Politics*, p. 301.
43 Ibid., pp. 301–302.
44 Anwar Ibrahim, "From the Halls of Power to the Labyrinth of Incarceration", p. 8.
45 Ian Stewart, *The Mahathir Legacy*, p. 66.
46 John Funston, "A Fateful September", p. 170.
47 Anwar Ibrahim, "From the Halls of Power to the Labyrinth of Incarceration", pp. 9–10.
48 "Mahathir Discusses Malaysia's Economic Crisis", *Time Asia Magazine*: *Malaysia Archives*, originally published 15 June 1998 <http://time.com/asia/2003/mahathir/mahathir980615_intvu.html> (accessed 1 November 2006).

49 Ian Stewart, *The Mahathir Legacy*, p. 77.
50 Anwar Ibrahim, "From the Halls of Power to the Labyrinth of Incarceration", p. 11.
51 "Affidavit – Anwar Sodomised Man 15 Times", *Malay Mail*, 3 September 1998 <http://global.factiva.com/ha/default.aspx> (accessed 31 March 2008).
52 "Affidavits Accepted by High Court", *Malay Mail*, 4 September 1998 <http://global.factiva.com/ha/default.aspx> (accessed 31 March 2008).
53 Anwar Ibrahim, "From the Halls of Power to the Labyrinth of Incarceration", p. 14.
54 Ibid., p. 14. A tape recording and transcript of the Supreme Council meeting, which were widely circulated, showed a small number speaking in support of Anwar. Email correspondence with John Funston, 6 April 2009.
55 In-Won Hwang, *Personalized Politics*, p. 305.
56 Ibid., p. 307.
57 Ian Stewart, *The Mahathir Legacy*, p. 105.
58 Statutory Declaration by Dr. Munawar Ahmad Anees, parts 1, 2 and 3, published 3 December 1998 <http://www.c2o.org/malaysia/democracy/reports/981203_stat_dec_munawar_01.htm> (accessed 19 February 2008).
59 Ian Stewart, *The Mahathir Legacy*, p. 106.
60 Satwant Singh and Sujatani Poosparajah, "We were Sodomised", *New Straits Times*, 20 September 1998.
61 Ibid.
62 "FAC News Unveils What the Royal Commission Uncovered", 4 March 2002 <http://www.freeanwar.net/jan2002/facnews040302.htm> (accessed 12 April 2009).
63 John Funston, "The Legacy of Dr. Mahathir", *Australian Financial Review*, 30 July 2004.
64 Rehman Rashid, "The Politics of Contempt", 17 December 1998 <http://members.tripod.com/Anwarite/rehman.htm> (accessed 3 March 2008).
65 Ian Stewart, *The Mahathir Legacy*, p. 114.
66 Statutory Declaration by Dr. Munawar Ahmad Anees, part 3.
67 "Justice in Jeopardy: Malaysia 2000", a report on behalf of the International Bar Association, the ICJ Centre for the Independence of Judges and Lawyers, the Commonwealth Lawyers Association and the Union Internationale des Advocats, pp. 60, 77.
68 Ian Stewart, *The Mahathir Legacy*, p. 132.
69 "Justice in Jeopardy: Malaysia 2000", p. 59.
70 Ibid., p. 48.
71 Resolution adopted unanimously by the IPU Governing Council at its 174th Session (Mexico City, 23 April 2004), cited in "Anwar Ibrahim's Long Struggle for Justice", a "Report on Datuk Seri Anwar bin Ibrahim's Appeal against Conviction Observed on Behalf of the Australian Bar Association and International Commission of Jurists", by Mark Trowell, QC, *INSAF, Journal of the Malaysian Bar* (2005) XXXIV no. 1, p. 37.
72 "Justice in Jeopardy: Malaysia 2000", pp. 44–45.
73 Dalilah Ibrahim and Chelsea L.Y. Ng, "'I WAS A SEX SLAVE'", *Star*, 3 December 1998.
74 Shamsul A.B. and Wendy A. Smith, "Serious Issues, Popular Desire: Paradoxes of Mahathir's Morality", in Bridget Welsh, ed., *Reflections: The Mahathir Years* (Washington: Southeast Asia Studies Program, The Paul H. Nitze School of Advanced International Studies, Johns Hopkins University, 2004), pp. 43–44.
75 Rehman Rashid, "The Politics of Contempt".
76 "Justice in Jeopardy: Malaysia 2000", pp. 45–46.

77   Ibid., p. 46.
78   Ian Stewart, *The Mahathir Legacy*, pp. 167–168.
79   "Anwar Ibrahim's Long Struggle for Justice", p. 27.
80   "The Anwar Appeal", press release by Param Cumaraswamy, U.N. Special Rapport-eur on the Independence of Judges and Lawyers, 22 April 2003, cited in "Anwar Ibrahim's Long Struggle for Justice", p. 30.
81   Letter to Ahmad Fairuz Sheikh Abdul Halim, Chief Justice, from Param Cumara-swamy, dated 20 June 2003.
82   "Anwar Ibrahim's Long Struggle for Justice", p. 64, fn 1.
83   Anwar Ibrahim's 21 August 2003 press statement, cited in "Anwar Ibrahim's Long Struggle for Justice", pp. 29–30.
84   "The Anwar Appeal", cited in "Anwar Ibrahim's Long Struggle for Justice", p. 31.
85   "Anwar Ibrahim's Long Struggle for Justice", p. 19.
86   "Justice in Jeopardy: Malaysia 2000", p. 77.
87   Param Cumaraswamy, Vice-President, International Commission of Jurists, quoted in 3 September 2004 press release, "Malaysia: ICJ Welcomes Ruling in Anwar Appeal".
88   "Anwar Ibrahim's Long Struggle for Justice", p. 20.
89   Leslie Lopez, "Malaysian Court Reverses Anwar Sodomy Conviction", *AWSJ*, 3 September 2004.
90   "Thinking Allowed: No Deal Between Pak Lah and Anwar", *Aliran Monthly*, 2004: 8 <http://www.aliran.com/monthly/2004/8i.html> (accessed 26 January 2006).
91   Transcript of Anwar Ibrahim trial before Judge Ariffin Jaka, 12 June 2000, pp. 2034–2040.
92   "Abuse of Power Over Corruption Probe: No", *Straits Times*, 9 April 2008.
93   Interview with Param Cumaraswamy, 16 January 2008.

Part III
Turmoil in Retirement

12
A Bare-Knuckle Brawl Over One Man's Legacy

When he retired on 31 October 2003, Dr. Mahathir said he was finished with politics. He declined an offer to remain in the Cabinet as a "senior minister",[1] an arrangement pioneered by Singapore's Lee Kuan Yew that enabled him to keep tabs on his successors. Dr. Mahathir had begun writing his memoirs while he served out his 16-month notice,[2] and looked forward to finishing them and accepting invitations from abroad that work commitments had hitherto precluded. He promised not to interfere in Malaysian government affairs. "No, I have already made it very clear that when I leave, I leave completely," he said.[3]

Dr. Mahathir had chosen carefully as his successor Abdullah Badawi, an experienced, modest and affable veteran, over the younger, better educated and more vigorous Najib Razak. Abdullah, 63, was familiar with Dr. Mahathir's thinking, having served in most of his cabinets in such senior portfolios as education, defence and foreign affairs. Najib, 50, a bit on the young side, Dr. Mahathir reasoned, could step in after Abdullah had served a single term.[4] Abdullah's only blemish was that he had backed Tengku Razaleigh Hamzah in challenging Dr. Mahathir for the leadership of UMNO in 1987. But Abdullah had not joined Tengku Razaleigh's breakaway faction, and Dr. Mahathir had forgiven him and restored his ministerial rank after three years and nine months on the backbenches. Before taking over, Abdullah envisaged no major policy shifts. He said, "My vision for Malaysia is Vision 2020," which was Dr. Mahathir's blueprint and target to join the First World.

Privately, however, Dr. Mahathir had second thoughts about Abdullah, who declined to give a commitment in advance to name Najib as his deputy, for the fairly obvious reason that Najib was his strongest rival in the party. In response to a letter from Dr. Mahathir, Abdullah said he could not decide until he became prime minister.[5] Dr. Mahathir discussed his misgivings with a confidant, former finance minister Daim Zainuddin, who suggested it was still not too late to hand the reins to Najib instead. But Dr. Mahathir worried that the public would condemn him if, at the eleventh hour, he ditched his fourth deputy. "I've already had three deputy prime ministers," he told

Daim. "If I do it again, people might say it's me, not my deputy," who is the problem.[6]

As Abdullah prepared to take office, he appointed trusted aides to run Bernama, the national news agency, and TV3, the country's biggest private television station. Three weeks into the job he sacked the editor-in-chief of the New Straits Times publishing group, Abdullah Ahmad, ostensibly for writing a commentary that offended a foreign government. In fact, Abdullah Ahmad was replaced because he was a Mahathir ally who was pressuring the new prime minister in print to confirm Najib. "Don't tie my hands," an irritated premier told Abdullah Ahmad. "I want a free choice."[7] Dr. Mahathir and Abdullah Ahmad feared his choice would be Muhyiddin Yassin, another UMNO vice president, who was close to the prime minister.[8] After two long months as prime minister, during which Malaysia had no leadership succession in place, Abdullah made Najib deputy UMNO president and deputy premier.

While that was the outcome Dr. Mahathir sought, he had just about lost faith in Abdullah. Subsequent events convinced him that he had made an horrendous mistake, and that it was incumbent upon him to force Abdullah to mend his ways or step aside.

Abdullah was known affectionately as Pak Lah – Uncle Abdullah, with his name shortened to the final syllable – a moniker that summed him up neatly: He was mild, moderate and, with the habits of a former civil servant, steeply inclined towards consultation and consensus. The contrast was striking with the energetic and confident Dr. Mahathir, who made decisions faster than he consulted his cabinet colleagues, and found targets of scorn and derision almost daily.

Ironically, it was Abdullah's need to prove himself – after all, he had been installed in the top job, unchallenged, by just one man – that provided the first systematic critique of Dr. Mahathir's record. Abdullah's agenda, which he gradually warmed to under the influence of a small coterie of unofficial advisers, had the effect of reviewing Dr. Mahathir's performance in a way that was beyond contemplation when he still held office. As some of the dark side of Malaysia's hard charge to modernity was exposed, Dr. Mahathir joined the debate, confrontational as ever, and it became nothing less than a bare-knuckle brawl over his legacy.

The appointment of Abdullah loyalists to key media posts assumed added significance as the drama unfolded and the two fought a political battle that kept the country variously enthralled, amused and appalled for the next three years. Devoting his "retirement" to undermining Abdullah's administration, Dr. Mahathir wrote another chapter in his extraordinary political career. It was bizarre at times, as he criticized policies and attacked ministers who, until recently, had been long-time cabinet colleagues and faithful followers. Forced to take sides, they protected their positions and observed Malay feudal tradition by lining up, to a person, behind their current leader, Abdullah. Finally, though, Abdullah was undone largely by his own incompetence and fading electoral appeal. In an effort to keep the heat on him, Dr. Mahathir quit UMNO in protest in 2008, only to rejoin in triumph in 2009 after helping force Abdullah into retirement early in his second term.

The subdued Abdullah won favour early for merely being himself and lowering the volume of politics. He took a conscious decision to limit his exposure to the media and not seek the saturation coverage that had become standard for the leader.[9] What would normally be an obstacle to leadership, his lack of sparkle, actually was an asset in the circumstances. After being lectured, hectored and admonished for so long, Malaysians relished a well-earned respite. Pak Lah's arrival helped engender a mood of relief, even elation, over the promise of a fresh start.

Yet once Abdullah settled comfortably in the prime minister's seat, he felt it necessary to emerge from Dr. Mahathir's shadow. Malaysians were gratified that the transition, the fourth since independence in 1957, had gone smoothly, once more confirming the essential and enviable stability of the political system. But they wanted to know if the pre-selected Abdullah was his own man. When he spoke, was it his, or his master's voice, they heard? The distinction was more than academic, for large numbers of them looked to the newcomer for change, despite the accolades that echoed for Dr. Mahathir.

Writer and journalist Rehman Rashid observed that the style of governance was giving way from magisterial to managerial in a Malaysia assembled on a build-operate-transfer basis: "Dr. Mahathir built it, and now he is handing it over to Abdullah Ahmad Badawi to operate, and eventually transfer to his own successor."[10] The belief that Abdullah would do little more than push buttons in the Mahathir machine was almost inevitable, considering that he had rarely expressed views that set him apart from Dr. Mahathir, and he no doubt had been chosen in part to protect his former boss's reputation and interests.

Clearly, Prime Minister Abdullah lacked legitimacy. He needed to step out and allow himself to be judged not only by his political party but also by the people of Malaysia, to gain the moral authority to match his political rank. Constitutionally, a general election had to be held by November 2004, while UMNO would hold its annual meeting, to include the triennial election of office bearers, in the second half of 2004. Abdullah set his sights on those two events, one tightly linked to the other, determined to acquire the sort of mandate that permitted nobody to doubt that he was governing in his own right, and as more than an interim or accidental premier.

There was no point in Abdullah trying to fill Dr. Mahathir's outsized shoes with bigger and better dreams for Malaysia. Nor did it make sense, at the other extreme, to present himself as a pale imitation of the larger-than-life figure he replaced. Abdullah settled for a measured approach that fit his personality and sought to reassess, renovate and, where necessary, reform Dr. Mahathir's Malaysia. While talking continuity, Abdullah's administration embarked on a process predicted by political scientist Khoo Boo Teik and characterized by him as de-Mahathirization – "suitably timed, carefully calibrated and delicately performed measures to distinguish itself from the old regime".[11]

While the measures were delicate enough at first, before long they took on a life of their own. And, given the sensitive nature of some, no time would have been suitable to introduce them if it meant avoiding embarrassment and bruised egos.

Abdullah began to stake out his own space by declaring war on corruption and inefficiency in government departments. It was a logical place to start, and not just because the cheer-leading media were promoting him as Mr. Nice and Mr. Clean. The Malaysia he inherited was awash with irregular payments, from petty bribery in the bureaucracy to outrageous commissions for defence contracts and multi-million dollar abuses in affirmative action policies. At the apex of this mountain of black cash was UMNO, a "one-stop shop for handouts and favours", as a critic put it.[12]

Shrewdly borrowing from former deputy premier Anwar Ibrahim's *Reformasi* campaign, Abdullah promised greater transparency and accountability and less red tape at the head of a "clean, incorruptible" administration that was "beyond suspicion". He pledged open tendering for government contracts, which would mean an end to one of the most notorious forms of cronyism. Announcing a national integrity campaign, he allocated RM17 million to establish a regional anti-corruption academy and pledged Malaysia would sign the United Nations Anti-Corruption Convention.

The enthusiastic reception for Abdullah's rhetoric confirmed the public's deep disquiet over Dr. Mahathir's failure to check the spread of corruption in its myriad and multiplying forms. Although he was never suspected of plundering the economy for personal gain along the lines of President Ferdinand Marcos of the Philippines, Dr. Mahathir could not escape responsibility for an entrenched culture of greed and graft. As a strong leader, he had set the tone as well as the standard of behaviour in his regime. For, as he once observed, "If a society does not want corruption, it should not create a climate so conducive to corruption."[13]

Despite being aware of corruption's corrosive nature, Dr. Mahathir had given higher priority to realizing his vision than ensuring honesty and integrity in the people who were supposed to deliver it. Long before he climbed the political ladder, Dr. Mahathir wrote a lengthy essay in which he described corruption as a "disease" and a "crime" that could weaken a country and allow it to be conquered. He blamed corruption, in the form of regular payments to local chiefs, for the fall of the Malay states into British hands in the nineteenth century. It was not sufficient to condemn corruption, he said; society should actively "cleanse itself of corruption".[14]

But once in the political fray, Dr. Mahathir compromised. As deputy prime minister, he had tried to persuade Prime Minister Hussein Onn not to prosecute for corruption Harun Idris, a former chief minister of Selangor, who helped Dr. Mahathir return to UMNO. Hussein, with a reputation for rectitude, sent Dr. Mahathir packing – and Harun to trial and jail.[15] As prime minister, Dr. Mahathir had promised to instill the fear of God into the hearts of civil servants on the take,[16] but again his actions belied his threat. He held nobody accountable for the half dozen financial scandals that cost Malaysian taxpayers tens of billions of ringgit during his time in office. Even friends noted his backsliding. Zainuddin Maidin, an associate from Kedah who was later appointed a deputy minister, said Dr. Mahathir had shown "extra anxiety not to lay himself open to accusations of abuse of power" by requesting guests not to give gifts at his second daughter's wedding in 1982. But ten years later, said Zainuddin, Dr. Mahathir had exposed himself to criticism over his children's participation in business, with some observers seeing "similarities" between him and Indonesia's President Suharto.[17]

Dr. Mahathir's stock response was that he lacked evidence to prosecute. "If you show us the proof, we will surely take action," he said a few years after taking office,[18] a line he used up to and beyond retirement. While it was undoubtedly difficult to prove corruption, Dr. Mahathir rarely indicated that exposing and punishing the corrupt was a serious objective. Indeed, he frequently sent signals to the contrary, indicating that meeting ambitious growth targets and raising the status of bumiputras was paramount. "I don't want the Malays to ask too many questions about the wealth of their fellow Malays," he once said. "Why don't we ask how the non-Malays acquired their wealth?".[19] Dr. Mahathir retained the services of a number of senior officials and ministers considered by the public to be corrupt, prepared to tolerate their perceived ethical flaws as long as they performed their assigned tasks. He rejected demands by the opposition and non-governmental activists that he give the Anti-Corruption Agency independent status, preferring to keep it answerable to him.

At the UMNO General Assembly in 2000, 19 years after he became president, Dr. Mahathir had broken down and wept over "money politics", which put a price on almost every party post. He explained later his "one great fear" was that a prime minister might come to power through corruption, and therefore "everything possible" should be done to ensure that only "clean leaders" were elected. Reminded that some vice presidents and Supreme Council members were suspected to have bought votes to get elected, Dr. Mahathir protested that "I cannot work on the basis of accusations. I must have clear evidence."[20]

In no time at all, Prime Minister Abdullah managed to obtain some of the evidence that had eluded Dr. Mahathir. Abdullah was aware that his anti-corruption campaign had raised expectations, but that a sceptical public doubted the authorities would net more than the usual *ikan bilis,* little fish, and reel in some recognized sharks. The separate arrest of Eric Chia, a prominent businessman, and Kasitah Gaddam, the Minister of Land and Cooperative Development in Abdullah's Cabinet, was meant to answer the sceptics. Chia was charged with criminal breach of trust when he was managing director of state-owned steelmaker Perwaja Trengganu Sdn. Bhd., while Kasitah was accused of abusing his position when he was executive chairman of Sabah Land Development Board. Both pleaded not guilty. Although their appearance in court only days apart was given maximum exposure in the local press and became a minor sensation, their prosecution in early 2004 raised doubts about Abdullah's commitment to a serious clean-up.

Chia was a close friend of Dr. Mahathir, who had personally recruited him in 1988 to run Perwaja, a pillar of Malaysia's troubled venture into heavy industry. Not long after Chia resigned in 1996, it was revealed that the company was insolvent with massive debts, and the Anti-Corruption Agency was called in to investigate. That the aging and ailing Chia was being charged eight years later looked odd, to say the least. In addition, the amount he was accused of diverting to a non-existent company in Hong Kong, RM76.4 million, was a fraction of Perwaja's losses and would not be able to explain what went wrong. As for Kasitah, he was an appointed senator and the least known member of the Cabinet, from Sabah state in East Malaysia, and his alleged offences also dated back a decade.

The convenient indictment of Chia and Kasitah, while no doubt welcomed by the public as a sign that the government was actually cracking down on corruption, also reinforced the impression that the Anti-Corruption Agency served a political purpose. And the disclosure by one of Abdullah's ministerial colleagues that 18 more high-profile cases were awaiting action only strengthened that suspicion. It appeared that translating investigation into prosecution might still depend on the advantages, if any, it offered to the political leadership.

While Abdullah deserved the sobriquet Mr. Clean in the sense that he had not enriched himself, his family and friends had benefited from the system of patronage he was supposed to be dismantling. A brother, who was in the catering business, had received a 15-year contract for the armed forces canteens when Abdullah was defence minister. Recently, the brother had been awarded the privatization of the national airline's catering service, with reports of a generous, guaranteed return for nine years. Abdullah's Cambridge-educated son, Kamaluddin, was identified as one of the country's fastest-rising corporate figures. According to a local business magazine, Kamaluddin, 36, the major shareholder in rapidly-expanding Scomi Bhd., a publicly listed oil and gas supplies services company, was the tenth wealthiest Malay in 2004, with assets of more than RM320 million.

Abdullah also had another reason to divert attention elsewhere at this time: serious U.S. allegations that Scomi Precision Engineering Sdn. Bhd., a company part-owned by Kamaluddin, had produced centrifuge components suitable for developing nuclear weapons. The Malaysian police and Abdullah were quick to deny the accusations, after they appeared in the international media in February 2004. They said Scomi Engineering did not have such capabilities, and had fulfilled a contract believing it to be lawful. But their claims carried little credibility. The Pakistani bomb-maker who ran a nuclear black market network, Abdul Qadeer Khan, had made several visits to Malaysia and logically would have met top officials. Kamaluddin also had close relations with the Dubai-based Sri Lankan, Buhary Syed Abu Tahir, described by President George W. Bush as the network's "chief financial officer and money launderer". Despite a clear conflict of interest – given his position as home affairs minister in charge of the police as well as prime minister – Abdullah ignored calls for an independent inquiry.

Much more substantive were Abdullah's economic-policy forays, venturing where angels had long feared to tread: close to Dr. Mahathir's toes. Abdullah indefinitely postponed the construction of a RM14.5 billion electrified, double-track railway line that was to have stretched the length of peninsular Malaysia. On the face of it, the decision was straightforward: Facing a nagging budget deficit, the government chose to shelve the deal, which would have been Malaysia's largest privatization venture, as it included the sale of the country's unprofitable state railway company. But this particular deal had sensitivity written all over it. Dr. Mahathir had approved the contract only days before his exit, giving it to a consortium led by the listed conglomerate, Malaysia Mining Corporation Bhd., which was controlled by a favoured friend, Syed Mokhtar Albukhary. Domestic critics contended that the proposed railway would not be commercially viable and would strain the government's finances, while China and India protested on other grounds: Kuala Lumpur earlier had signed letters of intent with units of their state rail companies and Malaysian partners to build the railway.

While government officials insisted that Abdullah's flip, following Dr. Mahathir's flip-flop, was not directed at any particular person or company and did not represent a rejection of Dr. Mahathir's policies, business executives and political analysts read it otherwise. Budget constraint was certainly a valid concern: After six straight years of deficit spending, Dr. Mahathir had left the country bleeding red ink. Overspending reached its peak near the end of his tenure, when the government blew almost its entire RM110 billion development budget for 2001–2005 in the first three years. In his last budget speech, Dr. Mahathir added a further RM50 billion for development in 2004–2005.[21] Inheriting a budget deficit for 2003 of 5.5 per cent of gross domestic product, considered worrying by some officials, Abdullah vowed to narrow and gradually close the gap.[22]

But balancing the books was also an excuse for Abdullah, who was bent on jettisoning the entire concept of mega-projects, which symbolized the excesses of the Mahathir era. The railway package had another strike against it, a fatal one, as far as Abdullah was concerned. Like most privatization projects granted under Dr. Mahathir, it had been negotiated privately on unknown terms, without an open bidding process and public disclosure when the award was pending.[23] And like many of the others, it had gone to a businessman widely perceived to be a crony, one who had won a total of RM22 billion in government infrastructure contracts in the past six months.[24] His credibility on the line, Abdullah bit the bullet.

A few weeks later, Abdullah cancelled another privatization venture awarded to Syed Mokhtar: a 60 per cent interest in Southeast Asia's biggest hydroelectric dam, Bakun in Sarawak, which carried a RM6.4 billion price tag, down from the originally projected RM15 billion. Although the dam would go ahead because construction had started, the "think big" credo at the heart of Dr. Mahathir's philosophy was out of fashion, if not dead. "Never mind that I may not build great monuments or glittering cities," Abdullah subsequently told a business group.[25] He said Malaysia needed to return to the basics of economic development, starting with agriculture and agri-based industries.

In another initiative to boost his popularity, Abdullah ordered a searching inquiry into the police force, a move that quietly addressed the wider issue of "institutional degradation", as regional analyst Manu Bhaskaran termed it. Public unhappiness over the performance of the police had long given way to disgust and resignation. At the top, the force had been politicized after serving the same party, UMNO, for more than 40 years, while at street level it had proved ineffective in stemming a rising tide of crime that included everything from murder to rape and armed robbery. As foreign residents complained about a growing sense of insecurity, locals noted an increase in police payoffs, violence and extra-judicial killings.

To indicate he meant business, Abdullah appointed a rarely invoked royal commission, headed by a judge and given sweeping investigative powers, to carry out the review. But the terms of reference contained no mention of corruption, and focused only on general issues such as "the role and responsibility of police in implementing law", organizational structure, and human resources needs. The overwhelming majority of the 16 members of the commission were close to the government or UMNO. They duly delivered a report that savaged the police force, though not until Abdullah had safely navigated his general and party elections.

The spotlight on the police inevitably drew critical attention to other institutions and services that had deteriorated over time. Other sections of the bureaucracy, particularly the education, immigration, customs and transport departments, had slipped. The Election Commission, nominally independent but located within the Prime Minister's Department like the

Anti-Corruption Agency, functioned as an arm of the government. Parliament, where the National Front habitually held a two-thirds majority that enabled it to amend the Constitution at will, appeared to be an empty shell, poorly attended by elected members and given little chance to scrutinize vital legislation. Saddest of all, Malaysia's once proud and independent judiciary had fallen into international disrepute after a head-on clash with Dr. Mahathir.

Although he conspicuously took the high moral road in distancing himself from Dr. Mahathir, Abdullah was motivated in large measure by self-interest: no less than political survival. Planning to call an early general election, he needed to win handsomely to face UMNO and confirm his place as president of the party. If he attended UMNO's General Assembly weakened or wounded in any way, he might be challenged for the party's leadership, and there was no guarantee what might happen if factional fighting convulsed the party. With vote buying endemic in UMNO, Abdullah lacked an established financial base if he were tempted, uncharacteristically, to play the money game.

Abdullah's electoral imperative was not just to lead the National Front to another victory. He could do that with minimal effort, since the opposition was not strong or unified enough, and did not have the resources to halt the entrenched, multi-party juggernaut. To secure his position as prime minister and not be considered a seat warmer for some ambitious UMNO rival, however, he needed to recover the support of the Malay majority that was lost in the last general election, after the persecution of Anwar Ibrahim. He had to show that UMNO once again spoke for the Malays. And, to do that, he must abandon some of Dr. Mahathir's unpopular predilections, if not Dr. Mahathir himself.

In the contest for Malay support with the opposition Parti Islam Se-Malaysia (PAS), Abdullah held a significant personal advantage over Dr. Mahathir, who had been demonized by the more-religious elements. From one of the most respected Muslim families in Malaysia – his father, grandfather and great grandfather were all prominent Islamic leaders,[26] and he held a degree in Islamic studies – Abdullah was an elusive target for PAS's conservatives. He was able to lead prayers, a significant symbolic act that Dr. Mahathir was unable to do – in fact, he lead prayers for the deceased PAS leader Fadzil Mohamad Noor in 2002[27] – and his less adversarial style was more effective and harder to counter. He did not brand PAS leaders "liars" and "hypocrites", as Dr. Mahathir had, and nor did he stage frontal attacks on the *ulama*. In political terms, when the competition was fiercest for the hearts and minds of the Malay community, PAS had lost the ideal opponent in Dr. Mahathir. Abdullah, with his impeccable religious credentials and sense of restraint, was worrying.

Creatively, Abdullah unveiled the concept of Islam Hadhari, a progressive form of the faith designed to undercut the appeal of PAS's allegedly more dogmatic and less tolerant Islam. Although vague in content – the religious affairs minister described it simply as a balanced approach to life – Islam Hadhari offered a set of principles for Muslims to participate successfully in a globalized economy. Closely associated with Abdullah and his clean reputation, Islam Hadhari was critical because Dr. Mahathir's strategy of trying to outbid PAS on religion had culminated in his declaration in 2001 that Malaysia was already an Islamic state. So it was a case of which Islam was the right Islam: the version pursued by UMNO, or that followed by PAS. With Anwar Ibrahim, the person who had given substance to UMNO's Islamic commitment, still in jail, Abdullah had to Islamize the party anew for its ongoing war with PAS.

The injustice suffered by Anwar was another troubling issue bequeathed by Dr. Mahathir that required deft handling if Malay support were to be recouped. Abdullah could have eased the pressure and undercut PAS and its allies by granting Anwar's request for special parole to go abroad for medical treatment for a back injury, aggravated when beaten in custody in 1998. But in the process of consolidating his own position, Abdullah was reluctant to do anything that might revive Anwar's political fortunes, a calculation that also reflected a degree of personal animosity between them. Instead, Abdullah took the opposite tack to Dr. Mahathir and stopped bad-mouthing the incarcerated Anwar, hoping his silence and the passage of time would allow the matter to fade away. After meeting secretly with Anwar's wife and learning that his condition was worsening, Abdullah ordered that Anwar be transferred from prison to a government hospital.[28] The Malaysian Federal Court's decision in September 2004, overturning Anwar's conviction for sodomy, lanced the boil, as one commentator put it, from Abdullah's standpoint: Anwar was free, but was not allowed to run for office for four years because his corruption conviction still stood.[29]

But while Abdullah enjoyed the praise heaped on him by international human rights and legal organizations over Anwar's release, Dr. Mahathir seethed. He called a press conference and declared he was "mildly surprised" by the court's decision. The clearest indication that he was deeply upset, however, was the presence at his side of his wife and three of their children, a most unusual event.[30] Later, Dr. Mahathir said he still believed Anwar was guilty.

With Malaysia's external relations, as in domestic affairs, the relaxed Abdullah found that a smile and a warm greeting went a long way. In the case of Singapore, Australia and the United States, a prime ministerial hand extended in friendship amounted to no less than a diplomatic breakthrough after Dr. Mahathir's prickly nationalism. Apart from the intrinsic value of being on polite terms with allies and neighbours, Malaysia realized practical gains by reducing the animus in contacts with them.

Abdullah lost no time in making a courtesy visit to Singapore, signalling that he wanted an end the impasse in their relations. He suggested they settle the easiest of their differences first and not let the hardest hold the rest hostage. "We have to pluck some low-hanging fruits before the *musang*," a nocturnal civet cat, "comes and takes them away," he said. For Singapore, it was vindication of a decision taken years earlier "to sit things out" until Dr. Mahathir had departed.[31] The improvement in atmospherics opened the way for two-way strategic investments, with Temasek Holdings, a Singapore state-owned investment company, leading a surge of capital northward. Four months after Abdullah took over, his government approved Temasek's purchase of a 5 per cent stake, valued at RM1.6 billion, in national phone utility Telekom Malaysia.

Similarly, Abdullah transformed relations with Australia by ending almost overnight what one Australian correspondent called "two decades of bilateral cold war". The two countries agreed to annual consultations between their foreign ministries and senior officials, with Abdullah making the first official visit to Australia by a Malaysian prime minister in 20 years.

In repairing contacts with the United States, Malaysia's largest trading partner and foreign investor, all Abdullah had to do, again, was substitute civil discourse for Dr. Mahathir's point-scoring on behalf of the developing and Islamic worlds. The Malaysians disagreed with Washington over the invasion of Iraq and some other issues, and that would not change regardless of who was in office in Kuala Lumpur. But pragmatic and interested in tangible returns, Abdullah travelled to America in mid-2004, met President George W. Bush and declared their ties "very strong".

Concerned about competition from Thailand and Singapore, which were negotiating free-trade agreements with the United States, Abdullah signed up for one himself. Dr. Mahathir had displayed considerable wariness about such pacts, arguing that in an era of globalization they mainly benefited the powerful industrial economies. He criticized Singapore for entering a free-trade agreement with New Zealand because, he said, it weakened the Association of Southeast Asian Nations and might allow Australian and New Zealand products access to the ASEAN market by the back door. While Malaysia under Dr. Mahathir had begun discussions with China and Japan on free-trade arrangements, Abdullah accelerated the process and tried to make up for lost time. He widened the discussions to include Australia, New Zealand, Pakistan, India and Chile, as well as the United States.

Keen to seek endorsement for his reformist programme before the end of the honeymoon period customarily extended to a new leader, Abdullah called a general election for 21 March 2004, less than five months after he became prime minister. Some of the gloss had begun to wear off when he re-appointed most of Dr. Mahathir's ministers to his Cabinet, a clear message that anti-corruption would not be pushed too far. And when it came to nominating UMNO candidates for the election, few of those commonly thought to be corrupt were excluded.[32]

Still, built around Abdullah's amiable and pious personality, the National Front's campaign stressed the by-now familiar themes of Islam and corruption.

The government went close to condemning the *ancien regime* by admitting in one full-page newspaper advertisement that Malaysia had become "rotten to the very core with no single aspect of life untouched by corruption".[33] The ads urged the electorate to give Abdullah a landslide so he could continue cleaning up the mess.

Dr. Mahathir, who did not seek re-election, was seen on balance as a liability and given a limited role. He canvassed for votes in parts of Kedah, his home state, and mainly in constituencies where ethnic Chinese were in a majority. On UMNO's advice, he did not venture into Kelantan or Trengganu, PAS's strongholds, or other parts of the Malay heartland.[34] The one-time Malay champion was now more popular with non-Malays.

While Abdullah eschewed the crude and offensive campaign tactics employed by the National Front in 1999, he had no hesitation in using the vast resources of the state, as usual, to overwhelm his opponents. He was aided by a redistribution of electoral boundaries that added 26 seats to Parliament in a way that would obviously favour UMNO while reorganizing some PAS-held seats to make it hard for the party to retain them. In addition to the gerry-mandering, the Election Commission was responsible for a litany of errors in the conduct of the entire electoral process that could be explained only by a combination of gross incompetence and a desire to benefit the government.[35]

Abdullah led the National Front to its greatest electoral win ever in terms of parliamentary seats, capturing 199 of the 219 on offer. The opposition won only 20 seats compared with 45 in the outgoing smaller Parliament. Although the National Front's 64 per cent of the vote trailed its 65 per cent previous best in 1995, it was up sharply from 56 per cent in 1999. The National Front regained control from PAS of the legislature in Trengganu state, where Abdullah was running the campaign, and went close to dethroning the party in Kelantan. PAS ended up with a mere 6 seats in Parliament, down from 27.

An analysis showed that while UMNO had scarcely crushed PAS in the showdown for the Malay vote, the outcome was still a strong endorsement for UMNO and a personal triumph for Abdullah. Malays were prepared to give Abdullah a chance with his moderate brand of Islam and reform agenda. They still hoped he was sincere in his declarations to eliminate corruption.

Where the country responded to Abdullah's promise of good governance, however, UMNO resisted, indicating it was out of touch with public opinion, or prepared to ignore it. At the UMNO General Assembly in September 2004, Abdullah dodged a ballot for the party's presidency only because Tengku Razaleigh Hamzah, the former finance minister who almost defeated Dr. Mahathir in 1987, could not persuade 30 per cent of divisions nationwide to nominate him as a challenger. Acting President Abdullah was confirmed in his post, as was Najib, his deputy, though Abdullah's failure to get key allies elected to top party positions made it less than a repeat of his general election success.

In the ballot for the party's three vice presidents, the likely future leaders, incumbent Muhyiddin Yassin, an Abdullah supporter, narrowly retained his position. Another incumbent favoured by Abdullah, Muhammad Muhammad Taib, lost. Two relative outsiders, Federal Territories Minister Mohamed Isa Samad and Malacca Chief Minister Ali Rustam, finished first and second, respectively. Abdullah retained a majority on the Supreme Council, though only because he was allowed by the rules to appoint up to ten members himself. Four cabinet ministers lost their seats on the council, while three old-line, pro-Mahathir politicians made surprising comebacks.[36] As delegates were giving Abdullah a standing ovation for his ringing cries to cleanse UMNO of political corruption, some of them were accepting cash and other payments in return for their votes. "Money politics" was worse than ever, delegates suggested, and could help explain the surprising poll results. Their view was confirmed later by an internal investigation that led to Mohamed Isa Samad, the poll topper, being suspended from the party for bribery.

With his huge electoral mandate, Abdullah persisted with policies that implicitly pictured Dr. Mahathir as irrational, irresponsible and profligate. Abdullah withdrew approval for a gambling concession that almost nobody knew had even been granted. The government said Dr. Mahathir, in his capacity as finance minister, had awarded the licence to Ascot Sports, a private company controlled by a tycoon who vied for the title of crony-in-chief, Vincent Tan Chee Yioun, not long before resigning. Dr. Mahathir denied that he was "personally responsible" for granting the licence.[37] It would have allowed Ascot Sports to conduct nation-wide off-site betting on local and international sports events for 20 years. The company paid a RM20 million fee for an operation that industry experts calculated would have generated annual turnover of RM1 billion from horse racing, soccer and other sports. While the government would have collected substantial revenue in taxes that was being lost to illegal gambling, Abdullah worried that the concession would expose the government to attacks by conservative Muslims, especially PAS, which had long campaigned to close existing gaming outlets.[38] Nobody explained why the public – and the Cabinet – had been kept in the dark about the original decision in 2003. Abdullah's aides said they learned about it only in 2004, when Tan informed them he was planning to start his new betting business.[39]

A wounded and angry Dr. Mahathir conveyed his unhappiness to close friends. "Mahathir's disagreement with Abdullah started with his delaying tactics over [appointing] Najib," said Abdullah Ahmad, who kept in touch with the former premier. "Next was the release of Anwar. The rest followed."[40] When Abdullah Badawi encroached on core elements of Dr. Mahathir's vision – Proton, the national car; the construction of a bridge to Singapore; and Putrajaya, the new capital – the former prime minister exploded in public. He was an adviser to Proton Holdings Bhd., the publicly listed company producing the car, and he used the post to go to the company's defence.

Proton was already under siege as trade barriers fell in Southeast Asia and the company progressively lost the protection that had long made it profitable. It faced a further threat if Abdullah was serious about cleaning up the ponderous, government-linked concerns that dominated the country's business scene and equity market. The task fell to Khazanah Nasional Bhd., the state-owned investment agency that held a controlling stake in Proton, and in the nation's power, airline and telecommunications companies. What happened at Proton showed how deeply politics was embedded in business under Dr. Mahathir's philosophy, and how hard it would be to disentangle them.

Contrary to Abdullah's assurance that Proton's board would have the final say in all management matters, Mahaleel Ariff, the Mahathir protégé who had been chief executive since 1997, began making decisions after consulting Dr. Mahathir alone. When the board decided not to renew Mahaleel's contract, Abdullah stepped in at Dr. Mahathir's request and overruled the board. Abu Hassan Kendut, Chairman of Proton, quit in protest. Later, the board successfully removed Mahaleel after he gave a newspaper interview and criticized the government for not providing enough protection for Proton.[41] Dr. Mahathir basically declared war on the government by defending Mahaleel and endorsing his criticism. He opened another can of worms by claiming "irregularities" in the opaque import-licensing system for foreign cars, by which, he said, the imports posed unfair competition for Proton.

With Mahaleel out of the way, Proton proclaimed its independence at the end of 2005 by unloading a 57.7 per cent stake in the debt-ridden Italian motorcycle manufacturer MV Augusta Motors. Proton's new management largely blamed Augusta for a pre-tax loss of RM158.8 million for the three months to 30 September 2005, the second consecutive quarterly loss and a sharp reversal from the RM439.8 million pre-tax profit for the six-month period a year earlier. The disposal of Augusta was a monstrous rebuke for Dr. Mahathir and Mahaleel, who together had purchased the famed but struggling motorcycle designer and maker less than a year earlier. Proton paid 70 million euros for Augusta and sold it for a token one euro.

In a joint statement, Dr. Mahathir and Mahaleel said their credibility and honesty were at stake. They questioned the rationale behind the sale and posed a series of questions that, they said, the company owed it to shareholders and the public to answer. In later comments, Dr. Mahathir took issue with Proton management's contention that Augusta did not have any synergy with the carmaker. Failing to elicit a response from Proton, Dr. Mahathir mocked Abdullah's new order: "I thought that this is supposed to be a very transparent world where everything is done in full view of everyone."

If Abdullah had been reluctant to take tough decisions that would put him into direct conflict with Dr. Mahathir over Proton, he surely agonized over plans for a second bridge to link Malaysia with Singapore. But on this issue, there was no fudging their differences. The Malaysians had argued with the Singaporeans for a decade to share the cost of replacing the old causeway with a bridge so that ships could pass through the narrow Johore Strait, but Singapore saw no reason to scrap the causeway, and this item became entangled with all the others on their bilateral agenda. In an act of brinkmanship close to retirement, Dr. Mahathir authorized a construction company to begin work on Malaysia's half of the bridge. Abdullah initially told the company to go slow,[42] before cancelling the contract in April 2006, outraging Dr. Mahathir and causing an irreparable breach between them.

To Abdullah, it made no sense to build a bridge to nowhere. Connecting it to the Singapore end of the causeway would invite legal action by Singapore, since it involved relocating water pipes and a train line, as well as demolishing half the causeway. Going ahead with half a bridge and hoping that one day it might be turned into a full bridge would subject Malaysia to ridicule and place it at Singapore's mercy. For Dr. Mahathir the nationalist, however, halting work was surrendering Malaysian sovereignty and kowtowing to the Singaporeans "as if you are scared of them". Dr. Mahathir pronounced Malaysia a "half-past six country", invoking a term whose origin was obscure but whose meaning he made crystal clear: a "country with no guts".[43]

Similarly, Dr. Mahathir disagreed volubly with Abdullah for suspending construction of a monorail in Putrajaya in the name of fiscal responsibility. Dr. Mahathir had been prepared to press ahead with the new city even during the Asian economic crisis, and he rejected the argument that the state was currently short of funds. Convinced the train line should be financed off-budget, if necessary, he pointed to "record" profits earned by state oil and gas company Petronas, to the flush Employees Provident Fund and to accumulating national reserves, as evidence that money was available.

Although Dr. Mahathir repeatedly had pledged not to interfere once he handed over, he justified his intervention on the grounds that Abdullah had broken their private, implicit agreement first. "Before I stepped down, we agreed that certain things needed to be completed, because this has been agreed upon," said Dr. Mahathir. "And he never said he would not. And then he reversed things that were decided, sometimes in the Cabinet."[44]

Dr. Mahathir was too angry to contemplate the sweet ironies of political life, that what goes around comes around. Thirty years earlier, Tengku Razaleigh Hamzah's career had been derailed by a gentleman's agreement, an "understanding" with Dr. Mahathir that became a misunderstanding. Now it was Dr. Mahathir's turn. It was not so much a case of teaching an old dog new tricks, as an old dog forgetting his tricks as he aged.

Dr. Mahathir took the view that while it was Abdullah's prerogative to add new elements, it was unacceptable for him to abandon a major policy or project already in place. "The style may change, but what was undertaken before should be carried out," he said.[45] For his part, Abdullah said it was "unrealistic to assume that I would let everything run on autopilot after becoming prime minister". Apart from challenges that keep changing, "there are also things that I wanted to implement for the country which may not have been a priority when he was prime minister", Abdullah said. Fortified by his huge election victory, "I think I have the people's approval to lead in the manner I believe will best benefit the country".[46]

The Dr. Mahathir confronting Abdullah was vastly different from the master politician the country had known for almost a quarter of a century. Apart from being an adviser to four government-linked concerns – Petronas, the Langkawi Development Authority and the Tioman Island Development Authority, as well as Proton – Dr. Mahathir lacked a power base and was 78 when he retired. His inability to acknowledge the nature of political power, that it flowed from the office and not the individual, was not a little sad considering how effortlessly he had once wielded power. Throughout his political life, he had been obsessed with perpetuating his own power, telling Hong Kong-based *Asiaweek* in 1997, "If you don't have power and you put out a very reasonable proposal, nobody will implement it. You have to have power."[47] Now, he was unable or unwilling to accept that power had passed to someone else. Dr. Mahathir was particularly hurt that his former cabinet members had switched their allegiance to Abdullah and endorsed alternative ideas, predictable in many a political system and completely consistent with Malay culture. "I thought they supported me because of what I was doing for the country," he said. "Now I know they supported me because I was prime minister." After complaining about being stabbed in the back, he said of Abdullah, "I chose him and I expected a degree of gratefulness."

In one crucial respect, though, it was the same old Dr. Mahathir: His way was still the only way. As he said, he had risked his neck in 1969 to point out that Prime Minister Tunku Abdul Rahman was "definitely doing something wrong", and it was disappointing that nobody in UMNO now was prepared to take a risk and speak out against practices that were "obviously wrong".[48] Even as a "pensioner", as the Sultan of Johore scorned him, Dr. Mahathir assumed that he should be the sole judge of what was wrong for Malaysia. Musa Hitam, the first of the deputies, joked that Dr. Mahathir was suffering from PMS – "post-prime ministerial syndrome" – causing him to think that "only he is right".[49]

In his sustained, frontal attack on Abdullah, Dr. Mahathir implicitly invited further examination of his own record, "to bring the magnifying glass to the collateral damage of his economic policies during his years in office", as academic Shamsul Amri Baharuddin said.[50] Or, as Karpal Singh, the opposition warhorse, put it, "I say those who live in glasshouses should not undress without drawing the curtains."[51] As always, Dr. Mahathir was fearless. No topic was taboo, despite its potential to rebound on him, and he was offended by repeated allegations "that the administration during my time was worse".[52] Dr. Mahathir's conviction and certitude were intact, but without the levers of state and party power to impose his views, his words echoed impotently.

The architect of Malaysia's mega-projects and duty supervisor for several world-class financial scandals dared accuse the budget-conscious Abdullah administration of wastage. The government's decision not to go ahead with half a bridge to Singapore had caused losses amounting to billions, Dr. Mahathir said. "This is the people's money."[53] He also portrayed the disturbing crime rate as part of the rot that had set in under Abdullah, a claim disproved by the royal commission into the police force, which found it was the most corrupt of all government departments and long incapable of protecting the public.[54]

Equally audacious was Dr. Mahathir's persistent targeting of Abdullah's businessman son Kamaluddin, and aspiring politician son-in-law Khairy Jamaluddin, both in their 30s, suggesting vast influence peddling. Oxford-educated Khairy, deputy leader of UMNO Youth, had worked as an adviser to the prime minister, but left to join an investment bank in which he bought a 3 per cent share. Dr. Mahathir said Kamaluddin's Scomi had RM1 billion of contracts with state companies, while Khairy, with no official position, had to approve all business proposals submitted to the government. Abdullah, Dr. Mahathir declared, would "pay the price" for turning the country into a "family business".[55] His accusations forced Abdullah to go on television to deflect charges of corruption and nepotism, an awkward position for Mr. Clean. Abdullah also said, "The projects awarded to Dr. Mahathir's children were far bigger than what Scomi received", a disagreeable comment for Mr. Nice.[56] Khairy sold his RM9.2 million bank stake, after associates felt compelled to explain how they financed him into it in the first place.

While Dr. Mahathir's barbs found their targets, by doing so he re-activated the controversy that swirled around his own family's commercial operations when he was in office. It was the corporate activities of three sons, Mirzan, Mokhzani and Mukhriz, that prompted critics to compare his administration with Suharto's corrupt regime in Indonesia. Without even acknowledging the most blatant example of favouritism, the RM1.7 billion bailout of Mirzan Mahathir's shipping interests in 1998, Dr. Mahathir moralized on the evils of corruption, cronyism and nepotism. As "a matter of a principle," he said – obviously in complete denial – he had not allowed his children or wife to do business with the government when he was prime minister.[57]

Dr. Mahathir was indignant that his critical comments were not being adequately reported in Malaysia. "Where is the press freedom?," he asked with a completely straight face in 2006.[58] The state of the press was about where he had left it three years earlier, firmly in the hands of the UMNO leader's political and corporate allies, who were reluctant to give a voice to critics inside or outside of the party. The reason "I am talking to myself", as Dr. Mahathir remarked, was due to the system of government ownership and control of the media he had imposed and consolidated over the years.

Dr. Mahathir was merely getting a taste of his own medicine when he was blacked out, or severely restricted, in Malaysia's mainstream media.

Dr. Mahathir courted ridicule by insisting, "During my time, the press was quite free."[59] In fact, to enforce his rule, he had sacked editors for not toeing his line and tightened restrictions on a press that historically was required to partner the government in the country's development. He twice toughened the Printing Presses and Publications Act, allowing the home affairs minister unfettered powers to control the press. He also amended the Official Secrets Act to permit almost any document to be classified "secret", and to require offenders convicted of disclosing the contents to spend at least a year in jail. With printing companies obliged to obtain a licence annually, many who had invested in expensive machinery refused to handle alternative publications offering incisive commentaries and critical perspectives.[60] For instance, the printer of five years of *Aliran Monthly*, published by the Penang-based public interest group Aliran, abruptly withdrew its services in early 1999. Over the next seven months, four other printers terminated their relationships with Aliran, amid reports of government intimidation.[61]

Apart from temporarily suspending the publishing permits of three leading newspapers in 1988, Dr. Mahathir's administration had closed permanently three Malay-language publications – the magazines, *Detik* and *al-Wasilah* and the tabloid *Eksklusif* – whose popularity soared after Anwar Ibrahim's dismissal in 1998. The government's abuse of prominent dailies to discredit Anwar saw their circulation and revenue drop significantly, as readers went on strike against biased and distasteful reporting. TV3 suffered the same fate. In contrast, sales of *Harakah,* a biweekly owned by PAS that closely tracked Anwar's fall, quadrupled to more than 300,000. To curb the paper's growth, the government reduced its frequency from twice a week to twice a month and enforced the terms of its licence, which allowed it to sell only to party members.[62] The paper's editor was convicted on a charge of sedition. The New York-based Committee to Protect Journalists put Dr. Mahathir on its list of the Ten Worst Enemies of the Press in 1999, citing his stranglehold on the mainstream media and efforts to stifle the handful of opposition organs allowed to publish.[63]

The foreign press fared little better. In 1985, a correspondent of the *Far Eastern Economic Review*, a New Zealand national, became the first journalist ever to be prosecuted in Malaysia under the Official Secrets Act. Within a month, a Malaysian reporter was arrested on a similar charge.[64] The following year, the government expelled two Kuala Lumpur-based correspondents of the *Asian Wall Street Journal* and banned the paper for three months, but relented after a court ruled against the expulsions. Distribution of the *Review, Journal, Newsweek, Time* and the *Economist* was sometimes delayed, or blocked altogether, by ministerial edict. Malaysia in 1999 became the first Commonwealth country in 50 years to jail a reporter for contempt of court: Murray Hiebert, a Canadian on the *Review's* staff in Kuala Lumpur, served four weeks of a six-week prison sentence for an article he wrote about a local lawsuit.

In an attempt to skirt the onerous licensing laws, two young Malaysian journalists in 1999 had started the country's first online daily newspaper, *Malaysiakini*. Their gamble: To promote his Multimedia Super Corridor in 1997, Dr. Mahathir had promised foreign information and communications technology investors he would not censor the Internet, a decision he later regretted. Nevertheless, the government sought to impede the venture by resorting to back-door methods, such as barring *Malaysiakini* reporters from official functions, press conferences and other events.[65] A police raid on the paper's offices in 2003, after a complaint by UMNO's youth wing that a reader's letter was seditious, made a mockery of Dr. Mahathir's promise. But the paper was back online less than half a day later, its confiscated computers and servers replaced with makeshift and publicly donated equipment, and its reputation enhanced. *Malaysia-kini* won the International Press Institute's 2001 Freedom Award for its independent coverage of Malaysia's political scene.

Seemingly oblivious to the irony, Dr. Mahathir turned in his hour of need to *Malaysiakini,* whose staff he had once labelled "traitors". He began the first of what became periodic interviews with the comment, "I never liked Malaysiakini.com. It was very critical of me before."[66] After that, he made extensive use of cyberspace, including news websites and popular blogs, before starting his own blog – www.chedet.com – to get his anti-administration message across.[67] VCDs of several of his talks were sold at roadside stalls.

Improbably, as even the opposition conceded "a greater sense of freedom and openness" after Dr. Mahathir stepped down,[68] he contended that Abdullah's Malaysia had become a "police state".[69] In an open letter to Malaysians, the former prime minister said anyone attempting to organize an anti-Abdullah function would be hassled and forced to cancel it. Actions or threats to deter them, he said, included sacking, transfer to remote areas such as Sabah, cancellation of contracts, harassment by the banks, summons by the police or the Anti-Corruption Agency, detention and repeated interrogation. "A climate of fear has enveloped this country," he said.[70] In truth, Malaysia was never more than a quasi-democracy, and Dr. Mahathir had done almost nothing to encourage it to mature into the real thing. As he concentrated power in his office, he had no qualms about stripping away the democratic trappings and baring his authoritarian claws. Nothing, before or since, had created a climate of fear like Operation Lalang in 1987, with the roundup of 119 politicians, intellectuals and activists.

While Dr. Mahathir insisted that only issues divided him and Abdullah, he made the dispute personal, branding Abdullah a liar, deceitful and shame-less.[71] Privately, with close friends, Dr. Mahathir used even stronger language, calling Abdullah a "hypocrite" and a "great pretender", pretending to be cleaner and more modest than his predecessor.[72] Dr. Mahathir's sheer nastiness made relations between their families awkward. Caught in the crossfire was Mokhzani, Dr. Mahathir's second son, who recalled that Abdullah had helped him get together with Mastisa Hani Mohamed Abid, whom Mokhzani married.[73] Despite what Abdullah called Dr. Mahathir's "stronger doses of venom", the prime minister remained on warm terms with Dr. Mahathir's wife, Dr. Siti Hasmah. Abdullah's wife invited Dr. Siti Hasmah to her old Putrajaya home, the official residence, even as the war of words turned ugly. Dr. Siti Hasmah accepted, keen to see what changes had been made by the new occupants, and delighted to accept a ride with Abdullah around the premises.[74]

Although he helped shaped the perception of Abdullah as an indecisive leader who relied heavily on a group of young advisers led by his son and son-in-law, Dr. Mahathir paid a price for his remorseless, scatter-gun offensive. While he retained a public following, elite political opinion turned against him when it became obvious that he was obsessed with ousting Abdullah, whatever the cost to UMNO and stability.[75] A brokered meeting with Abdullah in late 2006, billed as "peace talks", was pivotal. Apart from insisting on recording the private, two-hour discussion – mostly a stream of complaints by Dr. Mahathir – he resumed his onslaught the following day, before Abdullah had time to respond.[76]

The harder Dr. Mahathir pressed, the more his stature was diminished. He was hit in the face with pepper spray while attending a rally in Kelantan. The ultimate indignity was his attempt to persuade his old UMNO division, Kubang Pasu in Kedah, to elect him as one of seven delegates to the party's General Assembly in 2006. Although his name was first on the ballot paper, he came ninth out of 15 contestants – in the division he had headed for nearly 30 years. While Abdullah's followers, fearing Dr. Mahathir would try to instigate a revolt against Abdullah at the assembly, undoubtedly blocked his election, Dr. Mahathir compounded his humiliation by alleging vote-buying. "I know that bribery happens in any politics, but I did not think that the ruling party itself used money politics," he said, choosing to forget that the rampant use of cold hard cash had become common in his time and reduced him to tears.[77]

Dr. Mahathir's hectic schedule, including interviews, speeches and overseas travel, as well as opening a "concept bakery and bistro" with a Japanese partner, trying to criminalize war and convening a meeting in an attempt to solve the Muslim insurgency in southern Thailand, took a toll on his health. Despite his relatively youthful and extremely healthy appearance, doctors detected blockages in his arteries and warned him to slow down. After three minor heart attacks in under a year, Dr. Mahathir, 82, elected to have a five-and-a-half hour heart bypass operation in 2007, the second in 18 years. A resulting chest infection required him to undergo another three hours of traumatic surgery within three weeks. Malaysians tracked his recovery through daughter Marina's blog, updated twice daily. A week after the infected tissue was removed, she reported her father's moods were like the seven dwarfs: "grouchy, grumpy, whiny, snarly, whateverly, smirky and sometimes, sometimes smiley".[78]

While Abdullah no doubt enjoyed the periodic silence that hospitalization imposed on Dr. Mahathir, it did little to help the prime minister's political fortunes. Having promised so much so early, Abdullah was excoriated for failing to deliver on almost all fronts. After encountering resistance at UMNO's annual meeting in 2004, he ran out of what reformist zeal he genuinely harboured and allowed himself to be carried along by stronger party currents. His laid-back style, initially seen as endearing, became a liability and he was portrayed by opponents as listless, even lazy. Abdullah told one interviewer he was "not losing any sleep over" Dr. Mahathir's comments.[79] He was not losing sleep over much at all, according to anti-government websites, which circulated photos of him dozing through cabinet meetings and political gatherings.[80]

As Malaysia's ranking in Transparency International's corruption index slipped to 44 in 2006 from 37 in 2003,[81] Abdullah's lack of political will to tackle the entrenched system of "money politics" and abuse of power played out publicly over the case of Zakaria Mat Deros, the little known UMNO divisional chief in Klang. A one-time railway gatekeeper and office boy, Zakaria, 60, was the classic UMNO warlord, dispensing patronage and delivering votes. He attracted national attention by building an RM8 million mansion in a working-class neighbourhood, without obtaining planning approval and on land originally meant for low-cost housing.[82] With Malaysians flocking to Klang to gawk at the almost-completed palace, which would not have looked out of place in Hollywood or Beverley Hills, Abdullah emerged from an UMNO Supreme Council meeting to slap Zakaria on the wrist: He should quit as a municipal councilor, Abdullah said, but he could continue as a state legislator and UMNO divisional chief as his wrongdoing was not a party matter.[83]

A financial scandal over plans to establish a free-trade zone at Port Klang, the country's main port, also indicated that nothing much had changed in the way of large infrastructure projects.[84] Only after press reports that the state-owned Port Klang Authority had been saddled with huge losses did the government acknowledge a multi-billion ringgit bailout, in the form of a soft loan.[85]

With the royal commission into the police force, which delivered a 634-page report in mid-2005, Abdullah had a chance to make amends. It recommended sweeping reforms to fight corruption, with the establishment of a permanent, independent body to initiate and conduct investigations into graft and other abuses. But when the proposal for an Independent Police Complaints and Misconduct Commission was resisted by police, Abdullah prevaricated, and what remained of his anti-corruption drive disintegrated.

In a moment of irritation with his predecessor, Abdullah admitted that public confidence in the judiciary was low, but said that "this didn't happen during my time", alluding to events in 1988, when Dr. Mahathir intervened and brought the judiciary to heel.[86] Yet even when Anwar Ibrahim released a videotaped recording in 2007 showing a local lawyer, V.K. Lingam, boasting about his ability to broker judicial appointments, the government was reluctant to revisit the episode. After a protest march by lawyers, Abdullah appointed a toothless three-member panel to probe the authenticity of the videotape. With Anwar cleverly ratcheting up the pressure by periodically releasing more clips from the same videotape, Abdullah bowed to public demands in late 2007 for a full-blown royal commission. Its hearings in early 2008 proved sensational – Dr. Mahathir, his tycoon friend Vincent Tan, Lingam, two retired chief justices and a former minister all gave evidence – with a fuzzy picture emerging of a subverted judiciary. Dr. Mahathir's memory, usually as sharp as his tongue, let him down under oath: He said "I can't remember" or its equivalent 14 times during his 90-minute testimony, prompting opposition leader Lim Kit Siang to accuse him of "selective amnesia".[87]

More worrying for Abdullah was a deteriorating social climate in which the Indians and Chinese believed they were being denied political, religious and economic space. As positions polarized, some Malays also felt their rights were being challenged. The minorities were disturbed by what they regarded as creeping Islamization and by periodic displays of *ketuanan Melayu*, Malay supremacy, while the New Economic Policy was extended so reflexively that it was dubbed the "never ending policy". Extremists gained the upper hand as Abdullah proved ineffective in stemming an "increasingly intolerant" and "growing tide of Malay-Muslim communitarianism".[88]

With Abdullah's Islam Hadhari exposed as a political slogan to regain Malay votes rather than a new marker for social harmony,[89] an estimated 20,000 Indians poured onto the streets of the capital in November 2007. Led by the Hindu Rights Action Force, they defied a ban on the rally, pre-emptive arrests and police use of water canons, tear gas and baton charges to disperse them. At least 88 demonstrators were arrested, with five leaders later being detained without trial under the Internal Security Act for allegedly making inflammatory remarks. The government's heavy-handed response, consistent with its intolerant attitude to other peaceful protests, dramatically reversed sentiment in the Indian community, which had long been quiescent and pro-government.[90]

A memorable headline on an editorial by Steven Gan, editor-in-chief of *Malaysiakini*, summed up the popular reinterpretation of Abdullah near the end of his first term: "An incompetent, not-so-nice guy".[91] Yet almost nobody forecast the "political tsunami", as it was dubbed, that struck the government in a general election Abdullah called on 8 March 2008.

The National Front lost its two-thirds majority in Parliament for the first time and conceded control of five of the country's 13 states. The government won 140 seats in the new 222-seat Parliament against 199 in the outgoing 219-seat Parliament. A loose alliance of Parti Keadilan Rakyat, led by Anwar Ibrahim's wife, PAS and the Democratic Action Party, won 82 seats compared with 20 previously. They later formed a coalition called the People's Front, raising the prospect that Malaysia might develop a viable two-party political system. A vital factor was the charismatic Anwar, whose formidable organizational skills brought the parties together despite their misgivings about each other. While the timing of the election prevented Anwar from standing as a candidate by a few weeks, his unmatched oratory harnessed dissatisfaction in all ethnic communities and persuaded significant numbers to vote opposition regardless of race and religion.

The shocking results turned Malaysian political life upside down, creating uncertainty at state and federal level, in the ranks of the National Front and within each of its decimated component parties. It raised the possibility, previously almost unthinkable, that the UMNO-led government, in place for half a century, might lose office. As the People's Front took over state administrations in Penang, Perak, Trengganu and Selangor, joining Kelantan, already in opposition hands, Anwar reinforced National Front anxiety by engaging in psychological warfare. He predicted he would replace the central government within months by enticing at least 30 defectors, especially legislators from neglected Sabah, to join his People's Front and give it a majority in Parliament. The outcome also raised hopes that the era of race-based politics might be ending. Anwar had campaigned for a Malaysian Economic Agenda to replace the New Economic Policy and provide help to all needy Malaysians rather than bumiputras alone.

Adding to the turmoil in UMNO, Dr. Mahathir led a chorus blaming Abdullah for the rout and called on him, yet again, to quit. Tengku Razaleigh, the former finance minister, announced he would challenge Abdullah for the leadership. In the fluid political scene, where it was almost impossible to forecast what might happen next, Abdullah accepted responsibility for the dismal performance. He indicated he would step down in favour of Najib, his deputy, at some unspecified time beyond the annual UMNO General Assembly in December 2008 and before his next five-year term had expired.

Spurred by what amounted to a psychological defeat for the government, Abdullah pursued some of the reforms he had promised in his first term. As if to redeem his own legacy, he appointed as de facto law minister Zaid Ibrahim, a lawyer and former member of the Aliran reform movement, which itself had been a target of Dr. Mahathir's ire. Resisting pressures from within his own Cabinet and administration, Abdullah unveiled a package of measures that not only further impugned Dr. Mahathir's record but also set in motion events that could engulf the former prime minister in more controversy, if not legal proceedings.[92]

Abdullah expressed regret over the 1988 episode in which six Supreme Court judges were suspended, three of whom were later dismissed, including the head of the judiciary, Salleh Abas. At a Bar Council dinner attended by the three surviving former judges and the families of the others, Abdullah offered financial compensation to the sacked men, acknowledging "the pain and the loss they have endured".[93]

Abdullah was tiptoeing through a political and legal minefield in hoping to do enough to move on without seriously examining the past, arguing that to look back "would only serve to prolong the sense of crisis".[94] While some of the wronged judges or their relatives were pleased with the gesture, others indicated they would keep up the pressure to reopen the case. They wanted the government to apologize, which Zaid advocated, and they sought to expose those responsible for what he called "a serious blemish on our judicial history".[95] The implications, however, went far beyond that single event. Waiting on the sidelines were a number of influential People's Front politicians with sound reasons to think they also had been victimized by Mahathir-era courts and deserved the chance for redress. Among them were Anwar Ibrahim, Democratic Action Party leader Lim Guan Eng, who became chief minister of Penang after the election, and opposition parliamentarian Wee Choo Keong. They could be counted on to become more insistent in their demands for legal justice as they moved closer to the centre of political power.

The findings of the royal commission into the videotape scandal spelled more trouble for Dr. Mahathir. In a 191-page report, the five commissioners found evidence that top government officials, including the former prime minister, a lawyer and a businessman were involved in fixing the appointment of judges. "We are of the view that there was, conceivably, an insidious movement" by Lingam, the lawyer, "with the covert assistance of his close friends", Vincent Tan, the businessman, and Tunku Adnan Mansor, then a deputy minister in the Prime Minister's Department, "to involve themselves actively in the appointment of judges". In particular, the report said, they got involved in the appointment of Ahmad Fairuz Sheikh Abdul Halim as chief judge, Malaya, the third-highest position in the judiciary, and his subsequent promotion to president, court of appeal, the second-highest position. "In the process, Tun Mahathir Mohamad was also entangled," the report said.

On Cabinet's orders, the attorney general was instructed to investigate the six people identified in the report for possible offences, such as obstruction of justice, sedition and leaking state secrets. Not only was Dr. Mahathir under official investigation, but he was also closely tied to three of the others. Based on Vincent Tan's testimony, the commissioners said it was clear that Tan, Lingam, Adnan and Dr. Mahathir were long-term friends and business associates "whose lives are inextricably linked both personally and in the tentacles" of Tan's corporate empire "and various business projects" that required the former prime minister's backing.

Dr. Mahathir responded with a mixture of bravado and belligerence, while issuing a threat of his own. He saw the Abdullah administration's actions not as steps towards restoring public faith in the judiciary but as an attempt to "draw allegations against me for my alleged misdeeds" and to "shut my mouth should I find occasion to criticize the present government".[96] He welcomed any move to investigate him. "But don't give up halfway and claim there is no case against me," he said. "I want to go all the way to court. Let me expose many other things in open court."[97]

Soon after, Dr. Mahathir resigned from UMNO, saying he would rejoin once Abdullah was no longer leading the party. It seemed to be a desperate attempt to persuade UMNO's 3.2 million members to choose between him and Abdullah, and it contradicted his parting advice to them five years earlier to "be loyal" and "put the party first".[98] The most notable members who answered Dr. Mahathir's appeal to follow him were his wife and their wealthy businessman son, Mokhzani, who once was treasurer of the party's youth wing but was no longer active in politics. Another son, Mukhriz, who won a parliamentary seat in the election and joined his father in demanding that Abdullah resign, remained in UMNO.

Although Dr. Mahathir's standing, image and dignity had taken a battering, and he was left exposed to further reputational damage and possible criminal charges, he could never be counted out. Abdullah's indecisiveness following the election debacle created a longing among some Malays for the orderliness and predictability of the Mahathir era. With a distinct whiff of nostalgia in the air, Abdullah was forced to retire early in 2009, before a previously agreed 2010 deadline. He fell victim to an UMNO power play led by Muhyiddin Yassin, a vice president and former ally, subtly supported by Najib. Both were urged on by Dr. Mahathir, writing in his blog, who said they were the best two leaders to run the country.[99] Under the new arrangement, UMNO's General Assembly was postponed for three months, until March 2009. Abdullah agreed not to contest the presidency of the party and Najib was the only candidate to replace him. Muhyiddin defeated a rival in a ballot to become deputy party president.

The backroom choreographed leadership transition ended Abdullah's generally unhappy prime ministership, which was hobbled by his own ineptitude and lethargy, but also obstructed by entrenched UMNO interests opposed to reform. Although Abdullah near the end managed to push several bills through Parliament aimed at restoring confidence in the judiciary and strengthening the fight against corruption, almost no one had a good word to say for the watered-down pieces of legislation.[100] Abdullah was angered by the open politicking of Dr. Mahathir and Muhyiddin to get him to quit even earlier. He said Dr. Mahathir had left UMNO, but was still issuing orders to party members. "Who is he?" Abdullah said.[101]

Abdullah found out who Dr. Mahathir was on 28 March 2009, the final session of the five-day General Assembly. Wearing a striking mauve shirt and accompanied by his wife Dr. Siti Hasmah, Dr. Mahathir made an unscheduled appearance, entering the hall as Muhyiddin, the newly-crowned deputy leader, was speaking. More than 2,500 delegates rose spontaneously and gave the Mahathirs a thunderous ovation, bringing proceedings to a halt. Invited onto the stage later by Najib, Dr. Mahathir went through the motions of reconciling with Abdullah and was photographed between the two of them, holding their hands aloft in what was meant as a show of new-found UMNO unity. Dr. Mahathir announced he would rejoin UMNO, and Najib promised "a certain role" for him in the new administration.[102]

While the theatrics would scarcely end factionalism in UMNO, there was no doubt about Dr. Mahathir's restoration. When Najib announced his Cabinet after being sworn in on 3 April as Malaysia's sixth prime minister, Mukhriz Mahathir was made deputy minister of international trade and industry. Left out was Khairy Jamaluddin, Abdullah's son-in-law, who had a fortnight earlier defeated Mukhriz for the leadership of UMNO Youth, and who was the object of much of the elder Mahathir's ridicule. Dr. Mahathir was back near the centre of power.

Notes

1   Beh Lih Yi, "Be a 'Jantan', Leave UMNO, Mahathir Told", 26 June 2006 <http://www.malaysiakini.com/news/53031> (accessed 2 September 2008).
2   Interview with Mahathir Mohamad, 31 March 2008.
3   "Mahathir Confirms Heir, Rejects Official Role", *Kyodo*, 8 July 2002 <http://findarticles.com/p/articles/mi_m0WDQ/is_2002_July_8/ai_88685580/> (accessed 12 April 2009).
4   Fauwaz Abdul Aziz, "Q&A: Najib 'Scared' He Wouldn't be Picked as DPM", 9 May 2007 <http://malaysiakini.com/news/66986> (accessed 30 August 2008).
5   Ibid.
6   Interview with Daim Zainuddin, 18 October 2007.
7   Interview with Abdullah Ahmad, 16 August 2007.
8   Ibid.
9   Leslie Lopez, "He's No Mahathir, and That's OK", *Far Eastern Economic Review* (hereafter *FEER),* 25 December 2003–1 January 2004, p. 12.
10 Rehman Rashid, "Destinies Delayed (But Not Denied): Reflections on the Transition of Malaysian Administrations", in "Malaysia in Transition: The Battle for the Malay Mind", *Trends in Southeast Asia*, 8 (2003), Institute of Southeast Asian Studies, p. 5.
11 Khoo Boo Teik, "De-Mahathirising Malaysia: Abdullah Badawi's Debt to Reformasi", *Aliran Monthly*, 2003: 8 <http://www.aliran.com/oldsite/monthly/2003a/8k.html> (accessed 30 August 2008).
12 Rehman Rashid, "Malaysia's Transition to Abdullah", *FEER*, 4 September 2003, p. 24.
13 Mahathir Mohamad, *The Challenge* (Petaling Jaya: Pelanduk Publications (M) Sdn. Bhd., 1986), p. 151.
14 Ibid., pp. 140–153. Published originally as *Menghadapi Cabaran* (Kuala Lumpur: Pustaka Antara, 1976).
15 Interview with Mahathir Mohamad, 14 August 2007.

16 Zainuddin Maidin, *The Other Side of Mahathir* (Kuala Lumpur: Utusan Publications & Distributors Sdn. Bhd., 1994), p. 223.

17 Ibid., pp. 221, 224.

18 Rehman Rashid, *A Malaysian Journey* (Petaling Jaya: Rehman Rashid, 1993), p. 210.

19 Zainuddin Maidin, *The Other Side of Mahathir,* p. 240.

20 Mahathir Mohamad, *Reflections on Asia* (Petaling Jaya: Pelanduk Publications (M) Sdn. Bhd., 2002), p. 121.

21 S. Jayasankaran, "Behind the Politics, a Pressing Deficit", *FEER,* 4 March 2004, pp. 14–15.

22 S. Jayasankaran, "In Better Hands", *FEER,* 4 March 2004, p. 42.

23 Leslie Lopez, "Malaysia Premier Inherits Fallout From Rail Deal", *Asian Wall Street Journal* (hereafter *AWSJ*), 13 November 2003.

24 Leslie Lopez, "Taking the Reins in Malaysia", *AWSJ,* 31 October 2003.

25 "Spending on Development Projects Okay, Says Abdullah", *Straits Times,* 26 April 2006.

26 Chandra Muzaffar, "Malaysian Politics: The Emerging Scenario Under Abdullah Badawi", in *Trends in Southeast Asia,* 15 (2003), Institute of Southeast Asian Studies, p. 8.

27 Ibid., p. 8.

28 Leslie Lopez, "Malaysian Court Reverses Anwar Sodomy Conviction", *AWSJ,* 3 September 2004.

29 John Hilley, "Anwar and the Limits of Reform: Meaningful Problem-Solving Must See the Root of the Problem Itself", *Aliran Monthly,* 2004: 8 <http://www.aliran.com/monthly/2004b/8f.html> (accessed 26 January 2006).

30 "Mahathir 'Mildly Surprised' by Anwar's Release", *ABC News,* 3 September 2004 <http://www.abc.net.au/news/stories/2004/09//03/1191099.htm> (accessed 11 April 2009).

31 K. Kesavapany, "Promising Start to Malaysia-Singapore Relations", in Saw Swee-Hock and K. Kesavapany, eds, *Malaysia: Recent Trends and Challenges* (Singapore: Institute of Southeast Asian Studies, 2006), pp. 275–286.

32 John Funston, "The Malay Electorate in 2004: Reversing the 1999 Result?", in *Malaysia: Recent Trends and Challenges,* p. 145.

33 Ibid., 147.

34 S. Jayasankaran, "A Vote of Confidence", *FEER,* 1 April 2004, p. 18.

35 John Funston, "The Malay Electorate in 2004: Reversing the 1999 Result?", pp. 141, 149–151.

36 S. Jayasankaran, "Surprise Setback", *FEER,* 7 October 2004, p. 18.

37 Email correspondence with Mahathir Mohamad, 25 June 2008.

38 Leslie Lopez, "Gaming License Sparks Contention in Malaysia", *AWSJ,* 25 October 2004.

39 Ibid.

40 Interview with Abdullah Ahmad, 23 March 2007.

41 Leslie Lopez, "Malaysian Premier Quells Proton Revolt", *AWSJ,* 19 April 2004; "Mahathir's Clout Roils Malaysian Auto Maker", *AWSJ,* 4 February 2005; "Proton Ousts Mahaleel as Chief Executive", *AWSJ,* 26 July 2005.

42 S. Jayasankaran, "Tycoons in Trouble", *FEER,* 15 January 2004, p. 50.

43 "Mahathir Condemns 'Gutless' PM", *BBC News,* 2 May 2006 <http://news.bbc.co.uk/go/pr/fr/-/1/hi/world/asia-pacific/4963910.stm> (accessed 30 August 2008).

44 Interview with Mahathir Mohamad, 20 March 2007.

45 "Mahathir's Scathing Attack", transcript of press conference in Kuala Lumpur, *Straits Times,* 9 June 2006.

46   Email correspondence with Abdullah Badawi, 12 July 2008.
47   Azly Rahman, "Brand New Malay Dilemma", 12 June 2006 <http://www.malaysiakini.com/columns/52367> (accessed 2 September 2008).
48   Fauwaz Abdul Aziz, "Mahathir Vents Frustration on DVD", 11 May 2006 <http://www.malaysiakini.com/news/50965> (accessed 30 August 2008).
49   Star/Asia News Network, Bernama, "UMNO Veterans Warn Against Possible Rift", *Straits Times*, 10 June 2006.
50   Leslie Lopez, "Malaysia May Be the Loser in Public Feud", *Straits Times*, 9 June 2006.
51   "Dr. Mahathir Should Have Taken on Mantle of Statesman After Retirement, says Karpal", *Bernama*, 7 April 2008 <http://newsgroups.derkeiler.com/archive/Soc/soc.culture.malaysia/2008-04/msg00610.html> (accessed 8 April 2008).
52   "An Open Letter by Tun Dr. Mahathir", *Star*, 28 October 2006.
53   "Mahathir Attacks Government in Cyberspace", 24 April 2006 <http://www.malaysiakini.com/news/50184> (accessed 2 September 2008).
54   Leslie Lau, "Corruption in the Force", *Straits Times*, 17 May 2005.
55   Leslie Lopez, "Mahathir Set on Stepping Up Attacks Despite Loss", *Straits Times*, 12 September 2006.
56   Carolyn Hong, "Abdullah Saddened by Dr M's 'Stronger Doses of Venom'", *Straits Times*, 27 October 2006.
57   Fauwaz Abdul Aziz, "Dr M: PM's Sons Have No Business with Govt", 24 May 2006 <http://www.malaysiakini.com/news/51483> (accessed 30 August 2008).
58   Seth Mydans, "In Malaysia, Leader is Sidelined, But Not Silenced", *International Herald Tribune*, 5 July 2006.
59   "Mahathir's Scathing Attack", transcript of press conference in Kuala Lumpur.
60   Mustafa K. Anuar, "'Muzzled': The Media in Mahathir's Malaysia", in Bridget Welsh, ed., *Reflections: The Mahathir Years* (Washington: Southeast Asia Studies Program, The Paul H. Nitze School of Advanced International Studies, Johns Hopkins University, 2004), pp. 489–491.
61   "Asia 1999: Country Report: Malaysia", Committee to Protect Journalists <http://www.cpj.org/attacks99/asia99/Malaysia.html> (accessed 2 March 2006).
62   Mustafa K. Anuar, "'Muzzled': The Media in Mahathir's Malaysia", p. 487.
63   "Asia 1999: Country Report: Malaysia", Committee to Protect Journalists.
64   John Berthelsen, "Second Malaysian Journalist is Arrested Under Secrets Act", *AWSJ*, 4 November 1985.
65   Anil Netto, "Clampdown on Media Freedom", *Aliran Monthly* <http://www.aliran.com/monthly/2003/1d.html> (accessed January 1 2006).
66   "Q&A: I'm Disappointed, Says Mahathir", 23 May 2006 <http://www.malaysiakini.com/news/51427> (accessed 30 August 2008).
67   From 1 January 2009, http://chedet.co.cc/chedetblog/.
68   Soon Li Tsin, "Report Card: Pak Lah Fails", 31 October 2006 <http://www.malaysiakini/com/news/58798> (accessed 2 September 2008).
69   Hannah Beech, "Not the Retiring Type", *Time*, 6 November 2006, p. 39.
70   "An Open Letter by Tun Dr. Mahathir".
71   "Pak Lah has 'Habit of Lying': Dr. M", 11 September 2006 <http://www.malaysiakini.com/news/56587> (accessed 2 September 2008).
72   Interview with Mahathir associate, 30 May 2007.
73   Carolyn Hong, "Stage Set for a Battle to the Bitter End", *Straits Times*, 28 October 2006.
74   Interview with Siti Hasmah Mohamad Ali, 17 January 2008.

75 Leslie Lopez, "Attacks on Abdullah Starting to Hurt Dr. M", *Straits Times*, 2 November 2006.
76 Carolyn Hong, "Mahathir Hits Out at Abdullah One Day after 'Peace Talks'", *Straits Times*, 24 October 2006.
77 "Pak Lah has 'Habit of Lying': Dr. M".
78 Carolyn Hong, "Malaysians Lap Up News on ex-PM's Health", *Straits Times*, 3 October 2007.
79 Assif Shameen, "Abdullah Set to Realize Vision 2020", *Straits Times*, 13 September 2006.
80 Bernama, Agence France-Presse, "Abdullah Refutes Claims of Being Weak", *Straits Times*, 4 March 2008.
81 Associated Press, "KL is Winning Anti-Graft Fight, Says Abdullah", *Straits Times*, 13 April 2007.
82 Reme Ahmad, "Istana Zakaria – Klang's Latest Tourist Attraction", *Sunday Times*, 5 November 2006.
83 New Straits Times, "Klang UMNO Chief Quits State Post Over Scandals", *Straits Times*, 4 November 2006.
84 Leslie Lopez, "Govt Bailout Looms for Port Klang Project", *Straits Times*, 13 August 2007.
85 Ibid.
86 Carolyn Hong, "Abdullah Lashes Out", *Straits Times*, 7 April 2008.
87 "Dr M & Eusoff: Competing in Selective Amnesia?", 19 January 2008 <http://www.malaysiakini.com/news/77222> (accessed 21 January 2008).
88 Farish A. Noor, "Malaysia's Shame", *News Today*, 14 July 2007.
89 Joseph Liow, "Islam Hadhari: A Slogan Gone Cold?" *Straits Times*, 23 February 2008.
90 Chow Kum Hor, "Abdullah Loses Support of Indian Community", *Straits Times*, 26 January 2008.
91 Steven Gan, "An Incompetent, Not-So-Nice Guy", 27 November 2007 <http://malaysiakini.com/editorials/75321> (accessed 25 April 2006).
92 Leslie Lopez, "Abdullah to Unveil Judicial Reforms Today", *Straits Times*, 17 April 2008.
93 Ibid.
94 Ibid.
95 Zaid Ibrahim, "Fixing Malaysia's Judiciary", *Wall Street Journal Asia*, 20 May 2008.
96 "Apology for Chief Justice's Sacking: No", *Straits Times*, 9 April 2008.
97 Carolyn Hong, "Take Me to Court", *Sunday Times*, 18 May 2008.
98 Mahathir Mohamad, "Pantun Seloka", in *A Tribute to Dr. Mahathir Mohamad: A Great Leader and Statesman* (Kuala Lumpur: Various Channels Communications Sdn. Bhd., 2003), p. unnumbered.
99 Bernama, Star/Asia News Network, "Muhyiddin Best to be DPM, Says Mahathir", *Straits Times*, 13 October 2008.
100 Carolyn Hong, "Abdullah's Reform Bills Fail to Win Over Critics", *Straits Times*, 13 December 2008.
101 Carolyn Hong, "Abdullah Lashes Out at Mahathir", *Straits Times*, 20 October 2008.
102 Teo Cheng Wee, "Mahathir to Make UMNO Comeback", *Sunday Times*, 29 March 2009.

Cry for unity: In traditional dress, Mahathir appealed to Malays to close ranks at the UMNO General Assembly, 15 May 2000. The largest ethnic community was badly split over the treatment of his former deputy, Anwar Ibrahim.

Source: Bernama

Surprise: A weeping Mahathir was mobbed by delegates after unexpectedly announcing his resignation at the UMNO General Assembly, 23 June 2002. He later agreed to
stay on for 16 months, becoming the "lame duck" leader he vowed never to be.

Source: Bernama

Over to you: Mahathir officially handed the prime ministership to Abdullah Badawi, 31 October 2003. The smiles soon vanished as Mahathir criticized Abdullah's leadership and policies, and agitated for his replacement.

Source: Information Department, Malaysia

Fond farewell: Civil servants jostled to say goodbye to Mahathir as he left the prime minister's office for the last time. He occupied the post for more than 22 years, served consecutively by four deputies.

Source: Information Department, Malaysia

13
A Place in History

Universiti Utara Malaysia, a bucolic campus at Sintoc in Kedah near the northern border with Thailand, commends itself as a place to contemplate Mahathir Mohamad's legacy. As prime minister, Dr. Mahathir built this university, which specialized in management and quickly attracted a 22,000-student body, in his own parliamentary constituency. It was UUM that conferred an honorary degree on former British prime minister Margaret Thatcher in 2002 to acknowledge her warm personal bond with Dr. Mahathir, and it was UUM that was chosen to host the Institute of Tun Dr. Mahathir Mohamad's Thoughts after he retired in 2003.

But in the modest building where the institute is housed on the first floor, the silence that greeted a visitor in 2007 was almost deafening. The RM21 million in government funding requested by the institute had not materialized, and it was limping along with a staff of nine, seven of them administrative employees. The two professionals were part-timers, required to teach and conduct research in other UUM departments as well. Working with a slim allocation from the regular UUM budget, they lacked the resources to begin analysing the deeds of one of Southeast Asia's last strongmen. A bookcase told the story: It contained only a few of the dozens of volumes written by and about Dr. Mahathir. Having decided to establish the institute while Dr. Mahathir was still being lionized as the nation's leader, his political associates were reluctant to finance their commitment once he had departed.

The about-turn in sentiment was astonishing. For months before Dr. Mahathir had left the prime minister's official residence, many Malaysians almost tripped over themselves in eulogising him. Emotional tributes filled the newspapers and gushing editorials credited him with almost everything positive about the country. Muhammad Muhammad Taib, an UMNO vice president, described Dr. Mahathir as an "extraordinary leader" and declared, "Even in 100 years, or even 1,000 years, it would be difficult to find another like him."[1] In the week Dr. Mahathir actually stepped down, Kuala Lumpur was festooned with banners thanking him and wishing him well.[2] The annual General Assembly of UMNO in June, the last Dr. Mahathir attended as president, reverberated with bursts of song and rhyming couplets in his praise.[3] Delegates adopted a resolution urging the government to ponder, preserve and propagate the thoughts of the great leader, along with those of his predecessors, through the establishment of an academic institute.

Although the Cabinet had endorsed the idea and awarded the honour to UUM against competing bids from other universities, the Institute of Tun Dr. Mahathir Mohamad's Thoughts was effectively stillborn in late 2003. The ill wind that blew northward from Kuala Lumpur could be explained in part by the shift in political power and priorities that accompany any change in national leadership. In this case, however, there was malign intent as well. Deeply regretting what he considered a grave mistake in choosing Abdullah Badawi as his successor, Dr. Mahathir was waging open warfare on him. Abdullah, in return, was not about to do anything to enhance Dr. Mahathir's status.

Weighing Dr. Mahathir's performance requires an understanding that it spanned a full generation and included extremes of success and failure. Out of office, he did little to encourage or inform a balanced judgment of his record. While he spoke freely, he proved incapable of the candour and reflection that might have illuminated the controversies that defined his tenure. Showing no sign of mellowing, he admitted to few errors, other than trusting people who subsequently let him down. As in the past, he professed no interest in his "legacy", a comment that, like some of what else he said, could not be taken at face value. Dr. Mahathir was obsessed with the fate of Malaysia, and what he left behind was what he had worked for most of his adult life. As Abdullah deviated from Dr. Mahathir's platform, the former prime minister turned on him with a fury that would be assuaged only by Abdullah's resignation or defeat.

Like his heroes, Dr. Mahathir sought change on an historical scale. He admired Peter the Great of Russia, Japan's Meiji Emperor and Turkey's Mustafa Kemal Ataturk, as well as President Park Chung Hee of South Korea and China's Deng Xiaoping, not to mention "my greatest model", the Prophet Muhammad. The common thread was that that they brought progress and enlightenment to their backward communities. As Dr. Mahathir said, "These are people who changed, changed the community in which they lived, radically changed and literally dragged them into a new age."[4]

Emotionally, Dr. Mahathir belonged to the batch of Third World leaders who made their mark in the immediate post-independence period: Egypt's Gamal Abdel Nasser, Kwame Nkrumah of Ghana, Mobutu Sese Seko of Zaire, Julius Nyerere of Tanzania and Indonesia's Sukarno. Fiery nationalists who struggled for independence in the 1950s and 60s, they generally turned their backs on the West as they found like-minded allies in regional and international bodies they helped inspire, such as the Organization of African Unity in the case of Nkrumah and Nyerere, and the Non-Aligned Movement for Nasser and Sukarno. And, as they harshly denounced and sought to eliminate colonialism, they adopted variants of socialism, which eventually ruined their economies.

While Dr. Mahathir came of age politically when this group was at the height of its influence in developing-world politics, he achieved power in a different era. Dr. Mahathir's anti-West rhetoric in the 1980s and 90s, though reminiscent of the first generation's, was accompanied by a diametrically opposite view of economics. Although a strident nationalist, he was pragmatic and favoured the market system that had brought prosperity to the industrialized nations. Many of his criticisms of the West, even when delivered from a Non-Aligned Movement platform, were directed at the barriers preventing developing countries such as Malaysia from moving up the food chain and graduating to the First World. Like neighbours Lee Kuan Yew of Singapore and Indonesia's Suharto, Dr. Mahathir integrated his country deeply with the Western economies and achieved an enviable development record.

At the same time, Dr. Mahathir joined a lengthy list of regional leaders who practiced authoritarianism, including not only Lee and Suharto but also Sukarno, Thailand's Sarit Thanarat, Thanom Kittikachorn and Praphas Charusathien, Myanmar's Ne Win, Ferdinand Marcos of the Philippines and Cambodia's Prince Norodom Sihanouk and Hun Sen. Among the Southeast Asian leaders who escaped the socialist trap and gave themselves a chance of economic advancement in return for the political restrictions and stability they imposed, Dr. Mahathir was one of the most successful and enlightened. Only Lee Kuan Yew and his successor as prime minister of Singapore, Goh Chok Tong, clearly outperformed him.

Dr. Mahathir's approach, however, is unlikely to be replicated, either in Malaysia or elsewhere in the region. In many ways he was sui generis, a forceful, quirky outsider who happened along and possessed the attributes to capture the political system at a time when he could get away with it. Apart from the slim prospect of a similar personality appearing again anytime soon, Southeast Asian societies have become more complex as they have modernized and matured. In the age of the Internet, none of the leading Southeast Asian countries is likely to allow completely free rein to a leader given to arbitrariness, repression and severe lapses in governance.

For better and worse, Dr. Mahathir had a profound impact on Malaysia. When he retired, more than half the population had known no other national leader and many people, detractors included, simply could not imagine life without him. He was dominant for so long that nearly every aspect of the country reflected his preference or personality. Dr. Mahathir's influence was most visible in the thrusting Kuala Lumpur skyline, and in the impressive infrastructure that drew foreign investors in large numbers and created one of the world's top 20 trading nations. It was also present in a better educated, more affluent and mostly tolerant people, many of whom had plugged in with cell phones and satellite television and become global citizens.[5] But it permeated, too, the ranks of oppositionists and disaffected groups who often risked their livelihoods and liberty to disagree with him. "Dr. Mahathir changed not just the face but also the soul of Malaysia," observed sociologist Clive Kessler.[6]

In 2008, Malaysia faced greater political uncertainty than at any time since the racial riots that shook Kuala Lumpur nearly four decades earlier. Prime Minister Abdullah's National Front administration, punished in a general election in March for an ineffectual performance and broken promises, continued to sink ever lower in public esteem. UMNO's main coalition partners, the Malaysian Chinese Association, the Malaysian Indian Congress and Parti Gerakan Rakyat Malaysia, blamed the ruling party's "arrogance and excesses" for their defeats.[7] Abdullah's attempts to reverse the erosion of UMNO's legitimacy, by dusting off his earlier promises of reform, encountered internal opposition and floundered, leaving his partners frustrated and helpless.

While Abdullah sought to deflect pressures to quit by announcing that he would hand over to Deputy Prime Minister Najib Razak in 2010, UMNO remained divided, semi-paralysed and in danger of fracturing. Persuaded that Abdullah could not halt the party's slide, some influential members wanted him out sooner. But Najib had his own problems that made him less than an ideal candidate to restore UMNO's relevance and credibility, and he agreed to the timetable. Najib, also defence minister until September 2008, was unable to bury allegations, despite his denials, linking him to corruption in big-ticket weapon systems purchases, and to the case of a Mongolian woman, the former lover of one of his closest advisers, who was murdered in Malaysia.

Lurching towards another round of bitter factional fighting, UMNO had reached what political scientist Khoo Boo Teik called a well-known political condition: "the leader is too weak to impose his will, the led are not yet strong enough to depose him".[8] In the run-up to the UMNO General Assembly in December, the shortage of prospective leaders – members with ability, experience and stature – was all too painfully obvious. The only one to raise his hand to contest the party presidency was Tengku Razaleigh Hamzah, the former finance minister, who was 71 and had been out of the limelight for 20 years. Among the younger generation, almost no one enjoyed the standing needed to lift UMNO – and Malaysia – out of the quagmire. Besides, it would be extremely difficult to obtain the backing of 30 per cent of UMNO's divisions, a necessary condition for anyone to challenge Abdullah for the party presidency.

While UMNO's dire predicament and the electoral success of Anwar Ibrahim's People's Front could be interpreted positively, as the deepening of democracy and the prospect of a two-party political system taking root in Malaysia, stasis or upheaval seemed a more immediate prospect. True, many Malaysians had voted across ethnic lines, encouraging the belief that race-based politics might be receding. But desperate UMNO elements, fearful of losing power, resorted to the familiar aggressive defence of Malay rights, and the party itself pushed a Malay-centric line trying to entice Parti Islam Se-Malaysia to desert the People's Front. The real concern was that racial polarization might begin anew.[9]

Morally vindicated by the royal commission into judicial appointments, Anwar prepared to return to Parliament after his ban for being convicted of abuse of power expired in April 2008. His confident prediction, that enough National Front members of parliament would defect to enable him to form a government by 16 September, the anniversary of the formation of Malaysia in 1963, rattled UMNO and numbed sections of the political and bureaucratic establishment. Anwar left no doubt that he intended to pursue those he held responsible for his persecution. He filed a complaint with the Anti-Corruption Agency alleging that the Inspector General of Police, Musa Hassan, and Attorney General Gani Patail had fabricated evidence when Anwar was assaulted at police headquarters after his arrest in 1998.[10] With Anwar dictating the political pace, tantalizing followers and taunting opponents with the suggestion that he would soon take power, a sense of unreality and apprehension gripped the country as he was arrested again for sodomy.

As if learning nothing from events ten years earlier, police, some wearing balaclavas, used a dozen cars to ambush Anwar near his home without giving him time to attend a pre-arranged interview, accompanied by his lawyers, at police headquarters. He was held overnight in a cell and left to sleep on a concrete floor. His accuser was Mohamad Saiful Bukhari Azlan, 23, a university dropout who had worked for a few months on Anwar's staff. Anwar subsequently pleaded not guilty to a charge of sodomy and was granted bail. Calling the allegation a political conspiracy to prevent him from toppling the government, Anwar contested and won triumphantly a by-election in August for his old Permatang Pauh constituency, held since 1999 by his wife and vacated by her to allow his formal return to national politics. The poisonous political atmosphere, together with soaring inflation, undermined investor sentiment and sapped public confidence. Citing financial and political instability as larger concerns than the usual racial issues, social problems and crime, only 28 per cent of Malaysians were satisfied with the way things were at mid-year, down from 68 per cent five months earlier.[11]

Sniping from the sidelines as if he was just another citizen unhappy with the conduct of the country's political class, Dr. Mahathir accepted no responsibility for the threatening disorder that was, in fact, largely of his making. His failure to provide for the future leadership of Malaysia was entirely consistent with his penchant for political expediency and emphasis on the nation's hardware at the expense of its software. Musa Hitam, Tengku Razaleigh Hamzah and Anwar Ibrahim were capable contenders in UMNO, but Dr. Mahathir ousted them all – Musa technically resigned – to safeguard his position and pursue his development agenda without hindrance. With access to the top blocked, other ambitious or talented members languished at lower levels, departed, or were deterred from joining the party in the first place. Far from grooming a dynamic successor, Dr. Mahathir succeeded only in cultivating a "broad-based assemblage of loyalists not predisposed to thinking against the grain".[12]

When he became prime minister, Abdullah had been astute enough to recognize popular demands to end the worst abuses and repair some of the harm inflicted by a couple of decades of one-man rule.[13] He was rewarded in 2004 with the biggest mandate in Malaysian history. But when he failed so dismally to meet the expectations he inflated so liberally, his administration was dumped even more heavily in 2008. A more active and competent prime minister, with a stronger political base, might have been able to push through some of the promised reforms, but not the man handpicked for the task by Dr. Mahathir.

Even when he chose Abdullah ahead of Najib to be his deputy in 1999, Dr. Mahathir largely put his personal interests ahead of the country's. His retrospective contention that Najib at 50 was too young in 2003 to become premier rang hollow, given that Najib entered Parliament at 22 and joined the government at 32, and actually had been active in politics longer than Abdullah. As Dr. Mahathir's mood soured and he became more cantankerous, he claimed that Abdullah had not been his first choice. But since he had dismissed Anwar as morally unfit and the government was under pressure from the sectarian Parti Islam Se-Malaysia, Dr. Mahathir opted for the one who did not smoke or drink and had excellent Islamic credentials. Dr. Mahathir was mindful, too, that Abdullah personally did not like Anwar Ibrahim, and could be expected to block his return to active politics. Associates believed Dr. Mahathir tapped Abdullah also because he thought he would be the most grateful and easiest to manipulate from behind the scenes.[14] Instead, under the influence of ambitious young aides, Abdullah had moved his eager supporters into crucial positions during the 16 months that Dr. Mahathir was a lame duck leader, ready to chart his own course as soon as he took charge.

Dr. Mahathir's reaction to being politically outmanoeuvred for once, denouncing Abdullah in increasingly harsh language and refusing to retire graciously, did nothing for the former prime minister's reputation. He shunned the chance to play the part of elder statesman, indulging instead in mean personal politics, even as he registered some valid points. Worse for him, he was unable to influence events, beyond reinforcing the perception that Abdullah's administration was inept. Flailing away without any result, Dr. Mahathir later gave up temporarily on Najib as well, though not because he thought he was unsuited to lead Malaysia while dogged by scandal. Rather, he branded Najib a "coward" for not challenging Abdullah. Dr. Mahathir then pinned his hopes on Muhyiddin Yassin, an UMNO vice president. But he, too, initially accepted Abdullah's transition arrangement and ruled out a challenge, before engineering a peaceful handover to Najib from behind the scenes.

At no stage did Dr. Mahathir acknowledge his culpability in making it almost impossible for party rivals to contest Abdullah's presidency and allow for wider reform and regeneration in UMNO. Not only did Dr. Mahathir put in place the 30 per cent nomination quota to protect himself while in power, but he also arranged "bonus" votes for presidential nominees and gave the Supreme Council enormous advantage over the rank and file by allowing the council to postpone triennial party elections by up to 18 months.

By quitting UMNO in 2008, Dr. Mahathir tried to prompt a stampede for the exits by the party's elected representatives and leaders, who he hoped would remain outside the party until Abdullah was replaced, before return-ing to UMNO. It was one of those all-or-nothing gambits that worked as Dr. Mahathir's career ascended, but flopped as he lost power and his polit-ical touch deserted him. It was also an impractical and irresponsible tactic, given that UMNO was still the heart of the National Front, which had been recently re-elected to govern the country for another five years. Explaining Dr. Mahathir's misguided motivation, one long-time ally said, "He hates Abdullah more than he loves UMNO."[15]

The UMNO that Abdullah so fortuitously inherited and Dr. Mahathir so casually abandoned was nothing like the patriotic party that had led the campaign for Malaysia's independence half a century earlier. It had long lost its idealism and was rotting from within, "morally exhausted" and "ideologically hollow".[16] In addition to the ossification of the leadership, UMNO under Dr. Mahathir had become riddled with corruption as it went into business in a major way. Bereft of ideas, the party directed its efforts, not at addressing the changing needs of a more complex Malaysia, but at main-taining its hold on power and pursuing policies that primarily benefited a small and privileged circle.

Dr. Mahathir made UMNO more irrelevant by relying on the bureaucracy to perform what should have been party functions, and limiting UMNO's role in governmental affairs. For example, the 14,000-strong Social Development Department in the Rural Development Ministry served as the "eyes and ears" of UMNO in *kampungs*, while Dr. Mahathir ignored the tradi-tion that those who obtained the most votes in party elections were entitled to senior cabinet positions.[17] Even so, he overrode the other parties in the National Front coalition to the extent that many Chinese and Indians would no longer vote for junior partners. So while the National Front needed to reinvent itself to be effective, its minority partners would remain demoralized unless and until UMNO began the process by revitalizing itself.[18]

Although UMNO's claim to pre-eminence rested on majority support from the political dominant Malay community, the party proved resistant to change even as its historical base eroded. The general election in 1999, after Anwar's dismissal the previous year, when hundreds of thousands of members left UMNO to join the opposition, signalled the party's decline. Most UMNO leaders concluded that radical adjustment was necessary to meet the threat of Anwar's *Reformasi* movement for more democracy, transparency and all the sins gathered under the rubric of corruption. But Dr. Mahathir had resisted, insisting that what was needed was restoration not reformation.[19] While UMNO agreed to revise its constitution in 2000, two proposals that received strong support – direct election of top positions, such as the president, by some 300,000 party members, and dropping the requirements for a high percentage of divisional nominations for office bearers – were rejected by the Supreme Council.[20]

Abdullah's experience indicated that a rigid and inflexible UMNO was unable or unwilling to respond to the demands of a younger, better educated and more discerning electorate, despite the distinct possibility of defeat by defections or in future polls. Given the extent of its electoral setback in 2008, unless decisive action was taken to end UMNO's malaise, "It may even be terminal in the next general election," one party veteran warned.[21]

Broadly, though not all the participants and provocateurs were visible, UMNO and the vested interests that sustained the party were engaged in a life-and-death struggle with the forces of reform, skillfully marshalled by the articulate and resurgent Anwar Ibrahim. As the stakes increased, there was likely to be only one winner. Abdullah, caught in the middle, was jerked in all directions until he was thrown out.

Apart from turning UMNO into a powerful patronage machine that eventually slipped from his grasp, and leaving the party singularly ill-equipped to face a globalizing future, Dr. Mahathir cut Malaysia adrift institutionally. Similar to the way he personalized control of the party, he emasculated almost all institutions so he would meet no obstruction. He handed them to loyalists, shrank their authority, or bypassed them altogether. While that left the police, the courts and other agencies unable to discharge their public obligations professionally, his attacks on the doctrine of the separation of powers struck at "the very soul of principled, democratic governance".[22] In particular, the assault on the judiciary left fundamental flaws in Malaysia's constitutional system that would take time, in the best of circumstances, to rectify.

Unchecked, Dr. Mahathir created a culture that rewarded obedience and shortchanged integrity, allowing Malaysia to drift into a period appropriately described as "the lost ethical years".[23] For example, he extended Mohamed Eusoff Chin's term as chief justice beyond retirement in 2000, despite representations by the Bar Council that the judge had been photographed on holiday with a Malaysian lawyer in New Zealand in circumstances that raised questions of serious unethical conduct. A number of the most successful senior officials learned to anticipate what was expected of them and act before receiving orders. If they crossed the line of legality, as some did, they were likely to be even more responsive to prime ministerial demands. As one unhappy judge remarked, it was widely believed that Dr. Mahathir "kept a docket on everyone useful with a skeleton in their cupboard so that he can manipulate them on pain of disclosing the skeleton".[24]

Judged by his own high-minded rhetoric associated with Vision 2020, Dr. Mahathir failed Malaysia. One of the nine "strategic challenges" he set to enter the First World was "establishing a fully moral and ethical society, whose citizens are strong in religious and spiritual values and imbued with the highest of ethical standards".[25]

Although a significant number of Malays entered the professions, or made the transition from farm to boardroom, during his term, Dr. Mahathir expressed disappointment over his attempts to alter their mindset. "More of them should have succeeded," he said. Too many Malays took the easy way out to get rich by selling the contracts, stocks, permits and licences allocated to them, he said, instead of going into business as he intended.[26] Though valid, Dr. Mathathir's criticism let his government off the hook for the wholesale abuse of the New Economic Policy, which was a source of widespread discontent, particularly among Malays. It was his core supporters – the Umnoputras, in veteran opposition politician Lim Kit Siang's colourful term – who were the serial offenders, and almost nothing was done to prevent them hawking their state-bestowed bumiputra privileges, such as discounted share allocations, for quick profit.

When it came to strengthening Malaysia's macroeconomic muscles and sinews to realize Vision 2020, however, Dr. Mahathir scored convincingly. He engineered a socio-economic transformation, lessening the country's dependence on commodities and deepening its industrialization. Development was driven by local and foreign private investment, attracted by political stability, first-class physical infrastructure and enlightened policies that deregulated and liberalized the economy and encouraged higher value-added export-oriented industries. During the Mahathir era, before the 1997–98 Asian economic crisis, Malaysia received in absolute terms as much foreign direct investment as Thailand and Indonesia, which had a population base of three and ten times, respectively, that of Malaysia.[27]

The reduction in poverty and increasing affluence gave Malaysia the look and feel of a modern, prosperous nation, especially in urban areas. An expansion of the middle class, not least the Malay component, changed the ethnic landscape and helped dampen communal tensions in at least one segment of the population. One or two of the concrete symbols of Dr. Mahathir's dreams, always controversial, could become more contentious with the passage of time. While the highways, bridges, airports, seaports and industrial zones were necessary, multi-billion mega-projects such as the Putrajaya administrative capital were optional extras he personally ordered with a Petronas credit card.

As Malaysia draws nearer the time it will run out of oil and gas, projected for 2027 and 2049, respectively,[28] past extravagance and wastage could become an issue for future generations of Malaysians. Depending on economic circumstances, they may curse Dr. Mahathir for squandering their earnings in advance, or praise him for his foresight in building landmarks like European monarchs in the past.

Although Dr. Mahathir spoke modestly of his achievements, he obviously saw himself, like his heroes, as a man of history. He rated keeping ethnic relations "well under control" near the top, especially considering he was a Malay nationalist feared by the Chinese as "the ultra" when he took over. "But in the end, when I stepped down, there was relative harmony, good relations between the different races," he said.[29] Yet even this claim was flimsy, since clearly all was not well beneath the surface of social peace. Studies showed university students interacting less across ethnic lines, while UMNO's attempts to recover Malay support by stressing *ketuanan Melayu* often heightened communal tensions. And many Malaysians, especially Chinese and Indians, were disturbed by ongoing Islamization, propelled by conservative religious elements.

Dr. Mahathir also gave himself high marks for another goal he set at the outset: raising Malaysia's profile so that the country was known as well as its Southeast Asian neighbours, Indonesia, Singapore, Thailand and the Philippines. "Today, people know Malaysia. People know Malaysia has done well," he said.[30] Internationally, Malaysia had won a "premier" position among developing countries, being regarded as "the model" of an economy transformed from agricultural to industrial. "Malaysia has shown the way for the rest of the world," he said.[31]

Whether Malaysia would realize its Vision 2020 and graduate on time to the ranks of the developed world was less important than the fact that it was on the way. Dr. Mahathir supplied the compass. As he said, "If somebody doesn't give you a sense of direction, everybody would be going all over the place and nothing can be done."[32] Rising living standards, together with Dr. Mahathir's showpiece buildings and outspoken defence of Malaysia's interests, contributed to a sense of national identity, pride and confidence that had not existed before. He put Malaysia on the map, and most Malaysians were pleased about it.

With few illusions that he would be remembered fondly, Dr. Mahathir pointed out that people often change their opinions of leaders over time. Lawrence of Arabia, once a hero, was later "debunked", he said. In Dr. Mahathir's case, he would not be able to escape responsibility for many of the problems likely to plague Malaysian society in the future, from creeping Islamization to corruption and inequality. For while he held Malaysia together for 22 years, the political-administrative system atrophied and decayed under his personalized brand of governance. "People debunk so many things," he said. "That will happen to me also." Dr. Mahathir, approaching 83, paused and allowed himself a gentle smile: "But I won't be around to see it."[33]

Notes

1 "Malaysia's Mahathir to Quit", 25 June 2002, *BBC News* <http://news.bbc.co.uk/2/hi/asia-pacific/2064656.stm> (accessed 27 January 2006).
2 "Regional Economy: Malaysia After Mahathir", *Economist*, 4 November 2003 <http://www.chinadaily.com.cn/en/doc/2003–11/04/content_278370.htm> (accessed 1 November 2006).
3 Michael Vatikiotis, "The Last Hurrah", *Far Eastern Economic Review*, 3 July 2003, p. 12.
4 Interview with Mahathir Mohamad, 20 March 2007.
5 Bridget Welsh, "Mahathir's Legacy: A New Society?", in Bridget Welsh, ed., *Reflections: The Mahathir Years* (Washington: Southeast Asia Studies Program, The Paul H. Nitze School of Advanced International Studies, Johns Hopkins University, 2004), p. 355.
6 Clive S. Kessler, "The Mark of the Man: Mahathir's Malaysia After Dr. Mahathir", in *Reflections*, p. 15.
7 Khoo Boo Teik, "Leaving UMNO the Mahathir Way 2: Mahathir and Abdullah", *Aliran Online*, 5 June 2008 <http://www.aliran.com/index.php?option=com_content&view=article&id=616:leaving-umno-the-mahathir-way-mahathir-and-abdullah&catid=55:2008&Itemid=40> (accessed 29 August 2008).
8 Khoo Boo Teik, "Leaving UMNO the Mahathir Way 1: A Crumbled Trinity", *Aliran Online*, 3 June 2008 <http://www.aliran.com/index.php?option=com_content-&view=article&id=611:leaving-umno-the-mahathir-way-a-crumbled-trinity&catid=55:2008&Itemid=40> (accessed 29 August 2008).
9 Ooi Kee Beng, "Malaysia's Culture of Politicisation Still Alive and Well", *Opinion-Asia*, 25 July 2008 <http://www.opinionasia.org/Malaysiascultureofpoliticisation-stillaliveandwell> (accessed 27 August 2008).
10 The government announced in March 2009 that an investigation had cleared Musa and Ghani, a decision rejected by Anwar as a "cover-up". Agence France-Presse, "Anwar Beating: Two Top Officials Cleared of Wrongdoing", *Straits Times*, 12 March 2009.
11 Teo Cheng Wee, "Crisis of Confidence", *Straits Times*, 2 August 2008.
12 Maznah Mohamad, "Mahathir's Malay Question", in *Reflections*, p. 163.
13 Ooi Kee Beng, "When a Strongman Leaves...", *Weekend Today*, 26–27 July 2008.
14 Interview with Mahathir associate, 1 August 2008.
15 Interview with Abdullah Ahmad, 11 August 2008.
16 Khoo Boo Teik, "Leaving UMNO the Mahathir Way: Fearful Scenario", *Aliran Online*, 10 June 2008 <http:///www.aliran.com/index.php?option=com_content&view=article&id= 624:-leaving-umno-the-mahathir-way-fearful-scenario&catid=55:2008&Itemid= 40> (accessed 29 August 2008).
17 John Funston, "UMNO: What Legacy Will Mahathir Leave?", in *Reflections*, p. 136.
18 Khoo Boo Teik, "Leaving UMNO the Mahathir Way: Fearful Scenario".
19 John Funston, "UMNO: What Legacy Will Mahathir Leave?", in *Reflections*, p. 138.
20 Ibid., p. 139.
21 Abdullah Ahmad, "Still Relevant, Still Strong: But for How Long?", *Off the Edge*, July 2008, p. 36.

22 Tunku Abdul Aziz, "Waking Up from the Lost Ethical Years", 15 June 2008 <http://www.nst.com.my/Sunday/Columns/2267622> (accessed 16 June 2008).
23 Ibid.
24 "Mahathir and Judge Trade Barbs in Worsening Public Spat", *Straits Times*, 27 June 2008.
25 Dr. Mahathir Mohamad, "Malaysia: The Way Forward", in Ahmad Sarji Abdul Hamid, ed., *Malaysia's Vision 2020: Understanding the Concept, Implications and Challenges* (Petaling Jaya: Pelanduk Publications (M) Sdn. Bhd., 1997 edition), p. 405.
26 Interview with Mahathir Mohamad, 29 March 2007.
27 David Camroux, "Mahathir: National Hero, Global Bad Boy", EurAsia Bulletin Vol. 7, Oct–Nov 2003, pp. 9–11 <http://www.eias.org/publications/bulletin/2003/octnov03/eboctnov03.pdf> (accessed 27 August 2008).
28 Proved reserves to current production levels in 2008: 19.4 years of oil and 40.9 years of gas. Source: *BP Statistical Review of World Energy*, June 2008, London. Arguing against subsidies to keep the retail price of fuel low, the Malaysian government said in early 2008 that oil and gas reserves would run out by 2010: Bernama, Agence France-Presse, "Abdullah Refutes Claims of Being Weak", *Straits Times*, 4 March 2008.
29 Interview with Mahathir Mohamad, 20 March 2007.
30 Interview with Mahathir Mohamad, 31 March 2008.
31 Fauwaz Abdul Aziz, "Mahathir Vents Frustration on DVD, Pt 2", 12 May 2006 <http://www.malaysiakini.com/news/50975> (accessed 27 May 2006).
32 Eddin Khoo and Jason Tan, "Nothing Personal: Tun Dr. Mahathir Mohamad on Legacy", *Off the Edge*, February 2007, p. 41.
33 Interview with Mahathir Mohamad, 31 March 2008.

Index

358   *Index*